Economic Growth in Monsoon Asia

Harry T. Oshima

Economic Growth in Monsoon Asia

A Comparative Survey

UNIVERSITY OF TOKYO PRESS

Publication of this book was partially supported by a grant from the Council for Asian Manpower Studies.

Copyright © 1987 by University of Tokyo Press

ISBN   0-86008-402-7
ISBN   4-13-047014-0

Printed in Japan

Contents

List of Tables

List of Figures

Economic Growth in Monsoon Asia

INTRODUCTION

The Problem and Its Significance

Starting with national independence, the postwar decades saw kaleidoscopic changes in most Asian nations, perhaps the most momentous in the history of monsoon Asia. It began with the total defeat of Japan, the sweeping victory of the Communist armies in China and of socialism in India, wars for national independence and civil strife, inflation, and reconstruction. But as the decades went by the fears of Japan's collapse and the great hopes of the new systems in China and India faded. Instead, unexpected things began to happen, the most fascinating of which were the exceptionally rapid growth of Japan, Taiwan, South Korea, Hong Kong, and Singapore, and the resurgence, after a shaky start, of Thailand, Malaysia, and Indonesia. These turned out to be perhaps the most surprising performances the world has seen in the two and a half centuries of modern economic growth. No other grouping of nations with 150 million people has grown at a rate of GNP per capita of 6 percent per annum for as long as three decades. Increasingly, it is being conjectured that the new century will be the Pacific century, with the center of modern economic growth moving westward from the Atlantic—not, as some expected earlier, eastward toward the Ural mountains. As the growth of the West, both capitalist and socialist, slows down below that of Japan, per capita incomes in Japan are projected to rise above those of any country in the West by the mid-1990s.

One purpose of this volume is to learn more about this unexpected performance of East and Southeast Asia. Much has been written on the matter, and I seek to build upon this literature, hoping that a different approach may contribute to further understanding. The task is begun by asking how and why growth rates in Asia differed so much. The aim is to learn more about the growth of Asian countries through comparisons over time, hoping that the knowledge will be helpful in improving the future performances of other countries.

During the course of three postwar decades, there was an unexpected

3

differentiation in income levels in the three regions of Asia. By 1980, per capita income levels reached $2,000 in East Asia, $400 to $800 in Southeast Asia, but less than $300 in South Asia. This differentiation is historically unprecedented, and if it continues into the next couple of decades, Asia will see one group of countries in the postindustrial stage dominated by a modern service sector, another group completing the transition into industrial society, and a third still predominantly agrarian. An attempt to learn about the process by which this differentiation took place may be helpful to the slower-growing nations.

The Approach

The approach taken by this study is wide-ranging, in the hope that a wide net will be able to catch "as many fish" as possible—making it easier to sort out the general forces from those which are more specific to each country. Despite a number of similarities originating in the monsoon conditions of Asian production, countries vary in size, physical endowment, climate, topography, historical background, ethnicity, religion, and so on. It is difficult to assess the degree of generality or specificity in the successes and failures found in the postwar experience without looking at a large sample of countries. Despite the risks involved in a single investigator trying to cover such a wide spectrum of countries, the effort was made in order to draw a preliminary map on a large canvas with bold strokes. I hope that the effort will prove useful for others seeking to go deeper and more carefully into the specific issues, filling in the gaps, and eventually leading to a substantially redrawn map or a new one.

The approach is heavily macroscopic, viewing the forest both as a whole and in large subdivided lots. It seems necessary to start with a macro view of the forest if micro researchers are to have a map of the layout and not get lost in the forest, wandering from one tree to another, not knowing the size of the different parts of the forest nor which parts are growing and which are not. I hope to follow this volume with others that will go into the details of various aspects which can only be lightly touched on in this book.

Our main interest here is the secular long-run period. Decade-to-decade changes are much more affected by internal forces than the year-to-year changes in which external forces such as exports can be important. The ups and downs of cyclically induced exports cancel out in the secular trends, and whatever remains as persistent growth of exports is likely to be a function of improvements in the productive forces within the country. When Western markets opened up in the postwar decades, it was the superior productive power of the newly industrializing countries (NICs) that enabled them to take advantage of the openings, far more than other countries, and then to sustain their export growth, despite higher wages, with faster rises in productivity. The earlier rise in exports did help through larger scale economies, but as the chapters of this book devoted to specific countries show, this was a small part of the "bottom line." The NICs were able to open up and export because their industries were able to meet foreign competition; others could not because of low efficiency. The internal developments are emphasized more than in other studies, which stress trade liberalization as the primary force.[1]

The comparative approach is taken because existing growth and development theories are limited and leave out important aspects. They are inadequate guides to normative standards in assessing performance. The main part of this volume is devoted to binary (or two-country) comparisons, except for the chapter on Japan, which was the only country in Asia to begin the process of industrialization before World War I. Since there is no monsoon country to compare it with, Japan's postwar growth is compared with that of the prewar decades.

The guiding principle of the binary selections was to select two countries as similar as possible in size and characteristics, then to identify differences which emerged. Differences appearing between two similar countries are very useful in understanding their growth patterns. Just as a comparison of rates of growth or structural changes in apples and oranges, or in elephants and dogs, will not give many insights valuable for raising apples and oranges or dogs and elephants, so would comparisons of mini Singapore with giant India or of laissez-faire Hong Kong with socialist China lead to distorted conclusions. Unlike most comparative studies, the emphasis in the binary approach is on contrasts rather than similarities.

I study the underlying long-term forces that sustain economic growth by assuming that growth is largely the outcome of the interplay of technological and institutional changes, as emphasized by Kuznets. Since some of these forces cannot be satisfactorily quantified on the macro level, I resort to descriptive narration supplemented by whatever quantified proxies can be obtained. At bottom, technology and institutions have more qualitative than quantitative dimensions. The varieties

---

[1] One needs to be reminded that many Japanese industries were highly protected in the 1950s and 1960s but emerged in the 1970s to be formidable challengers to the unprotected Western ones; notable examples are the iron and steel and the automobile industries.

of each type of technology and institution are so great that they defy efforts to measure or even count them. It is said that different types of machine technology today number in the hundreds of thousands, possibly in the millions, though no one has undertaken a complete count. And there are no two institutions of the same type, even in a single country, that are exactly alike and operate with the same effectiveness. Even more difficult to approximate are the interactions, which at times are not even identifiable, much less describable. With qualitative forces so important, a variety of methods and approaches must be used, and a place made for informed and plausible speculations and conjectures.

When technologies and institutions are borrowed and adapted, time is required for them to be found or selected, imported, modified, disseminated, and effectively used. Longer time is needed for institutional changes, since Western imports are less suitable to developing countries where traditional ways of doing and thinking are the product of many generations. This implies that it is the institutional component that is most important in the interaction of technologies and institutions underlying the growth of developing countries.

In turn, the long gestation period needed for the basic forces to become effective agents of secular growth means that some of the major forces affecting postwar growth have roots in the distant past. We therefore need to step back into the prewar decades, into the century before World War II, when the forces unleashed by the first industrial revolution in the West during the 19th century began to speed up changes in the East. Their impact on Asian institutions took many forms in the various countries, probably no two of them alike. The behavior and response of the elites and lower classes in the postwar decades were conditioned in most Asian countries by colonial rule, in the context of the institutional heritage from the precolonial era. These longer term trends, rather than shorter term movements such as cycles and episodic ones, are emphasized in this study.

When institutions play such an important role in the growth of developing Asia, one cannot keep the analysis within the boundaries of economies, particularly if one wishes to go beyond the proximate to the ultimate forces. Understandably, economists tend to follow Matthews, Malinvaud, and others in leaving the final analysis of the ultimate factors to the other social sciences. But other social scientists do not know as well as economists do the proximate forces and their economic mechanism, and without this knowledge the ultimate forces are difficult to identify. Once these forces are identified, other social scientists are in a better position to join the discussion and extend the research deeper into their specializations. If we refuse to go beyond economics, the payoff in the study of growth will elude us, particularly for Asian countries still under the pervasive influence of long traditions.

The method used here is more inductive than deductive; thus inferences are drawn from generalizations much more than deduced from assumptions. This is to be expected in a volume largely historical, taking the issues to be analyzed from the records of the past and searching for answers in the changing complex of technologies and institutions over stretches of time. Since growth is defined to be sustained increases in real GDP per capita, the procedure is to look into the growth of GDP as it originates in the agricultural (A), industrial (I), and service (S) sectors.

Most of this volume was written in Manila, during the years since 1980, although some of the material is revised and extended versions of various papers published over the past three decades. Detailed statistical data, too voluminous to include here, are available in those papers, which are cited where appropriate.

Though scattered references are made to Indonesia, Burma, Bangladesh, and Vietnam, there are no systematic discussions of these countries although they are important. The time series data available were insufficient or inadequate, and the supplementary information and studies too meager for analysis and interpretation. Data and surveys have become more plentiful for Bangladesh and Indonesia from the 1970s, but not for the earlier decades. Without the latter, it is difficult to tell whether the experience of the 1970s constitutes real growth or only transitional change. Much of the Indonesian performance from the 1970s depends on petrol revenues, and there is little information as to what happened to underlying secular forces in the hyperinflation decades prior to the 1970s. Bangladesh achieved independence only in the 1970s, and with the social confusion and political uncertainties of nation-building, there was not much that could be done for secular growth. Similarly, reconstruction was the order of the day for Vietnam in the past decade. Burmese data are said to be unreliable.

The volume is divided into three parts. The first part, Chapters 1–3, contains the analytical framework to help with the selection of the strategic forces and processes used in discussing the growth of various countries in the second part. The framework is a detailed one because the growth patterns of various countries vary in complex ways, and it is difficult to understand them with the simple models of existing theories. The framework relates to proximate forces and their operational mechanisms in the historical background. The country chapters in Part II attempt to single out some of the more ultimate forces. In Part

III, the implications of postwar growth and structural changes are brought together to arrive at generalizations regarding the impact on income distribution and population, prospects and problems for the coming decades. My objective is to integrate the patterns of economic growth with changes in income distribution and population dynamics.

Synopsis of the Chapters

We start in Chapter 1 with an explanation of the poverty of monsoon Asia before the arrival of Western colonialists. We find that it was the nature of the monsoon winds, which brought heavy rains half of the year and very little in the other half, which gave rise to a type of agriculture different in many aspects from that of the West. The heavy rains led to paddy rice growing, which required a great deal of labor for transplantation and harvesting and which was responsible for the great population densities of monsoon Asia. This immense population, however, was unable to find adequate jobs during the drier half-year, and annual output per worker was low. The nub of the problem of the monsoon economy was to transform an economy operating at low levels of underemployment equilibrium to high levels of full employment equilibrium if it was to grow at full speed. The next chapter describes how this might be done.

Chapter 2 sets out to construct a detailed framework largely based on East Asian experience, after showing that existing theories of development worked out before the East Asian successes were not very helpful. The prevailing theories of dualism and unlimited supply of labor advocated shifting labor from agriculture into industries to begin the process of growth, not taking into account the nature of the surplus labor in monsoon agriculture. Since in monsoon paddy agriculture (before the labor force explosion of the latter 1960s) there was a shortage of labor during the peak seasons; the labor surplus was confined to the slack seasons. In our framework the process of growth is started by keeping labor in agriculture, providing more and better productive activities during the slack months through multiplecropping, and diversification with fruit and vegetable growing, root crops, poultry and other animal products, and fishery, together with greater off-farm employment from labor-intensive industrial production. The more plentiful work opportunities for farm family members during the slack months contribute to higher annual incomes and an expanding domestic market for industries and services, eventually leading to a fully employed labor force. With a tighter labor market, real wages start to accelerate and mechanization spreads to the vast majority of farms and firms, and the substitution of labor by small machines begins to raise total factor productivity and GDP per capita. Thus, growth, defined as upward change in GNP per capita (or per worker), speeds up after full employment is reached in agriculture. Accordingly, the optimum strategy of development starts out with agriculturalization as the best way to get the process of growth started in monsoon Asia with its pronounced seasonality in labor demand. The chapter attempts to delineate the framework in detail since without the specifics it may not be useful for policy purposes.

In Chapter 3, the record of growth since World War II is reviewed. The finding is that a group of countries in East Asia has been growing spectacularly over the three decades, and that another group in Southeast Asia began in the 1970s to follow in the footsteps of East Asia, but that progress was slow in South Asia. The central problem that emerges from the record—and that becomes the central problem of this volume—is how and why such great differentials in the pace of growth have occurred in the postwar era when all the monsoon countries grew so slowly in the previous centuries. We attempt to answer it using the approach discussed above, and then search for more ultimate factors in the historical background of the country chapters.

In the country chapters of Part II, we start with Japan in Chapter 4 and find that full employment was reached in agriculture in the latter 1950s with diversified cropping and off-farm employment. The much higher rate of growth in the postwar than in the prewar decades is traced to the extensive institutional changes started by the Allied Powers and continued by the Japanese. In particular, the demilitarization and democratization of institutions motivated manpower at all levels to great heights of diligence and innovativeness in the workplace, enabling Japan rapidly to import, adapt, disseminate, and use efficiently the technologies of the West.

Chapter 5 finds that the forces and mechanisms of rapid growth in Taiwan and South Korea were similar to those of Japan, but with a major difference. South Korea shifted too strongly and prematurely into industrialization in the 1960s, neglecting its agriculture, and then pushed into too many heavy industries in the 1970s. To cover the import of food and machines, Korea had to hastily build up exports by establishing large enterprises through subsidies and loans from abroad, ending up, in contrast to Taiwan, with big companies of dubious efficiency, the highest per capita debt burden in Asia, and social unrest.

Chapter 6 shows that the city-states of Hong Kong and Singapore grew quickly because, with little food produced domestically and without a large domestic market based on agriculture, they were compelled to rely on efficiency with free trade to earn foreign exchange for food imports. They were fortunate to have inherited one of the most efficient Asian service sectors which furnished external economies for industries in the form of financing, shipping, marketing, public utilities, housing and the varied government services. As in the other East Asian countries, there was a labor force with a strong work culture grounded in Confucian ethics. The city-states met the challenge of limited food, markets, and labor supplies with all-out efforts at efficiency and internationalization, unlike the giants of Asia which strove for self-sufficiency and self-reliance under conditions of unlimited supplies of labor, natural resources, nationalized industries, and extensive government intervention.

In Chapter 7, we take up the experience of the Philippines and Thailand. Starting out with one-half of the level of Philippine per capita income, Thailand, without a colonial past, steadily caught up with the Philippines, which after a fast start in the 1950s experienced retardation with heavy-handed import substitution. The free peasantry of Thailand, created by the Chakkri kings out of serfs and slaves, was largely responsible for this growth, with little state assistance, while the Philippines was dominated by landed oligarchies originating in the Spanish policy of giving lands to the datos, who proceeded to force the free peasants into tenancy.

Chapter 8 deals with the two economies of Asia whose agriculture was dominated by plantation crops, not rice. Although both started with relatively high levels of per capita income, Malaysia left Sri Lanka far behind as the latter concentrated its resources in a socialistic, welfare-oriented strategy while Malaysia emphasized agricultural development. To finance welfare expenditures, Sri Lanka taxed and regulated the British-owned plantations heavily. Malaysia left the planations alone, and they evolved into the most efficient rubber and palm-oil producers in the world, while assisting small rice growers and other peasants. Malaysia's industrialization was labor-intensive with minimal protection and regulation, and by the early 1980s Malaysia was evolving into an industrial society, with the agricultural labor force declining absolutely and with full employment, while Sri Lanka was troubled by ethnic unrest and unemployment.

Chapter 9 describes the slow growth of the Goliaths of Asia, India and China, when both countries became bogged down with costly and inefficient state-owned heavy industries which took away resources from the agricultural sector. The obsolete machines produced by the big industries and forced on the light industries destroyed their efficiency, though some of them had been the most efficient in Asia in the

1940s. This gave the NICs of East Asia the chance to move into the textile markets of the West, just as Thailand replaced Burma as the rice basket for southern Asia as Burma stagnated. The Goliaths ended the postwar era with two-thirds of the labor force still in agriculture, further from completing the agro-industrial transition than the ASEAN countries.

Part III selects for discussion some of the major implications of postwar growth. Chapters 10 and 11 seek to link economic growth and structural changes to income distribution and population changes. The impact of agriculture-based, labor-intensive industrialization is seen to be favorable for keeping income disparities low. This is because available resources are spread more evenly among farms and firms, and their rising efficiencies and full employment under conditions of liberalization and competitive market forces ensure the spread of the benefits to their employees. In contrast, capital-intensive industrialization in the early stages of the transition concentrates scarce resources in a few firms and a small number of employees, leaving little for the smaller farms and firms. And since the size of the domestic market depends on the latter in monsoon economies, home demand expands slowly and jobs are not generated for the new labor force. Under conditions of low income disparity and faster growth of GNP, savings are distributed more favorably for development since the smaller firms and farms have more finances for expansion and mechanization. The higher-income families have less wealth to indulge in luxurious living, and imports tend to be productivity-raising equipment rather than luxuries.

In Chapter 11, the impact on the demographic transition is shown to be favorable in that fertility tends to fall more rapidly when incomes and savings grow rapidly among lower-income families under a labor-intensive strategy of growth with full employment and increasing mechanization. Perceptions of parents in the lower-income groups shift toward providing more education for their children, and with increased income they are able to finance the direct and indirect costs of secondary schooling. After their children's education is completed, they are able to save for more security in their retirement. Fertility levels fall as peasants and working-class parents begin to substitute greater investments in education, and in physical and financial assets and insurance schemes, for more children. These, then, are some of the connections bringing together growth, structural changes, income distribution, and changes in fertility patterns.

Chapter 12 reviews the lessons from postwar growth and looks ahead to the prospect of a Pacific Century, describing the various trends which point in that direction. The prospects are good as Western and socialist Europe slows down more than Pacific Asia, but the road ahead will be bumpy as the global economy cannot be expected to be as robust as it has been in past decades.

Acknowledgements

In writing this volume and the numerous past articles underlying it, my obligations have accumulated over the past decades to a point where it is not possible to pay adequate respect to all who helped, but special thanks go to my wife Chiye, for straightening out my sentences, and to my assistants, George Cheng and Gloria Lambino. The first draft of the volume was sent in October 1984 to Mr. H. Fujimori, of the Institute of Developing Economies in Tokyo, who organized a series of meetings with country specialists at which lively discussions were held. Written comments on Japan from Professors M. Shinohara and Y. Kasai, and on Singapore from Lim Chong Yah of the University of Singapore, were very helpful.

Grateful acknowledgement is also made to former colleagues at Stanford University, the University of Washington in Seattle, the University of Hawaii, the University of Singapore, Thammasat University, and Gadjah Mada University, and, above all, to my colleagues at the University of the Philippines School of Economics, especially José Encarnacion, Alex Herrin, Edita Tan, and others who read various chapters and offered valuable comments. For major research support, I am indebted to the National Science Foundation in Washington, the Ford Foundation, and, above all, to the Rockefeller Foundation which (together with Ford) made it possible for me to spend the two and a half decades since the late 1950s working in Asia: at Hitotsubashi University in Tokyo (1959–61), the University of Singapore (1966–68), and the University of the Philippines, Thammasat, and Gadjah Mada (1971 to the present). I learned a great deal about research during the time I spent at the National Bureau of Economic Research, the United Nations National Account Division, the Food Research Institute at Stanford, and the Hitotsubashi Institute of Economic Research.

There are many other scholars to whom I owe much. But to the late Simon Kuznets I owe a lifelong debt for his support, his advice, and his writings, as is abundantly evident in this volume. To my parents I owe the opportunity to study for so many years in Hawaii and at Columbia University.

PART I

Analytical Framework

CHAPTER 1

The Nature of Asia's Monsoon Economy and Its Heritage of Poverty

*E*arly travellers to Asia from the West were struck by the "teeming millions" in Asian cities—a phrase which captures the basic characteristic of monsoon Asia, its large population packed densely into small houses but moving about vigorously, in sharp contrast to the sparsely settled, more leisurely pace in the West. Simon Kuznets has noted the low levels of per capita income in Asian countries compared with the preindustrial levels of Western countries in the 18th century on the eve of their entry into modern economic growth. The Statistical Office of the United Nations estimated 1949 per capita incomes for the Philippines, Thailand, India, Indonesia, South Korea, China, Burma, and Sri Lanka to average about U.S.\$50 in 1951/54 prices. This is about one-fourth the levels of the Western countries, estimated by Kuznets to be at a minimum of U.S.\$200 in 1952/54 prices (Kuznets, 1965: 176–79). In Chapter 4 below we have found Japan's income to be about 60 U.S. 1952/54 dollars in 1900. In terms of 1960–1965 average per capita caloric intake, Asia was the lowest with 2,070; per capita caloric intake was 2,170 for Africa, for North Central America 3,060, for South America 2,460, for Oceania 3,090, for Europe 3,210 and for the USSR 3,280.[1]

In Table 1.1 are shown data on farm family incomes of various Asian countries converted into 1960 dollars and compared with United States farm family incomes. Table 1.2 shows product per worker in agriculture, which after three decades of rapid Asian growth has not improved very much by the standards set by the United States. Even in the case of Japan, individuals in farm families earn only one-fourth the counterpart United States incomes, despite the fact that nearly half of the total incomes of farm families in Japan are derived from non-

[1] *FAO Production Yearbook*, 1976. Wickizer and Bennett (1941: 128–132) cite a number of dietary surveys in Asia before World War II showing extensive deficiencies in animal protein, fats, several vitamins, and minerals, resulting in the prevalence of a number of dietary diseases in nearly all countries of Asia including Japan.

Table 1.1   Average Annual Farm Income, Per Family and Per Capita, in 1960 U.S. Dollars

	(1) Av. Income per Farm Family in National Currency	(2) Av. Income per Farm Family in U.S. dollars	(3) Av. Income per Farm Family in 1960 U.S.$	(4) Index for Col. (3) U.S.$100	(5) Average Size of Farm Family	(6) Per Capita Farm Family Income in 1960 U.S.$	(7) Index for Col. (6) U.S.$100
U.S.A. (1960)	$ 4,531	4,531	4,531	100.0	4.50	1,007	100.0
Japan (1960)	¥ 409,500	1,138	1,138	25.1	5.72	199	19.8
Taiwan (1966)	NT$ 32,320	808	737	16.3	5.80	127	12.6
Korea (1965)	Won 112,200	422	396	8.7	6.31	63	6.3
Philippines (1965)	P 1,727	443	415	9.2	6.10	68	6.8
Thailand (1968/69)*	Baht 8,073	388	321	7.1	5.76	58	5.8
Indonesia (1976)	Rup. 174,684	421	219	4.8	5.85	37	3.7
W. Malaysia (1967/68)*	M$ 1,440	470	408	9.0	5.78	71	7.1

Note: These exchange rate conversions into U.S. dollars may undervalue the income of most of the Asian countries in terms of purchasing power parities. But even if they are doubled, they are still low. Data on exchange rates and U.S. cost of living index from *IBRD World Tables 1980*.

* Average annual income per rural family instead of per farm family.

Sources: *Historical Statistics of the U.S., Colonial Times to 1970*, Part I, p. 301 (for the U.S.); *Japan Statistical Yearbook* and *One Hundred Years of Agricultural Statistics in Japan* (for Japan); *Family Income and Expenditure Survey Report* (for Taiwan); *Major Statistics of Korean Economy 1977* (for S. Korea); *Family Income and Expenditure Survey 1965* (for the Philippines); Table 2.3.1 of Oey Astra Meesok, "Income Distribution in Thailand," CAMS Discussion Paper No. 76–12 (for Thailand); p. 17 of Lim Lin Lean, "The Pattern of Income Distribution in West Malaysia 1957–1970," ILO World Employment Programme Research Working Paper 2–23 (for West Malaysia); and Central Bureau of Statistics, *Income Distribution in Indonesia 1976* (for Indonesia).

agricultural sources. This is true also for Taiwan, but for the other countries of Asia only about one-fourth of farm family income is from nonagricultural sources.

This book hypothesizes that the monsoon paddy agriculture of Asia is of a different type from that of the West and that the technology and institutions which have evolved over the centuries in these economies and societies are also different. This form of agriculture has been largely responsible for the low income of Asian peasants by requiring very heavy amounts of labor during the peak seasons of plowing/planting and harvesting but leaving a huge labor force with little remunerative work not only in winter but also between the peak points of the wet season, i.e., after planting and before the beginning of harvesting—months during which infestation of insects and weeds are minimal since the rice crop grows in puddles of water. Thus, both the small size of densely settled farms and the pronounced seasonality in the demand for labor are the fundamental sources of the low income

Table 1.2   Product Per Worker in Agriculture, Industry, and Services, 1979

	(1) Product per Worker in Agriculture in U.S.$	(2) Index for Col. (1)	(3) Product per Worker in Industry in U.S.$	(4) Index for Col. (3)	(5) Product per Worker in Services in U.S.$	(6) Index for Col. (5)
U.S.A.	19,762	100.0	25,800	100.0	24,870	100.0
Japan	7,829	39.6	22,884	88.7	20,403	82.0
Taiwan	2,033	10.3	6,167	23.9	5,758	23.2
S. Korea	2,522	12.8	5,354	20.8	5,557	22.3
Philippines	834	4.2	2,880	11.2	1,994	8.0
Malaysia	2,419	12.2	5,989	23.2	4,683	18.8
Thailand	440	2.2	4,837	18.7	3,080	12.4
Indonesia	482	2.4	2,802	10.9	1,023	4.1
India	326	1.6	1,127	4.4	825	3.3

Note: Agriculture includes agriculture, forestry, and fishery; Industry in cludes mining, manufacturing, construction, public utilities and transport, storage, and communication; Services includes commerce and services.

Sources: *Key Indicators of Developing Member Countries of ADB*, April 1982 (for all countries unless otherwise indicated); *Japan Statistical Yearbook 1981* (for Japan); *Taiwan Statistical Data Book 1980* (for Taiwan); *Major Statistics of the Korean Economy 1982* (for S. Korea); *UN Yearbook of National Accounts Statistics 1979* and *ILO Yearbook of Labour Statistics 1980* (for the U.S.A.).

of Asian peasants, even though yields per hectare are not low by international standards. These incomes were too meager to provide food and release labor for establishing industrialization and generate enough demand for the products of industries during the 19th century when the Industrial Revolution was sweeping through much of Europe and North America.

The first part of this chapter discusses the major forces responsible for low incomes in Asia as they evolved in the past, beginning with the analysis of the low incomes in the agricultural sector, which was overwhelmingly the predominant sector throughout the past centuries, typically with more than three-fourths of the population. The relation of monsoon paddy (wetland rice) agriculture to the low incomes in the nonagricultural sector is then taken up.[2] The second part describes how monsoon Asia fell behind the West from around the middle of the second millennium A.D., and proceeds to a summary of the slow upward climb from the mid-19th century up to World War II. This historical perspective will serve as background to the later chapters on postwar developments.

The Poverty of Asian Monsoon Paddy Agriculture

We take up first the origin and evolution of the highly labor-intensive and seasonal monsoon paddy agriculture and its relation to Asia's great population densities, tiny farm sizes, and scarcity of arable land. Asians had no choice but to evolve paddy rice agriculture over many centuries since no other cereal crop was suited to the pattern of rainfall and humidity of monsoon Asia.[3] It was the monsoon winds which imposed on Asians this type of farming; in *The Pattern of Asia*, monsoon winds are described as follows:

> Each continent exhibits the seasonal reversal of winds and rains known as the monsoon effects, but nowhere are these reversals as notable as in Asia. In North America there is a smaller land mass in which cooling and heating takes place; in South America only a small part of the continent lies in the higher latitudes and the winter monsoon effects are minimized; as for Africa, no part

[2] This portion of the chapter is largely based on several earlier papers, and frequent reference will be made to them.

[3] Wickizer and Bennett (1941: 49) note that "few agricultural alternatives present themselves. Neither wheat, barley, rye nor oats will thrive as summer crops under such conditions of moisture and heat. Millet, grain, sorghums and maize do better but can equal rice only in areas of lower rainfall . . . and none can produce as much food per unit of land in the places where lowland rice thrives."

of the continent lies within the higher latitudes and the monsoon effects are restricted to relatively limited areas. Europe, as a westward-facing, ocean-fronting area is most strongly influenced by the westerly winds of the upper middle latitudes, and the climate of Europe is predominantly maritime all the year round, except in the Mediterranean region. In Australia, too, a relatively small area is involved and maritime influences tend to predominate throughout the year, except in interior Australia . . . (Ginzburg, 1958: 8).

The reversal in direction of winds and rains in Asia is due to the heating and cooling of the world's largest land mass, especially in the "vast complex of mountains and plateaus" centered in Tibet and bounded on the south by the Himalayas, on the west by the Pamirs, on the north by the mountains of Sinkiang, and on the east by the southwestern mountains of China—a range of mountains and plateaus extending 5,000 miles.

> The seasonal heating and cooling of this, the world's largest land mass, makes for major seasonal variations in climate. In winter, when the interior regions are cold, a semi-permanent high pressure belt forms within the northern interior of the continent, and strong, cold winds, outflowing as polar continental air masses from the anticyclones within the belt, bring winter to most of the continent. In summer, the rapid and continuous heating of the interior results in lower pressures and in the inflow of tropical maritime air from the continent's margin. Since the outflowing winds are land-originated and usually do not pass over large bodies of water, they are dry, and the winters also tend to be dry. Conversely, in the summer the generally weaker inflows of air from the eastern and southern seas are humid and carry with them the moisture that for much of Asia makes summer the rainier season (Ginzburg, 1958: 7).

The mountain core of this huge land mass "acts as the hub of a colossal wheel, the spokes of which are formed by some of the greatest rivers of the world, spiralling outward from the rain-catching and snow-capped slopes of the Hindu Kush, Pamirs, Himalayas, Karakorum, Altyn Tagh, T'ren Shan, and the other ranges of the highland core. The great rivers flowing eastward and southward define the Asia that is populous and developed." These rivers are the Indus, the Ganges, the Brahmaputra, the Irrawaddy, the Mekong, and the Yangtze, besides a number of smaller rivers. "Within the valleys of many of these rivers have developed the cultural cores of lasting civilizations and modern nations, and it is in them that most of the peoples of Asia live—and multiply." Nonetheless, "not only is most of Asia unattractive to settlement, but much of it is virtually unoccupied, although there are more people more densely concentrated in Asia than in any other continent."

Rainfall must be heavy enough during at least three months of the year that large puddles of water can collect for the rice seedlings to take root and then for the transplanted seedlings to grow to maturity. Where the rainfall is much heavier, as in parts of Sumatra and parts of Africa and Latin America, paddy rice growing is not feasible. The unique feature of Asian paddy culture may be said to lie in the monsoon winds which come, not to all sections of Asia, but to the heavily populated regions. The monsoon countries of Asia include nearly all of Southeast Asia and the densely settled portions of China, Japan, Sri Lanka, India, and Bangladesh. The monsoon regions exclude Hokkaido and Manchuria in the northeast, the Mongolias in the north, western China, Afghanistan, and Pakistan in the west, the southeastern islands of Indonesia, and India west and south of New Delhi. In Malaysia and Sri Lanka, as in Japan and Taiwan, there are light rainy months before the summer monsoons.

Figure 1.1 shows the rainfall patterns of the main regions of the world. The large mode for monsoon Asia contrasts sharply with the even rainfall patterns of Europe, North America, Latin America, and Africa. Of course, in parts of these regions, such as the Amazon in Brazil and parts of Sierra Leone, Gambia, and other countries in West Africa, there are heavy rains during certain months of the year, but these areas are sparsely settled compared with densely populated monsoon Asia. (Table 1.3 gives average annual rainfall for various countries of Asia. See also rainfall charts for each Asian country in Oshima, 1985.)

The usual concept of population density (total population divided by total land area) is less useful for our purpose than a narrower one pertaining to agricultural land and agricultural population, thereby excluding uninhabitable lands and cities with concentrated populations. The FAO regularly presents statistics on agricultural land and agricultural population for all regions of the world (see Table 1.4). If the latter is divided by the former, the estimates of agricultural population densities are obtained. In Asia, this density was 1.3 persons per hectare in 1975, compared with only 0.4 persons for the world as a whole. The Asian density was four times larger than that of Africa, six times that of Europe, and thirteen times larger than that of North and South

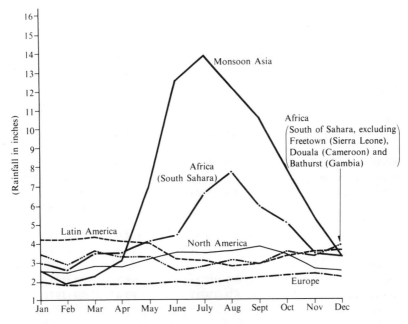

Figure 1.1.   Rainfall patterns in the major regions of the world.
Source: Royal Meteorological Society, U.K.

America. If we exclude those parts of Asia which do not belong to monsoon Asia as defined above—all of West Asia (i.e., the Middle East) Pakistan, western and most of northern China, about half of India and parts of Indonesia—the Asian density will rise to nearly 10 persons per hectare of agricultural land, or about 30 times that of Africa, 40 times that of Europe, and over 100 times that of the Americas. Moreover, most of the population of monsoon Asia is concentrated in the valleys and basins of the great and small rivers where paddy rice is grown. Where the less labor-intensive crops as on plantations are substantial, densities are low. In Sri Lanka, West Malaysia, Indonesia, and the Philippines, where plantation crops are important, another concept of density (in which plantation crop areas are excluded) shows densities to be double those of the broader concept.[4]

---

[4] In the FAO concept, agricultural land includes arable land plus land under permanent cropping, meadows, and pastures. If density is confined to arable areas only, in W. Malaysia density in 1970 was 8 persons per hectare (compared to 1.7 persons per hectare of all agricultural lands), 7.7 to 2.9 in Sri Lanka, 6.1 to 2.8 in Indonesia, and 4.3 to 2.5 in the Philippines. These computations are obtained by dividing hectares into agricultural populations in the FAO concept.

Table 1.3   Average Annual Rainfall, Area Planted to Rice, and Total
Population Density in Regions of Selected Asian Countries

	Total Population Density of Arable Land (persons per hectare)	Average Rainfall per Year (inches)	Rice-planted Area as % of Total Cultivated Land
Japan			
Hokkaido	4.9 (1979)	43.7	24 (1979)
Japan, excluding			
Hokkaido	25.4 (1979)	71.8	65 (1979)
India			
Northwest India [1]	1.9 (1961)	29.4	16
India, excluding			(1959–60 [2]
Northwest	3.9 (1961)	64.0	55
			(1959–60) [2]
Indonesia			
Sumatra	4.7 (1973) [3]	108.9 [4]	37 (1973)
Java-Madura	13.4 (1973) [3]	89.5	77 (1973)
Philippines			
Luzon	9.9 (1971)	98.2	54 (1971) [6]
Mindanao	6.0 (1971)	89.4 [5]	29 (1971)
Pakistan and Bangladesh			
Pakistan	3.1 (1970)	13.7	17 (1976) [7]
Bangladesh	7.7 (1970)	100.0	98 (1976) [7]

Notes: [1] Northwest India is composed of Uttar Pradesh East, Uttar Pradesh West, Punjab, Himachal Pradesh, Jammu Kashmir, Rajasthan, Madhya Pradesh West, Gujarat, and Saurashtra and Kutch. [2] Area planted to rice as % of area planted to total cereal. [3] Population density of total agricultural land (which consists of farm and estate agriculture). [4] Rain forest. [5] Rainfall for Mindanao is evenly distributed throughout the year, unlike that of the monsoon Luzon area. [6] Philippines, excluding Mindanao. [7] Area planted to rice as % of area planted to all cereals.

Sources: *Japan Statistical Yearbook 1981*; *Statistical Abstract of the Indian Union 1961*; *Agriculture Census 1973* and *Statistical Yearbook of Indonesia 1979*; *NEDA Philippine Yearbook 1978*, and *Census of Agriculture 1971*; *Area Handbook for Pakistan, Area Handbook for Bangladesh*, and *FAO Production Yearbook 1966*.

Another perspective on density can be obtained from the statistics on average size of farms, defined as land which is used wholly or partly for agricultural production and is operated by one person alone or with the assistance of others, without regard to title or location. FAO data (for 1972) on area of holdings divided by the total number of

Table 1.4   Agricultural Densities and Average Sizes of Farms in Various Parts of the World

Region/ Continent	Agricultural Population/ Agricultural Land (persons per hectare)	Agricultural Population/ Arable Land (persons per hectare)	Total Agricultural Holdings (million holdings)	Area of Holdings (million hectares)	Average Area of Holdings (hectares per holding)
World	0.4	1.4	138.5	2,387.6	17.2
Monsoon Asia	1.3	3.1	92.3	201.2	2.2
Africa	0.3	1.4	7.3	227.8	31.0
North and Central America	0.1	0.2	7.0	710.0	102.0
Latin America	0.1	1.0	6.8	544.2	80.0
Europe	0.2	0.4	24.7	221.3	9.0
Oceania	0.01	0.1	0.4	483.1	1,316.1

Notes: Arable land as defined by FAO refers to land under temporary crops (double-cropped areas are counted only once), temporary meadows for mowing or pasture, land under market and kitchen gardens (including cultivation under grass), and land temporarily fallow or lying idle. Land under permanent crops refers to land cultivated with crops which occupy the land for long periods and need not be replanted after each harvest, such as cocoa, coffee, and rubber; it includes land with shrubs, fruit trees, nut trees and vines, but excludes land with trees grown for wood or timber. Permanent meadows and pastures are land used five years or more for herbaceous forage crops, either cultivated or growing wild.

Agricultural land = Arable land + Land under permanent crops + Permanent meadows and pastures.

An agricultural holding as defined by FAO refers to all land that is used wholly or partly for agricultural production and is operated by one person—the holder—alone or with the assistance of others, without regard to title, size or location (livestock kept for agricultural purposes without agricultural land is also considered as constituting a holding).

Source: *FAO Production Yearbook* (1972), based on 1960 and 1970 agricultural censuses of each country.

holdings gives 2 hectares in Asia, 9 for Europe, 31 for Africa, 80 for South America, and 102 for North America[5] (Table 1.4).

[5] One of the few countries elsewhere in the world with Asian levels of density is Egypt, where irrigation from the Nile permits rice growing in paddies as in monsoon Asia, and transplanting was introduced in the 1930s. But since the water comes from the Nile, the rice can be grown year-round.

Underlying the densities of monsoon Asia was the highly labor-intensive nature of paddy rice culture. Labor requirements per hectare of paddy-rice grown varied from country to country, depending mainly on the extent to which work animals were used (or, in East Asia, machines), the extent of irrigation and of available transportation, and so on. Labor required per hectare in the prewar years was about 50 man-days in the Philippines, 80 in Thailand and Bombay, 100 in West Bengal, and 150 in Madras, China, and Japan. The lower figures for Southeast Asia (except Java) reflected the more extensive use of work animals and the limited extent of irrigation and transplantation, though even these figures were considerably higher than those for the wheat culture of the United States as early as 1800 (Oshima, 1971b). For the United States in 1900, before mechanization, only 5 man-days for wheat and 10 days for corn were needed.

The major reasons for the heavy labor requirements of paddy rice compared with wheat and other cereals were, first of all, the need (in order to get high yields) to prepare seedling beds and transplanting instead of broadcasting or drilling seeds as in wheat; second, the time-consuming methods of harvesting with a small knife or at best a sickle instead of cradles or scythes as in the Western wheat culture of the 19th century; and, third, the rigid work schedule enforced by the monsoon rains, which came and went at only certain periods of the year.

Typically, in Asian paddy fields, when the first rains come, the seedling beds are plowed and harrowed several times. The soil of the seed bed is hoed, plowed, or trampled into fine, soft mud before sowing. In most countries, the seeds are soaked in water and then broadcast after the water is drained. The water is replaced in the paddy after the seeds have germinated, and after about a month the young rice plants are pulled out, tied in bundles, topped, and taken to the paddies to be planted in the main fields. If the monsoons come too late, the seedlings become too old and may have to be replaced with new ones.[6]

During harvesting, reaping with knives and sickles is time-consuming. The use of the larger scythe employed in wheat harvesting is not feasible in the wet or moist paddy soil: moisture can spoil the grain as it falls to the ground after scything. Moreover, with the long-stalk *indica* rice used extensively in Southeast Asia before the spread of Japanese dwarfs

---

[6] In Japan in 1954, before mechanization made headway, plowing per hectare took 10 hours, seedling beds and transplanting 17 hours, weeding 15 hours, reaping 18 hours, threshing 10 hours, and irrigating 11 hours; transplanting and reaping/threshing were concentrated in a brief period. (Data from Agricultural Productivity Council, Tokyo.)

and IRRI semi-dwarfs, lodging was a common problem, leading to uneven maturing so that the heads had to be cut singly with small knives to avoid heavy losses due to shattering, lodging, and uneven maturing. Unlike other grains, the mature rice grain readily shatters. Thus, it is reported that before the war the Javanese peasant refused, despite strong urgings by the Dutch, to use the sickle in place of his small knife; recently, however, with the development of the IRRI short-stalk varieties, use of the sickle has been spreading, replacing large numbers of harvest workers.

Population density in the rural areas with their limited availability of new lands and the labor intensity of agricultural operations meant that farms were small. We shall see next that the seasonality of the monsoon limited the use of these tiny holdings to only about half the year, unless irrigation brought water during the dry seasons.

Heavy labor requirements concentrated in certain months of the year largely explain the greater densities of Asia compared with the West. The majority of Asian peasants must look for off-farm work when the dry months come, and some also after the busy months of planting and before harvesting, as crops growing in water do not require as much care as those crops grown in dry fields, such as wheat. Traditionally the rural people undertook handicraft production and work in forestry, fishing, hunting, and other off-farm activities; but with the importation of cheaper machine-made products, the peasants lost their urban markets, and their production of handicrafts was confined to village needs. In Western countries, the sparsely settled, low-density rural areas, together with the evenness of rainfall throughout the year, permitted farmers to complement their agricultural production with livestock raising as land (when wheat or other cereals were not being grown) was sufficient to allow growing of crops to feed livestock during the winter months. As will be noted below, the rise of capitalistic agriculture, especially in England from the 18th century, hastened the separation of agriculture from handicraft production and its combination with animal husbandry. This separation never occurred in monsoon Asia, even to the present, except in plantation crops such as rubber and tea which require labor all year around. Much of the available work was marginal, intermittent, irregular, of short duration, and of low intensity, and with so much labor competing for so little work in the dry months, remuneration was low.

The high population densities and the dry season preclude the development of animal husbandry as a seasonal complement to crop culture despite the year-round warm weather. "In the more densely populated areas, land is not available for growing both food and feed;

hence beasts of burden tend to be relatively scarce" (Wickizer and Bennett, 1941: 50). In Asia, the number of head of livestock per person is only one-fourth that in South America.

In addition to heavy labor demands for planting and harvesting, the monsoon rains impose a rigid schedule of labor requirements for the various operations. The early rains of the monsoon season are insufficient to soften the clay soils, hardened by the dry months. The brick-hard earth cannot be plowed even with buffalo power until the heavier rains begin to flood the paddies. This calls for timely and concentrated plowing, in addition to long hours of work with seed beds, so that transplantation will not be delayed beyond the optimal stage of seedling growth. Harvesting also must be carried out at the appropriate time; otherwise large losses will be incurred as over-ripe grain is more liable to shatter.

The heavy concentration of labor required during the few months of the monsoon and the tight work schedule mean that labor required for optimal yields typically exceeds by a wide margin the available adult male working population. (In areas where labor was available, both labor inputs and yields were highest, as in China, Japan, and Java; they were lowest in countries like Thailand where labor was not available for intensive cultivation.) This calls for the use of young, old, and female workers. These heavy labor requirements must have contributed to the rapid rise of population in the major, more temperate Asian regions such as China, India, and Japan, as the technology of monsoon paddy culture became increasingly labor-intensive in the centuries of the second millennium, with deeper and more careful plowing, more intensive transplanting, multiple cropping, and more intensive reaping. The process extended beyond Malthusian dynamics. Two rice crops on the same land during the year meant that with the same labor force much more could be produced and more people could be fed. But the increased hands could be put to more intensive cultivation to get higher yields per crop, so that in the latter case population and food supply went up more or less simultaneously. None of these operations (except for plowing) could use work animals, so that the demand for hands rose.[7]

In sum, the wet monsoons imposed on Asians a labor-intensive form of agriculture which over the centuries created greater and greater

[7] See Hanks (1972, Chapters 4 and 8) for discussion on how labor requirements per hectare rose and output per worker fell with the shift from broadcasting to transplanting rice in the recent decade in the central regions of Thailand, and for a description of the tight schedules of various operations. Chapter 11 of this book discusses the demographic transition in Asia.

demand for labor during the peak seasons. As a result, the increasing population densities meant decreasing size of farms, as crop land began to be scarce and diminishing returns set in. And the rising rural population found less to do during the dry months as the larger population sought more work. Thus, in Indonesia, per capita incomes are lower in the rural areas of Java and Bali (where densities are much higher) than in Sumatra, Kalimantan, and Sulawesi; similarly, in the Philippines incomes are higher in Mindanao, which is less densely settled, than in most parts of the country. The problems of income distribution will be discussed in detail in Chapter 10.

Low Incomes in Monsoon Asia's Industry and Services

The industries and services that evolved in Asia were also small and labor-intensive. On the supply side, since most of them could be operated at full capacity only during the slack seasons when labor was easily available, the use of expensive equipment, large buildings, and a regular staff of supervisors would have been uneconomical. In addition, the cheapness of labor during the slack seasons made labor-intensive operations in or near the home and farm feasible and economical. Land for workshops and stores was expensive in the lowlands in and around the river basins, the areas with greatest population densities.

On the demand side, while in the West larger farms made for longer distances between one farm family and another, in the densely settled lowlands of monsoon Asia villages were large groupings of farm families which could sustain many small workshops and stores. In the West, individual farmers had to travel to the nearby towns to market their produce and purchase supplies and consumption goods. This was possible since, with plenty of land, horses could be raised and cheaply maintained as the major means of transportation. This was not so in monsoon Asia; with land scarce, only the rich could afford horses, carriages, and rickshaws for transport into towns. In the United States around 1910 there was one horse to every 5 persons; in Japan the ratio was one to 33 and in Taiwan, one to 10,000. The inconvenience and cost of moving from one part of a city to another made necessary numerous small neighborhood stores and workshops to which the ordinary worker or consumer could walk. Thus, the traditional cities of Asia were clusters of towns with numerous market centers containing small, labor-intensive (often family-operated) stores and workshops (Table 1.5).

To the small units of industry and commerce may be added the small

Table 1.5   Percentage of Total Employment in Firms Engaging Fewer than 10 Persons

United States			Taiwan		
(1947)	Manufacturing	16*	(1961)	Manufacturing	46
(1954)	Manufacturing	8**	(1961)	Commerce	95
			(1961)	Transport	58
Japan			(1961)	Services	93
(1964)	Manufacturing	28	*Philippines*		
(1964)	Manufacturing	50*	(1961)	Manufacturing	76
			(1961)	Construction	93
Singapore			(1961)	Commerce	94
(1966)	Manufacturing	45	(1961)	Transport and Communication	64
			(1961)	Private Services	95
South Korea					
(1966)	Manufacturing	43			
Thailand					
(1970)	Manufacturing	70			

Notes: * % of employment in firms engaging less than 50 persons.
         ** % of employment in firms engaging less than 20 persons.

Sources: See Oshima (1971a) for the various economic and industrial censuses and surveys from which data are taken. United States data from *Statistical Abstract of the United States 1979*. Percentages were derived by subtracting from sector employment figures taken from the labor-force sample surveys the number employed in firms with more than ten persons engaged as reported in the economic or industrial censuses. The residual was assumed to be approximately the size of the sector comprising firms with fewer than 10 employees. The percentage is upwardly biased because there is a tendency for many firms with 10 or more employees to be omitted in the economic or industrial censuses, which are establishment censuses based on lists of addresses. On the other hand, part-time employees and part-year employees tend to be included in establishment censuses.

homes—"rabbit hutches," in the words of the OECD—closely bunched in Asian villages, towns, and cities. The small scale of dwelling units is due partly to the cost of land, construction, and transport but also to the smaller physiques of Asians than of Westerners, which may be related to more than genetics. In Japan, where nutrition has steadily improved in the postwar decades, education authorities are finding that the standard uniforms worn by students in primary and secondary schools are becoming too small for the students entering school in recent years. In the United States, second-generation Asian immigrants are bigger than their parents, and members of the third generation are even bigger.

In those parts of Asia just outside or at the edge of the monsoon territory, wheat/meat diets are prevalent and people are taller and heavier than those in the rice-eating sections of these countries. In the wheat regions (e.g., Manchuria and northern China, northwestern India, West Pakistan), much greater amounts of bread, meat, and milk products are consumed than in the rice regions where rice is supplemented by beans and fish products. Moreover, the lack of year-round employment in the monsoon area may have contributed to low incomes and low food intake, which over the long period may have been a factor in the failure of children in monsoon Asia to grow bigger. (For example, Korea used to be referred to as the "land of spring hunger.") It is also likely that evolutionary selection may not have favored the larger sized physique requiring greater caloric intake for metabolic functions of the body during the slack, dry season when work activity and food supplies were low; during the busy seasons, too, height was a disadvantage in bending down for transplanting, weeding, and harvesting.

In sum, the monsoons contributed to poverty indirectly by keeping the units of production small and labor-intensive in industry and commerce through low farm wages, seasonality, density, and high cost of land. But, as we shall see when we turn to the work ethics and culture of monsoon Asia, the influence of the monsoons was by no means all unfavorable.

Impact of the Monsoon on Work Culture and Social Stability

The heavy demand for workers during the busy seasons had a favorable impact on diligence and propensity to work, particularly on housewives and young workers who had to help with transplanting and harvesting when labor was in short supply. It became the accepted practice in Asia for most women and children to work in the fields alongside adult males. The scarcity of crop land and other resources and the exacting requirements of monsoon agriculture for high yields (careful plowing, rigid schedules and close timing, seedling growing and transplanting, multiple cropping, intensive reaping and threshing) probably contributed to the high quality of work habits and to thriftiness since it was necessary to save for the lean months ahead.[8]

[8] The high quality of Asian farming practices is attested to by the extensive successes achieved by farmers from Japan who went to California and to Brazil, Mexico, Peru, Venezuela, Bolivia, and elsewhere in Latin America before and after World War II.

Even more important was the impact of monsoon agriculture on attitudes toward cooperation, consensus, and harmonious relations, in contrast to the individualism and competition inhering in Western capitalistic agriculture, where the more even distribution of rainfall over most of the year permitted a more leisurely pace of planting and harvesting. Each Western farmer took care of his own needs with the help of his own equipment, animals, and hired hands. The distance between the large farms was an obstacle to sharing and cooperation, and self-help and self-reliance became the social values. In Asia, because of urgent labor requirements and tight scheduling and timing during the busy months, villages were compelled to depend on their kinfolk and neighbors for group work; thus evolved the ideals and tradition of working and living harmoniously, reinforced in the East Asian countries by the system of Confucian ethics. In my view, group-ism was the response to this need to work in groups of a dozen or so families during the busy seasons of plowing/planting and harvesting, as well as the need for group efforts in distributing water and maintaining irrigation works.

The family unit was too small to undertake the number and variety of tasks required during the short periods of the peak seasons. The various tasks involved in land preparation and in transplantation (pulling and heading seedlings, carrying and distributing them to the transplanters, guiding and feeding the workers, and so on) require special skills, different degrees of strength and muscle power, and ex-perience, which can best be met by specialization and division of labor between the sexes of different ages. Some tasks such as land preparation must be carried out by the strongest males, while overseeing of the transplanters can be done by elderly couples. The youngest workers can pull and distribute the seedlings, while females and younger adult males do most of the transplanting. With group planting/plowing, an element of flexibility can be introduced into the schedule by staggering the preparation of seedling beds, and therefore the transplanting of the individual plots of the participating peasant families; this also enables harvesting to be staggered. The enthusiasm generated by group work, often accompanied by singing and socializing, reduces the tedium and arduousness of long hours of work, thereby raising efficiency (Wong, 1979).

In addition to the need for group efforts during planting/plowing and harvesting, there were other operations unique to monsoon Asia, such as the cooperation required to maintain, coordinate, and expand irrigation infrastructure and distribute the water from the canals. Irrigation activities were necessary within the village (with tertiary and quaternary irrigation works), between the villages (with secondary irrigation), and between districts and provinces (with primary irrigation).

It has been noted by the classical economists Richard Jones, Adam Smith, and John Stuart Mill, and further elaborated by Karl Marx, that the need to maintain large irrigation and water-control systems by a central authority gave rise to nationwide political stability and unity in Asia. But much of monsoon Asia—Korea, Japan, Taiwan, the Philippines, Malaysia, and Java—lacks the large rivers such as the Indus, Ganges, Irrawaddy, Mekong, Yangtze, and Yellow, which get their water from the melting snow and rains of the vast plateau and mountain ranges of northern and western China and northern India and Pakistan. Moreover, most paddy farms, even in India, China, Burma, Indochina, and Bangladesh, obtain their water from smaller rivers which in turn are filled directly from the local monsoon rains.

It may be useful at this point to distinguish between nationwide political unification and local social stability. The network of primary and secondary irrigation works between provinces, districts, and villages may be said to depend on national political stability and unity, while the tertiary and quaternary networks are more closely related to local stability within villages. It is the necessity to cooperate and work together on irrigation works near and within villages, together with the requirement to work in family groups during the plowing/planting and harvesting seasons, that seems to underlie the historic stability of Asian village societies. Of the two, the latter contributes more to social stability within the village. Irrigation problems within villages—between farms upstream and those downsteam, or between farms in lower and higher terraces—or between villages are the sources of conflicts and disagreements; although normally resolved one way or another, they leave a residue of bad feelings and hostility between villages or sections of villages. Hence, relations between Asian peasants in neighboring villages are generally far from cordial. Within the village group, in contrast, the tradition of working together has given rise to concepts such as *gotong rojong* (in Java), *bayanihan* (in the Philippines), and "eating from the same pot of rice" (in East Asia)—all terms referring to group work within the village.

Where transplantation is widely practiced, as in East Asia and Java, the villages are much more cohesive and tightly structured than in parts of Thailand, Bangladesh, Burma, Cambodia, and India where deep-water rice-growing (due to the overflow of the major rivers) precludes transplantation of seedlings. In these areas population densities are low, as broadcasting or drilling does not require much labor and the yields are very low. Anthropologist John F. Embree reported

that Thai villages were loosely structured and villagers more independent than in Japan, but when other anthropologists investigated they
found that he was discussing villages south of Bangkok, where just
deep-water rice, not paddy, was grown, and that in other parts of
Thailand where transplantation was customary villages were cohesive
and structured and labor exchange was extensive (Embree, 1939;
Potter, 1979). Similarly, in upland rice areas where the rainfall is
insufficient for paddies, the absence of transplantation in dry farming
may make for less group cohesion.

In my view, these values of Asian groupism may turn out to be
valuable assets in a period of industrial technology which increasingly
requires cooperation between workers and management rather than
the individualist, confrontational attitudes more appropriate for 19th-
century technology. The modern industrial plant has become increasingly an organism of interconnected parts where stoppage in one part
means the whole plant must be closed down, unlike the 19th-century
factory. Instead of hundreds of identical machines horizontally and
separately placed, like spindles in spinning factories, the factory is
increasingly organized with different machines strung together in
assembly lines where stoppage in one machine closes down the entire
line.

Groupism implies that within the group, members help one another
so the group as a whole can compete with other groups. It also implies
that decisions are made, not in authoritarian fashion as in the modern
corporation, but with a high degree of participation by the main members of the group and through consensus which, in turn, calls for compromise. Effort must be made to maintain cordial, harmonious relations within the group if it is to operate effectively.

Just as Protestant ethics are the ethics of Western capitalism, Confucian ethics may be said to be the philosophy of the Asian monsoon
economy: harmony is seen as the key to social and political stability,
and compromise, moderation, diligence, and cooperation as the means
to achieve harmony.[9]

In sum, a unique type of agriculture different from those elsewhere
in the world evolved in Asia over the course of thousands of years.
Labor was abundant during the slack, dry months but scarce during
the busy, wet seasons. Agriculture had to be combined with handicrafts
and other nonfarm occupations; in contrast to the West, it never—

---

[9] But cooperation and harmonious relations can go too far when they preclude
competition and constructive criticism, as may be the case with Javanese entrepreneurs who do not like to compete, and with Filipinos and Malays who do not like
to criticize one another.

except in the plantations—evolved into a completely specialized industry. Fishing in paddies, rivers, and seas, rather than animal husbandry, complemented farming. The small size of farms and the long dry spells limited the earnings of rural Asians, while in the urban areas the small size of business establishments and their labor intensity contributed to low incomes. This poverty, together with the complexities and requirements of monsoon agriculture, however, called for strong work ethics and frugality, and a social philosophy quite different from that in the West. Countries which succeeded in overcoming the constraints imposed by the monsoons, while at the same time taking advantage of the strong work ethic, began to grow rapidly in the postwar decades. For the others, growth was slow. But before we go into the record of postwar growth, let us turn briefly to see what happened in the past.

Stagnation and Slow Growth before World War II

For many centuries leaders in both China and India regarded their countries as the leading centers of world civilization. Only during the last several hundred years did they begin to concede the superiority of the West. To understand the reasons for the decline of Asia relative to the West, we can look at East Asian, particularly Chinese, history, where better records are available (in part due to the Confucian penchant to seek guidance from the past).[10]

Historians of East Asia—John Fairbank, Edwin O. Reischauer, Joseph Needham, and others—point to the many signs of Asian technological superiority over medieval Europe: the silk trade across Central Asia to Europe and the various inventions from China (paper, printing, porcelain, the crossbow, cast iron, canal lockgates, the wheelbarrow, the sternpost rudder for steering ships, the compass, gunpowder, etc.). These were accompanied, among others, by institutional sophistication in bureaucracy, civil service examinations, culture and arts, philosophy and religion. Some of these technologies contributed to the emergence of the Renaissance, the Reformation, and the Commercial Revolution, which enabled the West to catch up and then push ahead of Asia. Fairbank and Reischauer note that China moved into an era of unprecedented cultural, political, and social stability between the 13th and 19th centuries when the West was emerging out of the stagnation of the Middle Ages. Why did China become so stable? Rather than geographic isolation, note Fairbank and Reischauer:

---

[10] This section is largely based on Oshima (1983a).

A more plausible reason is the very perfection that Chinese culture and social organization had achieved by the thirteenth century. The political, social and intellectual systems were basically so viable and so well balanced that not until this balance was destroyed by massive external blows in the nineteenth century was Chinese society again set in rapid motion. . . . It was during this period that they fell behind the West in many aspects of material culture and technology as well as certain forms of economic and political organizations. . . . Chinese society, though stable, was far from static and unchanging, but in this period the pace was slower and the degree of change less than in the West (Fairbank and Reischauer, 1960: 241–42, 291).

Joseph Needham explains the phenomenon as follows:

There is no special mystery about the relatively "steady state" of Chinese society either. Social analysis will assuredly point to the nature of the agriculture, the early necessity of massive hydraulic engineering works, the centralization of government, the principle of non-hereditary civil service, etc., But that it was radically different from the pattern of the West is quite unquestionable. . . .

To what then was the instability of Europe due? . . . I would prefer to think in terms of the geography of what was in effect an archipelago, the perennial tradition of independent city states based on maritime commerce and jostling military aristocrats ruling small areas of land, the exceptional poverty of Europe in the precious metals . . . . By contrast China was a coherent agrarian land-mass, a unified empire since the third century B.C. with an administrative tradition unmatched elsewhere till modern times, endowed with vast riches in minerals . . . and cemented into one by an infrangible system of ideographic script . . . . The greater population of China was self-sufficient . . . . Europeans suffered from a schizophrenia of the soul . . . while the Chinese, wise before their time, worked out an organic theory of the Universe which included Nature and man, church and state and all things past, present, and to come (Needham, 1969: 120–21).

For Karl Marx, it was "the Asiatic mode of production, the simplicity of the organization for production in these self-sufficing communities that constantly reproduce themselves. . . . This simplicity supplies the key to the secret of the unchangeableness of Asiatic societies, an unchangeableness in such contrast with the constant dissolution and refounding of Asiatic states, and the never-ceasing changes of dynasty. The structure of the economical elements of society remains untouched by the storm-clouds of the political sky" (*Capital*, Vol. I, pp. 350).

It was the widespread stability of Asian society in the centuries when capitalism was developing rapidly in Western Europe—beginning with agriculture and commerce in the 16th century and then through industry—which prevented Asia from benefitting from the changes which were propelling Europe to new heights of material and cultural well-being. To one group of writers, it was the high levels attained by Chinese society and culture that underlay its stability, a variant of this view holding that the traditional technology of China had reached the limits of its potential and could not progress further (Elvin, 1973). To another group, it was the geography, the environment, a centralized government with a nonhereditary bureaucracy, a strong state, and a unified script.

There were undoubtedly a number of reasons for Asian stability and subsequent stagnation. In historical phenomena so enormous as the issue under discussion (encompassing several centuries and vast regions and populations), the explanations can be complex with many forces involved. The view advanced here was suggested by study of the nature of the monsoon economy and the growth of East Asia in the postwar decades—a growth sparked by a revolution in monsoon paddy agriculture which in Japan had doubled yields per hectare while slashing labor requirements to less than one-third the level of prewar decades. It is prompted by a puzzle: if Chinese society, culture, and technology had reached the limits of their potential, why was it that attempts were not made to borrow from Europe various innovations in technology and institutions, as Europe had borrowed from Asia in the 13th through the 17th centuries?[11] Instead, many Asian countries sought to insulate themselves from Western influences with policies of isolation until it was too late.

Despite unprecedented advances, East Asia's rice farms were not transformed into capitalistic operations, remaining essentially peasant agriculture depending on family labor. The reason for this, I believe, is that the agriculture of these countries was a different type from that of the West, and that for this type of agriculture capitalism was not a

---

[11] Needham lists the following major innovations arriving in Europe from Asia from the 12th century on: magnetic compass, sternpost rudder, paper making, windmill concept, wheelbarrow, gunpowder, silk machinery, mechanical clock, segmental arch bridge, blast furnace, printing press, horizontal windmill, ball-and-chain flywood, canal lockgates.

suitable form of organization,[12] and the technology and institutions emerging in the postmedieval centuries in Europe could not be transferred to Asian rice farms. These views are in the directions of Marx's "Asiatic mode of production" but depart from his ideas in holding that it is not the simplicity but the complexity of Asian agricultural systems that made for stability and blocked the transfer.

Even in the centuries before Christ, the technology of rice grown in paddies began to move in the direction of labor-intensiveness, with deep plowing, terracing, green and organic manuring, ratooning, and small- and large-scale irrigation and drainage appearing in northern China. Then, in the early centuries of the first millennium, transplanting began raising not only yields but also labor requirements, as seedling beds, transplanting, thorough land preparation, water management, careful cultivation, and time-consuming reaping called for more labor. And in the first century of the second millennium came multiple cropping with the use of short-duration, drought-resistant seeds from Vietnam, raising even further the complexity (and the labor intensity) of land and seedling-bed preparations, transplantation, water management, reaping, and threshing, with tight schedules as one crop is harvested and the next put in immediately and with greater crop diversification. Elvin (1973: 129) concludes that "by the thirteenth century China thus had what was probably the most sophisticated agriculture in the world, India being the only conceivable rival." And in the centuries following, each of these began to be further improved, largely by the use of more labor. These improved technologies and methods were diffused over wider areas of China and beyond (Chang, Vegara, and Yoshida, 1976).

In contrast, the course of technological progress in Europe, especially in England after the 15th/16th century, was generally away from labor intensity. Beginning with enclosures for sheep raising, and then later livestock raising for food, increasing amounts of land were put into the growing of livestock feed (grasses, turnips, and clover). The growing of crops for winter feeding of livestock enabled the English farmer to combine farming with animal husbandry instead of hand-spinning and weaving—a combination which generated economies of scale as labor requirements per hectare diminished. The separation of farming from industry was not possible for the Asian rice farmer, since the great population densities demanded that all arable land be devoted at all times to the growing of food for human beings. Whatever feed

[12] Gunnar Myrdal, in his *Asian Drama* (1972), has suggested that rice agriculture in Asia should become capitalistic in order to improve productivity.

was available had to be fed to the oxen and buffaloes used in plowing. In places as densely settled as Java, the amount of available feed for buffaloes was insufficient, and most plowing had to be done by hand. And everywhere the average Asian had to pull his own cart or carry produce on his back before the advent of bicycles, railways, and other modern means of transport. As one foreign observer in Japan noted in the 1880s, when the Meiji government ordered the raising of a horse in each farm, the farmers complied at the sacrifice of food for the family. Thus, the most important institutional innovation to emerge from the agricultural revolution in the West, the combination of farming with livestock, was not feasible for China. Nor were the others. Drilling in place of transplanting would have caused yields to fall substantially; drainage systems were far more advanced and intricate in Asia; and it was multiple cropping rather than crop rotation and fallowing systems that Asia needed. Nor were improvements in scythes and cradles of any use as the easily shattering and lodging rice plant required knives and smaller sickles.

The most important institutional innovation, capitalistic farming, was also difficult to adopt. It was not that the Asian farms were too small (typically one to two hectares); more important, the husbandry was too complex. To feed the enormous population with so little arable land, the technology that evolved became not only intensive but intricate: deep and thorough plowing several times, the fine puddling and harrowing, elaborately prepared seedling beds, properly spaced transplantation, finely tuned watering, weed and insect controls, careful reaping of a crop prone to lodge and shatter—and all this carried out within a tight schedule imposed by the coming and going of monsoon rains. This is not the kind of work which can be done well by low-paid wage workers or adequately supervised by a few managers on a large farm. Nor can work animals and better equipment be substituted for the highly labor-intensive operations of transplanting and reaping. Only on small farms with close coordination and the cooperation of highly motivated family workers who receive all the returns after paying taxes, rents, and costs can productivity per hectare rise to high levels in the arduous and demanding husbandry of monsoon paddy agriculture.

Even as late as post-World War II, no country in Asia was able to convert peasant farming to capitalistic farming in monsoon Asia, although attempts were made in Java and elsewhere. In the 1870s and 1880s, the new Meiji government attempted to establish Western agricultural methods in Japan but found that the large machines were not suited to small farms and had to abandon the efforts, although some successes were achieved in spacious Hokkaido, Japan's northernmost island, which lies outside the monsoon zone. Plantations were operated capitalistically with a hired labor force in the Philippines beginning in the 19th century for the growing of less labor-intensive commercial crops like sugar, coconut, rubber, and bananas, but the large rice estates of the Spanish friars and the Filipino oligarchs were rented out to tenants in small parcels for their families to work on. China tried the large-scale commune system but is now shifting to the household responsibility system, with good results.

Industrialization

The big spurt that widened the material gap between the East and the West was not so much the agricultural revolution but the steam-powered Industrial Revolution of the 18th/19th century which began to mechanize industrial production, starting with textiles, in the Western world. Here, it would appear, were industrial machines from Europe which the monsoons could not keep out of Asia, at least not in the first half of the 19th century when industrial colonization had not made much headway in most of Asia, especially in China. Nevertheless, as long as the basic traditional village structure remained largely intact, the vast peasant population was needed for the peak seasons of agricultural work, and traditional transportation was inadequate for commuting to work in the cities during the seasonal slack. There was no choice but to continue to carry on with traditional off-farm work, principally hand spinning and weaving. Traditional agriculture hampered the growth of modern industries, and Asia fell behind in industrial production.

China's agricultural labor force was still around 70 percent in 1980, and the share could not have been lower than 80 percent in 1950. India's share was 75 percent in 1960. In the 18th and 19th centuries, the share of the agricultural labor force in China might have been as high as 90 percent, considering that Bangladesh's share in 1960 was 87 percent and Nepal's 95 percent. Great Britain's share in 1801 was already down to 35 percent (about that of South Korea in 1980) and fell steadily throughout the century to a low of 9 percent in 1901. As the low British share in 1801 suggests, it had been declining since the 1770s (Cipolla, 1976: 192). By the early decades of the 19th century, the number of agricultural families was declining absolutely, and the number of workers engaged in agriculture began to decline absolutely in mid-century.

To make possible the increase in the share of the industrial labor force from 29 percent to 39 percent (1801 to 1841) without increasing food imports for a growing population, output per worker in British agriculture had to rise throughout the 19th century. Deane and Cole (1969) estimate that farm product per worker rose at a rate of 1.2 percent a year in the first half of the 19th century and even more in the 18th century. It does not seem plausible to conjecture that, during the 18th and first half of the 19th centuries, with as much as 90 percent of the labor force in Chinese agriculture, output per worker was rising. But without this increase, it is difficult to assume that yields per hectare could rise faster than the population, which is said to have doubled from 1580 to 1850 (Elvin, 1973: 255). If so, where would the labor force and food to mount a drive for industrialization come from? And where would be the home market for the products of industries? Japan at the beginning of its industrialization drive had to colonize Taiwan and Korea in order to produce the rice for its industrial workers and create markets for its industrial products, as it found that capitalistic rice-growing was a low-productivity undertaking.

Conceivably, the labor could be supplied by poor peasant families, with little or no land, not too far from the cities. And there must have been some city dwellers without jobs who would have been willing to work in the factories, since population was rising. But two factors should be kept in mind if we are to understand the inability of China to industrialize with Western technology in the first half of the 19th century. First, the machines of the steam-powered industrial revolution were primitive and of low productivity. A factory housed a few machines and many workers—just the reverse of factories of the 20th century. The textile industry in England employed the cheapest labor available, pauper children and women who constituted most of the work force and who did the many simple jobs in preparing the cotton to be fed to the machines, processes which are mechanized today but then were not: combing, carding, trimming, spooling, warping, cleaning, sweeping, feeding, and tying. The low pay and long hours in steamy, dirty sweatshops were not attractive to most city workers, unless they were unemployed.[13]

Secondly, despite the lower productivity of hand-operated spindles and looms, the opportunity-cost of working on them in the villages was low. As noted, most of the workers who produced food in the rainy seasons had little to do in the dry seasons other than make cloth. To attract this labor for year-around work, the factories would have had

---

[13] For a description of the inconvenience and inferior productivity of steam-powered factories even as late as the latter 1800s, see Devine (1983).

not only to pay wages equal to those for cloth making but also to make up the cost of food production. And because of the high cost of machines and other overheads, the factories to be profitable had to be operated year-around, unlike the hand spindles and looms. Until the factories became much more productive, with more and better machines and greater economies of scale, the wages offered were not sufficiently attractive to tempt village labor to abandon the farms. As long as this labor produced its own clothing and other needs, the domestic market for industrial products was confined to the small urban market.[14]

This was the experience of the first textile factories in early Meiji Japan, which had to turn to the daughters of unemployed samurai for their labor force. And not much headway was made in textile mechanization until the turn of the century, after which the growth of industrialization was possible only with the import of large amounts of rice from the colonies (see Chapter 4). The Dutch in Indonesia had to force peasants to work on the plantations; the British in Malaya had to bring in labor from India and Ceylon; and throughout Southeast Asia, the colonial governments brought in Chinese workers to labor in the mines and in the handicraft shops and stores. Although the Dutch interpreted the backward-sloping supply curve of Indonesian workers as indolence, it was largely a reflection of workers going back to the villages during the busy seasons. It must be kept in mind that up to World War I, labor shortage was the rule throughout Asia, and it was only during the depression of the 1930s and the labor force explosion after World War II that large pools of surplus labor made their appearance.[15]

I am aware that historical research in recent times has shown that Marx's account of vast labor surplus flowing from the farms to modern

[14] Elvin (1973: 215) argues that the shortage of cotton prevented the growth of a mechanized cotton industry, which "would have had to take away supplies from the handicraft industries." If it could compete with the latter, why didn't it do so? The growth of new industries is the history of old industries giving up their supplies of inputs to the new ones which can better combine them into cheaper/better products. It is interesting to note that British factories in Bombay, using labor released from the exports of cotton yarns to India, were selling machine-made yarn to Shanghai and Japan, where they were woven by hand looms, during the latter part of the 19th-century.

[15] The migration of Chinese to Malaysia was for full-time work in the tin mines, and that of Indians was for full-time work on the rubber plantations of Malaysia and tea plantations in Sri Lanka—all of which paid more than part-time work in the rice paddies of India and China. No migration occurred to the part-time work of the sugar plantations in Indonesia and the Philippines, in contrast to the sugar plantations of Hawaii, which attracted Japanese and later Filipino peasants with year-around work.

industry (found in his first volume of *Capital*) exaggerated the picture of early British industrialization (Deane, 1980: 138–140). The problem is a difficult one as data on unemployment do not exist, but it is clear that British agriculture had to raise productivity in order to support the upsurge of population from the latter half of the 18th century (Cipolla, 1969: 165–167). The contention of this book is that for the spread of industrialization of the kind represented by the early, primitive, steam-driven mechanization to occur, a flexible supply of cheap, unskilled labor is a necessity; without the dissolution of traditional agriculture, adequate supplies of labor and food are not forthcoming, and real wages will not remain constant and low. Nor will there be an expansion of domestic demand for textiles and other manufactured goods—a necessity if profits are to be high and savings are to be reinvested. (This is the theory which Arthur Lewis mistakenly applied to post-World War II conditions, as discussed in the next chapter.) Matters changed in the 20th century, and more workers left the farms. The outpour accelerated with the more efficient electric/gas power-driven machines replacing steam-power in the early decades of the 20th century and with the rise of population.

Moreover, the supply of urban workers was insufficient. In West Europe, nonmechanized but capitalistic manufacture displaced guild production. Through division of labor, specialization, and simplification, large units were able to generate economies of scale, new tools and equipment, greater proficiency in workmen with fewer skills than craft producers, and better management. (See Adam Smith's discussion in *The Wealth of Nations*.) Such transformation from guild production to manufactures could take place in China only on a limited scale. In China, where the power of the guilds continued to dominate handicraft production until the 19th century, the transformation from guild production to manufactures could take place only on a limited scale.

At bottom, underlying the institutional stability of China (and that of other monsoon economies of Asia) and the difficulty of dissolving the traditional village communities with an agricultural revolution of the Western type was perhaps the difficulty of feeding huge populations with any other type of agriculture, given the agricultural technologies of the 16th to the 19th centuries. The enormous amount of labor used during plowing/planting and harvesting/threshing of the rice crop was not disguised unemployment. All of it—and more—was needed to produce the high yields to feed the peasant family and the "teeming millions" of monsoon Asia. Given the state of the arts and sciences, there was no other cereal crop which could produce the calories and proteins to enable the Asians to sustain themselves. Large-scale agriculture (capitalistically managed or otherwise) could not produce the necessary yields per hectare, as the Japanese found to their dismay when they attempted to introduce Western technologies after the Meiji Restoration.

John Lossing Buck's results from his survey of farms in China in the early 1930s revealed that the rice per acre produced in China was 67 bushels (nearly the same as Japan's 68), much higher than the 47 bushels produced in the United States. The highest was Italy's 93 bushels, but this was produced in a small area of choice rice land, Italy being largely a wheat-growing nation. The highest yields in wheat were those of Great Britain and Germany with 32 and 31 bushels respectively; China produced 16 and Japan, 25. Corn yields were highest in Italy and in the United States, with 28 and 25 bushels respectively. These figures represent yields in China with the use of traditional inputs, while other countries used modern inputs (chemical fertilizer, modern varieties, etc.).[16] If these figures were projected backward to the 18th century, when modern inputs were not available anywhere, it is clear that the large-scale agriculture of the West (for whatever crop) could not feed the Chinese population of 300 to 400 million.

Finally, with the old structure of the peasant production unchanged, the traditional structure of political power (with the imperial system on top, the bureaucracy below, and the gentry in the towns and villages) remained intact through most of the latter half of this millennium. This power structure did everything to preserve the old mode of production of which it was part and parcel and without which it would have become redundant. Thus, it was inconceivable for the agricultural and industrial revolutions of the West to be transplanted to Asian soil in the 19th century.

The arguments above may not agree with current views regarding the failure of China to move into modern economic growth. It may be, as some maintain, that traditional rice technology had reached the limits of its potential. There may be danger in putting too much emphasis on technology in pre-industrial Asia where major technological changes were few and far between during two or three millen-

---

[16] For China, see Buck (1956). Japanese rice growing in the early 1930s used new seed varieties developed in the experiment stations in the 1920s. Despite large imports of rice from the colonies, there was no significant decline in the agricultural labor force in Japan before World War II. Thus, in order to industrialize, the Japanese found that food had to be imported, and this impelled Japan to acquire colonies to which it could export industrial goods in exchange for food.

nia.[17] It was mainly with modern economic growth that technology came to the fore as a major factor in growth, and not until recently that it superseded capital in importance. Between the 17th and mid-20th centuries, China went on to feed a population which doubled, despite few major technological breakthroughs. Indeed, production could have more than doubled if there had been more and better irrigation, drainage, and multiple cropping, increased crop diversification, more use of animals and better plows and other implements, wider spread of highest-yielding traditional seeds, improved reaping, threshing, transport, and marketing, better flood control, and so on, as in Japan during the Meiji period and in the prewar decades in its colonies. Above all, institutional improvements such as agrarian reforms could have squeezed more production out of higher incentives to work. The importance of major technological changes even in Western agriculture in premodern societies was not great, and it was only after their acceleration in the 20th century that economists began to pay much attention to it in the growth of nations. Even as late as the mid-19th century, the writings of the classical economists and Marx did not take technology explicitly and fully into account in their theories (Kuznets, 1980).

It may be, as some maintain, that the old forces were too strong and the modernizing ones too weak to bring about such changes either in China, held together tightly by a common written language and a Confucian bureaucracy, or in India, united by Hinduism and caste; further, both countries were ruled by foreign dynasties: the Manchu in China and the Moguls in India. But these traditional forces were strong precisely because the new forces could not make much headway in monsoon Asia. Nevertheless, as Asia moved into the 19th century, small beach heads of modernization were being established here and there in the peripheries of island nations, such as in southern Japan where the forces of Satsuma and Chōshū fiefs were eventually able to overthrow the decaying Tokugawa feudal system and lead the Meiji government into modern economic growth.

---

[17] Historians of rice agriculture can point to only a handful of major innovations, such as the origin of irrigation works and flood controls, in China before the birth of Christ. The use of water buffaloes; the discovery of the hoe, iron plow, and spade; terracing of fields; transplantation; pedal-operated water pump; spike-tooth harrow; roller-compactor; and double cropping were developed during the 3,000 years or so of the history of rice technology in China. Moreover, their impact on productivity was minimal at the time of their discovery; it was only with their adaptations, improvements, and spread over decades and centuries that they made their substantial impact, and even so only in combination with labor, capital, and appropriate institutions. See Chang (1977).

To get to the nub of the problem, we make the assumption that population is increasing at a slow pace, and divide Asian economies into those which are closed to foreign trade (or where the share of foreign trade in total production is very small) and those which are open to foreign trade extensively. In the closed case, for the economy to be able to industrialize with population and labor force increasing very slowly, there must be a shift of peasants to the industrial labor force, and productivity in agriculture must rise so that food can be supplied to the new industrial work force. If food output is rising at 2 percent, industrialization at the rate of 2 percent a year (in terms of employment) can take place if workers are transferred at a 2 percent rate. The industrial output can then be sold to the more highly productive peasants remaining in agriculture. Industrial growth will be zero if agricultural productivity is zero. Large countries like India and China could not industrialize in the 19th century because growth of agricultural productivity was slow or nil. Italy, Spain, and the countries of eastern Europe were similarly tied down by feudalistic agricultural systems in the 19th century.

In the open economies where foreign trade is a large share of national output, the slow increase of population means that here also peasants must be shifted from agriculture for industrialization. But in these economies, to the extent that the industrial output can be sold abroad and food imported, domestic agricultural productivity need not necessarily rise as the transferred peasants can be fed from imports. To a large extent, small countries like Switzerland, Belgium, and Holland were able to grow in this way. But in order for this type of growth to be sustained, small countries must keep industrial efficiency at a high level from the beginning. As we shall see in Chapter 6, this was the pattern followed by Hong Kong and Singapore in the postwar decades.

The countries in which plantations were established in the 19th century faced different problems. In the Philippines and Indonesia, with agricultural productivity rising too slowly, most of the food for the peasants who were transferred to the plantation sector had to be imported using the export proceeds of the plantation crops. In the case of smaller countries like Ceylon and Malaysia, the British, unable to transfer farm workers fast enough for their expanding plantations, had to bring in workers from abroad to work on the plantations. Again exports from the plantations were the means by which food was imported. Rice from Burma and Indochina was brought in to feed the plantation work force. In the case of Japan, the pace of industrialization was sluggish before 1900 with the slow release of workers from agriculture but accelerated later as food imports from the colonies increased. There was little or no industrial growth in the rest of Asia as agricultural productivity grew slowly, if at all, in the period before colonization by the West.[18] Thus, the productivity of agriculture was a critical factor in the growth of industrialization in Asia as well as in Europe.

As the demand for labor increased with the rise of plantations in the various colonies, birth rates rose and population growth accelerated. These increases in population were probably related to the European population growth during most of the 19th century, which increased Western demand for the plantation crops of tropical Asia. In China and India, however, where there were few or no plantations and where industrialization proceeded at a snail's pace, population grew more slowly.

Before World War II, monsoon Asia outside the Japanese Empire fell further behind the countries of the West, which were growing rapidly with capitalistic agriculture and industry powered by the technologies of the industrial revolutions. In the West plenty of land and more even rainfall made it easy to convert small strip farms into large capitalistic farms even with simple technologies such as multiple-horse-driven iron plows and new crops, long before the emergence of more sophisticated power-driven technologies. Labor was made available for the simple factories which needed large amounts of unskilled cheap labor. This was not so for monsoon Asia, where the "teeming millions" were needed for the busy seasons if food production were not to decline and raise prices and farm wages. To keep them occupied in the slack months, they had to be put to work in labor-intensive handicraft production. In Chapter 3 we shall see what happened to monsoon Asia in the post-World War II decades as it gained independence and set forth on the path of modern economic growth.[19]

[18] According to the data compiled by Wickizer and Bennett (1941: 310–319), rice yields per hectare fell or remained constant during the first half of the 20th century in all of Asia except for Japan, Korea, and Taiwan, where they doubled.

[19] The picture in this chapter was painted with a broad brush, and applies to the vast majority of Asians and Westerners. There are, of course, exceptions such as the Western desert of the United States which receive little or no rain throughout the year, the northern countries of Europe where snow is on the ground much of the year, parts of Indonesia where rains come all year around, or parts of Malaysia and the Philippines where rainfall is relatively even. There are other less extreme exceptions as well since rainfall and agriculture can be influenced by other natural forces like local topography, soil conditions, or rivers.

CHAPTER 2

An Analytical Framework
for Monsoon Development

*A*s we saw in Chapter 1, the monsoons were the major cause of low per capita incomes in Asia. Confronted with rising populations and aspirations, the newly independent countries of Asia found that there was an urgent need to speed up growth and raise incomes as soon as possible. In the first part of this chapter, we review the theories of development and strategies that emerged in the earlier decades, when most of the new countries had barely had time to begin moving into modern development. Without knowledge of how the new countries were achieving growth, economists had to turn to the experience of Japan and the USSR in the prewar decades, and those of Western Europe in the 19th century. We now have the experience of East Asian countries to go by in assessing the usefulness of these theories, and based on that experience we work out in the latter part a framework for analyzing and evaluating the successes and failures enumerated in the country chapters of Part II.[1]

Brief Review of Development Theories and Strategies

Development theories may be distinguished from growth theories in that they are concerned with structural changes. Hence, they are more pertinent to developing countries whose structures and underlying institutions are the product of centuries of tradition and lack the flexibility to change with the times.

Early theories appear to be mainly concerned with the increase in national product per capita through shifts away from agriculture which was assumed to harbor excess labor. They are best exemplified by Ragnar Nurkse, the major pioneer in development theory, who believed that the surplus labor should be shifted from agriculture and applied to the formation of capital for public works, factories, and

---

[1] This chapter is based on Oshima, 1962; 1983b; 1984a.

47

machines. This should increase productive capacities and the aggregate demand needed for higher income-elastic products, thereby achieving a better balance in the economy (Nurkse, 1953).

In reaction, unbalanced growth theories argued that the under-developed countries did not have sufficient material and human resources to create all-round balances, as assumed by the balanced theories, and advocated that scarce resources of capital, entrepreneurship, and skills be concentrated on key sectors of the economy. Hirschman (1959) specified that the key sectors should be those with the greatest linkages (in the input-output sense) with other industries, and these turned out to be neither agriculture nor downstream light industries but those in the up- and mid-stream—the capital-intensive—industries, especially heavy industries. This conclusion was similar to the prewar ideas of the Soviet theoretician G. Feldman, who thought that since in the early stages of growth capital and foreign exchange earnings were scarce, focus should be on the capital goods industries whose development would eventually enable countries to produce the machines and materials needed to develop agriculture and downstream industries. The influence of these theories on policies was considerable in the major Latin American countries, in the communist countries, and in India.

These countries have grown slowly. Their capital-intensive industries have failed to reach levels of productivity which can supply machines and materials good enough for the lower stream industries to make much headway in the export market. Nor can the capital-intensive industries themselves export very much, and their absorption of so many resources has left little for agriculture. Hence, with slow growth in all the sectors, structural changes have also been slow. What, then, went wrong with the strategy?

Linkages are desirable if they are efficient, but if they are not, high costs and/or poor quality will "cascade" from upstream to the lower stream industries, penalizing the latter. Hirschman and Feldman perhaps depended too much on "infant industry" arguments (originating in the 19th century), trusting that in time the efficiencies of capital-intensive industries would rise. But in the 20th century the capital-intensive industries have become technologically extremely complex, both operationally and, more particularly, in research and development (Oshima, 1961; 1983a). The experienced, high-level manpower required to develop a whole range of such industries was not found even in large countries like India. The upshot was that these industries could not operate at adequate capacity most of the time and fell behind the product design and technology of the West and Japan as the decades went by. These countries, to invite downstream industries from abroad to use their large pools of surplus labor, have set up export zones to enable firms to avoid buying from their upstream industries which were producing highly protected, costly, but poor-quality yarns, chemicals, metals, paper and other materials, and equipment.

These early theories were less concerned with achieving efficiencies within each existing industry, as they assumed that agriculture was of low productivity and that the higher productivity of extensive industrialization would produce the desired rise in overall productivity through structural shifts away from agriculture. But if productivity did not rise continuously, the higher productivity of capital-intensive industries had more or less a "one-time-only" effect.

The dualistic theory of Arthur Lewis, the second major pioneer in development theories, and its emendation by Gustav Ranis and John Fei did pay attention to the growth of industrial productivity (Lewis, 1954; Ranis and Fei, 1964). The central thrust of these theories was based on the assumption that there is surplus labor in agriculture (or the traditional sector) that can be transferred to industry or elsewhere at constant wages so that the capitalist employer can produce with increasing profits, which are then to be invested in more and better technologies. And the migration of marginally employed workers (producing at zero or low marginal product) would leave a smaller work force in agriculture with output unchanged, thereby raising output per worker. The dualistic theories replaced the balanced/ unbalanced theories as the dominant explanation for rapid growth under conditions of unlimited labor supply.

Elsewhere I have pointed out that the Asian economies that grew most rapidly in the postwar period were those in which real wages in agriculture and industry grew from an early date; those in which real wages did not rise grew slowly. (Compare Figs. 2.1 and 2.2 with the figures in Chapter 3.) Labor was plentiful in Japan from the latter 1940s, Taiwan from the 1950s, and South Korea from the 1960s, but real wages rose in response to rises in yields per hectare. Real wages rose in these countries despite apparent slack because in monsoon agriculture during the peak months of planting and harvesting there is a *shortage* of labor. It is in these key months that there must be sufficient additional labor if productivity is to rise, calling for higher wages. In other months, the additional labor can seek off-farm jobs. If the labor force explosion from the late 1960s supplied labor which was not needed for the busy months, the workers moved out from agriculture; if jobs could not be found, they would be openly unemployed (not employed and not producing). If real wages in England in the early

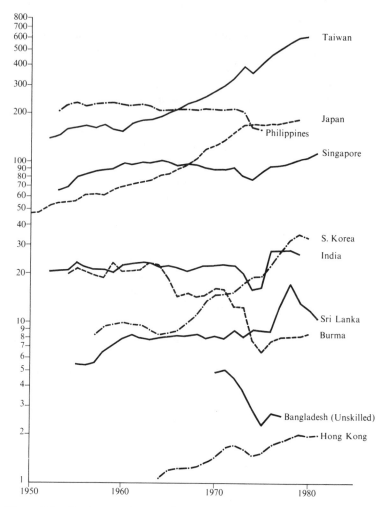

Figure 2.1   Real wages in manufacturing, selected Asian countries.
Sources: ILO Yearbook of Labour Statistics; IBRD World Tables 1980.

period of the Industrial Revolution were constant, it was because the
process of land consolidation and enclosure in the transformation to
capitalist agriculture was taking place, but this transformation has
not taken place in monsoon paddy agriculture during the postwar
decades, as noted in Chapter 1. The dualistic theories devised for
less developed countries are more pertinent for developed countries
which are at the frontier of technology and cannot substitute new tech-

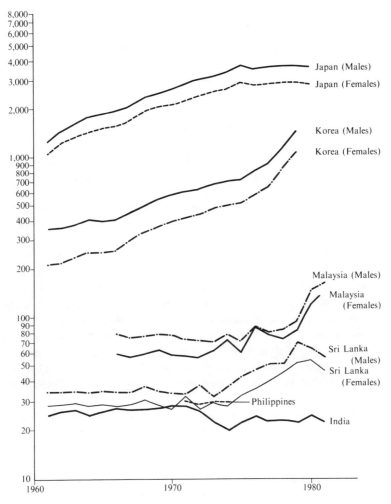

Figure 2.2   Real wages in agriculture.
Source: *ILO Yearbook of Labour Statistics.*

nology for labor when full employment is reached. But even before full employment the labor available is not surplus during the busy period; and wages did in fact rise, at least before the labor force explosion of the 1970s.

These early theories properly stressed the importance of structural change in underdeveloped economies, largely because of the back-wardness of the major sector, agriculture. Where they went astray was in concluding that there is an abundance of labor that can be shifted to the industrial sector without a fall in agricultural output. In China, Mao Tse-tung, following the dualists' assumption, attempted a massive shift in the Great Leap Forward in the latter 1950s, only to find that farm production fell sharply; we now know that the food shortages of 1958 to 1961 killed 10 to 27 million people, with the death rate rising from 11 per 1,000 in 1957 to 25 per 1,000 in 1960.

In the prewar Philippines and Indonesia, the shifts of Filipino and Javanese peasants from farms to plantations caused rice shortages which made imports from Indochina and Burma necessary. Even the more limited shifts in Malaysia and Sri Lanka produced rice shortages, and imports from Burma and Thailand became a regular feature in these countries also, as noted in Chapter 1. A development model should start with the problem of agricultural productivity, particularly in the case of monsoon agriculture where annual income and productivity per worker are exceedingly low. Attempts to sustain productivity increases from structural shifts will not be successful without first increasing agricultural productivity, unless the resulting increases in industrial output can be exported and food imported. This is difficult to do in the early stages of growth when industrial entrepreneurship and skills, capital, and scale- and external economies are not well developed. In this, the unbalanced theorists were right, but where they went wrong was to assume that scarce industrial resources can make a success of heavy industrialization. The sophisticated, high-level manpower needs of heavy industries were too much for the developing countries.

Kuznets's (1966) study of the growth of industrialized countries and those which followed have produced a number of insights and concepts from which we can benefit. In these studies, notably those of Abramovitz, Solow, Kendrick, Denison, Jorgenson, Matthews, and Malinvaud, the major objective of the long-run analysis was to explain the growth of real GNP per capita and the growth of population—the two characteristics identified by Kuznets as distinguishing modern economic growth from pre modern growth. These studies divided the sources of changes in per capita product into those relating to changes in the *quantity* of factor inputs (mainly labor and capital) and those relating to changes in the *productivity* of each of the factors. The results from these studies showed that major variations in product per capita were mainly related to variations in factor productivity and not to the amounts of factor inputs. In order to understand the changes in the secular trends of product per capita, attention came to be focused on the estimation and explanation of factor productivity, since the inputs of labor and capital in the secular long run changed slowly, governed as they were by the fairly stable growth of population and the savings propensity. Accordingly, the central focus of analysis came to be the rise of productivity in each sector within a framework of shifting sectors and subsectors.

In these studies, the growth of per capita product was explained as owing to either proximate forces—sources—or more ultimate ones—causes—underlying the movements of production. The exact division of sources and causes differed from one scholar to another, although there was a tendency to group various inputs into the category of sources (labor, capital, education, structural change), and to group the explanations of changes in the productivity of inputs into the category of causes, the major ones being changes in technologies, institutions (broadly defined as ways or patterns of doing and thinking), and exogenous demand. While the proximate forces, or sources, were quantifiable, the longer range causes were not easily quantified, and it was necessary to depend largely on narrative analysis in which the mechanism was described (or analytical description). Thus, the "bottom lines" in the studies of the growth experience of nations became rather ambiguous and indefinite since the major explanatory causes, technology, and institutions, were not measurable and their interactions difficult even to identify. (See Matthews et al., 1982, for Britain; Carre, Dubois, and Malinvaud, 1975, for France; Ohkawa and Rosovsky, 1973, for Japan; and Abramovitz, 1973, for the U.S.A.)

Econometric models thus proved to be of limited use as their results turned out to be highly unstable "in the face of minor modifications in data specification, observation period and estimation method" (Matthews et al., 1982: 202). All this meant that long-term analysis could not dispense with historical narration and analysis of the development of institutions and technology as these were important in understanding the size of the parameters, especially in long-term studies. To give an example or two of what is meant by historical narration, contributing to the rise in total factor productivity in the United States in the early decades of the present century (in contrast to its slow growth in the previous century) was the rapid spread from the 1920s of new types of mechanical equipment powered by electric motors and internal combustion engines displacing large numbers of unskilled workers on farms and in industry. Contributing to the quick dissemination of this equipment were the wage increases following immigration restrictions enacted as a result of strong pressures from the American Federation of Labor, together with the pent-up demand for manufactured products from World War I. In the case of postwar Japan, it was the new institutions introduced by the Allied Occupation and later modified by the Japanese that democratized and demilitarized basic economic and social institutions in the postwar years. Additional institutions were developed that succeeded in motivating peasants, workers, managers, and bureaucrats to great heights of productivity as technologies were efficiently imported, adapted, disseminated, and utilized. To keep this type of analysis from becoming too diffused, it was necessary to cast it in transition stages, to partition historical spans, facilitating the analysis of each portion.

Although development economists have been much more occupied with analyzing changes in product per capita than in the other characteristic of modern growth, population growth, the latter has been too conspicuous to be ignored. We need to understand the relation of population changes to economic growth since the Malthusian mechanism in the classical theories of growth was no longer valid in the postwar decades. As Kuznets (1980) has shown, there are many broad connections between modern economic growth and demographic changes. Population growth should be made largely endogenous if possible by linking the demographic transition to the industrial transition, making labor supply endogenous; imported technological changes can also become endogenous, depending on how efficiently institutions succeed in importing, adapting, improving, and disseminating applied technologies. Even though scientific knowledge and basic technologies cannot be endogenized, it is the technologies applied on the production floor and the farms that affect directly the GNP of a country. Therefore, we will borrow the concept of transition from the demographic framework and attempt to bring it together with the structural transition to study the nature and impact of productivity changes.

Both classical and Marxian theories written in the 19th century during the first Industrial Revolution placed more emphasis on capital accumulation than on technological changes. This was in keeping with the times, since in the infancy of industrial capitalism the need to accumulate both working and fixed capital to attain scale economies was more compelling than coping with technological changes, which were relatively few and slow. It was not until the second Industrial Revolution had advanced well into the 20th century that technological changes became comprehensive and incessant; instead of a few hundred machines, the economy had to cope with hundreds of thousands, many of which were extremely complex. And other types of technologies, agronomical, biological, and chemical, also became abundant and more complex as the 20th century wore on.

Neoclassical growth theories, by their focus on capital-labor substitution, did reflect the importance of technological changes. But they dealt with an economy in full-employment equilibrium and without any backward sectors such as agriculture. One-sector analysis may be appropriate for industrialized countries where the various sectors are developed to the point where sectors are homogenized and are connected by efficient nationwide markets. In dealing with growing monsoon Asian economies, we are dealing with economies which have no place for the steam-powered technologies of the 19th century. Instead, they must cope with electric- and gas-driven equipment, chemically produced materials, and biology-based technologies, in the setting of predominantly traditional Asian structures and institutions. Even two-sector analysis may oversimplify.

Most important, the foregoing theories pay scant attention to problems of manpower quality, assuming as they do fairly homogeneous lumps of manual labor power.[2] But each of the hundreds of thousands of mechanized and other technologies require manpower appropriately skilled to operate, repair, and guide it. As noted, the modern factory and plants have only a limited role for Marx's untutored proletariat, and the varied skill requirements bring to the forefront the importance of the quality—as distinct from the quantity—of manpower. Since quality varies over time and between countries, and work styles differ with life styles, the pace at which technologies are adjusted and disseminated and the efficiency at which they are used will depend very much on manpower quality. Even more so, manpower quality contributes to the effectivity in the operation of institutions, as manpower is the central component in the workings of institutions.

Matthews et al. (1982) list the changes in attitudes of workers and entrepreneurs in the postwar decades as an essential factor in the acceleration of the British economy in the postwar decades, while Malinvaud and associates (1975) point to the role played by the increased propensity to work at all levels in the higher growth of the French postwar economy compared with the prewar. As discussed in Chapter 4, I found that Japan's ability to motivate manpower was the key to its faster growth based on the interplay among accelerated investment, technological absorption, and institutional development. My skepticism about dualistic theories positing growth with constant wages stems from the difficulty such wages have at an underdeveloped stage,

---

[2] Under competitive conditions, entrepreneurs and their employees are assumed to put forth their best efforts in order to maximize profits or to survive. But the best efforts will depend on the norm of the society. In one country, it may mean 40 hours of work per week, in another 50, in others still more. Quality standards will also vary from country to country.

where they hover around subsistence levels, as incentives to motivate workers for the kind of work effort required with 20th-century technology.

The Dynamics of Rapid Growth, Structural Change, and Distributional Changes: The Agro-Industrial Transition

To bring some order into the differential pace of growth, which moves from one disequilibrium to another, and to keep track of the structural and other changes in the comparative study of nations, we divide historical periods into long-run equilibrium periods, such as the demographic transition. In the latter, underdeveloped countries move from a long period of high fertility and mortality levels to low levels of fertility and mortality. The period between these two levels is a transitional period where mortality falls first, followed by fertility. When fertility catches up with some lower stable levels of mortality, the transition is said to be completed.

In similar ways, we may think of an agriculture-to-industry structural transition where high levels in the shares of the agricultural labor force (about three-fourths of the total labor force, including farming, livestock, fishery, and forestry) begin to fall, and the transition is completed when the shares fall to levels around those of the rising shares of the industrial labor force (including mining, manufacturing, construction, transport, and public utilities in industry), roughly one-fourth to one-third. The economy may then be said to have completed the structural transition from a predominantly agricultural to an industrial economy. The second transition is from an industrial to a service economy when the service sector (comprising business, personal, and public services) overtakes the industrial sector in size. Most Western industrialized countries have completed the second transition; in Asia, only Japan has completed it. Taiwan completed the agro-industrial transition in the early 1970s, and South Korea in the late 1970s. (See Figs. 2.3–2.6.) The transition concept is a framework and not a theoretical device, to delineate the movements of the labor force in agriculture relative to those in the industrial and service labor force; it is akin to the tracking of birth rates relative to death rates in the demographic transition.

We use employment as the measure of the transition because in the case of the monsoon economies the completion of the transition roughly coincides with a situation where high levels of surplus labor decline to levels approximating full employment, and because these transitions are accompanied by a demographic transition. We are also concerned

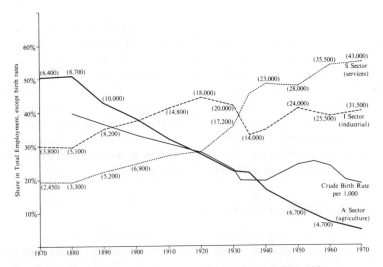

Figure 2.3   Industrial and services transition in Japan, 1906–1980.
Sources: Computed from Ohkawa and Shinohara (1979); updated by *Japan Statistical Yearbook 1981.*
Note: Numbers in parentheses are absolute numbers of employed persons in units of 1000.

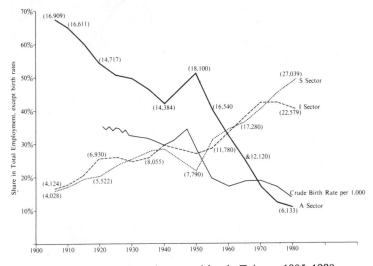

Figure 2.4   Industrial and services transition in Taiwan, 1905–1980.
Sources: Ho (1978), updated by *Statistical Yearbook of the Republic of China.*

with how full employment levels are reached and with what happens afterwards.

The concordance among the transitions is approximate, as there are elements of arbitrariness in their definitions. The structural transition, for example, is ideally suited for a closed economy as sector exports and imports vary among nations. (In the case of city-states with small rural sectors, the industrial transition is from the traditional service sectors to industries.) Nevertheless, there appears to be sufficient concordance for most countries to facilitate the tracing and tracking of the various forces and mechanisms operating in the transition. But the elements of arbitrariness should be kept in mind, and the transition concepts must be used with flexibility and care.

Starting the Growth Process

Productivity in the agricultural sector can be raised by reducing underemployment in the slack season in monsoon economies where idleness

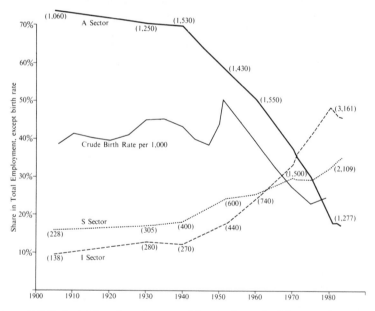

Figure 2.5 Industrial and services transition in the United States, 1870–1970.
Sources: Historical Statistics, The National Income and Product Account of the United States; OECD Labour Force Statistics.
Note: Absolute number of employed persons, in parentheses, are in units of 1,000.

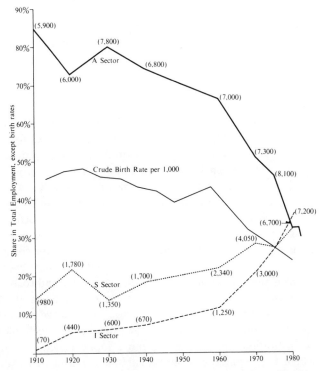

Figure 2.6   Industrial and services transition in Korea, 1910–1980.
Sources: Suh (1978); United Nations, ESCAP, *Population of the Republic of Korea*; various issues of *Statistical Yearbook of the Republic of Korea*. *Note*: Numbers in parentheses are absolute numbers of employed persons in units of 1,000 persons. For postwar years, data are for South Korea.

is found in the drier season of the year. Without adequate moisture, the large labor force intensively used during the rainy season finds insufficient work; what work is available is of low intensity and short duration, intermittent and irregular.[3] Remuneration is lower than in the busy months, when the peasant works long hours from dawn to dusk with 4 or 5 meals. Since this surplus labor is seasonal, it is annual productivity which is important, and since the family works closely together in a variety of activities throughout the year, on and off farm, as in fishing, forestry, services, and crafts, the annual productivity is

[3] This is not disguised unemployment of zero marginal productivity, since maintenance of irrigation, roads, tools, and houses also must be done. But because the farms are tiny, it can be done in a short time, in contrast to the West; handicrafts such as weaving take much time but are of low value (Oshima, 1971).

that of the family as a whole. Annual family productivity is convenient for the analysis of income distribution, savings, and birth rates, which pertain to the family as the unit of observation.

Since not much can be done to increase farm size in most countries, to increase the annual productivity of farm families in land-scarce monsoon Asia the main reliance must be on raising yields and the number of crops per hectare. Yields can be raised by adopting the best traditional varieties and practices; or, better still, modern varieties and practices can be adopted, with more use of fertilizers and insecticides, extension services to raise skills, and so on. There is need for dams and canals to irrigate dry-season crops, rural transport systems for marketing, and improvements in institutions such as farm cooperatives, irrigation associations, and extension services. Credit institutions are vital to assist with the purchase of seeds and other modern inputs, and where agrarian relations are strained by a powerful landowning class, reforms must be carried out if the cultivating peasantry is to be motivated to put forth its best efforts. Reforms are costly but are within the means of most governments with readily available assistance from the international banks for irrigation and roads. The skills for growing rice crops exist, and some of the physical infrastructure and institutions are already in place. To improve and extend them requires minimal demands on new knowledge, technologies, skills, and institutions, in contrast to more sophisticated industrialization, where the required centralized capital, sophisticated management, scientists, technicians, bureaucrats, skilled workers, urban institutions for external economies, and large markets are scarce or limited.

In the early stage of development, the demand for food by the expanding population is the most urgent, so that import substitution should start with the reduction of food imports for importing countries and the expansion of food exports for others—in both cases to obtain the foreign exchange to purchase the powered spindles and looms and other machines for labor-intensive industries. Above all, the strategy is useful for reducing income disparities since peasant families are found in the lower income groups in all countries. Being the largest group of consumers in the early stage of development, they comprise the main markets for the output of the nascent labor-intensive import-substituting industries. Hence, an increase in peasant production implies large increases in industrial and related service industries, all of which combined will translate into major increases in GDP. Thus, the strategy of developing agriculture and labor-intensive industries is the simplest and surest way to get the traditional economy moving into modern economic growth; at the same time it allows time for the schools to train in manpower skills, for government to establish physical infrastructure and modern institutions, and for the private sector to gain experience in using the marketplace for more sophisticated levels of development.

Towards Full Employment

The road to full employment is a series of steps. The first is constructing infrastructure for irrigation, drainage, transport, education, electrification, and basic industry; such construction generates more work during the slack months for the peasant family. Where new lands are available, they should be cleared for cultivation if they are not too marginal and costly, although new lands may not reduce underemployment during the slack seasons and the excessive clearing of forests may add to deforestation and environmental problems.

Next, as work becomes more plentiful throughout the year and annual farm incomes begin to rise, more can be spent on better seeds, fertilizers, insecticides, tools, and equipment. More labor will be required for cultivation, seedling bed preparation, transplanting, weeding, fertilizing, and water control for the main and subsidiary crops. As the irrigation infrastructure is completed, a major source of work will be the additional diversified crops that can be grown: pulses, vegetables, and fruits.

With rising incomes, the demand for livestock and for fishery and forestry products begins to rise. In the next step, more employment for these non-crop activities is created, and some of their output can be exported abroad as their quality improves with better processing and cultivation. In the fourth step, diversified agriculture gives rise to off-farm jobs for farm family members because diversified production generally requires more agro-industry processing (handling, grading, cooking, canning, packing), transporting, and marketing services than does rice (Oshima, 1984a; 1985). The acceleration effect of non-rice agriculture is likely to be large as it is linked to the construction of irrigation and drainage facilities, roads, and power plants; to agroprocessing of food, beverages, and wood products; to fertilizer, chemical, and other industries selling inputs to agriculture; and to retail, transport, and financial services involved in marketing agricultural products. The incomes generated from all these activities have large multiplier effects.

Finally, in the fifth step, higher incomes generate demand for industrial goods, especially garments, shoes, home utensils, farm inputs, and tools, creating a market for the import-substitution industries, which can now increase their scales of production. Migration to these industries and their supporting services from the rural sectors accelerates. As the above processes continue over the years, the increases in employment tend to outpace the growth of labor supply; the labor market starts to tighten and real wages begin to rise with the approach of full employment. The process must be sustained for longer periods in countries with higher levels of underemployment and higher rates of labor force growth.

In the five steps outlined above by which annual productivity, incomes, and employment expand—construction, higher yields and more crops per hectare, diversified crop production, off-farm employment, and migration to urban sectors—the full employment attained is not short-term nor transitional but long-term and sustainable because it is the outcome of long-lasting improvements and extensions of traditional rural infrastructure and institutions. This is a historic achievement of major significance for monsoon Asia—perhaps the most strategic, as the economy now moves into full speed on a higher level of labor utilization during the subsequent phases of the agro-industrial transition. For the first time, the economy has overcome the seasonal underemployment inherent in the monsoons.

After Full Employment

As the processes in the foregoing steps continue and are sustained over the years, farm wages, which have been climbing slowly here and there since the early part of the transition, accelerate, particularly because wages of unskilled workers start to increase as fast as those of others. When this happens, peasants are induced to use more equipment to economize on labor, since machines become cheaper to use than manpower. On tiny monsoon farms, the large machines found in Western farms are not feasible; instead, inexpensive, miniaturized equipment powered by small electric motors and internal combustion engines must be used. Total factor productivity begins to rise, as the elasticity of capital/labor substitution increases. The agricultural sector is now in a position to release labor to the industries in the urban sectors, while food production continues to increase as population and per capita income rise.

With higher domestic demand, more experience, and scale and external economies, the labor-intensive, import-substituting industries move out of their "infancy" and begin to find markets abroad. Unlike the more capital-intensive industries further upstream, these industries with simpler and fewer varieties of machines and other technologies are easier to master and take less time to learn to operate efficiently. The markets for their products are easier to find and penetrate.

As these industries become more competitive abroad and their exports accelerate, their expansion begins to outgrow the labor supply in urban areas. Since rural areas are also reaching full employment, the labor market tightens further and wages rise. There is a shift of workers from low-paying, informal work and from the home as housewives and others enter the labor market. The sectors serving commodity production also expand, and the demand rises for workers from the commercial, professional, and public services (as well as from transport, communication, construction, and other non-manufacturing industries). The growth of these sectors is closely related to the expansion in agriculture and manufactures because they service and facilitate commodity production and its distribution, although part of the output of these sectors is directly purchased by households for their own final consumption (Oshima, 1977).

Once the labor demand of the non-agricultural sectors exceeds the urban supply, even the replacement of labor with machines in the urban sector may not free enough workers to meet the labor demand for further growth, once the traditional handicraft and cottage industries and informal service sectors are reduced to minimal levels and the female participation rates level off. The slowdown in growth implied in the dualistic theories can be avoided by the release of more labor from agriculture. Once again the key role in the agro-industrial transition is played by the agricultural sector, as income elasticities for farm products fall and off-farm village crafts like spinning and weaving are abandoned.

At this point, there is a change in the type of mechanized technologies needed in the rice farms. As noted, productivity in the earliest part of the transition grew through biological and agronomical methods for raising yields, and through multiple and diversified cropping; as full employment was approached, the widespread use of power cultivators, threshers, sprayers, pumps, weeders, driers, and motorized transport saved time for those working on the farms. But as the young people leave for urban jobs, even the most labor-intensive operations of monsoon paddy farming, transplanting and reaping, begin to be mechanized. Much more than the other equipment, mechanical reapers and transplanters release a large number of workers at the busiest time of monsoon rice growing. With this substitution, the labor force on the farms begins to shrink sharply without reducing output, another landmark event in monsoon Asia. The young workers migrating in waves to the cities or commuting to jobs off the farms, accustomed as they are to hard work on complex tasks, represent manpower combining a strong work ethic with education and mechanical experience. About this time, the agro-industrial transition is completed and the economy moves into the next stage, the industrial-service transition.

Growth with Labor Shortage

As small-scale farm mechanization is completed, migration from the rural sector slows down, and the full-employment economy experiences labor shortages in which the growth and redistribution of the labor supply are insufficient to meet demand. Urban industries now must shift increasingly to technologies with higher intensities of scale, capital and knowledge, and move from lower-value to higher-value products requiring quality and sophistication.

In terms of branches of manufacturing, the structural change is from light material (food, textiles, wood products) to heavier material processing (cement, glass, metals), from light and simple machinery industries to heavier and more complex ones; the locale of production changes from cottages and small workshops to larger factories and plants. Small industries unable to mechanize move to the outlying small towns for cheaper labor which can commute to the factories from the nearby farms. At this point, off-farm employment for farm families accelerates and farm family incomes rise substantially. Members of the farm family work more regularly and for longer periods in the factories at higher pay, while continuing to help out in the farm operations during the busy days and over weekends.

Full employment may be said to be approximated when the wages of unskilled workers begin to rise as fast as or faster than the wages of more skilled workers. And when the ensuing migration from agriculture and shifts from the traditional informal service sectors begin accelerating, there are absolute declines in the work force in agriculture and the informal sector, and the economy moves into the last phase of the agro-industrial transition. When the migration from agriculture and shifts from the informal sector begin to decelerate and then fall to a trickle with the saturation in mechanizing transplanting and reaping on the farm and the substantial shrinkage of the informal sector, the economy is fully employed, and shortages of labor begin to appear here and there. The opportunities to introduce new technologies to substitute for hand work become scarce. New machines, faster and more powerful, replace aging ones, and the result is that labor and capital productivity grows more slowly within each industry; shifts to new industries accelerate, and structural changes become a major source of productivity growth.

By this time, the economy has overcome all of the obstacles imposed by the monsoon except the size of farms and service establishments, which are too small to use large-scale technologies. In addition, a full operating economy removes one disadvantage not easily observable: when manpower is used only part of the year under conditions of monsoon underemployment, the food consumed during the year is not used maximally for work energy. Whether manpower is used fully or only half the year, about half of the 2,500 calories the human body consumes a day must be set aside for the basal metabolic functions and for normal activities that must be undertaken even when the person is not working. The disposition of the rest of the calories varies with the amount of work done. There is a saving in basal metabolic calories, which do not vary with work done. Hence, GDP per calorie consumed tends to be larger under full employment conditions (Oshima, 1967).

At some point in the sustained growth of the industrial economy and the absolute decline of agriculture, the growth of the industrial labor force slows down and the labor force in the service sectors overtakes that in the industrial sector. We turn now to a discussion of the impact of growth and structural change on family incomes and savings and the growth of population and the labor force in the two transitions.

Impact of Rapid Growth and Structural Change on Income Distribution and Savings

The pattern of productivity and structural changes during the passage through the agro-industrial transition is ultimately favorable for income equality and savings in a labor-intensive strategy, where resources are spread more widely and evenly over small farms and firms.

Disparities between the agricultural and nonagricultural sectors before full employment should decline because the rise in yields and in number of crops per hectare, diversified cropping, and off-farm jobs will increase average farm family incomes, which are typically lower than in the other sectors. As mechanization in the industrial sector at first normally spreads slowly, the rising farm family incomes should reduce the difference between the average incomes of the two sectors.

Within the agricultural sector, disparities between larger and smaller farms may increase in the very beginning because the higher yields and increased use of irrigation will benefit largely the bigger and richer farmers, in particular those located near the urban centers. But as irrigation and roads are extended over larger areas nationwide, benefits from physical infrastructure, higher yields, and multiple/diversified crops accrue to more and more smaller farms, so that income disparities within the agricultural sector will cease to widen and then begin to narrow. Similarly, in the nonagricultural sector, the fuller use of resources and the dissemination of new technologies may begin at first within the larger units paying higher wages and then spread to the smaller units as capital becomes more plentiful. Within firms, the shortage of skilled compared with unskilled workers may widen wage differences. "Within disparities" increase at first and begin to taper off later, as in agriculture. Off-farm employment, although at first confined largely to rural families near the major railways and riverways, soon begins to spread to other areas as transport becomes more widely available. Hence, in the early stages of the transition disparities will widen, but with further growth will begin to stabilize and eventually narrow.

When full employment is approached, fuller employment per family, rising wages, and mechanization will raise average incomes in both sectors. It is difficult to say whether the two averages will pull apart or come closer. Considering the far greater importance of underemployment in the rural areas, full employment may benefit the agricultural families more. On the other hand, yields per hectare and multiple cropping will take a longer time to spread than mechanization and modernization in the urban areas. The outcome will depend very much on the scale and effectivity with which the state pursues agricultural development at the expense of industrial development. It is important to note that the sustained expansion of multiple cropping and off-farm employment is more likely to benefit the smaller farms. The extent of surplus labor per hectare for more cropping and for off-farm jobs is greater in small than in large farms mainly because the dispersion in the size of families is less than that in the size of farms. As rural institutions extend their services more widely, the smaller farms ultimately begin to benefit from education, extension, credit, and marketing facilities; similar benefits occur with the extension of mechanization, and in both cases more so if the appropriate institutions exist. These should favor the shrinking of disparities within the agricultural sector with full employment.

In the industrial sector, the mechanization of unskilled operations and the fact that wages of unskilled workers rise more than others should increasingly reduce the lower-paying jobs. (Farm mechanization also tends to raise the wages of landless farm workers.) Disparities between firms within industries and between industries are reduced with the spread of mechanization to the smaller firms and to low-income-generating industries. Hence, as full employment is approached, growth and structural changes will be favorable to income-equalizing tendencies. The decline in income disparities is more likely to start in the latter stages of the agro-industrial transition, the underlying reason being that the sustained spread of technologies, capital, skills, employment, and external economies from the services of governments, schools, extensions, transport, and so on increasingly affects the smaller units of production.

With labor shortages, the tendency for disparities to fall between and within major sectors may slow down as small-scale mechanization in agriculture reaches the limits of its spread and potential in the industrial sectors, and larger machines begin to replace smaller ones in the larger firms within industries. There is also a tendency for industries to shift to more capital-intensive types of industrialization. These may tend to increase somewhat overall disparities in family income.

As growth begins, savings begin to appear more and more among the lower-income groups, as they succeed in covering their expenditures and then begin to save to repay debts. With incomes continuing to grow, they are able to save to purchase the inputs needed for expanded production, and then to purchase equipment. With the growing perception that their children should get more education as modernization proceeds, workers' families are impelled to save for future education.

This contrasts with the situation in the West where savings for growth come mainly from the upper income groups. The reason lies in the much larger number of small units of production in a monsoon economy, where the small proprietors must save in order to expand and survive in a competitive situation. For the worker as well as the proprietor, working hard and saving for education are strongly emphasized in Confucian cultures. Accordingly, the increasing incomes received by the smaller farms and firms in monsoon Asia will give rise to an increase in saving even when income disparities decline, in contrast with the West where the main source of savings is the upper income groups.

Demographic Transition

The demand for labor increases in the early stages of the agro-industrial transition with far more cropping and intensified cultivation during the busy season. Birth rates will tend to go up, as in traditional times; more importantly, death rates fall sharply with the spread of modern medical technologies and better nutrition. But with full employment, mechanization begins to accelerate, and this sets in motion new forces which bring down birth rates.

Technological progress eventually reduces the demand for uneducated labor. Small machines increase the demand for female workers in labor-intensive operations requiring light-handed work. This raises the cost of rearing children as housewives go out to work. The demand for more education required by the new technologies—in biology, botany, and chemistry for the development of higher-yielding varieties and modern inputs, and in physics and mechanics for machine operations and repairs, together with more sophisticated literacy, mathematics, and accounting—compels parents to keep their children in schools beyond the primary levels. The higher educational costs, including the income forgone due to prolonged schooling of teenagers, can be paid out of larger family incomes, especially with wives working.[4] Parents pressure teenagers after graduation to work until they are older to help with the costs of more education. Marriages are then postponed to later years, reducing the childbearing period after marriage.

After the children are educated, the higher family incomes can go into more savings in banks, purchases of financial and physical assets such as land and homes, health and life insurance, and so on—all to meet the hazards of old age. There is thus less need for parents to depend for security on children when they grow up. Thus, the benefits of children, both in the shorter and longer run, decline while their costs go up; and quality rather than quantity of children becomes more important. As fertility continues to fall, the demographic transition is completed at roughly the same time as the agro-industrial transition. Falling birth rates and the later entry of the young into the labor force contract the labor supply in the latter portion of the transition, contributing to full employment and then to labor shortage, and to rising real wages and capital/labor substitution. Population growth becomes largely endogenous in this process, and the demographic transition is integrated into the agro-industrial transition. The main independent variables affecting the demographic transition are linked to the later stages of the industrial transition. Without the integration of the two transitions, it is difficult to explain the changing demand for child and

---

[4] It is the cost of additional education that leads to fewer children and more wives going out to work, although most demographers believe that is it the decision of wives, especially educated ones, to go out to work that leads to smaller numbers of children. For upper-income families the latter may be the case, but for the vast majority, whose family size must fall before the demographic transition is completed, it is the cost of education beyond the primary level that induces wives to go out to work. (See Chapter 11.)

female workers, the later years of marriage, and the decreased need of children for security during old age. Nor is it possible to explain the slower growth of the labor supply which affects wage rates and capital/labor substitution in the latter phases of the agro-demographic transition.

Manpower Quality in the Transition

A major source of productive growth is the persistent improvement in the quality of manpower during the agro-industrial transition. Traditional work skills, habits, and ways of thinking are modified and modernized, but the traditional strong work ethics and culture are retained. This transformation affects not just the young through widespread education but also the adult labor force through the mass media, community organizations, and, above all, the workplace. For most of the adults who are literate in the latter part of the transition, learning through the mass media is greatly facilitated and becomes even more important than a decade of schooling, while participation in discussion and decision-making in families, associations, cooperatives, labor unions, and community organizations improves social and political skills. Most important, new skills appropriate for modern production are learned on the job in the rapidly mechanizing workplace, whether farm or firm. The work habits, attitudes, behavior, and practices of modern production differ from those of traditional ways; greater responsibility, precision, cooperation, vitality, and willingness to learn are required to meet the demands for precision, speed, power, versatility, complexity, and variety of 20th-century technology. The sustained improvements of skills and work culture in the workplace cannot take place without steadily rising wages and improving working relations, nor can they take place under conditions of too much surplus labor since management is under less pressure to economize on labor costs. There is a complex interplay between improvements in manpower quality, productivity, and working conditions that is difficult to capture in a theory of wages, but there is no doubt that under conditions of rapid and sustained growth the quality of manpower keeps pace with the changes in technology and institutions, interacting and reacting with them in accelerating the growth of productivity.

Summary and Conclusions

The strategy that the foregoing analysis calls for is a heavy emphasis on agricultural development and labor-intensive industrialization in the early stages of the transition, with gradual shifts to more capital-intensive industrialization. Annual farm family incomes in monsoon Asia are too low for the sustained development of the industrial sector at the outset. Rising income and productivity per farm family with higher yields, more cropping, extensive diversification, and off-farm employment are needed to raise annual incomes for greater domestic demand for the output of industries which need time to gain experience, scale, and external economies before venturing into foreign markets. Increases in food production will tend to keep food prices and imports low; together with the release of farm workers after mechanization, this will help to keep industrial wages from rising too rapidly. The tendency for farm savings to rise with higher farm incomes will expand domestic savings for industrial expansion, contributing to lower interest rates and to less dependence on foreign borrowing. The growth of farm incomes will keep income disparities from rising, reducing the social tensions which are likely to increase with too drastic a structural shift to industrialization. As the agricultural sector begins to move, more attention can be shifted to industries that supply the needs of the farm sector, in particular food processing, modern farm inputs and equipment, clothing, household wares, construction, etc., most of which can be produced labor-intensively with simple technologies. The labor-intensive strategy makes it easier to leave the determination of most prices and wages to market forces instead of government forces whose intervention is likely to be heavy-handed and inefficient.[5]

If a country is to put heavy emphasis on industrialization in the early phase of the transition, as dualistic and other development strategies advocate, the growth of income from the small industrial sector will not be sufficient to expand domestic markets, savings, and foreign exchange, while food prices, wages, and interest rates will tend to rise. In the early phases of the transition, it is the agricultural sector that looms large and dominates the movements of macro aggregates and micro rates. The entrepreneurship, the skills, the physical infrastructures for externalities, and markets for scale economies for industrialization are too meager at the outset to support more than a modest effort at labor-intensive industrialization, and attempts to mount an ambitious program for industrialization at the earlier stages are likely to result in a collection of industries unable to efficiently supply industrial products.

[5] The Singapore government, for example, in its haste to move faster to capital intensity, tried to push up wages too quickly in the past decade, causing difficulties for the more labor-intensive industries.

The upshot will be an economy growing slowly or even stagnating, as it is forced to rely heavily on government intervention for protection, regulation, subsidies, and foreign loans, and showing wide disparities in family incomes and savings, extensive surplus labor, and social unrest. Efforts to shift to a strategy more appropriate for raising incomes and employment in agriculture and more labor-intensive industries will be met with a heavy barrage of super-nationalistic slogans from the vested interests of inefficient industries which have grown big and powerful on protected prices and shoddy products. The government bureacracy, so important in the selection and the management of development strategies, will become corrupted with the spoils of government regulations and handouts, and will be unwilling to shift to a less lucrative labor-intensive strategy. All the while the huge costs of capital-intensive industrialization will crowd out funds for human resource and physical infrastructure development and institution-building for balanced growth.

In the chapters to follow, we will use the foregoing framework to analyze the growth of Asian countries in the postwar decades. Since it was influenced most by the experience of Japan, Taiwan, and South Korea, the framework is most pertinent to the East Asian countries. For other countries, modifications must be made to incorporate their experience.

It is necessary to go beyond the framework that deals only with proximate forces, however, if we are to learn why various countries selected the particular strategies they did at the beginning of the postwar era. This question must be asked since strategies are an important part of the explanation for the differential pace with which nations grew. Much of the answer must be sought in the historical background, and the country chapters attempt to trace the more ultimate forces back to the prewar period.

CHAPTER 3

The Record of Postwar Economic Growth: Differential Regional Growth in Monsoon Asia

A s was noted in Chapter 1, after centuries of stagnation three groupings of countries began to emerge in the first half of the 20th century: in East Asia, the Japanese Empire, with Japan buying rice from Taiwan, Korea, and parts of China; in Southeast Asia, a group clustering around Singapore, with the surrounding plantation economies of the Philippines, Indonesia, and Malaysia importing rice from the countries of Indochina including Thailand; and in South Asia, British India and Ceylon importing rice from Burma. This general pattern of alignment was to continue into the postwar decades, crystallizing with a few modifications into the three basic regions of monsoon Asia: East, Southeast, and South Asia. The most striking phenomenon of postwar growth was the differential speed with which the three regions grew and which, if continued into the next couple of decades, will see the emergence of a developed region, a semi-developed region, and an underdeveloped region in monsoon Asia. This chapter describes quantitatively the record of rapid, moderate, and slow growth and structural changes of countries and regions in monsoon Asia.[1]

The Data and Their Reliability

Table 3.1 shows the annual average growth rates of gross domestic product (GDP) in constant market prices for the 1950s, 1960s, and 1970s and their postwar averages, together with growth rates of population and employment. Table 3.2 presents growth rates of GDP per capita and of GDP per worker, based on data in Table 3.1. In Table 3.3, growth rates of constant GDP produced in each of the three broad sectors are shown, and in Table 3.4 these growth rates are computed on a per-worker basis. Figures 3.1 and 3.2 illustrate the growth in constant and nominal prices for each year.

[1] This differentiation was discussed in Oshima, 1977a, 1977b.

Table 3.1   Annual Growth Rates of GDP, Population, and Employment in Asian Countries

	GDP				Population				Employment			
	1950s	1960s	1970s	Avg.	1950s	1960s	1970s	Avg.	1950s	1960s	1970s	Avg.
East Asia	7.1	9.6	8.2	8.3	3.2	2.2	1.7	2.4	2.8	3.4	3.9	3.4
Japan	8.0	10.9	5.0	8.0	1.3	1.0	1.1	1.1	2.0	1.5	1.2	1.6
S. Korea	5.1	8.6	9.5	7.7	2.0	2.5	1.7	2.1	3.2	2.8	4.5	3.5
Taiwan	7.6	9.6	8.8	8.7	3.5	2.7	1.9	2.7	3.0	4.2	4.7	4.0
Hong Kong	9.2	10.0	9.3	9.5	4.5	2.6	2.5	3.2	—	5.3	4.5	4.9
Singapore	5.4	8.8	8.5	8.1	4.8	2.4	1.5	2.9	2.9	3.1	4.8	3.6
Southeast Asia	5.0	6.0	7.2	6.1	2.5	2.7	2.5	2.6	3.5	3.0	3.8	3.4
Malaysia	3.6	6.5	7.8	6.0	2.5	2.8	2.4	2.6	2.9	2.1	4.0	3.0
Thailand	5.7	8.4	7.2	7.1	2.8	3.0	2.5	2.8	3.6	4.0	3.2	3.6
Indonesia	4.0	3.9	7.6	5.2	2.1	2.0	2.3	2.1	—	2.2	3.9	3.1
Philippines	6.5	5.1	6.3	6.0	2.7	3.0	2.7	2.8	3.9	3.7	4.2	3.9
South Asia	4.1	3.4	3.7	3.7	2.0	2.2	2.2	2.2	3.7	0.2	2.9	2.3
India	3.8	3.4	3.6	3.6	1.9	2.3	2.1	2.1	6.1	-0.9	2.8	2.7
Bangladesh	—	3.7	3.9	3.8	2.4	2.4	2.6	2.5	—	—	—	—
Burma	6.3	2.7	4.6	4.5	1.9	2.3	2.4	2.2	—	—	—	—
Sri Lanka	3.9	4.6	4.1	4.2	2.6	2.4	1.6	2.2	1.2	1.3	2.9	1.8
Nepal	2.4	2.5	2.5	2.5	1.2	1.8	2.5	1.8	—	—	—	—

Note: Regional and country averages are simple, unweighted averages.

Sources: Employment data are computed from various issues of the *ILO Yearbook of Labour Statistics*. Unless otherwise indicated, product and population data for the 1950s and 1960s were taken from *IBRD World Tables 1980* and those for the 1970s from *IBRD World Development Report 1982*. Taiwan's data for the 1970s were computed from various issues of *National Income of ROC* and *Statistical Yearbook of ROC*.

Table 3.2   Annual Growth Rates of Product Per Capita and Product Per Worker in Asian Countries

	Dollar GNP Per Capita		Annual Growth of Product Per Capita				Annual Growth of Product Per Worker			
	1950	1980	1950s	1960s	1970s	Avg.	1950s	1960s	1970s	Avg.
East Asia	155	4,446	3.9	7.3	6.6	6.1	3.8	6.1	4.3	4.7
Japan	190[1]	9,890	6.6	10.1	4.1	6.9	4.0	8.8	4.1	6.3
S. Korea	70[1]	1,520	3.1	6.0	8.0	5.7	1.9	5.8	5.0	4.2
Taiwan	110	2,150	4.0	6.3	6.7	5.7	4.6	5.4	4.1	4.7
Hong Kong	250	4,240	4.5	7.2	6.4	6.0	—	4.7	4.8	4.7
Singapore	—	4,430	1.3[2]	6.7	7.7	6.2	2.5	5.7	3.7	4.0
Southeast Asia	180	853	2.3	3.1	4.9	3.4	1.8	3.0	3.5	2.8
Malaysia	310[1]	1,620	1.0	3.3	5.3	3.2	0.7	4.4	3.8	3.0
Thailand	80[1]	670	2.8	4.7	5.1	4.2	2.1	4.4	4.0	3.5
Indonesia	—	430	1.9	2.3	5.7	3.3	—	1.7	4.2	3.0
Philippines	150[1]	690	3.6	2.2	3.4	3.1	2.6	1.4	2.1	2.0
South Asia	73	190	2.2	1.5	1.1	1.5	0.2	3.9	1.2	1.8
India	60[1]	240	1.9	2.2	1.2	1.8	-2.8	4.3	0.8	0.9
Bangladesh	—	130	—	1.1	0.3	0.7	—	—	—	—
Burma	50[1]	170	4.3	1.2	1.2	2.2	—	—	—	—
Sri Lanka	110[1]	270	1.3	2.5	2.3	2.0	2.7	3.5	1.6	2.6
Nepal	—	140	1.2	0.4	0.4	0.7	—	—	—	—

Notes: [1] Per capita net national product in U.S. dollars, average 1952–54, from UN Statistical Paper Series E, no. 4, *Per Capita National Product of Fifty-Five Countries: 1952–54.* [2] 1956–60 data.
Sources: Same as for Table 3.1.

Table 3.3   Growth Rates of GDP by Industrial Origin in Asian Countries (%)

	A Sector				I Sector				S Sector			
	1950s	1960s	1970s	Avg.	1950s	1960s	1970s	Avg.	1950s	1960s	1970s	Avg.
East Asia												
Average	4.2	3.9	0.6	2.7	12.2	12.6	10.1	11.6	7.5	7.8	8.1	7.5
Japan	2.4	4.0	1.1	2.5	13.7	10.9	5.5	10.0	8.8	11.7	5.5	8.7
S. Korea	5.5	4.4	3.2	4.4	12.3	17.2	15.4	15.0	3.7	8.9	8.5	7.0
Taiwan	4.8	4.1	1.6	3.5	10.7	14.7	12.5	12.6	10.0	9.1	8.3	9.1
Hong Kong	—	1.9	-4.6	-1.4[1]	—	7.9	8.2	8.1[1]	—	11.5	9.8	10.7[1]
Singapore	—	5.0	1.8	3.4[1]	—	12.5	8.8	10.7[1]	—	7.7	8.5	8.1[1]
Southeast Asia												
Average	2.7	4.6	4.6	4.0	6.3	7.5	9.9	8.1	4.8	6.6	7.5	6.5
Malaysia	0.9	5.8	5.1	3.9	3.7	7.0	9.7	6.8	1.3	7.2	8.2	5.6
Thailand	3.8	5.6	4.7	4.7	8.0	11.9	10.0	10.0	6.1	9.1	7.3	7.5
Indonesia	2.6	2.7	3.8	3.0	—	5.2	11.1	2.8[1]	—	4.8	9.2	7.0[1]
Philippines	3.3	4.3	4.9	4.2	7.1	6.0	8.7	7.3	6.9	5.2	5.4	5.8
South Asia												
Average	2.7	2.9	2.3	2.3	3.6	5.8	5.8	5.6	4.5	3.7	4.9	4.3
India	3.2	1.9	1.9	2.3	5.7	5.4	4.5	5.2	4.3	4.6	5.2	4.7
Bangladesh	—	2.7	2.2	2.5[2]	—	8.0	9.5	8.8[1]	—	4.2	4.9	4.6[1]
Burma	2.5	4.1	4.3	3.6	—	3.1	5.2	4.2[1]	—	1.5	4.7	3.1[1]
Sri Lanka	2.3	3.0	2.8	2.7	1.5	6.6	4.0	4.0	4.6	4.6	4.8	4.7
Nepal	—	—	0.5	0.5[2]	—	—	—	—	—	—	—	—

Notes: A Sector includes agriculture, forestry, and fishery; I Sector includes mining & quarrying, manufacturing, construction, electricity & public utilities; S Sector includes transport, storage and communication, commerce and services. Unweighted, simple averages. [1] 1960–80; [2] 1970–80.

Sources: IBRD World Development Report 1982, supplemented by *IBRD World Tables 1980* and various country publications on national accounts.

Table 3.4 Annual Growth Rates of Real Product Per Worker in A, I, and S Sectors (%)

	A Sector				I Sector				S Sector			
	1950s	1960s	1970s	Avg.	1950s	1960s	1970s	Avg.	1950s	1960s	1970s	Avg.
East Asia	3.3	5.9	5.4	4.9	6.3	6.3	4.4	5.7	4.4	5.5	3.1	4.5
Japan	3.2	6.2	8.0	5.8	10.2	8.9	4.0	7.7	5.6	7.0	2.4	5.0
S. Korea	2.1	1.8	3.2	2.4	0.9	7.9	5.8	4.9	0.9	5.2	4.8	3.6
Taiwan	4.6	3.2	4.1	4.0	7.8	6.6	4.8	6.4	6.7	2.4	3.7	4.3
Hong Kong	—	8.3	4.9	6.7	—	2.8	3.0	2.9	—	7.6	4.7	6.2
Singapore	—	10.1	6.7	8.5	—	5.3	4.3	4.8	—	5.5	3.0	4.3
Southeast Asia	2.0	3.7	3.4	3.0	1.2	2.9	3.2	2.4	0.8	1.7	1.1	1.2
Malaysia	0.8	6.1	4.1	3.7	0.8	4.9	3.1	2.9	1.2	3.4	2.9	1.7
Thailand	0.7	4.3	5.7	3.6	2.0	4.4	3.3	3.2	3.0	5.1	1.4	3.2
Indonesia	—	1.9	2.3	2.1	—	1.2	4.6	2.8	—	0.3	0.6	0.4
Philippines	4.4	2.6	1.5	2.8	0.8	1.0	2.8	1.5	0.6	-1.9	-0.7	-0.7
South Asia	-0.7	2.3	0.4	0.7	1.0	5.2	1.3	2.5	1.6	4.6	1.7	2.6
India	-3.6	2.9	0.4	-0.1	-0.6	5.4	1.1	2.0	0.5	4.9	0.7	2.0
Sri Lanka	2.2	1.6	0.3	1.4	2.6	4.9	1.5	3.0	2.6	4.2	2.6	3.1

Notes: A sector includes agriculture, forestry, and fishery; I sector includes mining, manufacturing, construction, electricity, gas and water, and transport, storage and communication; S sector includes commerce and services.

Sources: Employment data mainly from *ILO Yearbook of Labour Statistics*; product data from *IBRD World Tables 1980* and supplemented by various official publications on national accounts and employment.

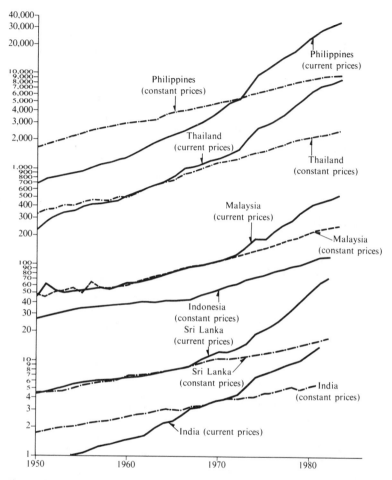

Figure 3.1   Postwar growth of GNP in selected countries in Southeast and South Asia.

Sources: Data are from *IBRD World Tables 1976* updated by *Key Indicators of DMC's ADB* (April 1984), with the following exceptions: Philippine data from *NEDA Philippine National Accounts*; Thailand data for the 1950s from *National Income of Thailand*; and data for West Malaysia and Malaysia in the 1950s from Bhanoji Rao, *National Accounts of West Malaysia 1947–1971*.

Note: Current price data for Indonesia are not presented because of its runaway inflation in the 1960s.

The growth rates in this and all other chapters are compounded or geometric percentages. The composition of each region differs some-

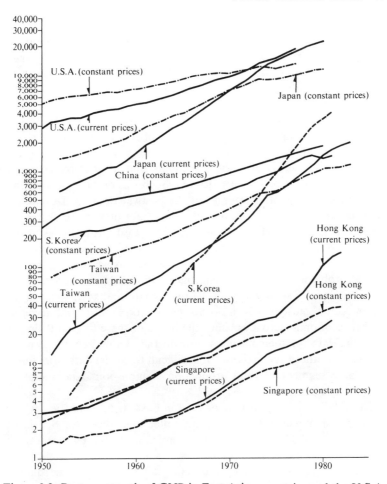

Figure 3.2 Postwar growth of GNP in East Asian countries and the U.S.A.
Sources: IBRD data tables and statistics from the governments of the various
countries.

what from the conventional definition, which seems to be made on a
geographic basis. The division used here is more of a socioeconomic
one; it treats Singapore as part of East Asia because of its predominant
East Asian ethnicity, and Burma as part of South Asia because of its
close economic ties with South Asia. Countries not included are those
for which long-term data are not available. In the case of China, the
official data are available but are puzzling and could not be reconciled
with the official estimate of per capita income levels in 1980, as discussed in Chapter 9. The major sectors, agriculture (A), industry (I),

and services (S), are defined in the conventional way, except that transport and communication are in the I sector rather than the S sector as in the IBRD and UN classifications. I follow Kuznets's usage, agreeing with him that because the transport and communication sectors are quite capital-intensive, it is more convenient to treat them as industries.

The decades following World War II witnessed great advances in the statistical compilations of many types of socioeconomic data. The most important set of economic data is in the system of national product accounts, and it is from these accounts that most of the estimates compiled in Tables 3.1–3.4 are derived. Such sets of data are available for most countries of Asia only for the postwar decades. Despite the great progress made, the data in the tables are of varying degrees of reliability. Extensive efforts have been made to improve the estimates by the various Asian statistical offices, whose professional skills have been substantially upgraded over the decades. Nevertheless, the statistical problem in monsoon Asia that is difficult to overcome is the huge numbers of small farms in the rural sector and small firms in the urban sector, most of which do not keep good records and accounts of their economic activities, since the heads of these tiny units do not need the data for their business; nor do they know how to keep the accounts. Without such records, it is difficult to collect data from them, so a large segment of total production in monsoon Asia cannot be adequately recorded.

The GNP data in constant prices for East Asian countries, where literacy and numeracy are high, are better than those for Southeast Asian countries. The data are best for Japan, which has by far the most extensive network in Asia of censuses, surveys, and administrative statistics, these sources being the major determinants of the quality of the statistical constructs. Japanese GDP statistics are not as good as the best from the industrialized countries in the West, though the censuses and surveys are more numerous. The reason can be traced to the larger proportion of small production units in monsoon Japan than in the West. The other countries of East Asia are covered by few surveys and sets of administrative data, and the quality of the data is lower; data from Taiwan are better than those from South Korea because tax administration is better. For the same reason Singapore's data seem to be better than Hong Kong's, although both city-states have the advantage of being small and without a rural sector where good data are difficult to collect. Chinese data, only recently made available to the outside, are of unknown quality but probably are the weakest in East Asia, and remain to be tested in widespread use by independent scholars. China's data are to a large extent the by-product of administration and may be biased, as they are compiled by officials and cadres whose performance may be evaluated on the basis of the collected data.

The surveys of South and Southeast Asia underlying the estimates of GDP are not only fewer but also poorer in quality than those of East Asia. Educational levels are generally lower, with less literacy and numeracy. Business and household records and accounts are not extensively kept, and survey respondents must rely mainly on memory to complete the questionnaires. The network of roads and transport to the remote villages and communities is less developed, with portions inaccessible to interviewers. Thus, the population censuses of South and Southeast Asian countries are frequently understated, and survey results are often unreliable when interviewers do not find the time or means to go out to remote areas and must fill out questionnaires by guesswork. The high quality of Japanese censuses and surveys is the product of long historical experience, good networks of transport and communication, high levels of literacy and numeracy, and a strong sense of responsibility and cooperativeness in the respondents, even stronger than that in the West. And the greater varieties and frequencies of surveys and censuses are due to the extensive use made of their results in planning, policies, and administration.

For most countries the estimates are better for the 1970s than for the 1960s, and better for the 1960s than for the 1950s; as funding improved and statistical staffs gained experience, the data also improved. There are many questions which can be raised about the computation of the national accounts apart from the underlying quality of the raw data. But space permits only a few general comments pertinent to evaluating the findings that the data point to. Complex conceptual and methodological questions inhere in the traditional structures of monsoon Asia for the estimation of wide-ranging aggregates such as GDP, which attempt to measure comprehensively the annual flow of goods and services produced in the entire nation each year, without duplication or omission, and then deflate the totals to eliminate the effects of price changes. There is a limit to what even the best-trained statisticians can do in the face of inadequate and insufficient data.

Many questions arise in the various steps in the computation, from the prices used to value the goods and services produced, the deductions made to arrive at net value of the output, the conversion of the products as they originate from their industries into final sales (or expenditures from the purchasers' viewpoint), and the methods of deflating and extrapolating to get at quantity changes, until the estimates finally emerge as shown in the tables. The numerous decisions made make it difficult to say whether the estimates of one country are understated or overstated, from one decade to another. A case can perhaps be made for assuming that, in general, the GDP levels of less developed countries are likely to be understated because coverage of the production of numerous minor, miscellaneous products and of the incomes of subsistence producers is poor, and that the inter country deflation based on foreign exchange rates undervalues nontradables, especially of subsistence producers. But this assumes that the statisticians in the national income offices do not make overgenerous adjustments to overcome the above deficiencies or are notinfluenced to deliberately overstate the growth rate for political reasons. Or it assumes that over time the price indexes used to deflate (or the use of underlying units to represent constant price estimates) do not take into account the quality improvements in agricultural and industrial output from one decade to the next. The general practice of estimating quantity changes in the output of the service sector by changes in the number of persons employed understates growth when the use of more equipment and training points to a rise in productivity per worker. But there are likely to be offsetting practices, such as the use of value-added per worker taken from the manufacturing sample surveys to represent output over time in the universe of the large number of small units (employing less than 5 or 10 or 20 workers).[2] In general, the changes over time are likely to be more reliable than the absolute levels at a point of time.

The weakest parts of the estimates in the production accounts of the national systems of all countries (including those of Japan) relate to the smaller producing units in industry and services, to the large variety of minor crops produced by small farms, and to the output from the small units in fishery, forestry, and animal husbandry. The output of the small units in monsoon Asia is proportionately greater than that in other parts of the world, such as Latin America, as shown elsewhere in this volume. The output of the organized sectors of the economy is far better covered than that of the unorganized sector.

The unreliable parts of the estimates of distributive shares in the system of accounts are likely to be the estimations of proprietors' income. The proprietors liable for taxes tend to understate, often by a wide margin, while for the smallest ones, who are not liable, the data are difficult to collect. Employee compensation for workers in the informal sectors is a "guesstimate" since there is little knowledge of

---

[2] I suspect this to be the case for the Philippines in the later period. See Oshima, 1983c.

the degree of regularity and seasonality of employment during the year, even when wages per diem are known. Not much better are property incomes, the weakest data being for the rental and interest incomes of persons and the best being for corporate incomes, though even the latter are understated in countries where tax administration is lax. Thus, statistics for the various distributive shares may be said to be of dubious value in many countries. It is understandable that statisticians in some countries in South and Southeast Asia shy away from serious attempts to compute all the distributive shares, contenting themselves with the estimation needed to complete the entries in the system.

The weakest parts of the expenditure (or output by use) estimates are the personal consumption estimates, especially for services. The best are government expenditures and the external accounts, both of which are based on statistics from budgets, settled accounts, and customs records, even though part of these may be dubious in countries where corruption and smuggling are rampant. The weakest parts of capital formation are inventory changes and construction in the informal sectors.

In short, the weakness of the GNP accounts stems not so much from conceptual/methodology problems as from the insufficient or deficient sources of information on the small, unorganized, informal sectors, which contribute substantially to national output in most of monsoon Asia. Although governments can do much more to improve the surveys, the main problem is the difficulty of collecting information from the vast number of respondents who find record-keeping difficult.

The foregoing implies that small differences between two points of time should not be taken seriously for analytical purposes, and that use of some of the data in finely tuned economic models may be hazardous. Nonetheless, these are data which have been extensively used by a large number of public officials, private businesses, international organizations, and scholars. In the process they have been tested and checked against other data, e.g., expected and actual government revenues, foreign trade, financial and other data. When the expectations from the use of these data are not met, or the data are used by particular groups with "axes to grind," questions have been raised in public that forced the estimators to examine or change the estimates. Moreover, the data have to be consistent with information on urbanization, social indicators, and living standards, e.g., statistics on electricity use, radio use, car ownership, life expectancy, infant mortality, birth and death rates, food consumption, literacy, and others which are related to levels and changes in national income. All these indica-

Table 3.5   Growth Rate of Real Per Capita GNP (1960 to 1980) and Social Factors (1980)

Country	Annual Real per Capita GNP Growth Rate (1)	Adult Literacy Rate (2)	Life Expectancy at Birth (yrs.) (3)	Total Fertility Rate (4)	Male Agri. Labor Force in Total Labor Force (%) (5)	Daily per Capita Calories Intake (6)	TDI of Quintiles (7)
East Asia	6.4	87	71	2.4	14	2,879	.49
Japan	7.1	99	76	1.8	6	2,912	.41 (1979)
China	3.7	69	64	2.9	41	2,539	.50 (1979)
Taiwan	6.5	90	72	2.5	13	2,812	.40 (1976)
Hong Kong	6.8	90	74	2.2	2	2,898	.57 (1980)
Singapore	7.5	83	72	1.8	2	3,158	.52 (1975)
South Korea	7.0	93	65	3.0	19	2,957	.55 (1976)
Southeast Asia	4.0	71	61	4.3	34	2,381	.67
Malaysia	4.3	60	64	4.2	24	2,625	.73 (1973)
Thailand	4.7	86	63	4.0	36	2,308	.62 (1975–76)
Philippines	2.8	75	64	4.6	37	2,275	.68 (1971)
Indonesia	4.0	62	53	4.5	38	2,315	.66 (1976)
South Asia	1.1	46	52	5.2	56	2,046	.60
India	1.4	36	52	4.9	55	1,880	.60 (1975–76)
Sri Lanka	2.4	85	66	3.6	39	2,238	.50 (1969–70)
Burma	1.2	66	54	5.3	—	2,174	—
Nepal	0.2	19	44	6.1	57	1,977	.78 (1976–77)
Bangladesh	0.3	26	46	6.0	71	1,960	.51 (1973–74)

Note: TDI derived as the sum of differences between shares of income and household of each quintile with signs ignored. To give an idea of the relationship between TDI and Gini coefficient, the latter is generally about three-fourths of the former.

Sources: IBRD World Development Report, 1982, 1983, and 1984 editions, except for Column (5) which is computed from *ILO Yearbook of Labour Statistics 1982.*

tors and many others usually are related in expected or predicted ways with slow or rapid growth—for example, a falling Engel coefficient is usually associated with per capita product growth. For example, in 1983, IMF economists criticized Philippine estimates of GNP growth rates as too high in 1981 and 1982, and these were substantially lowered after examination. But all these checks are approximate, and users of the estimates are warned to be constantly on guard for puzzling movements in the series.

In general the growth rates reported here are consistent with many other types of data from other sources, such as growth rates of government revenues, of money supply, of imports and exports, living standards, and social indicators (see Table 3.5). And as noted below, the patterns of structural changes are consonant with what Kuznets found to be associated with Western growth (Oshima, 1977b.)

The employment figures used here to calculate product per worker are generally better than the national accounting figures, most of which have been constructed out of a variety of data of different quality. They are taken directly from population censuses and labor force surveys held periodically (monthly in Japan; quarterly in Taiwan, South Korea, and the Philippines; once or twice a year in other countries). But there are difficult conceptual problems stemming from the fact that the labor force concepts were derived from the most developed economy in the world, the United States, whose labor markets and employment practices are quite different from those of monsoon Asia where seasonality is pronounced. In most Asian countries (with the exception of Japan), employment arrangements for most workers are dominated by short-term contracts—by the day, week, or month—and affected by seasonality and intermittence. Most of the small firms produce on the basis of orders daily or weekly from buyers; often workers are hired casually on a daily basis until the orders are filled. Since the respondents in the survey are usually asked about their employment situation in one reference week just prior to the interview, the data pertain only to that week, even though in the preceding weeks or months their employment situation might have been quite different.

Most troublesome is the seasonality in agriculture, where females and others work during the busy months but do not work or work only part-time during the slack season or, in the case of adult males, take on nonfarm employment in towns and cities. The survey week cannot be taken as representative of the whole year where monsoon seasonality is so pronounced. Even quarterly surveys may not be adequate. This is one of the reasons monthly surveys are undertaken in countries like Japan.

Table 3.6   Gross Domestic Capital Formation in Constant Prices and as Shares of GDP

	In Constant Prices (millions of national currency units)					As Shares of GDP				
	Avg. 1950s	Avg. 1960s	Avg. 1970s	Change (%) 1950s	Change (%) 1960s	Avg. 1950s	Avg. 1960s	Avg. 1970s	Change (%) 1950s	Change (%) 1960s
East Asia	—	—	—	283.7	187.7	16.8	25.3	31.7	71.7	29.0
Japan	6,239*	2,4714*	51,740*	296.1	109.4	28.9	36.0	33.3	24.6	−7.5
Taiwan	8,533	34,467	90,500	303.9	130.3	17.6	23.3	28.5	32.4	22.3
S. Korea	245*	833*	3,611*	240.0	333.5	11.4	23.2	29.4	1,03.5	26.7
Hong Kong	924	3,647	9,073	294.7	148.8	9.1	20.6	26.7	1,26.4	29.6
Singapore	—	984	3,115	—	216.6	—	23.4	40.7	—	73.9
Southeast Asia	—	—	—	120.9	161.8	13.9	18.0	25.3	25.8	46.3
Malaysia	—	1768	4409	—	149.4	—	18.1	26.1	—	44.2
Thailand	8,133	24,833	56,367	205.3	127.0	15.6	22.5	26.1	44.2	16.0
Philippines	3,881	8,115	18,718	109.1	130.7	15.3	20.1	28.7	31.4	42.8
Indonesia	317*	470*	1,599*	48.3	240.2	10.9	11.1	20.2	1.8	82.0
South Asia	—	—	—	81.2	41.4	12.9	14.1	18.3	16.6	28.7
India	34*	59*	87*	73.5	47.5	14.7	17.6	21.6	19.7	22.7
Sri Lanka	1,023	1,735	3,344	69.6	92.7	12.7	15.3	22.7	20.5	48.4
Burma	648	1,299	1,614	100.5	24.2	11.4	12.5	16.5	9.6	32.0
Bangladesh	—	4,249	4,291	—	1.0	—	11.0	12.3	—	11.8

Note: * Billions of national currency units.
Sources: Computed from various editions of *IBRD World Tables*.

Other problems in the labor force concept are persons switching industries with the seasons (e.g., from agriculture to fishing, industry, services); persons changing occupations as they shift from one industry to another; and unpaid family help doing intermittent work on farms, in shops, or in homes, irrespective of the season. Of course, these problems are not absent in other parts of the world, but they are minimal since casual work is largely confined to agriculture, since small enterprises and the informal sector are much less important. As is the case with national accounting statistics, the time series on changes in employment are better than absolute levels of employment at a point of time, as long as the patterns of seasonality, irregularity, and intermittence from one year to the next are stable. Here, too, small changes in employment and product per worker over time or small differences between countries are not to be taken seriously for analytical purposes. And although the data in Table 3.2 show that East Asia grew twice as fast as Southeast Asia and four times as rapidly as South Asia, the data for the latter two regions are too rough; all we can be certain of is that the differentials in growth rates in the three decades among the three areas were substantial.

Problems of Defining and Measuring Growth

Following Simon Kuznets, economic growth is defined as sustained increases in real GNP per capita or per worker. The increase is unidirectional and steady, in that the general movement is not overwhelmed by short-term fluctuations, either episodic, random, or cyclical (short or long). Such fluctuations as do occur, when removed, will reveal the trends whose slopes represent economic growth. Much of the influence of episodic or random fluctuations can be eliminated with decadal averages, but not the long swings, which in the United States in the 19th century were swings in the growth rates of GNP lasting about 15 to 20 years. Very few studies have been made on the long swings in Asia except in Japan, where swings beginning in the early 1900s were first identified by Shinohara (1982). A preliminary study for the Institute of Developing Economies found that long swing forces are important in the Asian countries which after independence undertook vast infrastructure construction programs, and predicted that in the latter half of the 1980s there may be a tapering off of construction, contributing to a slowdown in growth. Until we see what happens in the late 1980s, there is no way of correcting for long swings and eliminating them from the trends. But for the kind of broad historical analysis undertaken in this volume, the approximation to the

Table 3.7   Structural Change: Employment Share by Sector (%)

	Agriculture			Industry			Services		
	1950	1980	Annual Growth Rate	1950	1980	Annual Growth Rate	1950	1980	Annual Growth Rate
East Asia	34.9	13.7	−5.3	31.2	45.5	2.2	34.0	40.8	1.2
Japan	45.2	11.0	−5.3	26.6	40.5	1.6	28.2	48.5	2.1
S.Korea	57.2	34.2	−3.6	18.0	32.1	4.2	24.8	33.6	2.2
Taiwan	56.0	19.5	−4.3	20.8	48.3	3.6	23.3	32.2	1.4
Hong Kong	7.5	2.0	−6.4	58.8	57.9	−0.1	33.8	40.1	0.9
Singapore	8.6	1.6	−7.0	31.7	48.8	1.9	59.8	49.6	−0.8
Southeast Asia	72.1	55.9	−1.3	10.8	18.2	2.1	17.1	26.0	2.0
W.Malaysia	59.1	36.5	−2.2	16.5	30.4	2.8	24.4	33.1	1.4
Philippines	72.2	51.6	−1.1	11.0	20.8	2.0	16.8	27.6	1.6
Indonesia	73.3	60.9	−1.1	10.2	11.7	0.8	16.5	27.4	3.0
Thailand	83.8	74.4	−0.6	5.6	9.8	2.8	10.6	15.7	2.0
South Asia	73.9	70.9	−0.4	10.6	12.9	−2.3	15.6	16.2	5.3
Sri Lanka	56.7	50.4	−0.4	17.3	23.6	1.1	26.1	26.0	−0.1
India	70.6	72.5	0.1	13.0	14.1	0.4	16.4	13.4	−1.0
Nepal	94.4	89.9	−1.0	1.4	0.9	−8.5	4.2	9.2	17.0

Notes: The initial and terminal years for the following countries, instead of 1950 and 1980, are 1954 (initial year) for Japan, 1966 (initial year) for South Korea, 1956 (initial year) for Taiwan, 1961 and 1981 for Hong Kong, 1957 (initial year) for Singapore, 1957 and 1979 for West Malaysia, 1948 (initial year) for the Philippines, 1961 (initial year) for Indonesia, 1960 (initial year) for Thailand, 1953 (initial year) for Sri Lanka, 1951 and 1971 for India, 1971 and 1976 for Nepal.
Sources: Computed from *ILO Yearbook of Labour Statistics* except for Taiwan, data for which is taken from *Quarterly Report on the Labour Force Survey*.

trends is all that is needed.

Figures 3.1 and 3.2 show GNP in current and constant prices for each country. They do not appear to reveal cyclical movements, which are synchronous fluctuations in aggregate economic activities in nominal prices. Most short breaks in the smooth upward movements can be identified as episodic, random perturbations due to bad harvests, social unrest, or externally originating shocks such as oil price changes and cyclical fluctuations. But these do not make much dent in the onward, upward movements, even in the case of slower-growing South Asian economies. Thus, the trends are not, as Schumpeter once re marked, "shadows of cycles" but the reverse, and for most countries, cycles are not even shadows. Evidently the postwar decades in Asia have been one long secular movement, and the domination of growth forces has pushed out or buried cyclical, episodic, and other forces, although we have yet to see what happens to the long swing cycles. Accordingly, Figs. 3.1 and 3.2 testify to the paramount importance of studying the secular growth in the movement of Asian

Table 3.8 Structural Change: Product Share by Sector (%)

	Agriculture			Industry			Services		
	1950	1980	Annual Growth Rate	1950	1980	Annual Growth Rate	1950	1980	Annual growth Rate
East Asia	20.4	6.0	−5.8	32.5	43.3	1.6	47.1	50.7	0.7
Japan	22.3	4.0	−6.4	39.1	41.0	0.2	38.6	55.0	1.4
S.Korea	39.8	16.0	−6.3	30.5	41.0	2.2	29.8	43.0	2.7
Taiwan	33.3	7.6	−6.0	27.8	56.6	3.0	38.9	35.8	−0.3
Hong Kong	3.2	1.2	−4.8	47.5	40.8	−0.8	49.3	58.0	0.8
Singapore	3.5	1.0	−5.3	17.6	37.0	3.3	78.9	62.0	1.1
Southeast Asia	43.7	25.7	−2.4	22.1	35.8	2.4	34.2	38.6	0.5
W.Malaysia	44.3	25.2	−2.5	17.2	36.8	3.5	38.5	38.0	−0.1
Philippines	40.6	23.0	−1.8	24.8	37.0	1.3	34.6	40.0	0.5
Indonesia	49.0	29.5	−2.9	19.5	40.3	4.4	31.5	30.2	0.2
Thailand	40.9	25.0	−2.4	26.8	29.0	0.4	32.2	46.0	1.8
South Asia	59.3	47.9	−1.4	17.1	23.1	0.2	23.6	29.0	3.8
Sri Lanka	55.0	28.0	−2.5	19.0	30.0	1.7	26.0	42.0	1.8
India	50.3	48.9	−0.2	16.8	26.3	2.3	32.9	24.9	−1.4
Nepal	72.6	66.8	−1.6	15.5	13.1	−3.3	11.9	20.1	11.0

Notes: Same as those in Table 3.7A.
Sources: Computed from (1) *IBRD World Tables 1976* and IBRD National Accounts tape, (2) *IBRD World Development Report 1982*, (3) *UN Yearbook of National Accounts Statistics*, (4) Official publications of respective countries: *National Income Statistics of Japan, National Income of the Republic of China, National Income of Thailand.*

economies.[3]

Gross domestic product, or output produced within the territorial boundaries of a nation, and gross national product, or total output accruing to the nationals or residents of a nation, move in a parallel fashion for all countries except the smaller ones, a large part of whose output is produced by foreigners residing within their boundaries, or where a substantial share of the output (3 or 4 percent) is claimed by nonresident foreigners as in the plantations of Sri Lanka and Malaysia (Rao, 1960).

These aggregates in constant prices are divided by total population for each year to obtain per capita product as the measure of the growth of welfare. By correcting for population size, the size of a nation can be roughly taken into account for comparison between nations, or changing rates of population growth can be taken into account in comparison over time for a nation. Product per capita measures welfare

[3] Because of the strength of secular forces, three- or five-year averages in the initial and terminal points have not been computed in arriving at growth rates, as this will shorten the time span covered by the process of averaging, although exceptions should be made when random shocks are large, as in the case of South Korea in 1980 when the rice crop was ravaged by disease.

better than product per worker, and the latter, obtained by dividing GDP or GNP in constant prices by total employment, is a better measure of productivity per worker. The two move parallel over long periods of time for most nations except in the communist countries like China, in the postwar decades, where the stress on getting housewives out of the home and into outside jobs raises the labor force participation rate over time. In this case, per capita product rises faster than per worker product.

For productivity measurement, it is better to use product per worker and per unit of capital stock (i.e., concealed labor) or total factor productivity (taken in the simple conventional sense). Unfortunately, only a few countries outside East Asia have capital stock statistics, and for comparative purposes, we must depend on product per worker and capital formation data. We have put on graphs the movements in constant prices of gross capital formation, GDP, and gross capital stock for Taiwan, Japan, South Korea, and the Philippines (countries with capital stock estimates) and find that gross capital formation increases faster than GDP, or capital stock. This will imply that the use of comparative product per worker between nations as an approximation for the growth of total factor productivity (TFP) may be acceptable for over-time changes, as long as it is kept in mind that the higher the level of fixed capital formation for a country the greater the difference in the level of product per worker and TFP at a given point in time. (See data in Table 3.6.) Since the growth of TFP is computed by deducting from the growth rate of output the growth rate of labor input and the growth rate of capital stock, TFP growth is lower than the growth rate of labor productivity. Hence, the higher the growth rate of capital formation, the lower will be the growth rate of TFP compared with the rate of labor productivity, assuming no change in capital productivity.

One problem in deflated capital formation estimates is that the deflation of equipment expenditures is carried out by dividing the thousands of machines of varied types, sizes, and design into a dozen or so groups before deflation. With different machines varying in power, speed, fuel efficiency, and quality, such simple procedures may give results which are not likely to be too precise a measure of the growth of input of equipment in factor productivity. (See Chapter 5 for further discussion.)

The time frame may be conceived in the micro sense of the Marshallian long term, roughly the lifetime of a factory. It may also be thought of in a macroscopic sense as a period long enough for substantial changes in technologies and institutions to take place in the economy as a whole. In the postwar era, vast changes in technologies and institutions occurred in Asia; the two or three decades between the attaining of national independence and the slowdown that began in the early 1980s coincide with the duration of Kuznets's long swings. Or, if institutional changes and ways of thinking are taken to be crucial in their interplay with technologies, one generation (which approximates two or three decades) may be considered appropriate because of the changes in the labor force from one generation to the next.

Although this time span seems lengthy, long-term forces are in operation, interacting with short-term forces, over any period of time, whether a month or a year or a decade. During the Korean crisis of 1980, when real GNP dropped 3 percent, weather conditions were responsible for a poor harvest, while the recessions in the West caused industrial exports to fall. But longer-term forces were also at work, such as the inability of the government and peasants to cope with spreading crop diseases, the insufficiency of irrigation, and the failure of the heavy industries coming onstream to produce for export. Or, again, in the Philippine financial crisis of 1984, the factors at work included not only the need for huge debt repayments due to short-term borrowing at high interest rates in 1981, 1982, and 1983, but also the wasteful allocation and use of large portions of long-term capital borrowed from abroad during the 1970s, and the slow growth of productivity in agriculture and industry.

When we speak of the dominance of long-term over short-term forces in postwar Asia, we mean, for example, that the much greater efficiency of Korean agriculture and industry over that of the Philippines enabled South Korea to overcome the 1980 declines quickly and resume high growth rates in 1981, 1982, and 1983; in the case of the Philippines, in contrast, it is unlikely that previous growth rates of moderate speed can be resumed for another few years, despite wage levels only one-fourth to one-third those of South Korea. Long-term forces are those which work themselves out in decades, and even though statistically we need some kind of a decadal averaging process to shake off the shorter-term forces, they are present all the time.

Findings and Issues Raised

Table 3.1 shows that population in the postwar decades grew swiftly in Asia, by about 2.5 percent, and more rapidly in Southeast than in East and South Asia (2.5 percent compares with 1 percent in the 20th century before 1950). But GDP grew much faster than population so that per capita product accelerated over prewar rates, although there are only scattered data for the prewar period. Since population grew faster in the postwar than in the prewar decades, it was the much faster rise of GDP that accounts for the acceleration of GDP per capita in the postwar decades. For the region as a whole in the pre-World War II decades, the growth of product per capita was not much more than 1 percent and probably less. Rice production data for a dozen or so countries in Asia, excluding China, compiled by Wickizer and Bennett, indicate that the growth rate per year, 1910-15 to 1935-40, was 0.7 percent, or less than the population increase of about 1 percent.[4] This is consistent with the data on yield per hectare, which did not rise during the period. The increase was the result of acreage expansion. New commercial crops intended mainly for export rose, but rice had to be imported by the countries in the southern tier from the northern tier, making up for the insufficiency of local production in the southern tier when the workers shifted to plantation work in the Philippines, Java, and, to a lesser extent, Malaya and Sri Lanka. Under the Japanese Empire, much of the increased rice production in Taiwan and Korea went to Japan to feed the labor force in industries. As will be noted in Chapter 4, there was an increase in GNP per capita of 2 percent in Japan and 1 percent in Taiwan and Korea, or roughly 1.5 percent for the three countries, the result of better cultivation using higher-yielding rice varieties and of rapid industrialization. Since there was little or no industrialization or use of improved rice varieties in the other Asian countries, it may be plausible to conclude that per capita product rose by 1 percent or less in all other parts of Asia in the prewar decades.

The major finding in Table 3.2 is the high rate of growth of GDP per capita in East Asia: nearly 7 percent in Japan and nearly 6 percent in other countries. Such a growth rate implies a doubling of per capita real incomes in 12 years. Perhaps never, in the two centuries of modern economic growth, has any nation sustained growth rates as high as 7 percent for three decades, or any region as high as 6 percent for about 170 million people. In the century before World War II, the growth rates of product per capita of industrialized countries averaged about 2 percent; even in the best three decades, they averaged a bit less than 3 percent. The Soviet Union, in its best 30-year period, 1928–58, registered a rate of nearly 4 percent. In the three postwar decades, western Europe, the United States, Canada, and Australia grew at rates averaging 3.4 percent (Kuznets, 1971: 93).

One reason the rates of East Asia are so much higher than those of

[4] Wickizer and Bennett, 1941: Appendix Table 2. Countries included are Burma, French Indochina, Thailand, Korea, Taiwan, Japan, Java, the Philippines, Malaya, Ceylon, and India.

the United Kingdom, the leading nation in the 19th century, and of the United States, the leading nation in the 20th century, is that instead of having to develop new production technologies as those nations did, East Asia could import them from the West. This raises the question of why the nations of other regions failed to import technologies as rapidly as the East Asian countries. The growth rate of per capita product for Latin America, 1950–1980, was 2.2 percent; for Africa south of the Sahara, 1.3 percent; and even for the Middle East, less than 4.0 percent. The USSR and the non-market East European countries (for which only 1960–1980 data are available) and Southern Europe (including Turkey and Yugoslavia) averaged 4.7 percent, but were still below the 6 percent of East Asia.

Southeast Asia—or, more precisely, the ASEAN Four (Malaysia, Thailand, the Philippines, Indonesia)—grew a little less than 3.5 percent per capita per annum in the three decades from 1950 to 1980, a performance not as good as that of East Asia but still good enough to imply near doubling of per capita incomes in two decades, and better than the 2 percent or less for South Asia. Table 3.2 shows that there was acceleration in growth from one decade to the next for all the ASEAN Four except the Philippines, which started out strong but lagged in the 1960s and probably also in the 1970s (the 1970s figures may overstate actual performance). South Asia's growth, particularly that of Nepal and Bangladesh, was most disappointing.

If we apply variance analysis by taking the four countries of East Asia as a group, the four countries of Southeast Asia, and the five countries of South Asia, the differences in growth rates among the three groups are greater than the differences within each group. The F test shows that the differences between each of the groups is statistically significant at the 5 percent level and could not have occurred by chance. (Total sum of squares, 77.4; between each of the groups, 72.8, and within-group 4.6; computed F of 72.8 is significantly larger than tabular F of 4.25.)

It may be that within each group there are forces which bind the countries together much more than forces affecting Asia as a whole, or that there are common characteristics within each group more powerful than those common to all of monsoon Asia. Shorter distances within each region promote commercial relations with Japan in East Asia and with India in South Asia. In Southeast Asia, the prewar rice trade still prevails, though on a less extensive basis. Common or similar socio-cultural-ethnic forces may also be important within each region: Confucian ethics and Buddhism in East Asia; caste in South Asia; Islam and Malay ethnicity in Southeast Asia.

Above all, a common historical background still persists—for example, ties of friendship were forged during the period of Japanese colonialism and in the British colonial era in South Asia, and institutions left by the colonial powers remain partly intact in each region. The early start of Taiwan and South Korea in the postwar era was largely due to relatively high levels of literacy and education established by the Japanese, and the greater skills of the peasantry as a legacy of colonial efforts to modernize rice growing with better varieties and more physical infrastructure than in the rice agriculture of other Asian countries. Contributing to the rapid growth of Hong Kong and Singapore was the superb service sector left by the British, who made these cities the headquarters for their shipping, financial, trading, and political operations in East and Southeast Asia. In contrast, British rule in South Asia was exploitative. Unlike the Japanese, the British did little to promote education and rice growing, leaving the population in British India, Burma, and Ceylon hostile to capitalistic ways. The new governments coming into power after independence adopted socialistic ways, nationalizing industries and intervening in diverse ways in the operation of the economy. In Southeast Asia, British rule was benevolent in Malaysia,while the U.S. promoted education and left the Filipino peasants to the dictates of their own oligarchs; Thailand did not experience long periods of foreign occupation. Socialism was not attractive to the indigenous rulers of Southeast Asia after independence. Consequently, a large part of the differences in growth rates among the three regions was the outcome of the differences in colonial rule, as will be discussed in the country chapters.

There were, of course, divisive forces within regions—the conflict of Islam and Hinduism; old memories of colonial repression in Korea, Taiwan, Burma, and elsewhere; the competition represented by Chinese businesses in Southeast Asia—but they were overwhelmed by forces binding the countries together.

Structural Changes

The data on changes in shares of employment and of product in Tables 3.7 and 3.8 corroborate the findings in Table 3.2. Kuznets has shown that aggregate growth in the West was accompanied by declines in the shares of output and employment in agriculture (farming, fishing, livestock, and forestry) and rises in share of industrial product and employment (mining, manufacturing, utilities, construction, transport, and communications). Table 3.7 shows that in general the declines in product and employment in agriculture were more rapid in East Asia than in Southeast Asia, and were minimal in slow-growing South Asia. The Philippines showed the lowest structural change rates for Southeast Asia, consistent with its poor showing (for an ASEAN country) in aggregate growth rates (Table 3.1). Burma shows increases in agriculture and declines in industry. In the services sector, in line with Kuznets's findings for the West, employment shares increase faster than product shares, denoting a decline in productivity relative to those in the other sectors.

Kuznets explains these shifts from the A to I sector as follows: with the rise in per capita income and, thus, in demand, the differentials in the income elasticities of demand for various consumption goods historically favor industrial products over commodities. The shift in demand for industrial goods and services implies an increase in the size of the market, inducing increased productive capacity, economies of scale, specialization, and externalities in the industries for whose product demand is increasing. The connections are thus twofold: from higher incomes to the demand side via elasticities, and from the demand side back to production and income via high productivity and efficiency. Kuznets concludes: "While economic analysis may never reach down to the basic levels of production and spread of new knowledge and innovations, we may be able, through examining structural changes, to infer some of the ways by which efficiency was improved" (Kuznets, 1971: 85).

There is an additional element in the shift to services. Kuznets mentions the need for concentrating modern industrial production in one place—i.e., for urbanization—partly to generate scale economies and partly to benefit from external economies needed to cope with the growing complexities of the modern economy. In turn, urbanization, by itself, creates demand for police, sanitation, fire and flood prevention, public administration and other services. Rising per capita income increases the demand for high income-elastic services such as health care, education, and recreation, offsetting the decline of such services as paid domestic work. He speculates that productivity growth in services may have been slow because of the increasing use of less skilled employees and the existence of monopolistic elements in certain services during the earlier stages of growth, besides the difficulties in the application of mechanized technology to the mass production of services.

Therefore, it is surprising to find in Table 3.7A that the share of service sector employment in the ASEAN Four, which is still predominantly agrarian, is nearly 30 percent, almost as high as in industrialized Taiwan and South Korea. Thailand's share is low, but this is because of the exceptionally high share of agricultural employment (74 percent), the latter largely the outcome of a very broad definition of female participation in farming, as shown by the fact that share of value added in agriculture is only slightly higher in Thailand than in the other four ASEAN countries. It may be that the public, personal, and commercial sectors are overstaffed in Southeast Asia compared with Taiwan and South Korea. Partly because of much underemployment in the rural areas, unemployment in the urban areas, and very high growth rates of labor supply, the unwanted labor gravitates to the informal service sector where (unlike farming) no arable land is needed, and (unlike industry) little fixed capital and few skills are required. The large informal sector of monsoon Asia—menial services, petty trading, stall-keeping, peddling, hauling, scavenging—becomes the refuge of redundant workers. The public sectors in Southeast Asia also appear to be overstaffed compared with Taiwan and South Korea (Oshima, 1979).

The large size of the informal sector may partly account for the unusually high share of services in total product and labor in Asia. As noted in Chapter 1, women and children take part extensively in monsoon rice growing in the busy seasons, and their propensity to work carries over into the urban sector where they are more suited to service operations than even to the most labor-intensive types of manufacturing. And the low incomes earned in the informal sectors force families to send children and women to work in domestic services, stores, stalls, and so on.

Growth of Productivity

Underlying the rapid growth of per capita product in East Asia was the swift growth of per worker product; both grew only moderately in the ASEAN Four and slowly in South Asia. Since population growth in East Asia was much slower than GDP growth, the rapid growth of GDP per capita would not be possible without rapid improvement in the efficiency with which labor was utilized, which, in turn, was due mainly to the substitution of capital for labor. In Chapter 2 the mechanism and the processes involved in the rise of total factor productivity or the growth of product per unit of input were described. These changes in structure and productivity were accompanied by changes in distribution of family income and savings, and of birth rates, with lower income inequalities and higher savings rates and faster declines in total fertility rates in East Asia than in other regions. These changes will be discussed again in Chapters 10 and 11.

Divergence between the growth of per capita product and per worker product is substantial in a few countries listed in Table 3.2, with per worker product growing more slowly than per capita product, reflecting the faster growth of total employment than of population. This divergence in the growth of the two signifies that welfare grows faster than efficiency, that over the long run the population may be consuming more than is warranted by the production of goods, and that savings may be shrinking. As consumer demand rises, the productive system tends to shift to the supplying of consumer goods instead of investment goods; on the family income side, the slower growth of productivity, and therefore in earnings of the working members of the family, may mean that an increasing share of income is being spent rather than saved. This is the major dilemma of the giants of Asia, China and India, whose productivity growth is substantially lower than product per capita—only about one-half of the latter for the postwar decades.[5]

In the 1970s and early 1980s, the growth rates of private and government consumption combined exceeded the growth rate of GDP per worker by a wide margin in the ASEAN countries and Hong Kong. The discrepancy between the two tends to show up in balance of payments problems, government deficits, heavy debt burdens, and tendencies toward inflation.

Concluding Remarks

With such differentials in growth rates during the three postwar decades, the East Asian countries (and Malaysia) ended the period with per capita dollar incomes over $1,500; incomes in South Asian countries, however, were only about one-tenth and the others less than one-half that figure (Table 3.2). Structurally East Asia has completed the transition into industrial society, while China and most of the South Asian countries are at the early stage of the transition and others around the midpoint. If these differentials in growth rates persist into the next decade or so, monsoon Asia, which began the postwar period with minimal differences in per capita dollar income levels—with even Japan reporting only $190 for 1952 to 1954—will end this century with the three regions in different stages of development: East Asia in the process of moving into a service economy; Southeast Asia in the process of entering the industrialized economy; and South Asia still in the midst of an agricultural economy. The early years of the 1980s show

[5] Moses Abramovitz, in a 1981 article in the *American Economic Review*, pointed out that while in the first half of the postwar era, the growth of product per worker exceeded the growth of product per capita, the reverse happened in the second half, contributing to the difficulties of financing the public welfare expenditures in the government budgets of the industrialized countries of the West.

few changes in the trends shown in Table 3.1, with the exception of the Philippines and China, the former stagnating and the latter accelerating. These sharp differences in the postwar trends of growth and structural changes and their consequences and implications have not gone unnoticed by some of the leaders of the lagging nations, who are putting aside or modifying ideologies and dogmas, replacing them with more pragmatic policies as they learn from the experience of the leading nations. If so, there is a need to begin a more systematic examination of the growth experience and strategies of the various nations, comparing them as much as possible for the lessons they can yield. This is attempted in the next six chapters.

PART II

Comparative Country Growth

CHAPTER 4

Contrasting the Economic Growth
of Prewar and Postwar Japan

*I*t is often said by students of Japan's economic growth that postwar growth was a continuation of prewar trends, although there was an acceleration (Ohkawa and Rosovsky, 1973; Ohkawa, Johnston, and Kaneda, 1970). This chapter holds that it was more than a continuation and that fundamental transformations occurred in the technological and institutional setting of Japan in the 1950s which enabled it quickly to complete the industrial transition, enter the industrial society by the end of the 1950s, and then jump into the service society in the 1980s. Whether the postwar era was a break or a continuation may be partly a semantic matter since elements of both continuity and break are always present between adjacent eras, even in major upheavals such as the French, the Bolshevik, or the Chinese revolutions. The discussion in this chapter describes the forces making for breaks in well-known continuities and contends that a better understanding of prewar and postwar Japan is obtained by thinking of World War II as a major watershed, similar to the downfall of the Tokugawa *bakufu* at the time of the Meiji Restoration.

Although Japan's economy is basically a monsoon economy, as described in Chapter 1, with paddy rice culture requiring highly labor-intensive transplantation during the heavy rainy seasons, it is not as dry and hot as in Southeast and South Asia during the other half of the year. Unlike most other regions of Asia, Japan's western portions receive moisture-laden airflows from the Pacific Ocean, and there is precipitation throughout the year though it is lighter than the monsoon rains between June and September. The main rice-bowl areas of Japan around Tokyo, Nagoya, and elsewhere receive melting snow and monsoon rain water from the rivers originating in the western mountains. Hence, more remunerative work is available for Japanese peasants than in most other parts of monsoon Asia in the drier half of the year. Crops requiring less water than rice can be grown in central Japan facing the Pacific Ocean and in the southern regions, contributing to greater densities in these areas but also to higher per capita incomes.

The period of six decades or so preceding World War II was strongly conditioned by two and a half centuries of peace which preceded it in what may be dubbed the Confucian feudal system of the Tokugawa dynasty.[1] This was a society based on a classical feudal economy where bonds of loyalty and devotion in exchange for protection were even stronger than in European feudalism. It was ruled by an autocratic state rigorously administering an extensive system of minute regulations influenced by neo-Confucian teachings. The Meiji Restoration of 1868 brought back the Imperial Throne and relegated the shogunate to obscurity, clothed the Emperor with authoritarian powers, and abolished the feudal economy while retaining many feudalistic ways, including absolute loyalty to the Throne and devotion to the nation. But unlike the Thai absolute monarchy in the second half of the 19th century, the Meiji government vigorously and swiftly set out to modernize the economy by buying up the land from the nobility and giving it to the peasantry, then levying heavy taxes on farmland and using the proceeds to build the system of infrastructure necessary for industrialization: roads, railways, steamships, harbors, telegraph, postal system, schools and public utilities, military establishments replete with arsenals and munition factories, modern laws, courts, and constabulary, and public banks and a national currency. Large private enterprises with economies of scale were extensively promoted, supported by public enterprises generating external economies with the objective of developing as soon as possible a capitalistic system of industrialization (Sumiya and Taira, 1979; Lockwood, 1954).

Prewar Economic Growth

It used to be thought that Japan's prewar growth was impressive, even phenomenal—an example for developing economies to emulate. But recent estimates for colonized Taiwan and Korea show that their GNP growth rates were about the same as those for Japan, 3.5 percent for Taiwan (1903–1938) and 3.6 for Korea (1911–1938) as against Japan's 3.2 (1903–1938) and 3.4 (1911–1938) (Umemura and Mizoguchi, 1981). Nor is the rate of 3 percent particularly impressive when compared to Southeast Asian countries for the years 1950–1980, which showed about 6 percent, even when account is taken of varying cir-

---

[1] The Tokugawa period of peace and unity was in turn preceded by centuries of internecine warfare reminiscent of European feudalism.

cumstances. (See tables in Chapter 3.) For the prewar period, we have estimates only for the Philippines, of 3 percent for 1902–1938 (Hooley, 1968). Japan's prewar per capita growth rate of 2 percent is higher than the 1 percent for colonial Taiwan and Korea but lower than Southeast Asia's 3 percent. Japan ended the prewar era requiring nearly half of the labor force in the agriculture sector to feed its population, in addition to the food imports from its colonies. We review the reasons for the relatively slow growth of GNP for a newcomer as a prelude to a discussion of the contrasts with postwar growth.

Japan's pre-World War II experience illustrates the difficulties encountered by a traditional monsoon economy attempting to industrialize. Meiji leaders, aware of the much greater productivity per worker of Western agriculture and of the need to transfer labor from agriculture to modern industries, attempted to convert monsoon farming to Western farming by importing Western large-scale equipment in the 1870s and 1880s in order to release large masses of peasants for industries, as was done in England and other Western countries at the beginning of the Industrial Revolution. In order for this to succeed, small rice farms had to be combined on a larger scale. This, however, meant that yields per hectare would fall, and with the limited land, production would be insufficient to feed the population. That is to say, multiple-horse plowing might save labor, but the technology did not exist at that time for replacing hand transplanting and reaping, which were the most labor-intensive operations. The replacement of manual transplanting by drilling or broadcasting would sharply reduce yields. Some of the Western equipment was applicable to Hokkaido, which was too far north to be affected by the monsoons, but the policy had to be abandoned, and the later 1880s saw reversion to small-scale farming under landlord direction. Vigorous efforts followed to raise yields per hectare with the widespread dissemination of the best traditional varieties and practices, but Japan fell short of requirements and became a net importer of rice from the early 1890s on, as manpower was shifted to industrialization and militarization. The heavy burden of taxation and sharecropping rent made it difficult for peasants to buy sufficient inputs to improve cultivation, and the borrowings raised levels of indebtedness. Tenancy disputes rose from a few hundred in the decades before World War I to 2,000 in the 1920s and 4,000 in the 1930s. Real farm family incomes from all sources fell from 1,300 yen in the mid-1920s to 890 in the mid-1930s. Agricultural sector growth was only 1.8 percent in 1885–1900 and 1.3 percent in 1900–1940, less than one-half of the agricultural growth of ASEAN countries for 1950–1980.

Table 4.1   Average Annual Growth of GNP, Input, and Productivity in Japan, 1908–1980

	Output	Labor	Capital	Total Input	Output per Worker	Output per Unit Capital	Total Factor Productivity
Whole Economy							
1908–17	4.3	.6	3.3	1.7	3.7	1.0	2.6
1917–31	2.2	.8	3.6	1.9	1.4	−1.4	.3
1931–38	4.9	.9	3.2	1.9	4.0	1.7	3.0
1953–61	8.1	2.1	7.7	3.3	6.0	.4	4.8
1961–71	9.3	1.4	12.1	4.3	7.9	−2.8	5.0
1970–80	5.0	0.9	9.3	3.4	4.1	−4.3	1.6
Average							
1908–38	3.5	.8	3.4	1.8	2.7	.1	1.6
1953–71	8.8	1.7	10.1	3.9	7.1	−1.4	4.9
1953–80	7.4	1.4	9.8	3.9	6.0	−2.4	3.5
Nonagriculture							
1908–17	5.1	2.2	6.5	4.1	2.9	−1.4	1.0
1917–31	3.1	2.0	5.2	3.3	1.1	−2.1	−.2
1931–38	6.7	1.9	4.6	2.9	4.8	2.1	3.8
1955–60	10.8	4.1	6.6	4.9	6.7	4.2	5.9
1961–70	11.6	3.4	12.1	6.0	8.2	− .5	5.6
1970–80	5.7	1.8	9.4	4.1	3.9	−3.7	1.6
Average							
1908–38	4.5	2.0	5.5	3.4	2.5	− .9	1.1
1955–70	11.3	3.7	10.1	5.6	7.6	1.2	5.7
1955–80	9.0	2.9	9.8	5.0	6.1	−0.8	4.0
Agriculture							
1901–17	1.9	.1	1.5	.7	2.0	.4	1.2
1917–31	.4	− .03	1.0	.4	.4	− .6	.1
1931–37	.5	− .27	.7	.3	.8	− .2	.3
1955–60	4.7	−1.8	4.2	.6	6.5	.5	4.1
1961–70	1.9	−4.8	7.3	.1	6.7	−4.5	1.8
1970–80	0.4	−4.3	9.1	− .3	4.7	−8.7	0.7
Average							
1901–37	1.1	− .1	1.2	.5	1.2	− .1	.6
1955–70	2.9	−3.7	6.2	.3	6.6	−3.3	2.6
1955–80	1.9	−4.0	7.4	− .6	5.9	−5.5	3.5

Sources: For the whole economy, prewar data were calculated from Ohkawa and Rosovsky (1973), and, for the postwar period, Denison's (1967) data on employment and capital were used to compute conventional factor productivity. For the estimates on agriculture and nonagriculture sectors, Ohkawa and Rosovsky was used for the prewar period and Ohkawa and Shinohara (1979) was used for postwar data. All postwar data were updated using official estimates on product, capital, and labor from *Annual Report on National Accounts 1982* (for the 1970s).

Table 4.3 indicates a slight decline in the agricultural labor force, but this can be entirely accounted for by the mounting imports of rice from the colonies which by the end of the 1930s filled one-half of Japan's rice consumption demand. It was not that agricultural rice yields in Japan did not rise but that there was an increase in population which was partly due to the rise in birth rates induced by the expanded labor force needed for industrialization and militarization (Umemura, 1969; Minami, 1973).

Industry grew more rapidly, at 6.5 percent over the entire period. This was slower than the 8 percent of ASEAN countries and only one-half of the rate of industrial advance in the NICs during 1950 to 1980, despite the Meiji government's frenzied offerings of low-interest loans, dividends, guarantees, technical assistance, and, after 1900, extensive tariff protection. Before 1900, Japan was unable to use the latter because of Western treaties forbidding tariffs on imports, and attempts to have these treaties revised were not successful. Nevertheless, it is interesting to note that the industrial growth rate in the pre-protection, labor-intensive period (1885–1900) was just as high as in the capital-intensive period (1900–1940): 6.6 percent. For the most part, the industrialization technology was First Industrial Revolution vintage, i.e., steam-based mechanized equipment which was simple and clumsy compared with what was to come in the 1930s and especially after World War II. This was not the type of mechanized technology that was suitable for the overwhelming majority of industries and small firms of traditional monsoon economies. The steam-generating equipment was too costly to install for most firms, and only a few of the operations in the factories were mechanized. Thus, horsepower per worker in manufacturing was 0.06 in 1906 and 0.97 in 1935, compared with 1.44 in the United States in 1889 and 1.39 in Taiwan in 1954.

Moreover, the domestic market in a traditional monsoon economy with low farm productivity was too restricted for the products of larger-scale factories. Japan's average per capita income in 1952–1954, after postwar reconstruction and rehabilitation were completed and the economy had reached prewar peak levels (about that of 1935–1940), was estimated by the United Nations to be US$150. If we extrapolate this figure back to the 1880s by using the average annual per capita growth rate of 1.9 percent a year, we arrive at per capita incomes of $ 58 in 1952–1954 U.S. dollars. This is only one-fourth the minimum level of income ($200) that Kuznets (1980) estimated for the industrialized countries in their preindustrial phases.

The slow rate of growth of agricultural and industrial production meant that employment was growing too slowly, particularly in higher level jobs. The Meiji reforms in landholding and taxation separated a large number of samurai (about half a million) from their traditional sources of income. Many did not find sufficiently challenging occupations to shift to and became restive as there was no place for their traditional warrior skills. It did not take much time for ancient dreams of foreign conquests to surface and the clamor for action abroad to grow. Beginning with the expedition to Taiwan in 1874, there were no less than a dozen military campaigns outside Japan, and war became a regular feature of life in prewar Japan. Thus the Meiji slogan "rich economy, strong army," could also be understood as "rich economy for a strong army," as one expedition after another succeeded; even the peasants, groaning under the burdens of heavy rents, debts, and taxation, increasing population and land fragmentation, and low incomes, turned to foreign lands for their way out of poverty and frustration.

Under these circumstances, it is almost inevitable that the Meiji oligarchs, humiliated by the refusal on the part of the Western powers to change past treaties in such a way as to make it easier to develop an industrialized economy, turned to a growth strategy emphasizing the large-scale and heavy industries needed for military power. This was just the opposite of the kind of development strategy that should be pursued in the early stages of modern economic growth, as noted in Chapter 2.

The high cost of military adventures hoisted on a relatively poor economy made it difficult to remove the authoritarianism with which Meiji Japan started the modern era. The burden of the huge expenditures needed to modernize, industrialize, and militarize could not have been shifted onto the backs of the poor peasantry in a political democracy. I have estimated that something like one-third of the consolidated government expenditures of the prewar period (nearly 10 percent of national income, 1900 to 1940) went for military purposes, and that two-fifths of the total revenue collected was from land taxes, amounting to 10 percent of income originating in agriculture (1879 to 1911 in Lockwood, 1965: 359-89). Nor was it possible to relax the authoritarianism of agrarian and industrial relations and adopt a more participatory decision-making process, if returns to the peasantry and wages to workers were to be kept low in order to continue channeling vast resources to military adventures. But low incomes meant limited domestic markets for industrial products and hence a need for markets abroad. Thus, the haste to industrialize for military purposes was responsible for the poverty, unrest, and tensions which, together with the progression from constructive nationalism to militant, chauvinistic ultranationalism, led to the holocaust that ended in the atomic bombing of Hiroshima and Nagasaki.

To conclude, it may be argued that Japan had no choice in the prewar international setting but to resort to militarization. But was so massive a military buildup necessary for the defense of the country? Perhaps half or less would have sufficed, and the rest could have been returned to the peasantry for higher living standards and more farm inputs—both of which would have contributed to larger domestic markets for industry, faster growth of food production, and technological advance. Japanese experience may be a warning to other countries that monsoon conditions and low agricultural incomes do not permit the diversion of many resources for military purposes, and that militarization for long spans of time is not compatible with sustained, rapid growth of the overall economy since so much is wasted for nonproductive purposes.

Note must be taken of the major legacies of the prewar to the postwar decades. The experiment stations established in the late 19th century came up with the first scientifically bred high-yielding rice varieties which were to raise yields substantially in Japan, Taiwan, and Korea by the late 1930s and to begin the scientific revolution in rice culture that would be carried forward in the postwar era by the International Rice Research Institute at Los Baños, the Philippines. Peasants learned scientific skills and better ways of cultivation from the extension services established by the government. The skills learned by Japanese technicians using the simpler technology of the first industrial revolution, particularly in the chemical, metallurgical, and engineering industries, were to be the basis for mastering the more complex, extensive technology of the second industrial revolution that enabled Japan to move readily into the emerging electronic revolution in the 1970s. Above all, the values of cooperation and diligence in work group effort and harmonious relations were retained despite the authoritarian and aggressive atmosphere of a warlike polity and economy; as small firms and peasants were largely left to fend for themselves, they had to work together to obtain scale economies and externalities.

One important lesson is that authoritarian institutions cannot for long periods motivate workers and cultivators to sustained levels of higher and higher quality production, and that autocratic political institutions can make disastrous decisions that can inflict untold suffering. A strategy based on cheap food, produced by impoverished peasants in the colonies and at home, and on low wages for small-scale exporting industries whose exchange earnings are used to build up highly protected/subsidized large-scale and heavy industries does not yield high rates of growth in the long run. And the existence of surplus labor is an obstacle to higher growth rates for economies far from the technological frontier as low wages hamper the shift to more productive, mechanized operations in expanding domestic markets, while pushing impoverished workers to turn their attention to opportunities abroad and entrepreneurs to the lure of markets abroad.

Postwar Economic Growth

The statistics on postwar factor productivity in Japan rest on a large-scale project on prewar national income statistics of Japan undertaken at the Institute of Economic Research of Hitotsubashi University, initially funded by the Rockefeller Foundation in the mid-1950s.[2] The final volume of the project, *Patterns of Economic Development: A Quantitative Appraisal* (Ohkawa and Shinohara, 1979), is a summary of 14 or so volumes which are certain to serve as the most important source of quantitative information for the study of Japanese development.[3] Despite the wealth of data, however, Japan's statistics on factor productivity are rough and can only be interpreted broadly.

Table 4.1 shows that factor productivity growth was low in the prewar decades (about 1.6 percent a year) for the whole economy but rose to a postwar record high (1953–71) of 6.5 percent for nonresidential business economy and 4.9 percent for the whole economy. In the 1970s, the latter fell to 1.6 percent, but we leave the 1970s for later comments. Thus, there was a threefold rise in the growth rate of factor productivity. This level of growth is higher than in any of the nine Western countries for which Denison (1967) works out estimates for the 1950s.[4] As Table 4.1 shows, this was the result of an output growth rate which was nearly three times that of prewar decades, and a total factor growth rate twice that of prewar decades, with labor input growth twice and capital input growth three times that of prewar decades. Apparently the quality of the labor used in the postwar decades

---

[2] This section is a somewhat shorter version of my paper, "Reinterpreting Japan's Postwar Growth" (Oshima, 1982). The first version of the paper was published in a volume honoring Professor Miyohei Shinohara on his sixtieth birthday.

[3] These volumes are entitled *Estimates of Long-Term Economic Statistics of Japan Since 1868* (edited by Kazushi Ohkawa, Miyohei Shinohara, and Mataji Umemura) in Japanese but with column heads of statistical tables translated into English. The volumes are published by Tōyō Keizai Shimpōsha of Tokyo, starting from 1965; they required about a quarter-century of work in which more than 100 scholars participated.

[4] The countries are the United States, the United Kingdom, Federal Republic of Germany, France, Belgium, the Netherlands, Italy, Denmark, and Norway.

Table 4.2   Value of Production in Process and Engineering Manufacturing
and Consumption of Energy in Manufacturing: Japan, Prewar
and Postwar Decades

	Constant Prices Value of Production in Manufacturing (1934–36, millions of yen)			Total Energy Consumed		
	Total	Process	Engin-eering	Hp (1000s)	Billion kwh	Hp per Worker
1906	2,447.0	2,319.3	127.7	161.9		.06
1910	2,959.5	2,762.7	196.8	320.2		11
1915	4,029.4	3.703.2	326.2	635.8		.18
1920	5,689.0	4,789.7	899.2	1,447.5		.32
1925	7,043.1	6,379.0	664.2	2,594.2		.54
1930	9,261.3	8,163.8	1,997.6	3,723.0		.78
1935	15,093.9	12,613.2	2,480.7	5,221.9		.97
1939	20,620.5	15,678.4	4,942.0	9,397.8	11.7	1.49
1953	17,769.5	14,448.0	3,321.5		14.6	1.63
1955	22,429.6	18,714.6	3,715.0		27.5	2.97
1960	49,612.1	35,774.6	13,837.5		56.2	4.74
1965	97,630.9	69,112.9	28,518.0		92.5	6.43
1970	214,137.0	133,855.7	80,281.3		182.3	10.70
1975					217.7	11.40
1977					235.9	14.20

Sources: Data on value of production in constant prices and number of
workers were taken from Ohkawa and Shinohara (1979), pp. 303–6 and
pp. 394–95. Data on horsepower (prewar) were taken from *Estimates of
Long Term Economic Statistics of Japan Since 1868*, 12:223 (Table 27).
Postwar figures on per-worker horsepower were extrapolated from kwh
data given in various issues of *Japan Statistical Yearbook*, using 1939 as a
benchmark.

had improved so much that a unit of labor was producing more than
two times the amount produced in prewar decades. The outstanding
performance of labor in the postwar period suggests that not only the
skill of the labor force but also the other aspect of work quality,
work culture, rose. This implies that institutional arrangements in
the workplace underwent extensive transformation.

Particularly noteworthy is the 5- to 6-fold increase in labor productivity in agriculture. As we shall see in the next section, this sector, relatively stagnant and "sick" in the decades leading up to World War
II, became extremely dynamic after land reform and democratization
replaced landlordism and authoritarianism. Similarly, we shall see

that the threefold increase in overall labor productivity was accompanied by the rise of a unique system of industrial relations. Note also that in the 1930s factor productivity was already rising significantly, to 3.8 percent a year from the prior decades' rates of only about 0.5 percent.

All this does not mean that capital quality did not improve. In an industrializing economy such as Japan, unlike the United States, many sectors of agriculture and industry were not mechanized and at best were only partially mechanized by the closing years of the 1940s. This was true not only of agriculture but also of the small-scale industries. In the postwar decades, with rising wage rates, handwork and toolwork must have been mechanized.

The total factor productivity rates in the first period, 1908–1917, are fairly high for the early period, about 2.6 percent. This may be because this was the period when Japan's industries (especially cotton textiles), after being established in the previous decades, were becoming increasingly competitive internationally and reaching full capacity utilization. But to this conjecture must be added the caveat that the data for national product, labor force, and capital during this period may not be good enough for computation of total factor productivity since the first modern population census was held in 1920. The high level of factor productivity in the 1930s (3.0 percent) also represents in part fuller utilization of capacity from the depressed years of the late 1920s and early 1930s and also the build-up of capacity for militarization. But it was the beginning of rapid electrification of industrial technology.

The Role of Agriculture in Japan's Development

Reasoning that problems in the agricultural sector had had much to do with the rise of militarism, the Supreme Commander for the Allied Powers (SCAP) undertook a series of institutional reforms starting with a drastic land reform in 1947. The changes in the rural sector went far beyond land reform: there was democratization of cooperatives, of agricultural extension, of education, of local government, and of family life, thus destroying the power and privileges of the large landowners and opening up opportunities for participation and decision making to all farmers. Where large landowners had been the main beneficiaries of government services, now all farmers were affected through drastic land reform and democratization. Tension and bitter conflict between the upper and lower layers of rural society were replaced by discussion and consensus. The entire atmosphere of the village was transformed dramatically from that of the prewar decades, making unnecessary the militant peasant unions, which withered away overnight (Tohata, 1958). The increased incentives to work and produce for oneself (without turning over half the crop to others), the improvements in skills due to stronger motivation to learn and wider access to knowledge through democratized extension services, the economies of scale achieved by a more efficient and comprehensive system of cooperatives, the better response of local and central governments to the production and credit needs of all farmers, not just one-fifth or one-fourth—all these and many other events must have contributed to output growth of agriculture in the 1950s, without adding to the input of labor and capital as usually recorded in total factor productivity statistics. As one expert close to the villages put it, there was an unleashing of "the zeal for production," as compared with the bitter conflicts between landlord and peasants (a zero-sum game) before the war.[5]

The sequence of changes in agriculture was complicated by their rapidity and by overlaps among the forces of change. The new technologies and institutions increased yields; then came rises in real wages and farm incomes, domestic demand, crop diversification, and off-farm employment, all of which contributed to full employment, and these accelerated wage increases, mechanization, and migration in the 1950s.

The rise in productivity per worker was translated into real wage increases, even though in the early 1950s there was seasonal surplus labor. This is because there tends to be a shortage of labor in the peak periods in monsoon rice growing, when labor is most extensively hired or exchanged. Also, with the democratization of farm organization and relations, the power of the smaller farmers and their family helpers rose relative to that of the larger farmers who needed to hire the surplus labor of the small farmers. Thus, real wages of temporary farm workers rose from 1951 to 1961 at an average annual rate of 6.6 percent for male and 7.3 percent for female workers (or for both, 7 percent). This may be compared with Minami's (1973) computation showing average annual rates of increase of about 1.1 percent in the prewar decades, 1898–1938. In part, these surprisingly large postwar increases were achieved by an annual increase in real value added in agricultural production of nearly 4 percent a year (the highest increase recorded in Japanese history), simultaneous with the farm labor force declining by an average 1.7 percent each year. More-

---

[5] Hayami (1975) estimates that the number of days worked per year by the average farmer increased from 166 in 1950 to 183 in 1960—a 1 percent increase each year.

over, there was a differential between the prices of goods purchased (which rose by 10 percent) and prices received by the farmers (which rose by 15 percent), part of the difference being paid out as higher wages to farm workers. Unemployment levels were high in the late 1940s and early 1950s, in part due to the influx of expatriates from overseas, while at the same time underemployment or surplus labor characterized the agricultural slack periods. With improved irrigation and drainage, and rising per capita incomes and better income distribution, the structure of food demand was changing, and peasants were able to diversify their crops, away from rice, inferior grains, and root crops to higher-value fruits, vegetables, and livestock products, most of which were more labor-intensive than rice production, requiring twice the amount of labor input. The land reform was essential for rapid diversification as it freed peasants to use their land in their own interest, not the landlords'. Moreover, they were able to bring pressure on local and regional authorities for more infrastructure facilities such as roads and rail transport networks, without which the marketing of commercial crops would be expensive. The significance of diversification in monsoon Asia is that most of these crops are produced during the slack season, so that underemployment is reduced and incomes rise. In Japan, the value of diversified crops rose sevenfold from 1947–1952 to 1957–1962 when full employment was reached, and by 1980 equalled that of rice and other grains.

By the mid-1950s, with real wages rising due to increases in yields per hectare and multiple cropping, mechanization began, initially on the large farms, but later, as full employment was approached, real wages accelerated and mechanization spread to smaller farms. Fortunately, the basic technology for small-scale mechanization was available, largely from abroad, and a well-trained extension staff quickly spread the know-how. With farm family savings rising—partly because rents did not need to be paid but also because yields and crops per hectare began to rise—even the smaller farmers could afford to buy machines, with help from the cooperatives.

Adding to these forces promoting greater farm family employment and income was the rise of off-farm employment (Figure 1). If farm family income/employment is divided into on-farm and off-farm income/employment, with the latter defined as income received from outside one's own farm, on-farm incomes are seen to have grown mainly because of rises in prices, increased yields, multiple cropping, and diversification (and some limited increases in acreage). But in monsoon Asia, because of great densities and scarce land, the slow rise of yields, and the limits to land that can be profitably multiple-cropped, it

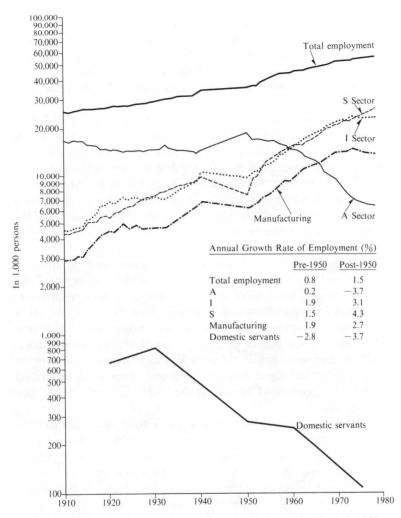

Figure 4.1 Changes in total employment by sector in Japan, 1910–1980.
Sources: Ohkawa and Shinohara (1979), updated by *OECD Labour Force Statistics*.

is difficult for total farm family incomes to keep up with the pace of nonfarm family incomes. The labor that is surplus in the slack seasons must look for work off-farm. In prewar landlord-dominated agriculture, tenants could work for their landlords at low pay, but after the war small farmers with limited land had to look for other off-farm work. Off-farm incomes accounted for one-third of total farm incomes in the 1950s but increased to half in the early 1960s. In the 1920s and 1930s they had been only one-fifth and two-fifths, respectively. In these ways, the faster rise of farm family incomes meant that rural employment was growing faster than the labor supply, particularly because labor-saving mechanization was minimal in the early 1950s.

In the 1950s, the major factor in the rise of off-farm incomes was the expansion in domestic demand, especially farm family demand, even though the growth rate of real consumption (8 percent) was less than that of exports (10 percent). The reason was that the export base was smaller than the agricultural sector, whose total originating income was 140 billion yen, compared to only 5 billion yen for total exports in 1947. Even in 1960, the former was greater than the latter, and it was only in 1964 that total export values came abreast of agricultural incomes. It is of course true that the rapid rise of exports hastened the process by which Japan completed the transition in the 1950s. But it is noteworthy that even in 1959 four-fifths of total wages and salaries from off-farm employment was from non-manufacturing (mining, construction, transport, commerce, fishery, forestry, and personal and public services), almost all of which cater mainly to domestic consumers. And within manufacturing, a considerable portion of the products of such industries as food processing, textiles, wood products, and housewares was domestically consumed. Hence, the role of exports may have been secondary in the growth of farm family incomes in the crucial 1950s when Japan attained full employment which in turn set the stage for accelerated growth in the 1960s and early 1970s. (See below for details.)

As Table 4.1 shows, the largest increase in total factor productivity in agriculture was achieved in 1955–1960, a record rise of 4 percent per year. This exceptional performance was mainly the outcome of product per worker rising at 6 to 7 percent a year, which, in turn, may be attributed mainly to a sharp rise in output with a decline in labor input. The much greater rise in output is due to rising yields, but also to the reduction of underemployment, particularly because of the shift to diversified cropping. Off-farm production is excluded from the A sector, but it is likely that the labor input figures do not capture the contribution of adult male workers, who, while commuting daily to nonagricultural work on weekdays, spent weekends, vacations, and after-work hours helping with farm work during the busy seasons.

In the 1960s and 1970s, the decades of tight labor markets and full employment, the problem of releasing labor to the rapidly growing nonfarm sectors became critical, in contrast to the problem in other Asian countries of absorbing labor. The obstacles to further growth, as suggested in dualistic theories, could have become insurmountable were it not for the availability of labor-saving mechanization which raised the elasticity of substitution and the fall in income elasticities in the demand for food staples. It is convenient to view this period as the transition from full employment to labor shortages, in which labor released from agriculture by capital/labor substitution, together with labor from low-paying sectors such as domestic service and handicrafts and from the home as wages for unskilled work rose, supplied the labor force in the expanding sectors of industry and commerce.

When labor from these sources began to dry up, the stage of labor shortage may be said to be reached, and this may have occurred during the 1970s.

Self-sufficiency in rice was attained in the early 1960s, thus obviating the need for imports, which in the prewar period came from Taiwan and Korea. This helped to wipe out large deficits in the balance of payments and facilitated the importation of machinery for more capital-intensive industrialization in the 1960s. The reduction in the farm labor force was largely due to an increase in the number of male workers who commuted to work or migrated. While in 1949 the labor force was evenly divided, by 1961 females exceeded males by 12 percent. Thus, when the men began to move or commute to the cities for better-paying jobs, the women were able to step into their jobs, and the operations that were too heavy or difficult for females became mechanized by machines small enough to be operated by women.

In the 1960s and 1970s, the main labor source for the expanding industries was agriculture, and only secondarily the mechanization of the home, services, and handicrafts. City-states like Hong Kong and Singapore without a substantial rural sector are forced to import labor as full employment is reached since the labor supplied from the home, services, and handicrafts is exhausted quickly. If we look more closely at the process of the substitution of machines for labor in agriculture, there emerge two distinct phases. Power threshers and hullers were the main equipment in the early 1950s. The migration from the farms began to accelerate in the latter 1950s as power cultivators released adult males for more lucrative nonfarm work. Power sprayers and dusters and trucks became necessary as the heavy spraying and hauling was done by the females and elderly males, particularly since wage increases made the hiring and exchange of workers difficult. Thus, underlying the sharp absolute decline of the agricultural labor force from the mid-1950s to the mid-1960s (Figure 4.1) and the massive migration while agricultural output was still rising was the substitution of power cultivators, sprayers, pumps, and trucks for adult male workers. But further release of labor in the 1970s required additional equipment, and mechanical transplanters, reapers, binders, and combines became necessary for transplanting and harvesting. The late entry of the transplanters and reapers may have been due to the difficulty of innovating and improving these as Western prototypes were not adapted to paddy agriculture. It was also related to further wage increases in the latter 1960s, with the pool of workers displaced by power threshers and cultivators becoming exhausted. By the end of the 1970s Japan's farms, from the largest to the smallest, were operating with a fairly complete array of machines and at the highest levels of yields per hectare, about 5 tons—the outcome not only of mechanized but also of biological, chemical, and agronomical technologies and of improved institutions and infrastructures. The revolution in monsoon agriculture had begun, and other countries were soon to follow in the footsteps of the Japanese peasantry.

Industrial Growth

With the completion of the industrial transition in the late 1950s the pivotal forces in accelerated growth shifted to the industrial sector. To comprehend the changes which led to the highest growth in industrial factor productivity in the annals of modern history (5 percent), again one must begin with institutional changes initiated in the latter half of the 1940s by the Allied occupation. Just as the land reform emancipated the peasants, the legalization of the labor unions and other democratization measures led to the "emancipation of workers." By 1948, half of all industrial workers were organized into unions and large increases in wages were demanded and secured (Sumiya, 1973). Union membership reached an all-time peak of 6.7 million in 1948, and labor disputes also reached an all-time high in the same year, involving 2.6 million workers. The result was that real wages shot up at rates of annual increase of 34 percent in the period 1947–1950, compared with 4 percent for the 1960s and 6 percent for the 1970s. The legalization of Japan's labor unions in 1946 was the first step in the reformation of industrial relations and management that led to the rise in factor productivity, just as the large wage increases in the United States during the early decades of the 20th century, when immigration was restricted, started a process which led to the acceleration in factor productivity (Oshima, 1984).

The next step was as important. The purging of zaibatsu leaders and the heads of other companies playing leading roles in the war economy brought forward a new group of young but professional managers divorced from ownership. Control of large enterprises shifted to professional management more amenable to the notion of "social responsibility." Accommodation to the strong pressure for more democratic industrial relations from the unions was the policy followed by the professional managers through an innovative and unique system of labor-management relations, appropriately rooted in the basic structure of Japanese social values. A system of lifetime employment, originating in the prewar decades, was firmly established and extended to cover nearly all the larger enterprises, together with a system of seniority wage payment, profit-sharing bonuses, and welfare facilities, and a system of cooperation, consultation, participation, and consensus in decision-making.

This system was able to meet the requirements of rapid industrial growth in the postwar decades: (1) by a network of extensive in-service training of various kinds (since the staff was permanently committed to the enterprise, management could safely invest in its varied skill development); (2) by the swift introduction of adapted new technologies, especially labor-saving mechanization from abroad (since the enterprise was committed to lifetime employment of the staff, the latter did not fear losing jobs and, in fact, favored the new technologies which raised their productivity and therefore their bonuses); (3) by improving work motivation, habits, and attitudes (through staff involvement in decision-making and cooperation, through large bonuses tied to profits, through encouragement of group participation—e.g. quality control circles, through welfare devices, and so on); (4) by reducing industrial disputes, strikes, and lockouts (through measures encouraging loyalty to the enterprise and staff solidarity); and (5) by emphasis on long-range profit maximization, planning, and decision-making (through greater control of enterprises by management).[6] All of these directly or indirectly added to postwar total factor productivity, increasingly so as these practices improved over time. But the major impact on factor productivity, as will be discussed below, was labor-saving mechanization.

The 1950s were important to Japan's postwar growth as real wages grew by 4 percent each year. Unemployment declined from 2.5 percent to 1.5 percent (1950–1960), and signs of full employment were emerging as wages of the lowest paid workers (casual and day workers) began to rise faster than the monthly cash earnings of regular production workers in manufacturing. The wages of female textile workers also

[6] See the article by H. Shimada in the *Japan Labour Bulletin*, July 1983, on how this system of industrial relations facilitates rapid industrial restructuring in times of contraction.

began to rise faster than the wages of male machinery workers. These signs in the latter 1950s signaled the approach to full employment. The faster rise in the wages of female and unskilled workers began to attract workers from agriculture, as well as wives and daughters from the home, so that, around this period, the absolute labor force in agriculture began to fall and the female participation rate began to move upward. These tendencies, as well as the reduction in the number of domestic workers who were moving to industrial jobs, in turn encouraged households, both urban and rural, to adopt labor-saving mechanization in order to supply labor to industries. Not until the pools of workers from households and the rural sector fell to very low levels was full employment transformed into labor shortages; this change probably started around the latter 1960s, after the waves of migration from agriculture diminished and the female participation rate reached a peak. Thus, the distinction between full employment and labor shortage is the slowing down in the decline of the farm labor force, with changes in the female participation rate, and in the accelerating growth of wage rates from 4 percent in the 1950s to 6 percent in the 1960s.

Where did the demand for all the industrial production come from to create full employment in the 1950s and labor shortages by the end of the 1960s? In the 1950s, the most important source was the domestic sector, which in 1951 purchased 1,400 billion yen worth of nonfood consumer goods: 700 billion yen worth of this was bought by nonagricultural families and 610 billion yen by agricultural families (the rest being bought by institutional consumers). Agricultural households in addition purchased 370 billion yen worth of capital and intermediate goods for agricultural use. Thus the largest source of demand was the agricultural household (with total purchases of 980 billion yen), followed by nonagricultural households (with 700 billion yen); the smallest was the export sector with 475 billion yen in 1951 in nonfood exports. However, the growth in purchases of the three sectors during the 1950s in constant prices was highest for the export sector (with average annual increases of 20 percent), followed by the nonagricultural household sector (with 16 percent growth), and the lowest for agricultural households (with 8 percent).

It should be kept in mind that a growth rate of 8 percent is an exceptionally good performance for agriculture, which cannot be expected to be as dynamic as nonagriculture and which, in the case of Japan during the period under consideration, was shrinking absolutely and transferring its population to the nonagricultural sector. Thus, the outstanding characteristic of the growth of demand in Japan which led to full employment in the 1950s was the growth in demand for nonfood commodities by agricultural households, and this was particularly the case in the first half of the 1950s when purchases grew twice as fast as in the second half. The first half was important from the point of view of demand because of the lower levels of export and of nonagricultural household demand and the recession brought about by the drastic measures taken to curb inflation in 1949. By 1960, the growth of the latter two sectors had made nonagricultural households the largest source of demand and the agricultural households the smallest source, foreshadowing the major role that nonagricultural household demand and the export sector were to play by the end of the 1960s in converting full employment into a labor shortage.[7] The swift increase in household purchases in both rural and urban sectors reflects the growing power of the lower-income groups, as a result of the Allied occupation reforms. As we shall see below, income disparities declined.

In the foregoing, we have attempted to explain the persistent upward movement of real wages, particularly those of low-paid workers, which triggered increasing mechanization. After rapid increases in the late 1940s due to unionization, we found that the growth of aggregate demand and then that of employment were major forces in the rise of real wages. We turn now to the nature of mechanization in the 1950s, which was a major source of total factor productivity growth.

As noted above, the increase in real wages, doubling between 1947 and 1950, started a wave of mechanization, as shown by the rapid rise in the output of the engineering industries (24 percent per year), the main producers of machinery. What may have happened is that wages per hour or per day exceeded the cost of operating new machines per hour or per day, including the cost of interest on funds if invested, depreciation, obsolescence, maintenance, repair, and other costs of machines. Thus, in the very short run, real wages can rise due to enhanced bargaining power; but these levels cannot be maintained in the longer run if productivity does not rise and firms are hit by cost increases in subsequent years. There were increases in consumer prices during the 1950s, of about 4 percent per year, but this rate is no higher than the increase in real wages in manufacturing in the 1950s. Apparently, much of the doubling of real wages in 1947–1950 was absorbed by productivity increases, mainly via labor-saving mechanization.

[7] In the above discussion, our concern is mainly with the factors increasing the demand for labor, ignoring the factors on the supply side such as the increase in years of schooling in the 1950s, from 6 to 9 years and then to 12 years for most youngsters. The growth of the domestic market in the 1950s enabled the more capital-intensive industries (automobiles, iron and steel, heavy engineering, chemicals) to expand to sizes large enough to benefit from the scale economies needed to compete in world markets, besides achieving maturity in the 1960s. See Kanamori (1968).

The reason for this lies in the management changes noted above. If management control of enterprises is strong enough that management is free to determine mechanization policies, then it will be rational to maximize profits in the long run by substituting machines for labor when wage rates rise beyond the hourly cost of using new machines, even though the initial costs for installing machines may be large and the risks involved may be greater than the use of workers from the point of view of the owners of the enterprises. Management may even be encouraged by the workers to shift to machines if the latter have permanent status and bonuses are tied to profitability of the enterprise, which may be enhanced by technological sophistication.

In the Western industrialized countries, especially in the United States, the machinery or engineering industries had substantially developed by the early decades of the 20th century. This was largely due to the widespread substitution of electric/gas-driven machines for the steam-driven ones of the 19th century and to the mechanization of handwork. The United States overtook the United Kingdom as an industrial power when the latter hesitated to convert to electric-driven technology, and U.S. total factor productivity rose substantially during the 1920s with the rapid mechanization of agriculture and industry.

The sources of the greater productivity of electric drive over steam drive for machines were several: electric drive made possible at the outset the designing of machines with higher and better controlled speed and greater accuracy, and later of larger machines, more automatic, serialized and standardized, suited for mass production. Still later these huge, automatic machines were connected to give rise to integrated operation of a number of factories, the most outstanding example of which in the process industries is the integrated iron and steel industry. It is also evident in the assembly industries such as the automobile industry as it evolved in the United States (but not in Japan, where subcontracting is widely practiced).

Japan, a latecomer in industrialization, had not invested heavily in steam-powered mechanization as the United Kingdom had in the 19th century. Japan's level of mechanization was very low in the early decades of the 20th century, so it could easily shift to electrically driven technology. By the late 1930s, the output of the engineering industries had surpassed the output of textiles, the leading industry of Japan. In large part, it was the substitution of machines for handwork that was related to the higher factor productivity of the non-agricultural sectors, from zero (or negative) productivity during the 1920s to a 3.8 percent a year increase in productivity in the 1930s.

Perhaps a better indication of the mechanization of handwork is the growth of electric power used per worker in manufacturing. The increased use of electric power per worker (measured in kilowatt-hours) is affected much more by machines displacing workers than by new machines replacing old machines or by the expansion of existing facilities (as when more spindles are added in a textile factory). In the last case, electric power use per worker will not rise, and in the second case, the new machines may use only a small additional amount of, or even less, power when the new machines are more fuel-efficient, and worker displacement may be negligible. It is in the first case, when electric power replaces muscle power, that the volume of electricity rises and, at the same time, the number of workers falls, so that electric power used per worker increases substantially. This is particularly true in the early stages of industrialization when small-scale machines are replacing hand tools. In the later stages, a rise in kilowatt-hours per worker will mark a shift from small-scale to larger-scale mechanization and increasing capital intensity. Thus, if the total volume of kilowatt-hours of electricity rises between two periods but not the kilowatt-hours per worker, this implies that the number of workers is rising along with the volume of electricity used, so that mechanized technologies have not changed very much as far as fuel and manpower uses are concerned. It could happen, however, that while the number of kilowatt-hours per worker remains stationary, value added per worker rises because the new machines themselves are more productive. In this case, as well as in the case where machines displace workers, total factor productivity rises, but in the latter case output per worker may increase faster than output per unit of capital, while in the former, output per unit of capital rises faster than output per worker, assuming that both factors are measured so that qualitative changes are ignored.[8] In Table 4.2, these data are presented for Japan, together with data on the engineering industries. The prewar data are in horsepower units since steam-driven machines were still important, although by 1940 steam power had fallen to about one-fifth of total power used in manufacturing.

Note the low levels and slow rise of horsepower used per worker in Japanese manufacturing before the war (Table 4.2). In 1869, the earliest year for which data are available, the United States was using 1.14 horsepower per worker in manufacturing. Japanese manufacturing

[8] The major sources of the productivity of machines are speed, size, and energy efficiency. The displacement of men working with tools raises total factor productivity mainly because of the much higher speed of machines over tools operated by workers.

Table 4.3   Distribution of National Product and Employment among Three Major Sectors in Prewar and Postwar Japan

	A (%)	I (%)	S (%)	Total (%)
National product in constant prices[1]:				
1910s	2,665 (29)	2,599 (28)	3,862 (42)	9,126 (100)
1920s	2,861 (22)	4,835 (38)	5,154 (40)	12,850 (100)
1930s	3,174 (18)	8,472 (49)	5,803 (33)	17,449 (100)
Prewar (1910s– 1930s) average	2,900 (22)	5,302 (40)	4,940 (38)	13,142 (100)
1950s	3,336 (18)	6,489 (35)	8,568 (47)	18,393 (100)
1960s	4,203 (10)	18,865 (46)	18,243 (44)	41,311 (100)
1970s	4,817 (5)	45,050 (49)	42,286 (46)	92,153 (100)
Postwar average	4,119 (8)	23,468 (46)	23,032 (46)	50,619 (100)
Employment (in thousands):				
1910s	16,011 (61)	5,302 (20)	4,892 (19)	26,205 (100)
1920s	14,461 (51)	7,137 (25)	6,500 (23)	28,998 (100)
1930s	14,567 (47)	7,983 (26)	8,420 (27)	30,970 (100)
Prewar (1910s– 1930s) average	15,013 (53)	6,807 (24)	6,604 (23)	28,424 (100)
1950s	16,287 (41)	11,838 (29)	12,099 (30)	40,134 (100)
1960s	12,129 (26)	17,905 (38)	17,336 (37)	47,370 (100)
1970s	7,119 (14)	22,191 (42)	22,992 (44)	52,302 (100)
Postwar average	11,845 (25)	17,311 (37)	17,446 (38)	46,602 (100)

Sources: Ohkawa and Shinohara (1979), updated by (1) *OECD Labor Force Statistics* (for employment figures in the 1970s), (2) and (3) Japan Economic Planning Agency, *Annual Report on National Accounts, 1979* (for current price data in the 1970s).

Notes: A = agriculture, forestry, fishery, livestock; I = manufacturing, mining, construction, utilities. trasnsport, and communication; S = commerce and public and personal services.

[1] Prewar data in 1934–36 millions of yen; postwar data in 1970 billions of yen.

did not reach this level until the first half of the 1930s; hence, only a small portion of manufacturing was mechanized in Japan before the 1930s, and even in the 1930s the use of horsepower per worker was no higher than in Taiwan in 1954 (1.4) or the United States in 1889, when steam-powered machines were prevalent. This suprisingly low level of mechanization in the prewar decades indicates that, for the most part, manufacturing in Japan was basically handicraft. One reason for this was the government's preoccupation during the early modernizing decades with the building of infrastructures and the establishment of capital-intensive military industries, but the major factor was the difficulty of applying steam-driven mechanized technologies in small, labor-intensive manufactures.

There was a threefold increase in the growth of horsepower per worker in the 1950s, from 1.63 in 1953 to 4.74 by 1960, an acceleration similar to that in the United States during the 1920s and in Taiwan during the 1970s. It was also in the 1950s that the engineering industries grew rapidly, even though Japan was importing vast quantities of machinery from the West. By the end of the 1970s, these industries, no longer heavily dependent on imports, were producing as much as all the rest of manufacturing put together.

Table 4.2 also shows that the value of manufacturing output rose 2.8-fold between 1953 and 1960, but that kilowatt-hour per worker rose 3.8-fold. This compares with output growth of 4.3-fold for 1960–1970 as against 3.2-fold for kilowatt-hour per worker. The greater increase in number of kilowatt-hours per worker in the 1950s over the growth of output means that machines introduced were more often replacing workers using hand tools (or bare hands) than was the case in the 1960s. This was related to the higher growth of total nonagricultural factor productivity in the 1950s than in the 1960s. The excess growth of kilowatt-hour use per worker over that of output denotes, as pointed out above, that displacement of human workers by machines was greater in the 1950s than in the 1960s, dominating the replacement of older machines or the expansion by addition of machines. In the 1960s, the exceptional capital growth of 12 percent (compared with 6 percent in the 1950s) and the greater growth of output over kilowatt-hour use per worker denote capital intensification via the replacement of older machines with newer, larger, and faster machines.

Professor Ryōshin Minami of Hitotsubashi University has shown that in Japan electric motors surpassed steam engines in terms of horsepower around the mid-1910s, and since then the former grew more rapidly than the latter, so that by 1940 the aggregate horsepower of steam motors was only about one-fifth of electric-motor horsepower. (Minami, 1976). All during these decades Japan imported electric-motor technology from the West, mainly the United States. Moreover, Minami points out, "Because small plants could not be equipped with large-capacity steam engines, tools and machinery continued to be operated by human power for a long time. The appearance of electric power had a revolutionary effect on these plants by enabling the replacement of human power, in many cases merely by extending an electric wire to an ordinary house and installing one small electric motor within the house." He goes on to cite data showing the smaller factories (50 workers or less) changing over from the predominant use of steam, gas, oil, and waterwheels in 1909 to over 90 percent use of electric motors in 1940.

The suitability of electric/gas-driven machines for small factories may have enabled the smaller establishments not only to survive but to grow in the 1950s and 1960s despite the rise in wages. Although their growth rate (in terms of persons engaged) was smaller than that of the larger establishments (100 and over), establishments employing 10 to 99 persons were able to double their labor force, and those with one to nine employees increased their labor force by 40 percent from 1951 to 1966. About 55 percent of the manufacturing labor force was still engaged in establishments with less than 100 workers in 1966.[9]

Thus, by an early shift to electric-driven mechanization and through the import of machines from the West, Japan was able to supply electric-driven machinery not only to the larger enterprises but also to the smaller ones, which were able to grow absolutely throughout the 1950s, 1960s, and 1970s. The use of electric/gas-driven machinery in place of handwork and hand-operated equipment increased factor productivity because of the speed of machine operation and, in other cases, of the larger size. Specialized machines producing one or a few components can be efficiently operated in small firms since economies of scale are low and machines are cheap, simple, and of the same kind and hence easily mastered, unlike the situation in many large-scale process industries, where the machines are expensive, large, highly complex, and varied.

In monsoon economies, as long as farms are tiny and highly labor-intensive and seasonality is pronounced, the labor-intensive industries must play an important role. To make use of slack labor during the dry seasons, the factories must not be located too far from the farms, but during the busy seasons the factories must operate at less than full capacity and some machines must remain idle. The population densities of the rice-growing areas could supply sufficient labor of one sort or another to keep the small factories operating all year round but at varying capacities. The cheap but efficient electrically driven machine technology was a godsend for monsoon Asia, which had to contend with large amounts of slack seasonal labor. Thus, in Japan, off-farm employment of farm workers rose continuously during the 1950s and 1960s until income from such employment exceeded income from agriculture for the majority of farming households.

[9] Even in 1975 the smaller establishments continued to hold their own: 55 percent of the total manufacturing labor force was in firms with fewer than 100 employees, and 34 percent was in firms with fewer than 30.

Moreover, as shown elsewhere, the labor-intensive industries are not only less capital-intensive than larger units but are capable of using more secondhand equipment, workers with less training, and locally produced raw materials. Thus the labor-intensive industries are important in the passage through the agro-industrial transition, as they use maximum amounts of labor but exert minimum pressure on the capital markets and the balance of payments.

In sum, the fast growth of industrial factor productivity was mainly due to the quick spread of small, efficient machines which were suitable not only for large but also for small enterprises, not only in the big cities but also in small cities and towns. But the efficient importation, adaptation, mass reproduction, dissemination, and utilization of these technologies would not have been possible without the institutional reforms which democratized industrial relations and management and promoted the development of small establishments. The service sector played an essential part in all this.

The contribution of the service sector, comprising public, commercial, and personal services to total factor productivity, can be either direct or indirect, through the commodity-producing sectors and by more efficient operation of the overall economy and external economies. Because these contributions are difficult to measure, services are usually left out of discussions on factor productivity, but an attempt to identify and describe them is made below.

Growth of the Service Sector

Through five wars, military culture permeated many aspects of Japan's institutions. A vast amount of the GNP went for military purposes, as noted above. The abolition of the military establishment meant that a substantial fraction of government expenditures could be shifted to economically productive uses, just as in the colonies of Taiwan and Korea where the abolition of colonialism meant that the surpluses going to Japan could be used for domestic purposes.

The Allied Powers' policy of democratizing political institutions and liberalizing and expanding social institutions was a success from the point of view of the economic growth of postwar Japan. It is true that some Western scholars felt that the achievements fell short of expectations; nevertheless, as the dialogue continued among scholars over the decades, Western-style modernization began to be seen as not the only form which political, social, and cultural advances can take (Glazer, 1976). The modifications introduced by the Japanese after 1953 to the Allied occupation reforms do not seem to have been retrogressions but rather improvements when viewed from an economic standpoint. Once again, as in the past, the Japanese were able to demonstrate their great skills in the adaptation and improvement of imported institutions.

Thus, the improvements made by the government in decision-making were vital to the success of postwar growth, unlike in the prewar decades when decisions for military adventures were damaging. As Vogel (1975) points out, through better methods of recruitment, more participatory decision-making, and intensive staff training in the postwar decades, the Japanese bureaucracy developed outstanding capabilities in information gathering, research, and analysis toward decision-making, policy, and administrative guidance—all from the viewpoint of long-range national interest rather than that of particular vested interests. A good example is the adoption early in the 1950s of a form of industrial planning in which industries strategic to Japan's long-term growth were selected each decade for concentrated assistance—electric power and steel in the 1950s, automobiles and electronics in the 1960s. Another example is the promotion of efficiency through import of technologies; still another, the promotion of competition and prevention of monopolies and cartels, which had been so common in prewar decades. Costly mistakes in industrial, agricultural, and other policies were minimized and efficiency in the allocation of resources maximized with the skillful manipulation of market forces and government intervention. Another example is the system of assembling expertise from many firms, institutes, associations, universities, labor unions, and the bureaucracy with the aim of producing new technologies as quickly as possible, adapting imported ones, and finding methods and know-how for large-scale production.

Reform converted the all-powerful, much-feared prewar police system into an efficient organization which has an enviable record of crime control: Japan is the only industrialized country with a declining crime rate in the postwar decades.[10]

Reforms in education have made the Japanese pre-university educational system one of the best in the world. Comparative surveys of high-school students in leading countries show that Japanese students are trained exceptionally well in science and mathematics. Even more important is the extensive training in vocational subjects together with a superb system of moral education, particularly in work ethics (Oshi-

---

[10] Nothing better symbolizes the postwar transformation than the change in the forces of order from the Imperial officer mounted on a horse and wearing a majestic hat and a long sword to the hard-working but friendly policeman without weapons going on foot from one household to another (Bayley, 1976).

ma, 1978). The stress on cooperative, careful, and high-quality work habits from the first grade on is carried over into the workplace. Japanese white- and blue-collar workers develop into a formidable work force, whether on the farm or the factory floor, in the office or in the shop. The contribution of the schools to the skills and work habits of the labor force—as well as to egalitarian values—is one of the most important sources of total factor productivity in postwar Japan (Cummings, 1980).

As Vogel (1979) puts it, Japan has avoided some of the huge costs of a full-blown welfare state by a minimal welfare program which gives "security without entitlement," leaving welfare activities to enterprises, cooperatives, and the family. And yet this system has enabled the Japanese by the late 1970s to attain levels of life expectancy as high as those of the leading welfare nations of the West.

The impact of this system of welfare on family saving should be noted in passing. In the West, under the influence of Keynesian views of excessive savings as one of the causes of depression, the fiscal system was reconstructed to reduce the desire of families to save against old age, ill health, and the possibility of unemployment. In Japan, however, a high savings rate has continued to characterize family economic behavior.[11]

Cognizant of the need for national consensus if growth is to proceed stably, the state, the bureaucracy, the mass media, and the schools have strongly promoted the values of compromise, cooperation, harmony, and consensus in achieving national solidarity. This is particularly important under conditions of such rapid change as Japan has undergone. Kuznets (1975) has noted that rapid economic growth entails rapid structural changes and widespread disruptions in which some groups benefit and others lose, and he has expressed surprise that Japan could pull through such a period without the disruption of national consensus.

In the rigidly authoritarian, traditional institutions of the prewar decades, consensus was difficult to maintain. In the postwar years, the destruction of authoritarianism allowed varying viewpoints to be expressed in extensive discussions in many newspapers and magazines and in the education-conscious television networks, which catered to

---

[11] Shinohara (1970) has traced the sources of high savings rates not only to upper-income groups but also to proprietors' and workers' families. Besides seniority, large bonus payments, and accelerated retirement pay as semiforced savings, the broadening of opportunities for improving one's economic status enhanced the desire of small proprietors to save in order to invest for expansion to meet extensive competition.

the needs of all groups, not just the intellectual classes. While these discussions and meetings took time and were costly, they were much less so than the disruptions of national consensus that occurred in many countries, the most costly example being the case of Iran. In Japan, though national and other decision-making took time, the implementation was swift, as both losers and winners participated in carrying out the decisions. The swiftness of implementation more than made up for the slowness of decision-making.

For example, in tackling the problem of urban pollution, the committee appointed to solve the problem included representatives of the chief polluters, e.g., the iron, steel and chemical industries, as well as of the people most adversely affected. Although it took some time for the consensus solutions to be worked out, the implementation was swift since the polluters were obligated to implement the decision agreed upon. Tokyo, once as smoggy as New York, recently received UN citations for major progress in pollution control.

The growth of product per worker in the service sector for the postwar decades, the 1950s and 1960s, works out to be 5 percent compared with –0.7 percent for the 1910s to the 1930s (Ohkawa and Shinohara, 1979). Despite the difficulties of deflating the service sector, the difference of nearly 6 percent is too large to be ignored. One reason for such large increases in labor productivity may be that during the immediate postwar years, 1945–1953, when there were high levels of unemployment, the commercial sectors may have been a refuge for workers unable to find work in agriculture and industry, leading to considerable underutilization of commercial capacities. If the phenomenon of disguised unemployment existed at all, it was not in agriculture where land is required nor in industry where capital is required, but in the service sector where very little of either is needed.

As full employment was approached and the expansion of aggregate demand eliminated the underutilization, the commercial sector was forced to employ additional staff. This may have taken place in the late 1950s when the underutilized capacities of the late 1940s disappered. If so, up to the mid-1950s the growth of factor productivity was not a real one since it was the result of rising capacity utilization. This interpretation is supported by statistics for average monthly hours worked in wholesale and retail trade (of firms with three or more workers), which rose from 186 hours in 1951 to a peak of 197 in 1960 and declined slowly thereafter. In the 1960s and 1970s, with full employment and labor shortages, the service sector began to mechanize with various office and store machinery and equipment and motorized transport. Moreover, with modernization, economies of scale began to be generated, as annual sales increased among the smaller units while the larger-scale retail stores' sales share increased from 18 percent to 23 percent between 1966 and 1980. Similar tendencies also appear to hold for personal service establishments, hotels, restaurants, and similar operations with full employment and labor shortages. The impact of labor scarcity in raising the intensity of work is likely to be substantial in the service sector, which tends to use surplus labor wastefully, paying low wages, as in Southeast Asia.

Impact of Factor Productivity on Changes in Production Structure, Income Distribution, and Demographic Forces

The extensive mechanization of Japan's industry and agriculture in the postwar decades and institutional changes dramatically altered the structure of production, as can be seen from Table 4.3. The output share of agriculture on the average (1910s, 1920s, and 1930s) was 22 percent of the national product, and this went down to 8 percent on the average (1950s, 1960s, and 1970s), even though the agricultural output was rising absolutely (from 3,336 billion yen in the 1950 to 4,817 in the 1970s in 1970 prices). The employment share of the agricultural sector, which averaged 53 percent in the three prewar decades, fell by approximately one-half (to 25 percent) in the three postwar decades.

Shares of output and employment in the postwar period changed much faster than in the prewar decades. Output increased owing to greater fertilizer use and shifts to higher-value crops. Using the data in Table 4.3, we can compute absolute output per worker (in 1934–1936 prices) for the three prewar decades and compare the output per worker in I (or the industrial sector) for the prewar decades. The output per worker in agriculture is 25 percent of the output per worker in industry in the prewar decades. For the three postwar decades this output rises to 34 percent. The rapid shrinking in the agricultural labor force with mechanization had raised the output per worker in agriculture closer to the industrial output per worker in the postwar over the prewar decades. As Kuznets (1966) has noted, this is a major factor in reducing income inequalities nationwide in the growth of nations; and in the case of postwar Japan, it is accompanied by an absolute decline in the agricultural labor force, particularly that portion receiving the lowest incomes—the small-scale peasants/farm laborers. If we are to shift to the distribution of family incomes, there is an added reason for concluding that farm family incomes came even closer to nonfarm family incomes than is shown by the data on output per worker. This is suggested by the fact that off-farm incomes of farm households rose from about one-fourth of total farm family incomes to about two-thirds in the 1970s. Thus, some of the output in the nonagricultural sector should be allocated to the farm families, and if this is done, total per-family output in agriculture may move to more closely approximate family output in the industrial sector.

Turning now to the I and S sectors, we find that their relative size as share of total product is the same in the prewar decades (38 percent for the I sector, 39 percent for the S sector) and also in the postwar decades (46 percent and 46 percent, respectively). The same is true of the relative size of the two sectors as shares in total employment; in the prewar years, the average shares were 24 percent and 23 percent, respectively, and in the postwar years, the averages were 37 percent and 38 percent, respectively. If the deflation of the S sector is assumed to be reliable, our previous analysis would lead us to conclude that in the S sector the rise in employment share was greater than the rise in the output share because of the labor intensity of Japan's S sector, which is made up largely of neighborhood stores as tiny as the paddy farms and operated mainly by a marginal labor force of housewives and family help.

Similarly, with the I sector, the rise in the employment share is greater than that of the output share (which, as in the S sector, must be lowered since part of the output is produced by farm workers) because of the labor intensity of the I sector, particularly the ability of small establishments to survive and grow at rates equal to the larger ones, as noted previously.[12] If we now look at computations based on the data for these sectors, the absolute output per worker for the prewar decades in the I sector is 6 percent lower than the output per worker in the S sector, but they are about the same in the postwar decades. The catching up from prewar to postwar decades of I output per worker to that of the S sector may be due to the rapid mechanization and institutional changes in the I sector. It also represents a factor reducing income disparities, both individually and by family.

Thus, if we view the three postwar decades as a whole, the average family incomes of the three sectors are roughly the same, in contrast to the great disparities in the prewar decades. (We follow the procedure

---

[12] These figures, being percentage shares, are affected by the rapid decline in the agricultural labor force in total employment. We had to use shares because the product series for the prewar period are in 1934–36 prices and those for the postwar period are in 1970 prices. The results above are surprising, and in the future, with data permitting, we need to look into the subsectors within the I and S sectors and attempt somehow to splice the prewar and postwar real product series.

of taking as a whole the prewar decades as against the postwar decades as a whole, as we are interested in the technological and institutional changes between the two periods.) Since these are average incomes in each of the three sectors, we can conclude that the "between" disparities in the size distribution of family incomes were substantially reduced in the postwar period over the prewar period.

Turning to the "within" sector disparities, one can say that there is little doubt that family income disparities in each of the sectors were reduced from those of the prewar decades. As the discussion of the three sectors shows, forces making for equalization through democratization programs dominated the 1950s and the 1960s. In the A sector, besides land reform, which immediately raised the incomes of the lowest group of the peasantry and lowered the incomes of the larger landowners, the replacement of farm workers in the peak periods of production by machines released them for jobs in the urban sector. Above all, the incomes from nonagricultural activities were larger for the smaller peasants than for the larger ones since the former had more time for nonfarm work, and they were nearly threefold larger in the postwar decades. The wiping out of the unemployment and underemployment so prevalent in the prewar decades reduced disparities within agriculture as well as within industry and the services.

In the industrial and service sectors, with the rise of unionization and full employment, wage increases for unskilled and semiskilled workers in the 1950s and during the whole of the 1960s reduced the income disparities among the workers in both sectors. The replacement of manual work by machines reduced the number of handworkers, who were paid the lowest wages. The bonus system, a form of profit-sharing, increased the share of workers over against the share of capital. But

Table 4.4 Distribution of Japan's Labor Force by Occupation (%)

	1920	1930	1962	1971
1. Professional, technical, managerial	5.4	6.1	12.3	13.3
2. Clerical, mining, transport	9.1	9.4	30.3	30.4
3. Sales, craftsmen, production, service	31.5	35.4	47.1	51.3
4. Farmers, lumbermen, fishermen	54.1	48.9	2.5	1.3
5. Laborers	—	—	7.7	3.7

Sources: 1962 and 1971 data from *Employment Status Survey* (Tokyo: Statistical Bureau, 1962, 1971); 1920 and 1930 data from *Population Census for 1920 and 1930* (Tokyo: Statistical Bureau, 1922 and 1932).

there were offsetting factors, as shown in Table 4.4. The five occupational groups listed in the table were formed according to cash income
received, as shown by the various *Employment Status Surveys* (1962,
1965, 1968, 1971), with the highest cash income receivers in group 1
and the lowest in groups 4 and 5. These differences in income are
thought to be stable as far as ranking goes even though the amount
of the differentials between occupations may shrink or expand, since
they are based on major skills which in turn reflect costs of training.
Note that the percentage in the highest-income occupations doubled
from the prewar decades, from around 6 to 13 percent. This may have
contributed to the increase in the share of the highest quintile from the
prewar decades, but the highest quintile share in prewar decades was
probably made up mainly of property incomes, so that this tendency
may have been offset by declines in the share of property incomes, at
least in the 1950s. The middle-income groups, 2 and 3, doubled from
around 42 percent in prewar decades to about 79 percent, and this
should raise the shares of the second, third, and fourth quintiles. But
the table shows that the most important factor making for equality is
the drastic reduction in the two lowest occupation groups, from 54
percent to about 8 percent.

One question remains: whether the steady rise in income inequality
shown by Richard Wada—from a Gini coefficient, showing income
concentration of total households, of 0.31 in 1956 to 0.41 in 1971 for
total households (including one-person households) and from 0.28 in
1956 to 0.35 in 1971 for ordinary households (excluding one-person
households)—may have wiped out the gains of the 1950s (Wada, 1975).
The discussion centers on ordinary households, for one can assume that
one-person households were not significant in the prewar decades. And
since we are concerned with the secular long run, one must take an
average of the Ginis in the 1950s, 1960s, and 1970s. For ordinary households the average Gini is 0.32 (0.37 for the total households) in Wada's
table. A Gini of 0.32 is not high by any standard, whether of Western
industrialized countries, of rapidly industrializing countries such as
Taiwan, South Korea, Singapore, or Hong Kong, or of developing
countries such as Thailand, the Philippines, and West Malaysia, the
last three with Ginis around 0.5 in the 1960s. If we take the Ginis of the
last three countries as representative of prewar decades in Japan (on
the grounds of similarities in occupational and industrial structures of
the labor force), then one may conclude that the Gini of household
income distribution in Japan in the prewar decades centered in the
1920s might have been around 0.5, and that the reduction to the 0.3–

0.4 level in the postwar decades was exceptional. For the Gini measures relative changes in household incomes through cumulation of relative changes; it is insensitive to small changes which often are offset with counterchanges. A drop from 0.5 to 0.4, a 20 percent change, in the secular long run requires major transformation in technologies and institutions.

The widespread mechanization of handwork in agriculture and industry has implications for income elasticities of demand. The use of powered instruments means a reduction in the intake of caloric carbohydrate foods, which fell from an average of about 410 grams per capita per day in 1950–1955 to 315 grams in 1979. The reduction is even greater if account is taken of the larger proportion of working age (15 years old) to total population, which was 57 percent in 1950 and 64 percent in 1979, and of the increasing average size of the physique of the average Japanese. This, together with structural changes, meant that income elasticities of demand for the most important part of food consumption were falling sharply as the average worker required less caloric foods, and that less income was spent on foods as incomes rose (lower Engel coefficient), with favorable implications for personal savings, which were the highest in the world in the 1960s and early 1970s.

As in the U.S.A. (and some other industrialized countries), the sharpest declines in birth rates were related to the periods when postprimary education spread to the majority of families. In the United States this came during the 1920s with the rapid spread of labor-saving mechanization. The Japanese, for all their Asian social values, appear to have been subjected to the same forces. In the distant past and in the Meiji era when long-run demand for labor went up, birth rates rose, but this time the rise in the demand could be met by using machines which reduced the demand for unskilled and semi-skilled labor. It was the spread of mechanization to the primary and secondary sectors that caused pressure from both the government (through compulsory junior high school education) and the parents for children to attend junior and senior high schools. In 1920 the number of pupils enrolled in postprimary education as a portion of total households was only 13 percent, and in 1930 it was 20 percent; but the number reached 47 percent in 1950 and a peak of 52 percent in 1955, declining to 50 percent in 1960. Live births, which declined at an annual rate of only 0.9 percent in the 1920s, in the 1950s dropped by 4.8 percent a year, the sharpest fall in the postwar decades. Live-birth levels stabilized in the 1960s around levels reached toward the end of the 1950s.

Summary and Implications

The process which resulted in large postwar increases in total factor productivity began with a series of reforms initiated by the Allied occupation (and improved by the Japanese after 1952). These reforms attempted to demilitarize Japan through democratizing the basic institutions of prewar times. The land reform and other agrarian changes, the legalization of labor unions, the purging of the traditional leadership of the large enterprises, and other measures in industry led to large increases in real incomes and wages of lower-income groups in agriculture and industry in the late 1940s. In the 1950s, the increases in domestic demand due to the greater purchasing power of peasants and workers led to full employment and further rises in wages of lower-income groups and more machine substitution. In the 1960s the process was carried further through acceleration of exports, as well as of domestic demand, and a labor shortage ensued, with further rises in the wages of lower-income groups. This, in turn, forced farmers and management to substitute mechanized technology for human labor as the cost of employing workers per day rose beyond the cost of using machines per day. Mechanization took the form of replacing workers in the peak periods of plowing, planting, and harvesting, which enabled agriculture to release workers to industry. One measure of spreading mechanization in the 1950s was the increase in kilowatt-hours of electrical energy used per worker. Fortunately for Japan, the machinery industry was already making good progress in the 1930s, with a quick shiftover from steam-driven mechanization to electric- and gas-driven mechanization. Thus, in the postwar decades, industry was advanced enough to be able to import and adapt electric-driven machine technologies from the United States. In the tertiary sector, the reforms introduced by the Allied powers and modified by the Japanese were able to improve the efficiency of government employees and public institutions like the police and the schools. And political democratization led to decision-making procedures which were able to maintain national consensus in the midst of the incessant and disruptive changes induced by rapid growth.

Structural changes were extensive in the postwar decades as Japan completed the industrial transition in the late 1950s. The changes were so far-reaching that they were not merely related to changes in the economy as a whole; rather, there were several breaks in the absolute trends, either reversals or kinks. The most noteworthy were the sharp declines in the agricultural labor force with mechanization, in the number of unskilled laborers in industry, and in the income elasticities of caloric foods. These changes in turn had widespread repercussions on the structure of incomes whose distribution became much more equal than in the prewar decades. The increasing need for postprimary education induced by electric/gas-driven machines sharply increased the cost of raising children, while the decreased need for handworkers reduced the demand for uneducated workers.

With the oil crisis and the slowdown in the industrialized countries and in world trade since 1973, Japan's growth rate in the 1970s fell to about one-half that of the previous decades, 4.5 percent compared with about 10 percent for overall GDP. This points up the importance of the liberal trading practice of the industrialized countries in Japan's accelerated growth in the 1950s and 1960s. But it may also be indicative of the slowdown in the availability of new technologies from the West as Japan edged closer to the technological frontier. Nevertheless, Japan's growth rate for the 1970s was about double that of frontier countries such as the United Kingdom, the United States, the Netherlands, Germany, Sweden, and Switzerland, and highest among the 18 industrialized countries listed in the IBRD World Development Report.

For the 1980s, a growth rate of about 4 percent is officially projected. Probably this rate can be substantially raised if the productivity of small-scale agriculture and service sectors can be increased. Japan's GDP per worker in 1978 was only two-thirds that of the United States, West Germany, France, and Belgium. Even though Japanese manufacturing product per worker in 1978 was about as high as those of the other countries, the situation was the reverse in agriculture, and it will be necessary to shift to larger-scale farming if agricultural productivity is to keep pace with that in the nonagricultural sectors. Similarly, in the large and growing service sector, the small shops presently catering to small groups of customers in the densely packed cities must grow in scale if productivity is to come up to Western levels.

Large-scale technologies are available in the West. On California rice farms, bulldozers for soil preparation; airplanes for planting, fertilizing, and insect control; harvester/thresher combines; and railcars for transporting have reduced man-hours per hectare to less than 10, compared with several hundred man-hours in Japan, with yields about the same, 5 to 6 tons. In the commercial sector, small neighborhood stores in the United States have been largely replaced with huge shopping center complexes containing specialized department stores and self-service supermarkets. The success of postwar agricultural development and democratization in Japan has made farm families content with small-scale farming combined with off-farm employment. The political power of the small farms and shops in the consensus and participatory politics of Japan's democracy slows down the transition to large-scale farming and merhandising.

And yet the transition from small-scale to large-scale technologies must be speeded up if the imbalance with the large-scale manufacturing sector is not to worsen. The unduly large amount of labor tied up in the agriculture and service sectors compels the industrial sector to move too quickly towards greater capital and technology intensity with automation and robotization, which in turn contribute to technological unemployment and disruption of union-management relations as workers become increasingly apprehensive of losing jobs. Together with the rise in the cost of living, the slow rise in productivity and incomes in the small-scale sectors tends to slow down the growth of the domestic market, driving Japan's manufacturers to seek markets abroad. It is therefore not without justification that the United States and other industrialized countries complain of the inroads made in their markets by Japan's manufactured goods in the 1970s and 1980s. At the same time, other countries in Asia with low wages and surplus labor cannot sell to Japan and therefore will not be able to buy Japan's machinery.

The overwhelming impression that stands out in the Japanese experience is the unique development of the motivation to work at all levels of manpower. By no means low in the prewar period, the new and improved institutions appear to be directed toward further raising the work culture of the labor force. Rapid, sustained growth is not possible in monsoon Asia, where small farms and firms are responsible for the bulk of GDP, unless the smallest units are energized. This was carried out in postwar Japan through institutions which raised the human conditions of the workplace, going beyond material conditions and aiming at the desire of human beings to be esteemed, creative, consulted, and challenged.

To conclude, democratization and the demilitarization policies succeeded in creating opportunities for the lower classes. Compared with the society and economy of the prewar decades, a vibrant society was created with an economy so dynamic that it has begun to challenge the supremacy of the West with technological capabilities that can begin to revolutionize monsoon Asia and lead it into the Pacific century. No society can cut off its past, but few have set out so dramatically on new paths as Japan. Its postwar performance was more than the continuation of the past, and in the process something new has emerged.

CHAPTER 5

Similarities and Contrasts in
the Rapid Transition of Taiwan and South Korea

*T*aiwan completed its industrial transition one decade after Japan did, around the end of the 1960s, and South Korea followed Taiwan another decade later.[1] Although delayed by the Korean War in the early 1950s and by its heavy industry strategy in the 1970s, South Korea was actually ahead of Taiwan in industrialization by the end of World War II. The completion of this transition in Taiwan and South Korea was exceptionally fast compared with that of other countries with an agricultural base (except for Japan, which had a head start of several decades). This was due to a highly developed rice economy, education during the Japanese colonial period, longer experience in industrialization than most other Asian colonies, the influx of entrepreneurs and technicians from North Korea, China, and elsewhere after the Communist governments came to power, and a strategy of development which emphasized agricultural and labor-intensive industrialization in the 1950s and 1960s in both countries. All this is well known and amply documented in the extensive literature on the growth of these countries. Hence, the emphasis in this chapter will be on the differences in their patterns of development, rather than on similarities. In the 1970s the development paths of the two countries parted and different patterns emerged, although the circumstances leading up to that point of departure are not yet fully understood.

The various similarities described in the literature include an annual growth rate in per capita GDP at constant prices of 5.7 percent (1950–1980). This impressive record over three decades, second only to Japan, Singapore, and Hong Kong, was accompanied by rapid shifts from agriculture; substantial reductions in income disparities, in birth and death rates, and in unemployment compared with prewar decades; and sharp rises in total factor productivity, in educational enrollment, literacy, and life expectancies—all signs pointing to the widespread

---

[1] This chapter is an extended version of Oshima, 1986.

distribution of the benefits of growth as seen in Japan, Hong Kong, and Singapore, but not in Mexico, Brazil, and other NICs.

Institutionally and historically, both Taiwan and South Korea have had long traditions of Confucian culture with strong work ethics. Both were colonies of Japan before World War II. Upon independence they reoriented old institutions and devised new ones to produce growth for their own benefit. Both began the growth process with extensive land reform, which reduced the power of the landed oligarchy. A large influx of migrants, including experienced entrepreneurs and technicians, proximity to Japan, and close relations with the United States all aided the beginnings of recovery and growth. Both are monsoon economies with meager natural resources, light rainfall during the winter and spring months, and ethnic and social homogeneity, similar to Japan and in contrast with the countries of Southeast and South Asia.

Differences in historical and natural endowments should be noted. Because of its subtropical climate, the Republic of China has always been better suited to agricultural development than is Korea with its harsh winters. Moreover, because Korea is adjacent to Manchuria it was a suitable staging ground for the Japanese invasion of North China and thus more industries were established in colonial days in the Korean peninsula than in the Republic of China. There were also important historical differences in earlier centuries. During five centuries of the Yi Dynasty preceding the Japanese conquest, Koreans, like the Filipinos, were ruled by a degenerate dynasty which became increasingly corrupt and oppressive, forcing the people to depend upon kinship loyalties for protection and to resort to rebellion against the state and lawlessness. Factional strife among the ruling elite and rebellion by the people continued during the Japanese oppression.

Colonial Legacy

The Japanese developed industries more in Korea than in Taiwan, and agriculture more in Taiwan than in Korea, but both grew fairly rapidly. As noted in the previous chapter, GNP grew somewhat more rapidly in the colonies than in Japan from the 1910s to the 1930s (Mizoguchi and Umemura, 1981). Japan established capital-intensive industries, chemical, metal, machinery and other engineering industries in the north and light industries in the south. The degree of industrialization in the two colonies on the eve of World War II was quite unusual, mainly because Japan needed to industrialize its colonies in order to wage war on China; Korea was used as a staging ground to supply the troops in China, and Taiwan became a source of manpower when labor shortages began to occur in Japan with the acceleration of fighting in China. It is true that many of the larger industrial facilities established by the Japanese were destroyed in World War II and the Korean War, and that the top echelon of officials in these large enterprises were Japanese. Nevertheless, as Mizoguchi and Umemura (1981) pointed out, the 1944 Census reported over 7 million managers and 28 million craftsmen in Korea. These were the people who later manned the labor-intensive manufacturing enterprises which in the late 1940s employed a workforce one-fifth as large as that in agriculture. They composed the backbone of South Korea's strong labor-intensive industries, the products of which penetrated Western markets in the 1960s and throughout the 1970s (Repetto et al., 1981).

Taiwan's early industrialization was due in part to the Korean War. But it is not clear how much the war retarded Korean industrial growth. Although it lasted for three years, the greatest damage was confined to the first year, after which there was a stalemate "within a 10-mile strip" near the border. Recovery was quick, and by 1953 production had surpassed the level reached just before the war. Before 1950, U.S. assistance was restricted to relief and education, and "existing plant and equipment were barely usable." Foreign economic aid quadrupled between 1953 and 1961 compared with the 1946–1952 level, financing 80 percent of fixed capital formation. Besides the $2.6 billion received in 1953–1961, $1.6 billion in military aid was rendered, most of which was used for industrial construction. One can speculate that the massive aid more than offset the war-incurred damage, particularly because the assistance continued throughout the 1960s. Another contribution was made by the many U.S. firms and experts from whom the Koreans were quick to learn new technologies and techniques (Mason et al., 1980).

Japan developed agriculture in both Taiwan and Korea, in order to import cheap rice from both and sugar from Taiwan. Many things were introduced in the agricultural sector: new rice seeds, chemical fertilizers, irrigation, roads, research, and credit. TFP in the 1920s and 1930s increased by about 2 percent. Yields per hectare rose, and while they were higher in Taiwan than in Korea as a whole, in what was later to become South Korea the rise in yields probably matched that in Taiwan.

There was a fundamental difference in the governance of the colonies by Japan. This is suggested by the assessments of the Japanese period by Samuel Ho (1978) on Taiwan and Sang-Chul Suh (1978) on Korea. The former's evaluation was much more favorable than that of the latter. The occupation of Taiwan was accomplished fairly smoothly, but there were tensions and frequent clashes in Korea, where a large

Table 5.1   Average Annual Growth of Product, Input, and Productivity in Taiwan, 1911–1980   (%)

	Product (1)	Labor (2)	Capital (3)	Total Input (4)	Product per Laborer (5)	Product per Unit Capital (6)	Marginal Capital per Laborer (7)	Total Factor Productivity (8)
Whole Economy								
1911–20 to 1931–38	3.78	1.49	5.30	3.01	2.26	−1.52	3.80	0.77
1952 to 1980	9.10	3.10	7.40	4.39	6.00	1.70	4.30	4.71
1952 to 1969	8.60	2.70	4.50	3.24	5.90	4.10	1.80	5.36
1952 to 1960	8.20	1.70	2.50	1.94	6.50	5.70	0.80	6.26
1960 to 1969	8.90	3.60	6.30	4.41	5.30	2.60	2.70	4.49
1969 to 1980	9.80	3.60	11.90	6.09	6.20	−2.10	8.30	3.71
Primary Sector								
1952 to 1980	3.60	−0.60	6.20	1.44	4.20	−2.60	6.80	2.16
1952 to 1969	4.70	0.70	5.60	2.17	4.00	−0.90	4.90	2.53
1952 to 1960	5.20	0.60	4.60	1.80	4.60	0.60	4.00	3.40
1960 to 1969	4.20	0.70	6.50	2.44	3.50	−2.30	5.80	1.76
1969 to 1980	1.90	−2.60	7.00	0.28	4.50	−5.10	9.60	1.62
Secondary Sector								
1952 to 1980	12.00	5.30	11.80	7.25	6.70	0.20	6.50	4.75
1952 to 1969	11.40	4.60	10.40	6.34	6.80	1.00	5.80	5.06
1952 to 1960	10.70	2.90	7.80	4.37	7.80	2.90	4.90	6.33
1960 to 1969	12.00	6.10	12.70	8.08	5.90	−0.70	6.60	3.92
1969 to 1980	13.00	6.50	13.90	8.72	6.50	−0.90	7.40	4.28

(Table 5.1, continued)

*Tertiary Sector**

1952 to 1980	9.30	4.70	6.30	5.18	4.60	3.00	1.60	4.12
1952 to 1969	9.80	4.80	3.00	4.26	5.00	6.90	-1.80	5.54
1952 to 1960	10.00	3.30	1.60	2.79	6.70	8.40	-1.70	7.21
1960 to 1969	9.70	6.20	4.20	5.60	3.50	5.50	-2.00	4.10
1969 to 1980	8.40	4.50	11.40	6.57	3.90	-3.00	6.90	1.83

Notes: (2) Labor and (3) Capital were given weights of .6 & .4 in the prewar period and .7 & .3 in the postwar period in combining inputs.

* Tertiary Sector including Transportation and Communication.

Sources: (1) Prewar data on GNP from Mizoguchi as cited in Kuznets; labor and product per labor from S. Kuznets in Walter Galenson, ed., *Economic Growth and Structural Change in Taiwan* (Ithaca: Cornell University Press, 1979), p. 22. Capital stock estimated by using Mizoguchi's investment data quoted from Table A-2 of Samuel P. S. Ho, *Economic Development of Taiwan, 1860–1970* (New Haven: Yale University Press, 1978), p. 286, and capital stock estimated by R. Goldsmith's formula.

(2) Postwar data (1952–69) calculated from Shirley W. Y. Kuo, *The Economic Structure of Taiwan 1952–1969.*

(3) 1969 to 1980 product and employment data are official estimates taken from *Statistical Yearbook of ROC 1981.* Net capital stock estimates were derived by using fixed capital stock in 1975 as a benchmark and extrapolated utilizing real fixed capital formation data in *National Income of ROC 1981.*

Table 5.2   Average Annual Growth of Product, Input, and Productivity in South Korea, 1920–1980   (%)

	Product (1)	Labor (2)	Capital (3)	Total Input (4)	Product per Worker (5)	Product per Unit Capital (6)	Marginal Capital per Worker (7)	Total Factor Productivity (8)
Whole Economy								
1920–1938	3.5	0.6	7.9	2.8	2.9	−4.4	7.3	0.7
1953–1980	7.4	3.4	8.8	5.1	4.0	−1.6	5.6	2.3
1953–1961	3.9	2.0	3.3	2.4	1.9	0.6	1.3	1.5
1961–1969	8.8	3.3	9.9	5.3	5.5	−1.1	6.6	3.5
1969–1980	9.0	4.5	12.4	6.9	4.5	−3.4	7.9	2.1
Agriculture								
1920–1938	2.0 (1.4)	0.5 (0.5)	(1.5)	(0.4)	(0.9)	1.5 (0.9)	(−0.1)	(0.9)
1953–1980	3.4	0.6	8.0	2.8	2.8	−4.6	7.4	0.6
1953–1961	3.4	1.3	5.7	2.6	2.1	−2.3	4.4	0.8
1961–1969	4.2	0.6	9.4	3.2	3.6	−5.2	8.8	1.0
1969–1980	0.8	0.7	8.5	2.1	1.5	−7.7	9.2	−1.3
5-year average centering on 1980	(2.7)	(0.1)	(8.7)	(2.7)	(2.6)	(−6.0)	(8.6)	(0.0)

(Table 5.2, continued)

Non-agriculture

1920–1938	5.9	4.3	8.9			1.6		
1953–1980	9.1	5.8	8.9	6.7	3.3	0.2	3.1	2.4
1953–1961	4.4	3.5	3.0	3.4	0.9	1.4	0.5	1.0
1961–1969	8.0	6.9	9.9	7.8	1.1	−1.9	3.0	0.2
1969–1980	13.4	6.6	12.5	8.4	6.8	0.8	5.9	5.0

Notes: Prewar estimates are for the whole of Korea and are based on T. Mizoguchi, "GDP and GNE Estimates of Japanese Empire," Hitotsubashi Discussion Paper No. 35, March 1981. Sung Hwan Ban's estimates for prewar South Korean agriculture (1920–39), as obtained from Yūjirō Hayami, V. W. Ruttan, and H. M. Southworth, *Agricultural Growth in Japan, Taiwan, Korea, and the Philippines*, are given separately in parenthesis. Postwar estimates were calculated from *National Income in Korea 1978* (for growth of product), *ILO Yearbook of Labour Statistics* and *UN Statistical Yearbook for Asia and Pacific* (for growth of labor), p. 399 of W. Hong, *Trade Distortions and Employment Growth in Korea*, Seoul: KDI, 1979 (for growth of net fixed capital stock). All data were updated to 1980 by using *The Bank of Korea Monthly Economic Statistics*, no. 3 (1981). Labor and capital were given shares of .7 and .3 respectively in calculating total input (as Hong did in his estimates). Because 1980 was a bad crop year, five-year averages centering on 1980 are used for agriculture.

number of Japanese immigrants took up jobs and farms, becoming employers and landlords. Some scholars believe that about half the land in Korea came under the control of the Japanese.

Thus in the case of Korea major elements of a class struggle were added to colonization; exploitation was added to suppression. Tenancy rates increased from 39 percent in the 1910s to 55 percent in the 1930s, forcing the impoverished peasants to migrate to Manchuria and Japan where they were discriminated against and ostracized. The distribution of income probably worsened in Korea during Japan's occupation; in Taiwan real wages rose steadily throughout the prewar decades and tenancy fell (Suh, 1978).

The different styles of Japanese occupation were a major factor in the development of the two countries in the postwar decades. After the confusion of the immediate postwar years the independent governments sought to develop as rapidly as possible. New insitutions were established, of which the most important were new agrarian relations, a comprehensive educational system, large military forces, financial institutions, and so on. In Taiwan, the development of agriculture was continued after the initial land reform, and the peasantry was able to contribute substantially to national development. This was not so in Korea, where despite strong demands by the United States, the Rhee and the later governments ignored the peasantry and relied on industrial entrepreneurs who developed under Japanese rule and were prepared to undertake industrial development. Net output of Korean manufacturing in 1939 and 1940 was already 40 percent of agricultural output, with textile, metal, machinery, and chemical products equalling about two-thirds of manufacturing output (Mason et al., 1980).

Tables 5.1 and 5.2 show that the growth of capital inputs for prewar Korea was higher than for Taiwan (7.9 percent compared with 5.3 percent) and since Korea's capital growth in agriculture was only 1.5 percent, most of the overall capital growth must have occurred in industry. This is consistent with the view that industrialization had progressed further in Korea than in Taiwan. The growth of factor productivity in the prewar decades was slower in Taiwan and Korea than in Japan by about 50 percent. This may have been related to the large outflow of agricultural products to Japan which, after independence, became available for domestic consumption. All the skills learned in the Japanese colonial period in agricultural and industrial production along with the physical and institutional infrastructure contributed to the ability of these countries to take advantage of the various opportunities which opened up in the postwar era far better and more quickly than the countries of South and Southeast Asia in which the colonial regimes failed to develop agriculture and industrialization to such a great extent.

Growth of Total Factor Productivity (TFP) in Taiwan and South Korea

Tables 5.1 and 5.2 show data on total factor productivity (TPF) in the Republic of China and the Republic of Korea. The sharp acceleration in the growth of TFP from the prewar to the postwar era (0.8 percent to 4.7 percent a year for the Republic of China; 0.7 to 2.3 percent for the Republic of Korea) is unusual in the secular growth of nations. However, what stands out in Tables 5.1 and 5.2 is that TFP growth in Taiwan was nearly double that in South Korea in the postwar years, although their prewar growth rates were about the same. Part of this difference is accounted for by the slower start of Korea as a result of the Korean War in the early 1950s. Taiwan's TFP growth was 5.4 percent in the 1950s compared with Korea's 1.5 percent, and a large part of the difference is attributable to higher growth in Taiwan's agriculture (3.4 percent to Korea's 0.8 percent). If the rate during the 1950s is excluded, TFP growth was 4.1 percent during the 1960s and 1970s in Taiwan, still substantially larger than Korea's 2.8 percent. The difference is more than accounted for by the higher growth of TFP in Taiwan's agriculture, which equalled 1.7 percent compared with 0.8 in Korean agriculture. Differences in growth strategy accounted for the much higher growth of TFP in Taiwan, no matter which time period one considers.[2]

This chapter is concerned with the difference in the patterns of growth indicated by the foregoing findings, in particular during the earlier periods when agricultural development was emphasized more in Taiwan than in South Korea and later when heavy industry was emphasized in South Korea. The latter's experience has recently aroused a great deal of interest among the ASEAN nations which have begun to consider a shift to capital-intensive manufacturing. Studies of Korea's growth have lent weight to the view that an industrialization strategy in the early stages of growth can contribute as much to a country's development as an agriculturalization strategy. This chapter will

---

[2] The heavy industry strategy of Korea is reflected in the higher ratio of construction to equipment, 63 percent compared with 47 percent for Taiwan in 1980. Since the estimates of TFP are conventional, capital stock estimates are used. Construction yielding benefits over longer periods of time tends to be less productive per unit of time.

emphasize the difficulties encountered by Korea in the postwar decades, in contrast to development of Taiwan, and argue that in view of the nature of monsoon agriculture, Korea should have put more resources into agricultural growth earlier on.

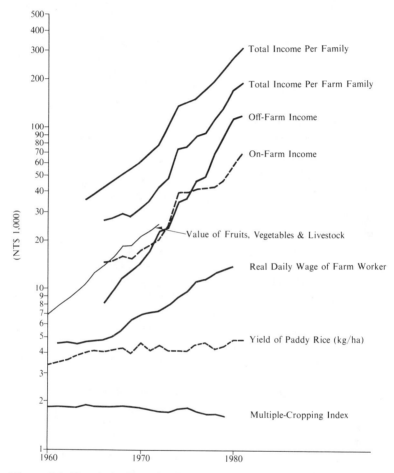

Figure 5.1. Trends in farm family income, wages, yields, cropping index: Taiwan

Sources: Various issues of *Statistical Yearbook of ROC* and from *Basic Agricultural Statistics*, Council for Agricultural Planning and Development, March 1983.

Notes: All data in current prices unless specified. Total Income Per Farm Family and On-Farm Income before 1970 were adjusted by extrapolating with current agriculture product per farm family.

In Part I I said that the poverty of monsoon Asia was due not so much to a year-round labor surplus as to seasonal unemployment. By eradicating this underemployment with more work in the monsoon agriculture slack seasons, the annual income of peasants can be raised. With this higher income they can purchase more inputs such as fertilizers to increase yields per hectare. And when full employment is

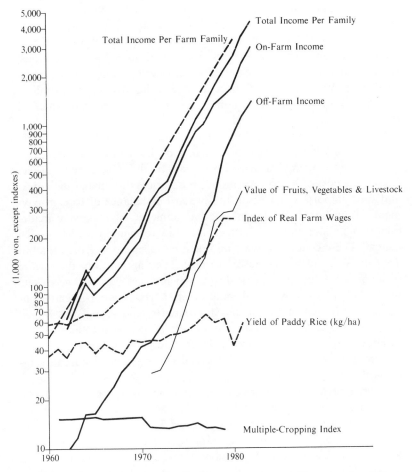

Figure 5.2. Trends in farm family income, wages, yields, cropping index: South Korea

Sources: Various issues of *Korea Statistical Yearbook* and *Report on the Results of Farm Household Economy Survey*. All data in current prices unless specified.

reached, capital/labor substitution can take place, and the economy can proceed along neoclassical growth lines. Otherwise, the policies involving a shift of farm workers to industry will be premature because annual farm incomes will be low, the domestic market will be too small for industries to make much headway, and food will have to be imported to compensate for the shifted farm workers. First, yields per hectare must be raised, cropping per hectare increased with shifts to higher value diversified crops, and off-farm employment expanded before full employment and a sustained rise in farm family incomes can be attained. Because of the slower growth of agriculture in Korea than in Taiwan from 1946 to 1950 and the Korean War disruptions, Korea should have made greater efforts to develop its agriculture in the 1950s and 1960s, instead of concentrating so heavily on industrialization. In 1960, Korean farm family incomes were about one-half of those in Taiwan (Figs. 5.1 and 5.2).

Inadequate local demand forced Korean industries to turn too hastily to foreign markets, necessitating large subsidies to promote big firms at the expense of smaller ones. Insufficient food for industrial workers caused the cost of living to rise since food prices dominated the index, and food imports weighed on the precarious balance of foreign payments. Low farm incomes meant that domestic savings were inadequate to finance industrial expansion and foreign loans had to be sought. These conditions were all much more severe in Korea than in Taiwan. Without the resources to mechanize agriculture, the release of labor for industries slowed down. When wages began to accelerate in the late 1970s, this fueled inflation. Exports of labor-intensive industries were not enough to pay for imports, and Korea was forced to move into heavy industrialization in the 1970s. With so much going to large firms and in heavy industries there was not much left for agriculture and small industries, and social tensions and disturbance increased.

Thus, Korea ended the postwar era with much larger foreign debts, price rises, devaluations, smaller international reserves, and higher income disparities and birth rates than did Taiwan (Figs. 5.5 and 5.6). The neglect of agriculture is a major reason that in the early 1980s Korea was struggling with a heavy debt burden, excess capacity in heavy industries, and continuing social unrest. It has been fortunate to possess a large shelf of efficient labor-intensive industries with one of the hardest-working populations in the world, extensively educated and trained. When the yen rose to high levels, Korea was able to seize the opportunity to export and resume growth.

Agricultural Development

Both Taiwan and Korea started out with heavy unemployment in the 1950s due to the sudden influxes of cross-border compatriots noted above. By the late 1960s in Taiwan and the latter 1970s in South Korea full employment had been attained. Farm family incomes in Taiwan recovered quickly after the war, as agricultural production rose at a rate of 10 percent a year from 1945 to 1952. Between 1952 and 1960, it rose by 5.2 percent a year and in the 1960s by 4.2 percent, but fell to 1.9 percent in the 1970s. These rates of growth (about 5 percent annually before 1970) exceeded the growth of the labor force by 3 percent, so that by the latter 1960s, the unemployment rate had fallen to 2 percent compared with 4 percent in the early 1960s. Export growth was also rapid but it started from very low levels, being 14 percent of GNP in 1960, one-third in 1970, and two-thirds in 1980. Industrial exports had exceeded domestic demand by around the mid-1960s. In the 1970s farm incomes grew slowly while off-farm incomes of farm families rose rapidly, and the growth rate of total incomes of farm families reached 7 percent in the 1970–1979 period (Fig. 5.1). In the 1950s and 1960s, total farm family incomes rose at a rate of about 4.5 percent a year.

South Korea's real farm output grew at an annual rate of 3.4 percent from 1953 through 1961, partly in compensation for the low levels during the Korean War and its aftermath, but fell in the first half of the 1960s to 2.8 percent each year. Then in the latter half of the 1960s, there was an acceleration to 10.8 percent, which in the 1970s fell to 5.8 percent. The overall rate for the period 1960 to 1979 was 4.9 percent, while the labor force grew by 3.3 percent. But because of its poor start South Korea did not reach full employment until the late 1970s when its unemployment rate fell to 3 percent. This was nearly a decade later than Taiwan, despite Korea's rapid growth of exports from 5 percent of GNP in 1960 to 15 percent in 1970 and 30 percent in 1980. As discussed below, full employment was reached through land reform, as yields per hectare, the number and kinds of crops per hectare, and income from off-farm employment increased. In both countries, as in Japan, the amount of new land brought under cultivation was negligible.

Extensive land reform was carried out in Korea, Taiwan, and Japan early in the postwar period under strong U.S. pressure. Real incomes of small peasants rose as rents were abolished and the former tenants were motivated to put in more labor per hectare to enlarge the residual returns which now accrued mostly to them. Probably this was not a major direct factor in increasing employment. Land reform in Taiwan, as in Japan, was a significant factor in an indirect way through the political power it took away from the landed elite and bestowed upon the smaller peasants in the form of credit, extension services, better distribution of water supplies and other inputs, and an improved physical infrastructure which allowed multiple cropping, diversification, and commercialization of Taiwan's agriculture.

Secondly, the backlog of new technologies (higher yielding varieties, better cultivation, and new fertilizers and cultivation methods) developed by experimental stations and research centers after the 1940s were labor-using and had a large impact on labor absorption. This is because in the period before full employment was attained the use of mechanized technologies was limited on small farms where surplus labor existed and draft animals were scarce. The increase in yields, not only of rice but of other crops as well, meant that more had to be reaped, threshed, processed, and transported.

Third and more important was the increase in the multiple-cropping ratios which rose to a peak of 1.9 in Taiwan in the mid-1960s, and to 1.6 in South Korea at the end of the 1960s (Figs. 5.1 and 5.2). Though the overall rise in all three countries was not particularly large, the impact on the smaller peasants was great. The multiple-cropping index in Taiwan rose from 1.3 for farms with more than 5 hectares to 1.55, for farms with 2 to 5 hectares to 1.8, for farms with 1 to 2 hectares to 2.0, and for farms with less than 0.5 hectare to 2.1. Average days worked on the farm rose from 143 days per worker a year in the period 1921–1940 to 189 days from 1956 to 1970. In South Korea, labor input rose by about 40 percent between 1950 and 1965.

Finally, perhaps the most important factor in larger farm incomes and increased employment was crop diversification and commercialized farming. As rice yields and production rose, rice was substituted for the inferior grains (barley, millet, etc.) and sweet potatoes. Improved irrigation, roads, and other infrastructure allowed farmers to diversify into vegetables, pulses, fruits, sericulture, and animal and forestry products, with the output being sold to urban consumers. There was a general substitution of higher value crops for lower value ones such as grains because as yields rose rice replaced other grains, root crops, and other inferior carbohydrates in the diet. The higher value crops (and livestock) were labor-absorbing since machines were not used to replace or save labor. Two to three times more hours of labor per hectare were required for these new crops compared with the figures for rice. These structural shifts due to crop diversification were crucial in rural labor absorption and in reducing underemployment in monsoon

Table 5.3   Gross Value of Crops and Livestock in Taiwan, South Korea, and Japan
(Value in billion current national currencies, shares in percentage of total value in parentheses)

	Taiwan		South Korea		Japan	
	Average 1955–1960	Average 1965–1970	Average 1961–1966	Average 1971–1976	Average 1947–1952	Average 1957–1962
1. Rice	5.9 (41.0)	13.0 (34.4)	151.9 (46.6)	791.2 (41.0)	641.2 (54.4)	852.2 (47.4)
2. Other Grains	1.7 (11.8)	3.9 (10.3)	45.4 (13.9)	163.1 (8.5)	128.8 (11.0)	139.8 (7.8)
3. Other Crops	2.3 (15.6)	4.2 (11.2)	68.0 (20.8)	382.4 (19.8)	210.5 (17.9)	311.7 (17.3)
Subtotal (A)	9.9 (68.4)	21.1 (55.9)	265.3 (81.3)	1,336.7 (69.3)	980.5 (83.4)	1,303.7 (72.5)
4. Fruits	0.4 (3.0)	3.3 (8.7)	5.9 (1.8)	70.7 (3.7)	37.2 (3.2)	90.7 (5.0)
5. Vegetables	0.6 (4.2)	3.1 (8.3)	26.2 (8.0)	256.5 (13.3)	101.8 (8.7)	164.8 (9.2)
6. Livestocks	3.5 (24.3)	10.3 (27.1)	28.8 (8.8)	266.0 (13.8)	56.7 (4.8)	240.3 (13.4)
Subtotal (B)	4.5 (31.5)	16.7 (44.1)	60.9 (18.6)	593.2 (30.8)	195.7 (16.7)	495.8 (27.6)
Total Agriculture	14.5 (100.0)	37.8 (100.0)	326.1 (100.0)	1,929.7 (100.0)	1,176.2 (100.0)	1,799.5 (100.0)
Diversity Index	3.73	4.36	3.40	3.96	2.84	3.45
% change: diversity index		16.9		16.5		21.5
B/A	0.46	0.79	0.23	0.44	0.20	0.38
Changes in B/A (%)		71.7		91.3		90.0

Notes: (1) Diversity Index is computed using the Formula $1/\sum_{i=1}^{n}(y_i/y)^2$, i.e. the inverse of the sum of the squared ratio of each major branch in total value of agriculture production in current prices.
(2) In measuring structural change, Subtotal A which consists of rice, other grains, and other crops is considered the product of lower income elasticities and Subtotal B (fruits, vegetables and livestock) the product of higher income elasticities. South Korea's changes in diversity index and shares are overstated as it imported large amounts of rice and other grains.
(3) Similar tables were worked out for the Philippines, in both current and constant prices, for the the periods 1967–72 and 1977–82. Diversity indexes decreased from 3.69 to 3.53 (4.3% decrease) and B/A fell from .43 to .37 (14% decrease) in the current price version.

Sources: Taiwan data computed from Table T-2 of Y. Hayami and associates, ed., Agricultural Growth in Japan, Taiwan, Korea, and the Philippines. South Korea data computed from Yearbook of Agriculture and Forestry Statistics, various years. Japan data computed from Estimates of Long-Term Economic Statistic of Japan Since 1868, vol.9 (Agriculture and Forestry).

agriculture because these higher-value, nongrain crops require labor during the traditionally slack months. Many of the diversified crops are sold outside farm villages and require additional labor for processing and marketing. Production is not restricted by local consumption as much as is that of other crops. The increased production of nongrain crops implies a structural shift from low-income to high-income crops, and they are important factors in increased incomes and productivity in the agricultural sector.

Table 5.3 shows the index of structural change measuring crop diversification in Japan, Korea, and Taiwan. This index, similar to the diversification index computed as the reciprocal of the sum of the squared fraction of the value of major crops to the value of all crops, is a measure of agricultural structural changes based on the ratio of the percentage share of income-elastic crops (fruits, vegetables, livestock products) to the share of less income-elastic crops (rice and other cereals and other crops). The change was highest for Japan, followed by Taiwan and then South Korea, with the ratio of fruits, vegetables, and livestock products to grains and other crops reaching a level of .79 in Taiwan between 1965 and 1970 and .44 in Korea between 1971 and 1976. For Japan the index between 1947 and 1952 and between 1957 and 1962 when full employment was reached was 90 percent; for Taiwan between 1955 and 1960 and between 1965 and 1970 when full employment was reached it was 71.7 percent; and South Korea had the same index as Japan. (In the Philippines, where full employment has not yet been attained, it was − 14 percent.) These indexes are indicative of the direct role of diversified agriculture in employment absorption. The indirect roles of off-farm employment in agro-processing and the expansion of domestic demand are probably as important but are difficult to measure.

With increases in productivity, real farm wages began to rise in Taiwan from the early 1950s and in South Korea from the early 1960s (Figs. 5.1 and 5.2). Underlying these early rapid increases in the postwar decades were the historical heritages of institutions and infrastructure: systems of extension, credit, education, experimental stations and research centers, roads, electrification, irrigation, and so on. This heritage enabled all three countries to raise rice yields by approximately 25 percent during the 1910s, 1920s, and 1930s, at a time when yields were stagnant or falling in most other countries in Asia. The higher yields and productivity in the postwar years were due to marked improvements in institutions, technologies, and infrastructure, starting with land reform.

Off-Farm Incomes and Employment

The second method used to attain full employment in monsoon Asia was to increase off-farm employment opportunities (Figs. 5.1 and 5.2). Because new agricultural land was unavailable, multi cropping potentials quickly exhausted, and improvement of cultivars slow, family incomes and employment tended to rise slowly, too slowly to keep pace with non-farm incomes where productivity increased through the application of Western technologies. Perhaps because of this, Japan experienced a slow rate of increase in on-farm incomes in the 1960s and in the late 1970s, as did Taiwan in the late 1960s.

The rise in productivity and employment on the farm had a decisive impact on national income, and thereby contributed to the rise in aggregate domestic demand. There was a rapid rise (6.8 percent per year) in the rate of growth of real consumption in Taiwan during the 1950s. This was somewhat less than the annual rate of growth of exports (8 percent), but considering the much greater base from which consumption started out as compared to exports, the impact on national consumption was considerable in the 1950s. Hence, in Taiwan the rise in real farm incomes contributed through the expansion of the industrial and service sectors to the increase in off-farm employment which accelerated during the 1950s and 1960s, as was the case in Japan. In South Korea, consumption growth was 6.5 percent and exports grew by 28 percent between 1960 and 1970; consumption was only three times exports in 1960.[3] In part, the slow growth of Korean off-farm employment was due to its small consumption base and the regional concentration of the industrial base centered in two or three cities.

Off-farm employment before full employment is attained mainly occurs in construction and services and secondarily in manufacturing, which are mostly non-mechanized and labor-intensive. This is because most off-farm jobs must be seasonal with the workers returning to farm work during the peak seasons. In manufacturing employment, food processing and other agriculture-related industries and the garment and woodwork industries dominate. It is only after labor shortages and rapid wage rises that factories operating year-round find it necessary to move to outlying cities and towns to seek workers and pay more for off-farm employment. At this point farms must be mechanized to release labor for year-round work.

---

[3] From 1952 to 1962, off-farm incomes more than doubled from 1,600 per family to 3,900 in 1952 prices. *Taiwan Farm Family Survey of 1967* (JCRR, Taipei: 1970), p. 37. Consumption and export data are from the official national accounts.

Labor Release after Full Employment

Unless agriculture can release farm workers to other sectors (both industry and service) through labor-saving mechanization, migration will be restricted as the sustained increases in real farm family incomes

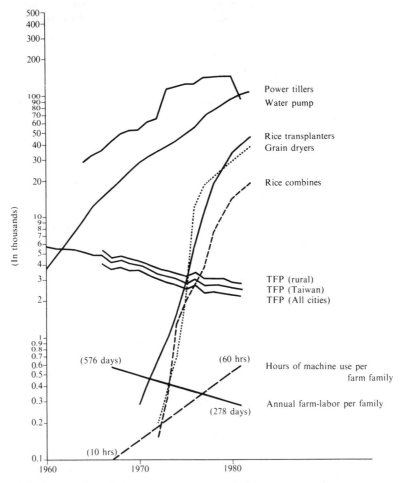

Figure 5.3   Agricultural machines owned by farm families in Taiwan.
Sources: Mechanization data from Tien-song Peng, *The Development of Agricultural Mechanization and Its Strategies in Taiwan*; fertility data from *Taiwan-Fukien Demographic Fact Book*; farm and mechanical labor per family from *Report of Farm Record-Keeping Families in Taiwan*, 1967 and 1981 issues.

continue to exceed the growth of the labor supply. With full employment, real wages in both the agricultural and industrial sectors acceler-
rate, as seen in Figs. 5.1 and 5.2 for farm wages and in Chapter 2 for
industrial wages. The accelerating real wages induce farm families and
industrial firms to turn to mechanized equipment to replace or save
labor. This occurred in Japan in the 1950s, in Taiwan from the late
1960s, and in South Korea from the 1970s, as machines became cheaper

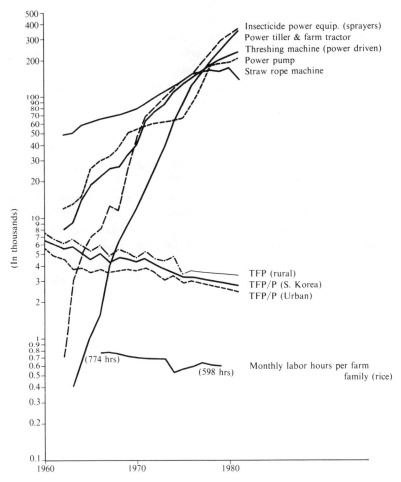

Figure 5.4   Agricultural machines owned by farm families in South Korea.
Sources: *Major Statistics of Korean Economy 1982*; TFP from *Korean
Institute for Family Planning* and *Statistics on Population and Family Plan-
ning in Korea*.

to use than manpower. As in Japan, this substitution made extensive use of miniaturized equipment powered by small electric motors and internal combustion engines and formed the basis for the rise in the elasticity of substitution and the acceleration of total factor productivity in all three countries. Figure 5.5 shows the rise in horsepower per worker in industry. In Taiwan it rose from 1.4 in the mid-1950s to 4.7 by the mid-1970s, and in South Korea from 1.1 in the early 1960s to 4.7 by the mid-1970s, indicating that mechanization spread quickly.

As noted in the previous chapter, from the point of view of direct substitution of machine power for manpower, it is the machines used during the busy times of monsoon paddy rice cultivation that are most effective in releasing labor, not the power sprayers, dusters, weeders, and driers which tend to reduce labor hours by speeding up operations in between the busy peaks. The latter machines are introduced first as wages of hired workers during planting and harvesting rise. Later on, with the migration or commuting of young workers to off-farm jobs, transplanting and reaping—the most labor-intensive operations of monsoon paddy growing—become mechanized. Figure 5.3 shows the sequence of the introduction of the different types of farm machinery in Taiwan.

Figure 5.1 shows that multiple cropping reached a peak around the mid-1960s and by the late 1960s began to decline as full employment was reached and there were insufficient workers for the lower-value inferior crops such as root crops. In South Korea, this point was reached around the 1970s.

By 1980, off-farm incomes in Taiwan had risen to 64 percent of total farm family incomes, but in South Korea the figure was only 25 percent while in Japan it was 79 percent. South Korea lagged behind Taiwan since accelerated growth occurred later and also since Korean development strategy depended much more on industrialization than on agriculture.

Although by 1980 both countries had approached the saturation level with respect to power cultivation and threshing, about half of farms were mechanically transplanted and reaped in Taiwan although in Korea the mechanization of the most labor-intensive paddy operations had not yet commenced (Figs. 5.3 and 5.4). Mechanization levels on Taiwan farms were low in the 1960s, but after full employment was attained there was a rapid shift from hand to power transplanting and reaping accompanied by an accelerated growth in off-farm incomes in the 1970s. South Korea was far behind Japan and Taiwan in mechanization, though its yields per hectare were as high as in Japan and higher than in Taiwan. In 1980 Korea retained one-third of its labor force in agriculture compared to one-fifth for Taiwan and one-tenth for Japan, despite the fact that the share of off-farm income was less than one-half that of Taiwan and one-third that of Japan.

Taiwan-Korean Contrasts in Early Agricultural Development

The rapid growth of farm family incomes in all three countries was achieved through physical infrastructure construction and the establishment of various institutions. The network of rural roads from the prewar period was extended to cover nearly all villages, in addition to the construction of additional railways, highways, and harbors; the rural areas were nearly completely electrified in Japan by the early 1960s, in Taiwan by the early 1970s, and in South Korea by the late 1970s. Most important for achieving higher yields and cropping intensity was the extensive construction of the irrigation infrastructure, which in 1975 covered 66 percent of farm households in Japan, 50 percent in Taiwan, and 45 percent in South Korea (FAO, 1981).

With independence from colonial rule, development of institutions was rapid in Korea and Taiwan. Land reform achieved the greatest success in Japan, some in Taiwan, and least in South Korea. The main reason for the differences was the extent to which rural institutions were improved to provide inputs hitherto supplied by landlords, and the extent to which peasants' work incentives and motivations were raised. The previous chapter showed how well rural institutions in Japan were developed to promote the growth of production. In Korea, however, the structure of agricultural and rural institutions was monolithically controlled at the top by the central government with little leeway for grassroots participation and initiatives. This was not only true for the various local government agencies but also for cooperatives and other rural institutions. While in the short run such tight controls may permit for efficiency in initiating and implementing policies, as in the adoption and quick dissemination of HYVs in the 1970s, in the long run policies established from Seoul were often unsuitable to the varying local conditions and to specific needs at the farm level as in the case of HYVs in the latter 1970s which were unable to resist blasts and collapsed in 1979 and 1980. The capabilities of peasants to make changes and improvements were not as extensively developed as in Taiwan and Japan. Authoritarian controls of farmers are also likely to lead to less than optimal allocation of government development funds, which appeared to have been insufficient for agriculture throughout most of the postwar decades.

Table 5.4   Average Farm Family Income and Savings by Size of Farm in Japan, Taiwan, and South Korea

Farm Size	Farm Family Income (1)	Off-farm Income (2)	Savings (3)	% (2)/(1)	% (3)/(1)
JAPAN					
Large (1.5 ha)					
1957 (¥1,000)	516.7	77.1	37.7	14.9	7.3
1980 (¥1,000)	4,514.6	2,145.5	708.0	47.5	15.7
Medium (1 to 1.5 ha)					
1957 (¥1,000)	373.2	92.5	21.2	24.8	5.7
1980 (¥1,000)	4,379.7	3,091.4	741.8	70.6	16.9
Small (<1 ha)					
1957 (¥1,000)	301.7	162.5	14.6	53.9	4.8
1980 (¥1,000)	4,565.0	4,215.9	971.6	92.4	21.3
TAIWAN					
Large (1.5 ha)					
1958 (NT $1,000)	28.5	4.1	10.0	14.4	35.1
1980 (NT $1,000)	363.4	154.2	157.1	42.4	43.2
Medium (1 to 1.5 ha)					
1958 (NT $1,000)	21.5	5.2	6.4	24.2	29.8
1980 (NT $1,000)	269.8	145.0	83.0	53.7	30.8
Small (<1 ha)					
1958 (NT $1,000)	17.9	9.0	4.4	50.3	24.6
1980 (NT $1,000)	224.2	157.0	56.2	70.0	25.1
SOUTH KOREA					
Large (1.5 ha)					
1968 (Won1,000)	301.7	43.1	67.4	14.3	22.3
1979 (Won1,000)	3,545.6	637.8	920.5	18.0	26.0
Medium (1 to 1.5 ha)					
1968 (Won1,000)	202.1	38.3	36.8	19.0	18.2
1979 (Won1,000)	2,467.1	664.3	535.8	26.9	21.7
Small (<1 ha)					
1968 (Won1,000)	131.3	45.9	11.1	35.0	8.5
1979 (Won1,000)	1,711.5	793.6	261.3	46.4	15.3

Sources: Various issues of *Farm Household Economy Survey* (Nōka keizai chōsa hōkoku) of Japan, *Report on the Results of Farm Household Economy Survey of South Korea* and *Report on Farm Record-Keeping Families in Taiwan*.

In Taiwan, below the authoritarian central political apparatus, the structure and operations on local levels were more democratic and participatory, not as much as in Japan but more so than in South

Korea. This was especially the case with agricultural institutions at the farm level such as the farmers' associations. The former head of the cooperatives association that spearheaded and guided agricultural development just as MITI did for Japanese industrialization has noted that cooperatives were "now of farmers and by farmers," and that "farmers rid themselves of the landlord-centered tradition of decision-making regarding production and marketing," and "are becoming more enterprising." These are similar to developments which occurred in Japan but not in South Korea (Shen, 1974).

Nevertheless, because the upper tier of Taiwan's political apparatus was undemocratically controlled, central government institutions behaved more like those in South Korea than those in Japan. The government taxed the farmers heavily (via land taxes, import duties, and commodity taxes), maintained extremely high fertilizer prices (monopolized by the government), and levied high import taxes on agricultural machinery. Perhaps a greater voice for the peasants would have left more income for human resource development, which Taiwan needs today more than some of its inefficient heavy industries such as iron and steel, petrochemicals, and automobile plants.

The funds forthcoming from Taiwan's central government for rural roads, major irrigation works, extension services, and agricultural education and research were probably as limited as in South Korea. Central government investment expenditures in Taiwan (including bank loans) for agriculture during 1976–1981 was only 5.7 percent, compared to Korea's 11 percent for the same period. Even when the more advanced stage of Taiwan's agriculture and the larger share of the labor force in Korean agriculture (34 percent to Taiwan's 20 percent) in 1980 are considered, the central government investment share was no larger than that in Korea. The share of households covered by irrigation in Taiwan in 1975 was only 5 percent higher than in Korea, and much of this was due to the efforts of local governments and farmers' associations, which also were responsible for the construction of facilities for various marketing services, fertilizer mixing, health, industry, feed processing, pesticide plants, and other activities besides bearing most of the costs of agricultural credit, extension, education, research services, and various investments. A good case can be made that the better performance of Taiwan's agriculture over Korea's was due not to the central government but to the efforts of local governments and farmers' associations. This is important in motivating farmers to produce efficiently and diligently, thereby increasing output without the need for additional input of labor as defined in Table 5.1.

Taiwan's farmers contributed more to overall growth than did their counterparts in South Korea. First of all, starting from the earlier period, Taiwan's agriculture contributed substantial amounts to total investment through net capital outflows while these were small in South Korea. The personal savings rate was 40 percent higher in Taiwan, despite high taxes and fertilizer costs. The smaller financial contributions from agriculture forced Korea to depend on its foreign borrowings to finance industrialization, as discussed below. Secondly, the rapid growth in production (and its diversification) from 1945 enabled Taiwan not only to save foreign exchange through fewer food imports and food self-sufficiency but to become a major source of exports. This meant that there was no need for the frenzied promotion of industrial output exportation with various subsidies and state assistance to big firms that was necessary in Korea.

Also reducing the need for increased industrial exports was the larger size of the domestic market (households) for industrial products in Taiwan. Both in 1966 and 1975 average farm family incomes (in U.S. dollars) were a little more than double the average in South Korea, with the Engel coefficient about 5 percent lower in Taiwan. Using the purchase of clothing as representative of the demand by farmers for industrial products, the average farm family in Taiwan purchased 15 percent more clothing in 1966 and 1975 than did a similar family in Korea.

Finally and most important, the inadequate development of agriculture bottled up a larger share of the labor force in the Korean farm sector, as discussed above. One insight from the postwar experience of Korea and Taiwan is that one major source of TFP acceleration is related to the absolute decline in the agricultural labor force under conditions of rising farm output, full employment, and expanding employment in industry, thus raising the elasticity of capital/labor substitution. In Taiwan the product per worker in agriculture increased by 4.2 percent, but in South Korea, where an absolute decline occurred only in the late 1970s, product per worker rose by only 2.1 percent (Tables 5.1 and 5.2). Similarly, on U.S. farms during the early decades of this century, TFP accelerated with the increasing use of tractors and other machines. This did not occur in Singapore, which has a tiny agricultural sector. Apparently when appropriate mechanized technologies are available, labor shortages induce the rapid substitution of farm labor which can then shift to urban employment at higher wages. Before mechanization the farm sector product per worker is substantially lower than that of other sectors, and the shift of workers raises the output in the nonagricultural sectors while the use of machines maintains and even raises output levels on the farm, thereby increasing the per-worker product of those remaining on the farm. Structural change, together with efficient equipment and a lower share of structure in capital formation, become the major sources of TFP growth.

Korea's hasty shift to industrialization has been justified on the grounds that its agriculture was nearly as highly developed as Japan's, and its amount of arable land the smallest in the world. This view is supported by data showing that Korean yields are higher than Taiwan's. Japan's average rice yields were higher than Korea's in the 1960s, 1970s, and early 1980s. Taiwan's yields were 10 percent lower largely because more extensive double cropping of rice entailed a trade-off between short maturation varieties and lower-yielding, better-tasting ones. Taiwanese did not like the taste and quality of rice developed at the International Rice Research Institute (IRRI), and today Korean consumers are also increasingly rejecting it. In the mid-1950s, before the great migration in Japan, arable land densities were about the same. Nor should the development of agriculture be judged by rice yields alone but by a host of other factors including multiple-cropping, diversification, mechanization, and off-farm employment as well.

That there is further potential for agricultural development in Korea was shown by the need to increase output of diversified crops which central planners from Seoul overlooked (but now are trying to rectify), and to increase rice yields. In the first half of the 1960s rice yields totalled 4.2 thousand metric tons, and these increased by 50 percent in the second half of the 1970s. In three decades, Korea's investment in agriculture was 30 percent less than Taiwan's. More investment would have permitted higher rice yields and greater diversification of crops (vegetables, fruits, and feed for livestock). Instead Korea opted to continue importing large amounts of food, about one-third of the excess of total imports over exports in the 1970s, in the hope of being able to finance imports with industrial exports. Even with food imports, its per capita supply was only 2,200 compared with 2,400 in Taiwan and 2,500 in Japan in the first half of the 1960s when the decision was made to go all-out for industrialization.

Industrial Development

In the immediate postwar years, independence from colonial controls enabled Korea and Taiwan to industrialize. They proceeded to develop industrial policies, institutions, and infrastructure intended to support labor-intensive industrialization. Domestic industries were protected in the 1950s but compelled to export in the 1960s. The 1970s saw movement into more capital-intensive industries, which accelerated in the latter 1970s in both countries, although much more so in South Korea than in Taiwan, as the industrialized countries began to protect their markets. Kwh per worker in Korea, which was about one-half that in Taiwan in 1964, equalled the Taiwan figure in 1979.

In trying to analyze the slower growth of nonagricultural TFP, we are confronted with the problem that there are no data for South Korea's industrial TFP (conventional) as separate from the service TFP for the entire period, while data for Taiwan are available. Thus, an analysis must be pieced together from various other data. Service product per worker in Korea grew faster than in Taiwan, 5 percent compared with 3 percent. The share of service sector investment in total capital formation was approximately one-third in both countries; thus, the difference in nonagricultural TFP growth in the two countries is related not to the service sector, but to the industrial sector. Compared with Taiwan's 4 percent (1952–80) (Table 5.2), TFP data available for South Korea's manufacturing sector for 1966–1975 show that it increased at a rate of 2.1 percent yearly, in part because of large minuses in the heavy, chemical, iron and steel, nonferrous basic metal, transport equipment, and paper/pulp industries. From 1975 to 1979, labor productivity in light manufacturing grew at 12 percent a year, compared with 10 percent in heavy manufacturing, dropping from 14 percent in the 1971–1975 period.[4]

There are a number of similarities in Korea's and Taiwan's pattern of industrial development. Import-substitution growth began to reach saturation around the end of the 1950s and manufacturing output growth slowed. Both countries began to take major steps to shift to export promotion around the early 1960s, and both were remarkably successful. Compared with other colonized Asian countries, industries were more highly developed during the colonial period, and a substantial group of technicians, skilled workers, and entrepreneurs, as well as factories and infrastructure, remained to form the foundation for industrialization in the 1950s. In the early postwar period Taiwan received a large influx of immigrants with industrial experience, and Korea received compatriots from the north and Japan. Both countries were recipients of grants from the United States in the 1950s to make up for deficits in the balance of payments and the budget. They then came under heavy pressure from the United States to reduce deficits by increasing exports beginning in the 1960s. An opportunity to comply came when quotas were fixed on Hong Kong and Japanese textile

---

[4] 1975–79 labor productivity was computed from *Korean Statistical Yearbook*, 1980, pp. 76–79.

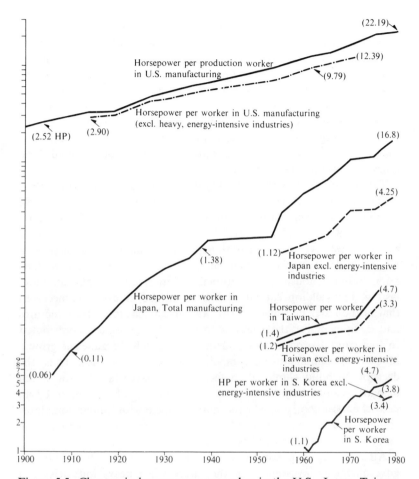

Figure 5.5 Changes in horsepower per worker in the U.S., Japan, Taiwan, and Korea, 1900 to 1980.

Sources: U.S. data computed from *Historical Statistics of the U.S.* and updated by *1980 Annual Survey of Manufactures—Fuels and Electric Energy Consumed*. Japan data computed from *Long-Term Estimate Statistics* and updated by *Japan Statistical Yearbook*. Taiwan data computed from various censuses of commerce and industries. Korean data computed from various issues of *Korean Statistics Yearbook*.

exports by the United Kingdom and the United States in the late 1950s. The full employment in the United States and Japan in the 1960s allowed investment from these countries to flow into Korea and Tai-

wan, and they became major sources of supply of labor-intensive manufactures, such as textiles, garments, shoes, plywood, and electronics.
Mass distributors from the United States like Sears, Montgomery
Ward, J.C. Penney, and other chain stores and Japanese trading companies and joint ventures began to do business in the two countries,
teaching local entrepreneurs to produce high-quality goods for export,
especially garments and then consumer electronics. Without all these,
export promotion would not have been successful and perhaps would
not have been undertaken in the first place, as the experience of the
Philippines suggests. Being under less pressure to export, the Southeast
Asian countries with large plantation export sectors showed little
interest in industrial export promotion.

The pressures to export manufactures were heavier on Korea than
on Taiwan. The less developed agricultural sector in Korea was unable
to supply (in per capita terms) farm exports, savings, and a domestic
market for industrial products. From 1975 Korea embarked on an
accelerated heavy industrialization program and invested heavily in
huge complexes of plant, equipment, railways, storage facilities, harbors, utilities, housing, recreational facilities, and so on—all long-
lasting, low-yielding capital stocks. It can be plausibly conjectured
that in the latter half of the 1970s, the investment in costly structures
and equipment for the heavy industrialization program contributed
to low capital productivity and did not help to increase the growth
of TFP in manufacturing compared to previous decades. Thus, the
decision to build shipbuilding facilities for large tankers for which
demand is not likely to increase in the future, the enormous Ulsan
petrochemical complex, which cannot compete with similar complexes
coming onstream in the Middle East, and a new heavy engineering
complex were major mistakes in the 1970s.

All these large expenditures for heavy industries were justified by the
government as investment for the future when heavy industries will
have grown out of infancy and South Korea will move into a fully
industrialized economy like that of Japan. But the underlying assumption that the primary, basic industries such as iron/steel, petrochemicals, paper/pulp, aluminum and copper smelting, and heavy engineering are subject to the infant industry argument may be questionable.
Large countries like India and China with their larger markets and
scientific communities have failed to develop their heavy industries

[5] The role of the U.S. mass distributors like Sears and later European department
stores and supermarkets in the development of exports in Japan in the early 1950s,
Hong Kong in the late 1950s, and in the 1960s in Taiwan, Korea, and Singapore may
have been crucial in the rise of NIC exports, especially consumer electronics.

to maturity and export during the past two and a half decades. The technology and management of these industries have become extremely complex, and each integrated industry comprises a dozen or so separate branches of industry. Not only huge R & D expenditures but also a certain minimum of highly developed downstream industries to work with are required, especially in the machinery sector. Japan has been able to develop midstream, capital-intensive industries, but China and India have not. Taiwan's iron and steel plants are already obsolete; Korea's Pohang complex, built only a few years ago, is beginning to be outdated. When Korea's president visited Japan in September 1984, eight of the 20 new technologies he requested from Japan were for the iron and steel industry.

Even in the short run these heavy industries are highly risky enterprises above and beyond the technological factor. The iron and steel industry is increasingly becoming a "sunset" industry, like railroads and shipping in the past, as one developed nation after another nationalizes or subsidizes it. Even the most efficient iron and steel industry (in Japan) finds its rate of return falling and is forced to diversify into other industries. The Koreans (and also the Taiwanese) have been able to operate at full capacity and penetrate foreign markets under subsidies of about 20 to 30 percent, but they face the prospect of rising tariffs. Since the iron and steel industry is necessary for military purposes, the industrialized countries are not likely to give it up.

Industries like petrochemicals, paper/pulp, and copper smelting face problems of raw material supplies which must be obtained cheaply to be competitive. It is difficult for countries like South Korea to develop these into viable industries, as raw material prices are too high and plants are too small to produce competitively. Because cheaper sources of supply and larger plants are available elsewhere, Korean industries will become increasingly expensive and must be subsidized in order not to "cascade" high-cost products down to lower-stream fabricating industries. In the heavy engineering industries such as electric generators and transformers and automobiles, the need is for the creation of a large group of smaller subcontracting firms for quality production of components and parts, along with R & D for improved designs and innovation. In these industries excess capacity and poor product quality further increase the problems for the future.

Another problem with heavy industrialization is its cost. Gross fixed capital formation in constant prices for heavy industries in the period 1975–1979 amounted to three-fourths of the totals for agriculture and light industries. If government-financed infrastructure, especially for heavy industries, is included the shares may be equal. Loans

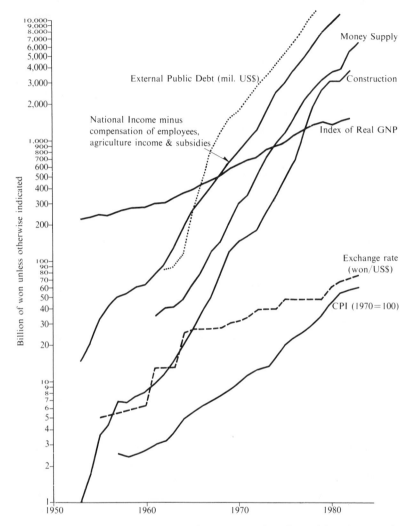

Figure 5.6. South Korea: Postwar changes in various financial and economic series

Sources: National Income in Korea 1982, IBRD World Tables 1980, and *Key Indicators of the Asian Development Bank* (April 1984).

to heavy industries rose from 40 percent of total loans in 1975 to 54 percent in 1980, implying that accelerated expansion of heavy industries in the late 1970s entailed a reduction in the share of financial resources going to light industries and agriculture. The heavy industry share of

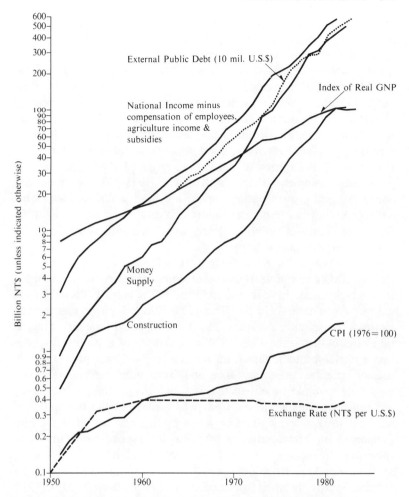

Figure 5.7 Taiwan: Postwar changes in various financial and economic series. *Sources: National Income of the ROC, IBRD World Tables 1980,* and *Key Indicators of the Asian Development Bank* (April 1984).

total loans and investments rose by 5 percent (plus perhaps the 2 percent increase in the share of other sectors largely supporting the infrastructure), entailing a 7 percent reduction in the share of agriculture and light industry (to 37 percent in the period 1972–1976 and to 30 percent, 1977–1979). Investments rose from 1,134 billion won to 2,687 in 1975 prices, or 2.4-fold, compared to 1,200 billion won to 2,100 for light industries, or 1.8-fold.

Another unfortunate consequence of the haste at which the export of industrial output was pushed in Korea was the concentration of industry in a handful of giant firms located in two or three cities. This prevented the growth of off-farm income and employment of farm families needed to permit farm family incomes to keep pace with the growth of urban incomes. Kim and Sloboda have noted that "rural industrialization that has occurred has been concentrated in the rural hinterlands of the metropolitan cities." In contrast, G. Ranis has shown that Taiwan's industrialization has been extensively regionalized, as a result of its labor intensity, good network of roads, and rural electrification. Taiwan had 50 percent more paved roads and railways per square kilometer than did Korea in 1973–1974. A more balanced regional growth pattern would not have left Korea with what Vincent Brandt has termed a country of "rural isolation." Brandt has found the degree of isolation closely correlated with variations in regional farm per capita income.[6]

Another reason for Korea's large labor force in agriculture was the slow spread of mechanization, as noted above; net rural-urban migration, which should have increased in the 1970s, actually declined from 2.3 million in 1966–1970 to 1.7 in 1970–1975. More mechanized cultivators, transplanters, reapers, and threshers could have raised migration rates closer to the 1966–1970 level in spite of grain price policies that contributed to higher farm income levels. Grain price supports mainly benefited the large farms and farms near metropolitan areas with only minimal benefit to the vast majority of the predominantly self-sufficient, smaller farms from which most of the migrants and off-farm workers came. This is shown by the fact that while the proportion of on-farm (excluding off-farm) incomes of farm families to their nonfarm incomes remained constant throughout the 1970s (falling somewhat in the latter half of the 1970s), the Gini coefficient of nonagricultural family incomes worsened from 0.36 to 0.41, 1970 to 1975, owing to the substantial rise (about 10 percent) in the share of the highest three deciles. The impact of price supports may be minimal in keeping workers on the farm when the on-farm incomes of most farmers are not rising as fast as wages in urban areas, as the experience of Japan in the 1960s has shown. It may be concluded that Korean capital growth in industry accelerated in the 1970s compared with previous decades, but this did not lead to an increase in output.

Besides the impact on TFP, the failure to release enough farm workers through mechanization contributed to labor shortages when the unemployment rate fell below 4 percent in the late 1970s. Real wages

---

[6] All cited in Repetto et al. (1981).

rose faster than labor productivity in manufacturing (20 percent as against 11 percent, 1976–1979), and consumer prices accelerated, necessitating a major devaluation in 1980. Throughout the postwar decades, consumer prices and foreign exchange rates rose much faster than in Taiwan (Fig. 5.6).

The slower growth of TFP and farm family incomes contributed to the slower growth of personal savings in South Korea compared with Taiwan. Excessive growth of capital formation without sufficient domestic savings forced Korea to borrow large sums abroad as the deficits in the current account averaged tenfold more than in Taiwan (3.4 percent compared with 0.3 percent), resulting in an external public debt twice as much as Taiwan's (29 percent of GNP compared with 13 percent). Since these debts carry large interest burdens, debt servicing is likely to be one of the constraints in the 1980s (Figs. 5.6 and 5.7).

Finally, though both countries were able to complete demographic transitions and reduce income disparities, Taiwan ended 1980 with a much lower total fertility rate (2.5 compared to Korea's 3.0), while South Korea's income disparities began to rise in the 1970s. (See Chapters 10 and 11.) The world recession in the early 1980s hit South Korea much harder than Taiwan, and the Korean per capita GDP in constant prices fell below the 1979 level in 1980 and 1981. Fortunately, Korea's leaders were quick to reverse their strategies, now favoring the support of agriculture and fewer capital-intensive and more technology-intensive industries such as electronics and other machinery industries where the highly trained laborers with strong work ethics appear to have a comparative advantage.

Finally, the sources of the social tensions that have frequently erupted in the form of student demonstrations were in the rural areas. Demonstrations were led by students from the provinces, and the strongest support for them came from the farmers.

At bottom, the unstable growth with greater inflation, devaluation, external debt, income inequality, and social tensions in Korea compared with Taiwan (or Japan) are traceable to its premature industrialization strategy aggravated by its impulsive jump into heavy industries before its agricultural sector was ready to support so much industrialization (see Figs. 5.6 and 5.7). Despite the fact that the growth rates for the two countries were the same, South Korea's construction expenditures rose much more sharply, particularly in the 1970s. The acceleration was largely due to infrastructure and plant construction for heavy industrialization since the national transport network and irrigation works were not as developed as in Taiwan. Apparently the returns from construction in the 1970s with low capacity utilization and subsidies were not as large as in the 1960s or as in Taiwan, and national income minus wages, farm incomes, and subsidies grew more slowly. Since construction expenditures entail payments of wages and purchases of local materials beyond the available savings, they contributed to Korea's steeper rise in the cost of living index and external borrowings compared with Taiwan's. Thus, Figs. 5.6 and 5.7, together with the transition figures in Chapter 3, show how different the impact was from the strategies pursued by the two countries despite their numerous similarities. It shows how important it is to pursue agricultural development in the early stages of transition and then to switch slowly to an industrial strategy at exactly the right point of time in the transition.

The question may be asked: how was it that South Korea made such a mistake and Taiwan did not? This is not easy to answer, and many elements are involved, including historical forces which have made Korean society, both North and South, more action-oriented than Japanese or Chinese society. In 1974, 1975, and 1976 the North Koreans also suddenly began to buy huge amounts of heavy industrial equipment (nearly $2 billion) on a turnkey basis. Without the capability to operate this equipment, they soon defaulted on loans to Japan, Germany, and other Western countries, and found themselves cut off completely from the transfer of technologies. A major contributory element to the South Korean situation was the authoritarian decision-making atmosphere under President Park Chung Hee, a great admirer of prewar Japanese achievements. Major shifts such as the one to heavy industrialization have vast impacts on agriculture, light industries, labor, consumers, and the intellectual community. Such decisions cannot be made strictly on scientific and rational grounds since it was impossible to foresee the jump in oil prices in 1979, the slump in the world economy, the rise in the cost of foreign borrowing, the bad weather in 1980, and so on. It may be that South Korea's military, worried about the North pushing into so many heavy industries, decided to act swiftly to counter the North. But this would not have been possible without the military authoritarianism of Park Chung Hee's regime. If full consultations were made, compromises could have minimized the shift to heavy industries and would have saved billions of dollars.

The Korean style could be referred to as command planning, similar to the communist style, with decisions made from the Blue House and minimal consultations in the interest of trying to do things "right away." As L. Jones and Il Sakong (1980) noted: "We conclude by characterizing the Korean implementation system as a Myrdalian 'hard' state. . . ." To change to more participatory ways, government controls of financial institutions, farmers' organizations, and of politics may have to be relaxed. Above all, changes in industrial relations institutions are required. They cannot continue to be, as Eberhard Liebau describes, so authoritarian:

"Especially since the early seventies . . . the government has pursued an industrial relations policy of coercive containment of socioeconomic conflicts and problems. To secure its one-sided concept of maximizing economic growth against any social disturbances, government imposed a freeze on any further development of industrial relations by banning autonomous collective bargaining and any collective action and by strictly controlling and weakening the trade unions. Since then almost any kind of industrial conflicts had to be administered by a badly prepared and poorly qualified bureaucracy with the consequence that most of the conflicts did not find adequate resolution and continued burning under the surface. Under these circumstances there was no chance at all for the workers as well as no encouragement for the employers to develop their organizations in order to find suitable structures and mechanisms for the resolution of open or hidden disputes and grievances [leading to] the sudden outburst of heavy' industrial disputes and outburst of severe inner-trade union conflicts by the end of the year 1979. . . ." (Liebau, 1980).

In the last sentence, the author was referring to the rise in labor-management disputes which quadrupled in the 1970s and which burst out into a rash of strikes, sit-ins, and other forms of demonstrations in 1980, despite their illegality. Just as V. Brandt found that "the more critical obstacle to successful rural development has been a lack of institutional mechanism to provide the organizational linkages to bring about an effective coordination of efforts," so in industrial development there must be good working relationships between labor, management, and government.

Despite authoritarian central government rule, Taiwan's labor-management relationships were closer to those of Japan than of Korea. Reversing the prewar practices, labor unions were legalized and collective bargaining was required, but strikes were prohibited. Unionization was slow to start but as larger units of industrial production came into existence, unions began to be organized, and by the end of the 1970s there were one million members in 1,600 unions. But collective bargaining, being a contradiction of the non-confrontational values of monsoon Asians, was slow to take root, and the government had to encourage the formation of factory councils to handle day-to-day disputes to promote work efficiency and welfare. By 1973, there were 246 councils operating in factories (Djang, 1980).

Employees were infrequently dismissed, and this, together with increases in practices such as year-end bonuses (averaging the equivalent of two months' salary) and various fringe payments, contributed to good morale and efficiency.

The relation between government and business enterprises in Taiwan is also closer to that of Japan than Korea since it is more cooperative and consultative and less authoritarian. An example of this is the National Vocational Training Fund whereby half of the proceeds of a payroll tax is reimbursed to industries willing to establish approved vocational training centers which, together with substantial on-the-job training, made possible the rapid expansion of the skilled labor force that has been important in accelerated industrial growth.

With the rural sector reaching full employment in the latter 1960s, and the industrial sector growing rapidly, overall unemployment in Taiwan fell to its lowest level in 1973 with an excess of demand for industrial workers over the supply of job seekers reaching its peak. Wages of the lowest-paid workers began to increase more rapidly than those of higher-paid workers, with monthly wages in lower-paying industries such as food, textiles, and leather products rising faster than in the other industries (21 percent against 18 percent).

There are no direct data on the rates of displacement of workers by machines or replacement of old machines by new ones. But there is other information indicating that displacement was extensive. According to the annual Industrial Commercial Census, the machinery industries grew from the 1950s annual rate of 9 percent to 30 percent from the mid-1960s through the early 1970s, although part of their product was exported. That mechanization was taking place in the labor-intensive industries is shown by the fact that horsepower per worker in beverages, tobacco, textiles, garments, furniture, leather, printing, metal, and transport equipment which stood at 1.0 in 1954 rose to 2.4 in 1971 and then doubled in a few years by 1976 with full employment, equalling a growth rate of 14.4 percent per year as compared to 3.2 percent in the 1954–1971 period. Taiwan's industrial growth was labor-intensive. Value added per employed person in manufacturing was $860 in 1971, only one-twentieth the United States figure and a little less than one-tenth of Japan's total in 1971. Even in the most capital-intensive, knowledge-intensive industries, it was only one-half that of Japan in 1976. South Korea sought to catch up with Taiwan, not only by shifting rapidly into heavy industries but by the importation of metal-working machinery which rose 26 percent each year from 1953 to 1977. Measured by horsepower per worker, Korea's 1955 level was only 40 percent of Taiwan's until the end of 1970s when they became equal. The growth rate of labor and net total factor productivity in the 1970s was twice that of Taiwan, which started industrialization earlier without the interruption of a civil war. Although favorable to labor productivity, Korea's attempt to develop quickly both the light and heavy industries ended in a near disaster. Wages rose much more rapidly than productivity as the scarcity of industrial labor ended with inflation, devaluation, and a huge foreign debt by the end of the 1970s, and industry was concentrated in the hands of 50 large enterprises.

Summary and Concluding Remarks

Before the onset of the world recession, both Taiwan and South Korea moved swiftly toward industrialized society with the industrial labor force exceeding that in agriculture. There was a difference in the patterns as Korea shifted more strongly to industrialization in the 1960s with a heavier emphasis on capital-intensive industrialization in the 1970s. This difference shows up in the TFP growth which in South Korea was much lower than in Taiwan. In this chapter, I have chosen to account for this difference in TFP growth by focusing on the reasons for the slower growth of total output and the faster growth of total input in South Korea, rather than by dealing directly with the residual as in growth accounting. The interest is more in input substitution elasticities, and no attempt is made to partition off the various sources such as education and scale economies. Educational levels were about the same in both countries, with Korea slightly ahead in rates of enrollment in secondary and higher education and in literacy levels. Not much difference was to be expected from their scale economies. Both economies were predominantly small scale in industry, services, and agriculture, and with a population twice as large in Korea but with lower per capita income. In foreign aid received from the United States, the amount per capita was higher in South Korea, but this excess largely made up for the destruction in the Korean War.

The findings point to the relative neglect of agricultural development and a too-early shift to industrialization, especially heavy industrialization, as the underlying explanation for the slower growth of output and the faster growth of total inputs in Korea as compared to Taiwan. Agricultural output would have grown faster if more attention had been paid to growing higher-value non-grain crops, to improving agricultural institutions such as cooperatives which generate scale economies in small-unit production, to building the more extensive rural infrastructure needed for higher yields, to promoting more multiple cropping and more diversified, commercialized agriculture, and, above all, to creating more off-farm employment and migration. The rapid decline in the agricultural labor force (accompanied by increases in output) through mechanization was a major source of TFP growth in Taiwan, as it was in Japan in the 1950s and 1960s.

Korea's premature emphasis on industrialization left its farm families with incomes too low to absorb industrial output and to save enough to supply the required capital to industry, and unable to produce enough to feed the population, forcing the country to look abroad for markets, loans, and food. Korea started the 1980s with the highest foreign debt per capita in Asia (Taiwan had the lowest), unused capacities in heavy industries, and mounting unrest and tensions as income disparities grew. The continued heavy dependence on exports forced the government to keep the large conglomerates afloat with loans and subsidies even though many of these were inefficient and shaky with heavy debt burdens.

Korea is fortunate in having manpower with an exceptionally strong determination to work and excel, but the future may be difficult. Perhaps it may be time to let some of the big firms go bankrupt and switch to more stable and balanced growth with much more attention paid to the sectors which have been left behind, especially small farmers and businesses. The argument that the big firms must be bailed out to maintain employment is a lame one. They should be declared bankrupt and assets sold to others to provide the jobs for future growth. Only in this way can more credit be made available for the peasants and small firms, and domestic incomes and aggregate demand increased.

A more satisfied populace may serve the aims of national defense better than incessant attempts to maximize exports. Macrostrategies of development affect the whole population from the top of the hierarchy to the bottom, across all classes, and over the length and breadth of the country. The prewar Japanese experience and that of Korea demonstrate the utmost importance of maintaining a finely tuned balance in the development of agriculture and industry if social consensus is to remain intact for sustained, stable growth.

With the global economy slowing down, Korea would have been in great difficulty in the latter 1980s had it not been for the spurt of the yen to high levels in 1986. The outlook for Korea's exports, as well as those of the other NICs, is extremely good as the NICs replace

Japanese exports everywhere and as Japanese firms move production out of Japan—to the NICs, in many cases. Labor shortages are likely to occur in the future, and this may be the time for South Korea and Taiwan to open up their markets for diversified agricultural products and lower-value industrial products to South and Southeast Asian exports, as labor is shifted to sophisticated industrial products and services.

CHAPTER 6

Hong Kong and Singapore:
Accelerated Growth with Limited Supplies of Labor and Food and a Small Domestic Market

B esides the Malaysian outpacing of Sri Lanka, the catching up of Thailand to the Philippines, and the spectacular growth of Japan, Taiwan, and South Korea, the other major surprise in postwar Asian growth was the impressive growth of the small city-states of Hong Kong and Singapore compared with the lackluster growth of the giants of Asia, India, and China. When Singapore separated from the Malaya Federation in the mid-1960s, most Singapore economists were pessimistic over the future of Singapore with its population of less than 2 million and were envious of the huge internal markets of China and India with their several hundred millions.

However, it appears that over the years large countries can be handicapped by a number of factors which can outweigh the advantages of large internal markets. The smaller the country, the greater the ease of communication, resulting in savings in public utilities and transportation. Much more important, it is easier to reach nationwide consensus on strategies and policies for development and to implement them administratively. In countries like India the central political leadership must devote most of its time to the huge provinces with obstreperous oligarchies in the numerous cities and to the vast rural hinterlands of various provinces. Even though the Chinese Revolution wiped out provincial oligarchies, the leadership in Peking must still contend with the power of the provincial bureaucracies. It took Indonesia two decades to achieve national cohesion with the might of its armed forces at the cost of being saddled with a military heirarchy of questionable capability in national development governance. A small country like Singapore is not without heterogeneities and diversities in ethnicity, religion, and language. But whereas the leadership needs to deal with one set of heterogeneities, in a veritable league of nations like India there are many sets of heterogeneities. Historically in India it was Hinduism, and in China the use of the character script and Confucianism, that helped in holding these vast empires together. (In Indonesia it was the military power of the Dutch and the force of Islam.)

In terms of external and scale economies, a small country is usually an island, an archipelago, or a peninsula with easy access to marine transportation. Due to 20th century technology, ocean transport is superior to land transport for long-distance hauling. Inputs can be bought more cheaply from overseas sellers than from other provinces, and scale economies can be acquired with overseas markets. But this requires that industrial efficiency to meet international standards must be achieved as quickly as possible without a period of "seasoning" through sales to the domestic market.

In the process of growth the greater importance of the institutional over the technological factors in the size of nations is illustrated by Western experience before the 20th century. The rapid rise of an island nation like the United Kingdom and of small nations like Switzerland, the Netherlands, Belgium, Sweden, Norway, and Denmark, which all had populations of less than 5 million in the 19th century, compares with the slow growth of Czarist Russia, Spain, Italy, Austria-Hungary, Poland, Rumania, Germany before Bismarck, France before the revolution, and Italy, which were all held back by the power of the large feudal nobility in the hinterlands. Even though territorially large, the United States, Canada, and Australia had no feudal nobility to obstruct modern economic growth. And unlike the Latin American countries and the Philippines, Thailand wiped out the rural oligarchies. It is not so much the size of a country and its domestic market, but its power structure, that seems relevant.

City-states feel a compelling need to export, first to earn foreign exchange in order to import food and other raw materials (such as hides, leather, vegetable and animal oils, crude rubber, wood and pulp, fibers, minerals, and fuel materials), and then to pay for the import of equipment and machinery to sustain the industrialization drive after the labor market tightens. This can only be done through greater efficiency in the production of goods and services by depending on highly competitive private enterprise in an open economy that can import tariff-free food and other consumer goods, thus keeping living costs and industrial input costs low. By subsidizing housing and education, the costs of shelter and good manpower are also kept low.

In the beginning of postwar growth, the service sector was predominant in the economy of the city-states, and it had to be efficient, first to supply external economies to the commodity sector in the form of efficient financial, transport, communication, training, public utilities, and governmental services, and then to export services to earn foreign exchange. Thus, the service sector earned foreign exchange by supplying merchandising and financial services to the traders and financiers of other countries, by carrying foreign goods in international shipping and transport services, and by becoming a center of tourism and of headquarters of international companies doing regional business. Between 1974 and 1983, the services in Hong Kong earned accumulated net foreign exchange of HK£70 billion, helping to pay for net imports of goods worth £96 billion; in Singapore, from 1970 to 1982, net service exports amounted to £58 billion compared with £77 billion in net imports. The unique characteristic of the service sector in the city-states was its ability to earn foreign exchange. Further, in the absence of an agricultural sector, it must be the source of surplus capital and labor for the initial industrialization effort. It can be hypothesized that the key sector in the initial stage of the development of city-states was the service sector with its modern institutions of merchandising, marketing, financing, and public services, and the accompanying physical infrastructures, just as in the early stages of the development of rural states it was the agricultural sector that held the key to takeoff. Unlike vast agrarian nations such as India and China with their large domestic markets, the city-states could not from the outset ignore exports, particularly because with a small domestic market their industries and services had to acquire scale economies largely through external markets.

But the extraordinarily rapid growth of the city-states was partly due to certain important advantages that the absence of a large hinterland conferred. There was no powerful, traditional landed oligarchy to contend with politically, but rather merchant and financial houses which saw advantages in developing export-oriented industrialization. They exploited the great advantage of the strong work ethic nurtured by Confucian culture.

Nevertheless, these were no more than potential blessings in disguise, in the same way that the lack of land and resources was a challenge to Japan, Taiwan, and South Korea to develop intensive rice growing with high efficiency. The response of the labor force to these challenges must be positive if they are to be converted into real blessings. For the policymakers, there were few options open, given the limited supplies of food, raw materials, and labor, the small internal market, and the strong pressures for rapid growth from a dynamic population willing to work and save to establish an open, free market economy based on individual and private enterprise.

Historical Legacies

Unlike the other British colonies in Asia, Singapore and Hong Kong were not originally established as places where the British could profit from plantations and other agricultural enterprises by exploiting large forces of Asian labor. They were intended to be port cities where British mercantile houses could conduct commerce and finance between China, Malaya, Indonesia, India, and other Asian countries as efficiently as in England. Hence in both colonies the British established systems of courts and laws evolved in England and conducive to the efficient and smooth operation of business enterprises. These arrangements soon attracted an increasing number of people from China. Brushing aside various discriminatory obstacles, they grabbed whatever opportunities opened up in the colonial system, and soon there was a mushrooming of Chinese merchant houses and banks and the growth of a large class of Chinese clerks versed in modern business practices and skills. Despite some problems, this was a far cry from the agrarian abuses that left large segments of the agrarian colonies hostile to the British in South Asia. The predominantly commercial character of the city colonies required a broader system of public education to train workers for the service occupations. With the opening of educational facilities and rising family incomes, the ideals of learning taught by Confucianism, which places the scholar at the peak of the class pyramid, came within the reach of Chinese families, and a highly literate and educated population had emerged by the eve of World War II. Free trade and laissez-faire capitalism made hard work and efficiency necessary for survival in the competitive markets, and manpower with high capability developed. The service sector, not only commerce and finance but also public and personal services, emerged from the prewar decades as probably the most efficient and modern in all of Asia.

The Chinese who came to the city-states, like those who migrated to other countries around the rim of the South China Sea (Nanyang Chinese), from the 19th century worked hard and saved. In alien environments and under foreign governments, they knew that they could not depend on the banks, government, and other institutions of the new countries for assistance in their businesses or to cope with family misfortunes. Through diligence, frugality, self-reliance, and their own initiative and effort they struggled to move ahead and soon began to thrive under British colonial rule. Not all prospered, but those who did established institutions to cope with the new environment. The owners of the family enterprises in the main developed paternalistic but humanistic industrial relation systems, providing for nearly all the basic needs of their workers: housing and feeding them, taking care of their health, educational, and recreational needs, and sharing with them their trials and tribulations. This encouraged most of the employees to work willingly from dawn to dusk throughout the week, thus attaining high levels of productivity.

Various associations and groups were established to share finances, technological information, and marketing know-how, and contacts were extended to counterpart groups in other areas around the South China Sea. This network was very useful to the Chinese community in the region. In the family-centered economy of the Nanyang Chinese, under the suspicious and hostile foreigners, secrecy and self-reliance were paramount and strength depended on a large family labor force. Birth rates were high, especially among the higher income groups, and this with constant immigration allowed the populations to increase.

Finally, one legacy of the past essential to the understanding of the postwar decades was a century of effective political institutions, including legislative councils to advise the heads of the colonies. This was a restricted but effective consultative and participatory institution established in the 19th century which, though it fell far short of a democratic governance, enabled the voices of different ethnic and economic groups to be heard. Together with an open economy, impartial administration of law and order, and the network of associations, this was an important step towards egalitarianism. But the fact remains that the highly motivated, pragmatic immigrants with their ideals of Confucian political ethics played an important role in keeping the British governments efficient, effective, and responsive. All the foregoing adds up to the inheritance of an economy with a strong and efficient system of competitive markets. Many agrarian developing countries started out without such markets, which work well in the West because of the forces and institutions that have created them.

All this presents a sharp contrast to the legacy countries like Sri Lanka, Burma, India, Indonesia, the Philippines, and Vietnam inherited. In the city-states, most of the prewar institutions were retained in the early postwar decades and extended, modified, and adapted later on. Indeed, in the case of Hong Kong not even independence was sought as the populace feared being absorbed by the giant neighbor, and the colonial government largely retained most of the old systems, improving them as new challenges emerged.

Nevertheless, in the early years of the postwar period, the prospects for Hong Kong and Singapore looked dim compared with those for

Sri Lanka, the Philippines, and Malaysia. Without industries and a large plantation sector for export and to spark growth, even the future of the strong service sector, which was still heavily dependent on the expansion of the commodity sector, looked well-nigh hopeless, as the entrepôt trade began to shrink as neighboring countries attained independence. The closing of the huge British military base in the 1960s was an additional blow to a Singapore beset with unemployment. How these adversities were overcome in the next three decades and how the service sector in the city-states emerged as the strongest and most efficient in all of Asia are described in the following sections. It is well to note that increases in productivity in the service sector have been the most difficult to achieve in Western economic growth, in large part because mechanized technologies were less applicable than in commodity sectors, although the emerging electronic revolution will change this situation. After having raised productivity to high levels in the past decades and with current labor shortages, the city-states are now in a position to take full advantage of the electronic revolution in services; unfortunately, the same cannot be said for most countries outside of East Asia and Malaysia, which have surplus labor.

The Record of Postwar Growth

Basic growth data are shown in the tables of Chapter 3. Hong Kong early registered the highest GDP growth rate in all of Asia for the period 1950–1980, with 9.5 percent, higher than Taiwan's 8.5 percent and Singapore's 8.1 percent. Its population and employment growth were also highest in Asia, 3.2 percent and 4.9 percent, respectively. But the growth of product per capita was exceeded by Singapore, whose rate was 6.0 percent as compared to 6.2 percent. Japan had the highest at 6.9 percent. Hong Kong's product per worker grew at 4.7 percent annually, equal to Taiwan's and higher than Singapore's 4.0 percent. The highest was in Japan, which grew 6.3 percent. The better performance of Hong Kong than Singapore is related to its earlier start. But it must be said that the Hong Kong data for the 1950s are not wholly reliable since population censuses and other surveys are not available and Singapore data are available only from 1966.

Dr. Tsao Yuan has worked out total factor productivity estimates for the Singapore economy as a whole, 1966–1980, and has found that the growth of TFP was extremely low—in fact, there was no growth.[1] She found this puzzling when compared with South Korea's

---

[1] There was actually a small minus growth of about 0.2 percent, with growth of 0.5 percent, 1966–1972, and –0.9 percent, 1972–1980.

4 percent per year for 1960–1973, and discussed various factors that could account for the absence of factor productivity growth, some of which will be taken up below. In Chapter 5, we saw that Korean TFP grew with the massive shift of the labor force from agriculture to industry, that is, a shift of workers whose *level* of TFP may have been as low as one-half or less of the nonagricultural sectors. In contrast, the agricultural sector in Singapore during the period in question was very minor so that the sources of TFP growth from the shift were virtually nil. Hence, one cannot expect productivity growth to be as large as in economies, like South Korea, in the midst of rapid transition from a predominantly agricultural to a predominantly industrial economy. Nor is the shift from the service sector to the industrial sector an important source of productivity growth since the income per worker in these two sectors is roughly the same.

It is for such reasons that in the United States TFP growth was high in the early decades of the 20th century when the agricultural labor force began to shrink rapidly as farms were mechanized. In Japan in the 1950s and 1960s, and Taiwan in the 1960s and 1970s, it was the substantial decline in the A sector which was the major source of the high TFP growth, as seen in Chapters 4 and 5. It was also a major contributory element in the slowdown in TFP growth in Japan in the 1970s after the A sector shrank below 10 percent of total employment. No estimate for Hong Kong's TFP is available to compare with those of the Tsao study. But the expectation from the above discussion is that TFP will be very much lower than in South Korea and Taiwan but probably higher than that in Singapore because the growth of capital stock played a lesser role in the more labor-intensive growth of Hong Kong. For these sectors, adequate data are available only for the 1960s and 1970s. The growth of industrial product was higher in Singapore while the growth of service product was higher in Hong Kong. The same can be said of product per worker in the two sectors. The agricultural sector was minor for both countries, averaging only 4 percent of GDP in the 1960s and 1 percent in the 1970s for both: an 8.5 percent growth of product per worker in Singapore compared with 6.7 percent in Hong Kong.

There was not much difference in the dimensions of growth of product per worker in the two countries. There are no survey data on employment in Hong Kong in the 1950s, but if the 1960s and 1970s figures are used, product per worker grew at 4.7 percent for both. One difference was that in Hong Kong use of workers as against capital was far greater than in Singapore. The growth rate of employment was 4.9 percent annually (1960 to 1980) in Hong Kong compared with

3.6 percent (1950 to 1980) in Singapore. If the 1950s are included for Hong Kong, it is likely that the rate may have been 5 percent or higher since the growth was labor-intensive. Singapore used much more capital in the 1960s and 1970s, 29 percent to Hong Kong's 20 percent of 1965 to 1980 GDP. Much of this was the result of an influx of foreign investment, indicated in an approximate way by the large difference in the excess of imports over exports during the three decades, which for Singapore was 13 percent of GDP compared with Hong Kong's 5 percent for 1950 to 1980.[2]

What is noteworthy is the 10.7 percent growth rate in service productivity in Hong Kong from 1960 to 1980, which was by far the highest in Asia. Taiwan and Korea were second with 8.7 percent rates, followed by Japan with 8.6 percent and Singapore with 8.1 percent for the 1960s and 1970s. In the industrial sector, Hong Kong's 8.1 percent and Singapore's 10.7 percent for 1960–1980 were far below those of Korea (16.8 percent) and Taiwan (13.6 percent).

The completion of the industrial transition in these city-states with minor agricultural sectors took the form of the labor force in the industrial sector exceeding the service sector. This probably occurred in Hong Kong in the early 1950s, since by the 1961 Census 59 percent of workers were already in industry compared to 34 percent in service. In Singapore, the transition came later, due partly to the slow growth of industrialization in the 1950s and early 1960s and partly to the slower shrinkage of the entrepôt trade in Singapore compared to the complete stoppage in Hong Kong after the Communist government was established in China in 1949. Singapore's industrial labor force rose to more than 48.8 percent in 1980, only slightly lower than the 49.6 percent in the service sector, and thereafter began to decline slowly to 48.1 percent in 1982, even though absolute numbers continued to rise. In Hong Kong, too, industrial employment reached its peak in the 1976 Census figure of 59.4 percent and then declined to 57.9 percent in the 1981 Census, while employment began to rise in the service sector from a low of 34 percent to 40 percent.

The difference in the transition of the service sector from that of the agricultural sector in Japan, Taiwan, and South Korea is largely due to the fact that the greater share of the output of the service sector is more income-elastic than that of agriculture, particularly in commerce, finance, and professional and public services. Only in the low-wage

[2] Data in this paragraph are from official national account statistics and appendix tables. A better indicator of net inflow of foreign investment is net private nonmonetary capital in the balance of payments, but Hong Kong does not publish such data. For Singapore, it is 11 percent of GDP for the period 1966 to 1980.

informal sectors such as petty trading, stall-keeping, menial personal services, domestic services, and small eating places are there declines in employment as full employment is approached. Thus, unlike agriculture, the service sector cannot be expected to release many workers to the industrial sector. This is another reason that city-state economies are likely to reach full employment and then experience labor shortage quickly after a few years of rapid industrial development. There is no large pool of low-paid labor in the rural sector as there is in agrarian economies, where after full employment another decade passes before the rural sector's release of labor becomes sluggish.

A 1966 employment survey in Singapore reported unemployment to be about 10 to 11 percent. By the end of the 1960s the economy had begun to register signs of full employment, and by the mid-1970s labor shortages began. Employment data are incomplete for the 1950s in Hong Kong, but full employment was probably reached in the latter half of the 1950s, when real wages accelerated. (The first half was constrained by the UN "trade embargo" of China.) This is indicated by the estimated increase in total migration which reached a peak of a quarter million in 1954–1958. Labor shortage was delayed because of the intermittent inflow of legal and illegal migrants from China throughout the 1960s whenever the labor market tightened. In a limited sense the Chinese hinterland served as a labor force reservoir for Hong Kong. Nevertheless, by the early 1960s full employment was reached, as shown by the 1961 Population Census, which reported the unemployment rate to be 1.7 percent. As in Japan, Taiwan, and Korea, after full employment growth GDP accelerated in both city-states, from 9 percent in the 1950s to 10 percent yearly in the 1960s in Hong Kong, and from 5 percent to 8 percent in the 1970s for Singapore, with rising real wages and the substitution of machinery for workers.

Hong Kong started its industrialization drive a decade or so earlier than Singapore. Singapore did not become a city-state economy until the mid-1960s since it is part of the Malay peninsula and there is unrestricted movement over the causeway between the two. Hence, Singapore for a time tried import-substitution industrialization without much success. It was affected by the pre-independence political confusion of the Malaysian Emergency in the 1950s. Once separated from Malaya, the imperatives of city-state economics compelled Singapore to take Hong Kong's path to industrialization, which included the imposition of low, or no, tariffs (because the domestic market was too small to make it worthwhile to protect existing industries, and there was little agricultural production to protect) and the low maintenance living costs with cheap imports of food, other consumption goods, and low-cost industrial materials, parts, components, and equipment to keep production costs low to expand exports. These and other similarities derive from the nature of city-state economies, and the Singapore economy began to resemble the Hong Kong economy—in effect, a huge export zone. Though a latecomer, once started, Singapore would have followed Hong Kong's pioneering path to industrialization had it not been for one factor. Singapore has historically been the center of a region with the world's largest concentration of plantations producing tropical export crops (Malaysia, Sri Lanka, Indonesia). Its merchant and financial houses were highly specialized in the marketing and financing of commercial crops, unlike Hong Kong which marketed and financed processed Chinese foods, handicrafts, and other manufactures from the vast Chinese mainland. In the following sections are described some of the differences in the pattern of industrialization that resulted from this and other factors.

The Interplay Between the Service and the Industrial Sectors

It was in part a historical accident that Hong Kong was able to export industrial products early in the 1950s, second only to Japan which started in the late 1940s.[3] Among the refugees fleeing to Hong Kong in 1948 and 1949 was a large group of experienced Shanghai entrepreneurs who were able to start off the manufacturing industries in Hong Kong without the need for protection and subsidy. Most important of these were the textile manufacturers with their skilled workmen who before World War II had been responsible for the largest textile industry in China, second in experience in Asia only to those in Osaka and Bombay. These manufacturers had ordered immediately after the war the newest textile machines from the United States and United Kingdom, and these were routed to Hong Kong about the time of the communist takeover of China. The Shanghai enterpreneurs were able to rent floor space, to borrow capital from the Hong Kong banks, and together with their skilled staff to train unskilled Hong Kong labor. They soon began to export to nearby countries, then to the United Kingdom, and a few years later to the United States. Their marketing advice came from merchant houses. (In effect, what Shanghai

---

[3] The discussion on Hong Kong draws heavily from T. Geiger and F. M. Geiger (1976). They interviewed public officials and industrialists in Hong Kong and Singapore and obtained insights on the development of Hong Kong which would have been difficult to receive through mailed questionnaires.

textile makers were doing was to continue their prewar activities, competing with the Osaka and Bombay rivals from Hong Kong.) In 1948, there were only 8,000 spindles, but in 1951 there were 210,000. They and others were soon expanding into the export of garments, shoes, furniture, toys and games, and small machines and equipment, besides highly processed foods by the end of the 1950s. By the late 1950s, "voluntary quotas" were imposed on Hong Kong textile exports by the United Kingdom and United States, and protectionism in East and Southeast Asia forced Hong Kong manufacturers to move their enterprises to other countries, especially to Taiwan and South Korea, which helped to start these countries off on their export-promotion strategy.

The Geigers (1976) in their interviews with Hong Kong entrepreneurs were able to learn the process by which industrial entrepreneurs got their start and became efficient. The skilled blue- and white-collar employees of the ongoing industries made every effort to learn the entire process, and while still employees began to take small orders which were filled in their homes and other shops. Besides the Shanghai enterprises, there was another source which in the 1950s and 1960s became even more important for the industrialization of a Hong Kong faced with increasing restrictions on textiles and later on garments. This was the large U.S. and other Western mail-order, stores, department stores, and chain stores and other mass distribution firms which came to Hong Kong to teach entrepreneurs to produce a wide variety of good quality merchandise to be purchased in large batches for sale in their mass markets.

In particular, the Sears, J.C. Penneys, Montgomery Wards, and others of the West who were dissatisfied with the cartel pricing of Philco, Seimens, and Philips sent their engineers and marketing exports to Hong Kong in the late 1950s to teach Hong Kong producers to make radios, TVs, and other consumer electronics whenever the cartel patents expired. Parts, materials, equipment, and components not made in Hong Kong were imported from Japan. This combination, the importation from Japan and marketing in the mass markets with know-how taught by Western experts, became the pattern by which Hong Kong grew into an industrial society of high efficiency in the 1960s. After full employment in the early 1960s, when Hong Kong wages were double or quadruple those in Taiwan or South Korea, Western mass distributors moved on to Taiwan and South Korea to start the export-promotion drive in those countries. Export promotion incentives were helpful, but without the skills transferred to their entrepreneurs exports would have been slow to experience substantial growth.

Unlike the service sectors in the Philippines, which also started to industrialize in the late 1940s, the merchant and banking houses of Hong Kong assisted nascent industries with their marketing abroad and financing. The government persuaded businesses to participate in trade fairs and exhibitions in the United States and Europe and was active in export promotion, while business associations and others set up training programs. Through these and other efforts to improve export performance, the efficiency of Hong Kong's service sectors, the merchant, banking, and insurance houses, the professional consulting firms, and the nonmanufacturing industries generating external economies, transport, communication, construction, electric power, and other utilities, rose to new heights rivaling those of Japan. Despite the laissez-faire philosophy of the colonial government, it did not stand in the way of active assistance. Its numerous departments took the initiative in bringing together business groups to furnish necessary information and other services.

Because colonial government heads were appointed by London, the government established various participatory and consultative bodies which in many respects may have been more responsive to the needs of the citizenry and private institutions than in countries where governments elected by popular vote were corrupt and ineffective. Of these institutions, the most noteworthy was a wide network of over 130 advisory committees attached to various government agencies. The functions and operations of these committees were similar to those in Japan.

This network, complemented by a system of business associations, contributed not only to smooth cooperation between business and government but also to government efficiency in its overall management of the economy and to efficiency of private enterprise management. The modern economy is too complex and the world economy too massive and dynamic for any single bureaucracy, no matter how big and formally well trained, to comprehend adequately for efficient regulation. Perhaps the best in-service training for the bureaucracy in a modern economy is regular consultation and cooperation with the business sectors, in the same way that participation and cooperation on the factory floor is the best way to train blue- and white-collar workers for efficient production. One major limitation of the Hong Kong system, unlike in Japan, was the failure to give better representation in the advisory boards and committees to the small business groups and the nonbusiness groups, such as consumers, labor unions, and academia.

The efficiency of the service sector enabled it to become an important export sector, notably through the large number of tourists who came to Hong Kong. (In 1980, 2.4 million tourists visited Hong Kong, exceeded only by 2.6 million visitors to Singapore.) Hong Kong became the chief financial center in Asia with the largest number of regional headquarters of multinational firms, which found it the most convenient place to conduct regional business despite high rents and salaries. The earnings of these organizations and the Hong Kong traders' overseas business, together with earnings from tourism and from the maritime freight and transport services carrying foreign goods, comprise a significant share of total foreign exchange earnings, although data are not available for even a rough estimate. Probably no service sector anywhere brought in as much foreign earnings relating to GDP as that of Hong Kong.

There was no migration of industrial entrepreneurs into Singapore in the early period of postwar growth. Like most colonial countries, it inherited only a small group of industrialists, and the large group of merchants and banking houses found the trading and financing of tropical commercial crops preferable to shifting into risky industrial enterprises in which they had no previous experience. Moreover, entrepôt trade along the coastal regions of Malaysia and Indonesia continued to flourish throughout the 1950s and 1960s and kept the smaller traders and merchants occupied. But mounting unemployment in the early 1960s forced Singapore's leaders to throw its economy wide open to foreign entrepreneurs and enterprises. Not only labor-intensive industries (plywood, textiles, garments) came in but also branches of multinational companies during the late 1960s and throughout the 1970s (in shipbuilding, oil refining, and electrical and electronic products) as various methods to improve the business climate were adopted and vigorously implemented. The entry of multinational branches meant that Singapore's industrialization was much more capital intensive than Hong Kong's, consonant with the higher levels of wages (about 30 to 40 percent higher in the mid-1960s). In a matter of years, the labor market began to tighten. Although the unemployment rate was high in the mid-1960s the labor force in Singapore was the smallest in Asia, about one-half that in Hong Kong.

With much higher wage levels than the other NICs, with militant labor unions intent on agitating for higher wages and fewer hours in the best British tradition, with leftists agitating among the Chinese-speaking majority, with turbulence and hostility in neighboring countries, and with the British military establishment ready to dismantle and pull out, the leaders of independent Singapore had to take swift action. They handled the situation with a firm, at times even

Table 6.1   Annual Average Expenditure by Government Function in Singapore

	1950s			1960s			1970s		
	Amount (Mn. S$)	% of Total	% of GNP	Amount (Mn. S$)	% of Total	% of GNP	Amount (Mn. S$)	% of Total	% of GNP
General services	31	17.6	1.8	68.5	8.9	1.5	105.8	3.7	0.8
Defense, justice, and police	34	19.3	2.0	124.4	18.8	3.2	740.3	26.1	5.7
Education	35	19.9	2.0	128.9	21.0	3.6	321.2	11.3	2.5
Health	21	11.9	1.2	74.8	11.3	1.9	138.1	4.9	1.1
Other social and community services	13	7.4	0.8	49.7	7.5	1.3	163.8	5.8	1.3
Economic services	16	9.1	0.9	44.4	6.7	1.1	129.6	4.6	1.0
Agricultural, non-mineral resources, industrial and commercial development	—	—	—	6.5	1.0	0.2	36.2	1.3	0.3
Transport and communication	—	—	—	26.7	4.0	0.7	58.0	2.0	0.4
Other economic services	—	—	—	11.2	1.7	0.3	35.4	1.2	0.3
Others	26	14.8	1.5	170.0	25.7	4.4	1,242.1	43.7	9.5
Total	176	100.0	10.2	660.7	100.0	17.0	2,840.9	100.0	21.7
Social exp. as % of total		39.2			39.8			22.0	
% of GNP		4.0			6.8			4.9	

Sources: Data for 1960s and 1970s computed from *Singapore Yearbook of Statistics*, various issues; data for 1950s computed from Lee Soo Ann, *Economic Growth and the Public Sector in Malaya and Singapore 1948–1960.*

rough, hand, particularly in wiping out corruption and inefficiency in the bureaucracy, in solving traffic problems, and in eliminating poorly performing industries. Unlike in Hong Kong, Singapore rulers found market forces ineffective and consultations too slow in bringing about the desired results. There was no need for widespread consultation through advisory committees to help with technological development and marketing as in Hong Kong, for the multinational enterprises coming into Singapore were selected for their expertise in technology and marketing, unlike the Chinese enterprises in Hong Kong.

The Singapore government has never been a laissez-faire government. It is closer to a strong, active government like those in Taiwan and South Korea. All three have taken vigorous steps to get the economy moving, regulating when the need arose and setting up public enterprises. In 1959, there were as many employees in government as in private enterprise. Even today, the Singapore government takes pride in calling its economy a socialist one. But unlike other socialist governments, all the public enterprises earn profits while private enterprises are highly respected and market forces increasingly resorted to.

It is pertinent to note that both governments, although relying largely on private enterprise and competitive market forces, did not hesitate to intervene—one through the network of consultative institutions, the other through public enterprises and regulations. In both cases, the intent was to strengthen market forces and improve the operations of the markets. When the labor unions in Singapore began to use their power to obstruct the workings of the labor market, legislation was enacted to forbid certain union practices inimical to productivity growth. In Hong Kong the government sent business delegations to various countries to learn more about markets abroad and acquaint foreign buyers with the Hong Kong market. To enhance competition, the entry of foreign enterprises and importation of goods and skills were largely unrestricted in both Hong Kong and Singapore.

Income Distribution

In both Singapore and Hong Kong family income disparities fell from the mid-1960s to the mid-1970s. Despite the substantial fall (of about 10 percent), the average levels in both periods tended to be higher than in more agrarian countries such as Taiwan and South Korea. The reason for this can be traced to the nature of city-states without a monsoon agricultural sector. In countries like Taiwan, South Korea, and Japan, average farm family incomes were high, because of not only high yields but also income from off-farm employment during the dry seasons. More important, the within-sector disparities were low because of low inequality in land distribution, absence of tenancy and landless workers, and higher incomes earned in off-farm jobs by the lower income groups. Not only was there no such agricultural sector in the city-states but the existence of a large service sector with wide-ranging average incomes among the branches of the service sector raised inequality within the sector. Thus, the average income per worker in finance and real estate was 3.5 times larger than in the service sector as a whole; the average in personal services was only half, and that in trade was slightly higher than the average of the service sector as a whole.[4] This kind of subsector variation was not found in monsoon agriculture or in industry. The data are for Singapore in 1970, but similar variations were found in the Hong Kong data for 1971.

The foregoing relates to between-disparities. Disparities-within in the subsectors of the service sector tended to be larger than for the other sectors because firms in the other sectors used fewer unskilled workers relative to skilled and white-collar. Thus, the proportion of blue-collar or low-income workers to white-collar or higher-income workers was low compared with the commodity-producing sectors where manual workers greatly outnumbered the white-collar ones in the production process. This meant that the frequency distribution curve relating income to number of workers in the service firms was much more sharply peaked with a smaller base than in the A or I sector firms. The Gini coefficient of finance and insurance in Hong Kong in 1971 was among the highest, 0.57, compared to 0.36 for manufacturing and 0.38 for agriculture, while commerce was 0.46 and personal services was 0.50.[5]

Nevertheless, with the modernization of the service sector through large banks, hotels, department stores, and others employing large number of clerks, laborers, and other low-skilled workers using equipment, inequality within the subsectors declined in both city-states between the 1960s and 1970s. Here the same process as in manufacturing took place, whereby the use of machines by relatively unskilled workers replaced those with more expensive skills.

Moreover, with full employment female participation rates rose and more housewives in lower-income households were able to obtain jobs, thereby raising family incomes. In Hong Kong, female participation rates jumped from 37 percent in 1961 to 43 percent in 1971 and 44 percent in 1977, and in Singapore from 30 percent in 1970 to 47

---

[4] Computed from data in 1970 from the official national accounts of Singapore.
[5] For Singapore similar differences in the Gini ratios are found, but the data for commerce are not disaggregated between commerce and finance.

percent in 1980. But this decline in Gini for the city-states may not continue into the 1980s if the between-sector disparities do not decline. In Hong Kong the S sector average incomes rose faster in 1980 than in 1970 and the excess of the average of S over I increased by about 10 percent. But in Singapore sector disparities declined, and with the female participation rate continuing to rise, Singapore's Gini may have fallen in the late 1970s. In Hong Kong, where not only sector disparities rose but also the female participation rate failed to rise, there was a rise in inequality of about 10 percent from 1971 to 1980.[6]

Birth Rates

Total fertility rates fell to a low level of 1.7 in Singapore in 1982 (along with Japan's, the lowest in Asia) and to 2.1 in Hong Kong. They have been falling for some time, perhaps from the later 1950s or early 1960s. Mortality began to decline much earlier, from the early decades of this century. The demographic transition was completed by Hong Kong around the end of the 1960s and by Singapore in the early 1970s.

Despite declining mortality about half a century earlier before the fertility declines, the demand for labor relative to supply in Hong Kong and Singapore was high in the prewar decades (except for the early 1930s) as these trading cities began to expand. The rising birth rates were insufficient to meet the large labor demand, and there was no migration from China and India except in the early 1930s. In the postwar decades, fertility began to fall when the labor demand was largely for educated workers in mechanized factories and modernized offices and stores. Increasingly, parents began to realize that children needed more education if they were to obtain good jobs when they grew up.

Occupations requiring more education (professional, technical, administrative, managerial, sales, and clerical work) rose from 36.7 percent of all jobs in 1957 to 41.5 percent in 1981, and the number of blue-collar workers declined from 63.3 percent to 58.5 percent in Singapore despite industrialization, while in Hong Kong the rise was from 27.8 percent to 30.7 percent for the white-collar and the decline from 72.2 percent to 69.3 for the blue-collar occupations. This increased the cost of raising children as they were sent to schools beyond primary grades and not to workplaces to earn incomes. The percentage of child-

---

[6] For Hong Kong 1980 data, see *World Development Report 1982*. The total disparity index for quintiles for 1980 is 0.68 compared with 0.62 for 1970 computed from the *Census of Population, 1971*.

ren in the secondary education age group rose sharply from 20 percent in Hong Kong and 32 percent in Singapore in 1960 to 65 percent for both in 1981.

Moreover, in contrast to the prewar decades, there was a shift in the socioeconomic structure of the labor force in the form of a decline in the proprietary, own-account, and family-help group relative to the employer-employee group. Self-employed/family help workers in Hong Kong fell from 14.8 percent to 7.8 percent from 1961 to 1981; the employer-employee group rose from 85.2 percent to 92.2 percent of all workers, and in Singapore from 22.6 percent to 13.3 percent and 77.4 percent to 86.7 percent, respectively. A major force underlying these shifts in labor force status was the need for greater capital for machines, other equipment, and structures required by modern industry and commerce. If data were available for the prewar decades the shift would appear even larger. In the own-account families in which a large family could supply cheaply and readily the workers needed to operate shops and offices for long hours throughout the week, fertility was highest among the various classes of workers.

Also, as noted above, female participation in the labor force has increased sharply compared to prewar levels, not only because of full employment and the labor shortage but because the factories were able to use women in jobs using small machines and electric equipment. In the prewar decades, most industries used steam-powered machines which were too heavy and cumbersome for females. Similarly in modern offices and stores, an increasing number of females found suitable jobs. Modern apartments, consumer appliances, and rapid mass transportation afforded housewives the time to leave their homes and work in factories, offices, and shops, thus enabling them to increase family incomes, in part to pay for more schooling for their children as technological progress made more education necessary. At the same time, the opportunity cost of staying home and raising children increased. Family size began to fall.

All the above, together with rapid growth under conditions of declining income disparities, meant that even incomes of the lower-income families rose substantially. The impact on desired family size was varied. Higher incomes opened up new leisure opportunities (the mass media, travel, eating out) which could be enjoyed by childless couples. In the past, increasing incomes for lower-income families meant that more money could be invested in more children who were sources of family enjoyment, of family income, and later on of security for parents' old age. But as the demand for child workers fell and the cost of raising children rose, higher incomes could be saved to invest in dwellings and in additional education for fewer children as a better source of security, particularly when mortality declined over the decades. Even more important for security in old age was the compulsory investment of a portion of income in old age pensions and in health schemes in the city-states. The rapid fertility decline in the 1970s in Singapore meant easier access to government housing.

Summary and Concluding Remarks

The successes achieved by the city-states of Hong Kong and Singapore were not expected in the 1950s by economists who were prone to emphasize the size of the domestic market as an essential condition for the success of long-term industrialization and to minimize the importance of the service sector. The successful completion in the postwar decades of the industrial transition in the city-states demonstrated that, starting with ample external economies from the services sector, the manufacturing industries were able to achieve scale economies by exporting a large share of output. The emphasis of governments, entrepreneurs, employees, and the populace on efficiency in order to export was dictated by the absence of a rural hinterland from which to import food, fuel, water, raw materials, and other absolute necessities. Later on, after industrialization had made some headway and full employment approached, the absence of a rural hinterland with an abundant supply of cheap labor called for more foreign exchange to buy machinery from abroad to substitute for labor. In this drive the legacy from the colonial period and a populace with a strong work ethic were important contributions to the successful transition, in addition to the presence of efficient mercantile and financial houses and the absence of provincial landed oligarchies.

The relevance of the city-state experience for countries with large rural hinterlands will be discussed in Chapter 9 on India and China. Something may be said here of the pertinence of each city-state's experience to the other since the characteristics of the two are sufficiently alike for mutual lessons to be learned. Singapore may in the future be able to profit from the system of formal consultations through a large network of advisory councils and committees that the Hong Kong government has employed. The success of Japanese industrial policies is rooted in the system of widespread consultation and participation instituted by MITI (and the bureaucracy in general), based on the rationale that decisions are better made with more heads than fewer. Up to now, Singapore has been singularly fortunate in possessing leaders like Lee Kuan Yew and Goh Keng Swee. But when they pass from the scene, it is not likely that leaders of the same caliber will be found among the new generation. Nor are new leaders likely to have the political support that the present leadership managed to accumulate over the past three decades. It may be that a system of wider consultations may be worth trying, especially because the affluence and social successes achieved in Singapore mean that time is not as pressing as in the past, and the better educated and sophisticated generation in the higher echelons of the labor force will have views worth tapping. In any case, time lost in consultations can be easily retrieved by swifter implementation of policies, as Goh Keng Swee has noted in discussing Japanese methods.

The lesson Hong Kong can learn from Singapore is that it is not necessary to be dogmatic about adhering to a laissez-faire philosophy for successful development. Consultations with the smaller enterprises and labor unions may uncover methods for improving the lower efficiency of the smallest enterprises and raising wages and working conditions of their employees, thereby improving their work incentives and motivation. Reliance solely on market forces may be inappropriate when the bargaining power of small entrepreneurs is weak and may destroy many potentially able enterprises which will be needed in the future as the population expands. One strength of Japanese industry is the extensive system of small subcontracting firms, many of which would not have survived without appropriate outside assistance. The Japanese and Singapore experience has shown that Asian workers in strong labor unions can contribute immensely to economic growth. Nor are income taxes such obstacles to growth as the Hong Kong government appears to think. The failure to financially assist technological research in electronics and venture capital by the government has put Hong Kong behind the other NICs in the sophisticated restructuring and advance of its electronic industry which was far ahead in the early 1970s. Businesses can learn to play for lower stakes, as in Singapore and Japan. It is the failure of the low incomes in the large manufacturing sector to catch up fast enough with the higher incomes in commerce and finance that is linked to the rise of family income inequalities from the 1970s to 1980s. In Hong Kong, product per worker in manufacturing is the lowest of all sectors and only one-third of the average for the S sector, while in Singapore it is about 10 percent lower than the S sector average according to official national accounts.

For all other countries in Southeast and South Asia, small or large, there are valuable lessons in Singapore's transformation of the inefficient and corrupt bureaucracy of the 1950s into one of the most efficient and cleanest in the world; dictatorships and republican governments alike may find the system of consultation and advisory committees employed by Hong Kong a better way of establishing and implementing industrial policy than regulations and nationalization. The experience of Hong Kong and Singapore (together with that of South Korea, Taiwan, and Malaysia) also demonstrates that foreign multinational enterprises can be beneficial in the industrialization of less developed countries without, however, necessarily compromising the sovereignty, integrity, and independence of the host nation. The latter is more a function of the integrity of the nation's political leadership, the soundness of the financial system, and the diligence of indigenous entrepreneurships. And, finally, the city-states' all-out concern for economic efficiency shows that the payoff is enormous in the rapid completion of the industrial transition, no matter how large a country's hinterland may be.

Another practice of the Singapore leadership worth pondering in other countries is its vigilance against inappropriate tendencies in the British institutions inherited from the colonial period, not only in the British-style bureaucracy but also in the institutions of higher and lower learning, trade unionism, defense establishments, financial systems, and so on. Singapore's leaders have not hesitated to eliminate tendencies they find detrimental to Singapore's development. Time has proven them to be right; in fact, in Britain itself questions raised by Singapore's leaders two decades ago are now seriously being discussed. Many Asian countries have not done much to adjust inherited Western institutions, and in some cases the modifications have been in wrong directions. To Western intellectuals, the constant calls for integrity, diligence, and devotion to the national cause may appear arrogant and self-righteous, but that these were necessary has been proven by the widespread financial malfeasance of public officials in Asia, of which the Philippines is only one extreme case. In traditional Asia, exhortations by respected leaders are listened to, although the question arises of whether in the future the highly educated modern populace of Singapore may not respond better to persuasion than to exhortations.

The moral of the tale of the two city-states concerning income distribution and fertility declines is that rapid, sustained growth accompanied by full employment is associated with the quick spread of technologies of the second industrial revolution whose cumulative effect is essentially similar to that described above in the other dynamic economies of Japan, Taiwan, and South Korea. In a nutshell, the impact of the spread of mechanization and modernization in the city, homes, offices, and stores on lower-income families was to increase expenditures on education and savings and thereby mitigate the need for large families.

Finally, the service sector played a crucial role in export-oriented growth. Countries should not neglect to ensure extensive competition for the various branches of the service sector. Cartel-like arrangements such as found in Philippine banking need to be dissolved by bringing in more foreign banks from ASEAN and elsewhere to furnish competition and ensure continuous improvements in efficiency. Here, as well as in department store policy, the examples set by the city-states should be studied.

There is a tendency for economists to concentrate on the commodity-producing sectors at the expense of services, which may be a holdover from conditions in earlier centuries. Starting with the Physiocrats in the 18th century, the service sector has been viewed as unproductive. This line of thinking was carried over by Marx into the 19th century and into the 20th by his followers. There may have been some justification for the Physiocrats in their time to argue that the consumers of services were largely the leisure class who did little or no work. This is not the case today, however, when lower-income families' expenditure patterns include personal services of all sorts, and the expansion of the system of exhange commodities means they must be transported and marketed through layers of middlemen. Nor can public services be dispensed with in the highly organized economies and societies of today.

As per capita incomes continue to rise, the demand for modern forms of services will rise. Today the more advanced commodity production is larger when the service sector is more efficient. In countries where per capita incomes are low and grow more slowly than the population, the informal service sector is one of the few sectors providing employment to those not wanted by the commodity sectors. Therefore public funds should be used to improve the productivity of service sectors.

CHAPTER 7

Thailand Catches Up with the Philippines

In the pairing of the Philippines with Thailand, several structural similarities and differences seemed important. The area and population were similar, with both countries approaching a population of 50 million in 1980. The levels of literacy and life expectancy were about the same. Per capita dollar incomes also were approaching $700 in 1980 in both countries, and a little less than one-fourth the value added in GDP was from agriculture.[1] Above all, both were classic monsoon economies with a half year of dry weather. With such similarities, the difference in growth rates which enabled Thailand to catch up with the Philippine level of per capita income presented an interesting issue, particularly so because the Philippines started the early postwar years with about twice the per capita income of Thailand. I shall also refer in this chapter to Burma, which like Thailand has a very large rice sector, and to Indonesia, which like the Philippines has an important plantation sector. The Philippines, like Sri Lanka and Burma, was a colony of foreign powers for a very long period, in sharp contrast with Thailand, which has never been a colony. Both, unlike Indonesia, had a fast start in the 1950s, with the Philippines becoming independent in 1946.

With the "catch-up" by Thailand, both countries ended the postwar decades somewhere around midpoint in the agro-industrial transition process, with a labor force in industry only one-half that in agriculture, and with per capita income one-half that of Malaysia and South Korea, but nearly double that of Indonesia and a little more than double that of Sri Lanka.[2] Both countries, like Indonesia and Burma, continued to be troubled by unemployment and, especially, underemployment; despite the fall in the relative share of employment in agriculture, there

[1] See World Development Bank, 1983, especially the appendix tables. This chapter draws heavily on Oshima, 1983c and 1983d.

[2] Data from tables in Chapter 3. See below for discussion on the peculiarities of Thai employment data in agriculture.

199

were no signs of absolute decline in agriculture even in the early 1980s, in contrast to Malaysia. The Philippines ended the postwar era faltering badly, with a severe financial crisis in the early 1980s and poor prospects for the rest of the decade, while Thailand in the early 1980s was still growing vigorously. There is a good possibility that before the decade ends Thailand will be completing industrial transition ahead of the Philippines and Indonesia. All this is despite the fact that the Philippines led the growth of the ASEAN countries in the 1950s, when its physical infrastructure, literacy, life expectancy, and bureaucracy were among the most advanced. In contrast, Bangkok in 1961 still had all the earmarks of an ancient Oriental city, full of large buildings made of wood, hardly any concrete structures, narrow streets, and many canals running through the city. It is with this contrast in the performance and fortunes of the two countries that this chapter will be primarily concerned.

Historical Background

Before the reforms of King Chulalongkorn in the latter half of the 19th century, the system of land tenure in Thailand was basically the same as that of the ancient Indo-Chinese kingdoms and Japan. Land was, in principle, owned by the monarchy and was assigned to the nobility in large parcels of several thousand acres, which were mainly tilled by the slaves of the nobles and by forced labor (corvée) of peasants who also worked small plots of their own nearby. Any land of the nobility not tilled for three years reverted to the monarchy. In the Chulalongkorn period, beginning around the late 1860s, reforms were initiated, and eventually the slaves and serfs became free peasants tilling their own land. Without the serfs and slaves, the number of large estates declined sharply over the course of time, as the untilled land reverted to the monarchy and then to the peasantry. These reforms, together with the centralization of administration in the Bangkok government, destroyed the political power of the nobility who had ruled the provinces independently of the central government. The new administration began the modernization of the bureaucracy, staffed by Western-trained Thais who replaced the old nobility whose titles expired after five generations. The Thai peasants not only were free to cultivate their own land, with the growth of population and with the rise in demand for rice from the plantation countries to the south, but also were able to clear forests and establish new rice farms (Ingram, 1971; Steinberg et al., 1971).

This process enabled the Thai peasantry to develop independence and self-reliance, quite different from the Javanese and Malay peasants who were overly protected, confined to their village communities as part of the colonial policy, and shut off from nearby lands which were taken over for plantation crops. Their experience was also different from that of the Ceylonese peasants whose communal lands were taken over by the plantations, or of the peasants in Burma where land tenure was governed by Western laws of private ownership and who found themselves losing their lands as they became unable to repay loans from Indian lenders and other middlemen, particularly in the important delta region of the south. Plantations were not established in Thailand (except for a few in the extreme south near Malaya).[3]

But the most unfortunate peasants were those of the Philippines, who, in Central Luzon and other fertile rice valleys, "never had a chance," in the words of American historian John A. Larkin. The Spaniards for centuries governed the rural areas through the *principalia*, formerly local chieftains, who were made tax collectors over the freemen. Those unable to pay taxes became serfs and lost their land. The chiefs, together with the Catholic Church and later the Chinese mestizos, began to amass large tracts in the form of haciendas. In the 19th century, they expanded their holdings as they took over the land of the peasants who fell into debt. The indigenous concept of communal ownership was early replaced by alienation through private, fee simple ownership. Thus, like the Ceylonese, Burmese, and Vietnamese peasantry and unlike the Malay and Javanese peasantry, more and more Filipino peasants began to lose their land and fall into share tenancy. The preempting of other lands by the Spanish Crown left little land for the peasants to move to when population began to expand in the 19th century as the demand for labor increased with the emergence of plantations, while tenants in debt were tied to the soil like serfs and compelled to do extra work. This process was the opposite of that in Thailand where serfs became freemen.

A unique aspect of 19th century Philippine history was the rise of a large indigenous landed oligarchy owning vast tracts of hundreds and thousands of hectares of both rice and plantation lands. Unlike the British, Dutch, and French colonialists, the Spaniards—coming from a feudalistic Spain and having no experience as capitalistic entrepreneurs—were neither interested in nor capable of establishing and operating plantations. In their place, the mestizos, especially the

---

[3] It may be that Thailand, with a longer dry season, was not suitable for perennials and plantations except in the extreme south and thus was not coveted by the Western colonial powers.

Chinese, took advantage of the accelerated rise in world demand for tropical commercial crops in the latter 19th century and became the new social and economic elite of the Philippines; without their co-operation not only the Spaniards but also the Americans, who took over the Philippines in the first half of the 20th century, would have found it difficult to manage the country politically.[4]

In the American colonial period, the weakening power of the Catholic Church and the opening of American markets further strengthened the indigenous elite, whose land holdings expanded as most of the Church lands were taken over by the colonial government and fell into their hands. After World War II, with the spread of education, public health, and physical infrastructure (part of which was destroyed by the Japanese but rebuilt with United States aid), with a modernized bureaucracy and years of experience in some forms of republican political institutions, and under the unified leadership of a powerful, indigenous elite, the Philippines was able to move immediately into an era of modern economic growth. But the peasantry in Luzon, the center of national power, was restive, unable to shake off the weight of centuries of exploitation by colonial rulers and their own elite. The 1948 Census of Population reported that in Central Luzon, in the main rice-producing section of the Philippines, only one-fifth of the farms were owner-cultivated and in Southern Luzon two-fifths, compared to about one-half in the rest of the country (with three-fourths in Mindanao). The rest were sharecroppers and part-tenants, largely the former.

The Thai peasantry was better off, with no foreign rulers and a greatly weakened rural nobility. Relieved of the burden of corvée labor and free to expand into nearby areas, it was largely responsible for the accelerating rice production which more than doubled between 1900 and 1950.[5] But Thailand's physical infrastructure, both urban and rural, was not developed for a modernizing economy, and its institutions were largely traditional, with the monarchy as a unifying, stabilizing power but with a weak, decimated ruling elite which had little experience in commerce, industry, and modern agriculture.

---

[4] The indigenous oligarchs, in order to control the police, without whose help the system of exploitation could not be perpetuated, entered politics and became political oligarchs as well. Historians report over 200 rebellions and uprisings during the Spanish periods continuing into the American period—a record probably unmatched in Asian history (Corpuz, 1965).

[5] Ingram (1971) points out: ". . . the land was brought under cultivation by individuals acting on their own initiative and not to any significant extent by government or private resettlement programs. . . . Uncultivated land was free to anyone who could clear and cultivate it; the main cost was the labor of clearing since no fertilizer was used."

Record of Postwar Growth

The tables in Chapter 3 show that the Philippines' growth of per capita GNP (3.6 percent) was the highest in the ASEAN countries in the 1950s, higher than Thailand's 2.8 percent. In the next two decades, however, the Philippine performance was the poorest, averaging 2.8 percent, with Thailand the best among the ASEAN agrarian Four with 4.9 percent. This enabled Thai incomes to catch up with the Philippine per capita incomes by the early 1980s. The *1985 World Development Report* gives $820 per year for Thailand and $760 for the Philippines in 1983, and the difference had widened to $200 by the end of 1985.[6]

Underlying the better performance of Thailand was the faster growth of its agriculture and industry in the 1960s and the acceleration of the non-agricultural sectors in the 1970s. Agricultural productivity per worker in the 1960s and 1970s grew at twice the rate of the Philippines, industrial productivity at about the same rate, and service sector productivity at four times that in the Philippines service sector. Crude efforts to correct for the use of capital give an estimate of the growth of total factor productivity during the three decades of about 1 percent higher for Thailand.[7]

The main concern in this chapter is that Thailand's performance was the best among the ASEAN agrarian Four in terms of the growth of GDP and GDP per capita for the three decades, and that of the Philippines, the worst. Thai performance was better than Malaysia's because of the slow start of the latter during the 1950s, and far better than Indonesia's because of the latter's faltering beginnings in the 1950s and 1960s, due largely to problems of nation-building and national unity. How did the Philippines, with a strong start in industrialization and a vigorous plantation sector, slow down in the later decades, ending up as the poorest performer among the ASEAN agrarian Four, and with the darkest prospects for the 1980s? The answer may have something to do with the low growth of labor productivity—2.0 percent compared to Thailand's 3.5 percent.

It should be pointed out that the estimates of GDP from the national

[6] World Bank figures for 1980 incomes show Philippine levels to be about 10 percent higher, but they do not take into account the fact that Philippine exchange rates were overvalued by about 10 percent or more compared with the Thai exchange rate. When this is taken into account, the two levels were about $640 in 1981.

[7] See Table 6.1. For the Philippines, there is a Ph.D. dissertation by Aurora Sanchez, "Philippine Capital Stock Measurement" (School of Economics, University of the Philippines, 1982), which shows a negative growth of TFP, −1.6 percent per year, 1960–1980. These estimates are in line with the above results.

accounts for both countries are not as good as those for East Asia, perhaps not as good as those for Malaysia and Sri Lanka, but better than for Indonesia, and especially weak for the earlier postwar decades. Elsewhere I have speculated that the Philippine estimates of GDP may be overstated for the late 1970s. The method of estimation for the small unit sectors in nonagriculture may overstate the growth of the informal sector because the estimated annual product per person engaged in the informal sector may impart a growth rate of national product perhaps one percentage point too high for the late 1970s. If so, the Philippine growth rate of GDP per capita may fall below 3.4 percent into the 2.0 percent range, inasmuch as the informal sector is very large.[8]

This conjecture is consistent with the data shown in Table 7.1. The rationale of this table is that in the course of development, the percent share of agricultural employment decreases as income per capita rises in the economy as a whole. This relation has been found to be quite stable and universal, being based on Engel's law, which states that with the rise of real incomes the percent spent on food declines. This in turn is related to the low income elasticities of the demand for food, especially the carbohydrates which dominate food expenditures during in-

Table 7.1   GNP Growth and Agriculture's Share

		% Decrease in Agriculture's Employment Share 1970–1980 (A)	Growth Rate of Real GNP per Capita 1970–1980 (B)	(A)/(B)
Philippines	1970s	2.0	3.4	0.6
Philippines	1960s	5.0	2.2	2.3
Malaysia	1970s	13.0	5.3	2.5
Thailand	1970s	7.0	5.1	1.4
Indonesia	1970s	6.8	5.7	1.2
India	1970s	3.1	1.2	2.6
Taiwan	1970s	16.5	6.7	2.5
S. Korea	1970s	16.8	8.0	2.1
Japan	1970s	7.4	4.1	1.8

Source: Data from *IBRD World Development Reports* and official sources.

[8] In Oshima, 1983c, establishments with less than ten persons comprised about three-fifths of nonagricultural employment, or about 2.9 million, obtained by deducting from total nonagricultural employment of 5.1 million (as reported in the Labor Force Survey) the total reported in the 1972 Census of Establishments. The International Monetary Fund found the official announcement of growth rates for 1984 and 1982 too high, and subsequently the government cut them by about one-half.

dustrial transition. In the last column of Table 7.1, which divides the percent decrease in agricultural employment by the growth rate of the economy during the 1970s, the percent decrease in agricultural employment per 1 percent of increase in GNP per capita is obtained. What stands out in the table is the low percentage in the fall of agricultural employment in the Philippines in the 1970s, only little over 0.5 percent. This is only about one-fourth of the employment decline in the Philippines in the 1960s, when the growth rate of GNP per capita was less, and also about one-fourth that of India, Taiwan, and South Korea in the 1970s. It is only one-half that of Thailand and Indonesia in the 1970s. (The 1.8 of Japan is low because by the early 1970s Japan's agricultural employment—after rapid mechanization in the 1950s and 1960s—had sunk to a level so low that its decline became very sluggish.) The high rates for Taiwan and South Korea are due in part to the rapid rise in yields per hectare and mechanization in the 1970s, besides the Engel effect on the demand side. Accordingly, if we assume the lower Thai and Indonesian rates to be relevant for the Philippines, we can speculate that the growth rate of GDP per capita may be overstated by one-half.[9]

Another interesting set of data is from the International Rice Research Institute publication on rice statistics (Palacpac, 1980). Dividing the wage rate per day by the retail prices per kilogram of rice, the publication gives the amount of rice that can be purchased by the wage rate per day. It was 3.9 kilograms in mid-1971 and then fell to 2.7 kilograms in mid-1976 and 2.8 in mid-1977, then rose to 3.2 in mid-1978 and to 4.1 in early 1979. Note that even in 1979 the real increase from 1971 is not much more than 10 percent for the entire decade, whereas the per capita real income data from the national accounts show a rise of 35 percent in the same period. In Thailand, where the estimates begin from mid-1976, the rise is from 5.5 kilograms to 11.9 kilograms in mid-1977 (due largely to the doubling of the wage rate). Similar increases are indicated for Malaysia, where 13.2 kilograms is shown for mid-1978. For Central Java and Sri Lanka in the latter 1970s, it was 2.5 kilograms, and 1.5 for India. The average level of the Philippines of 3 or 4 kilograms (compared with more than 6 for Thailand) puts the Philippines below Malaysia but only slightly higher than Sri Lanka and Java where the per capita dollar income data taken from the na-

[9] The difficulties may be in the employment data. But the official labor force surveys each year in the 1970s show the changes in agricultural employment to be stable, and they appear to be easier to accept than the national accounts data. The sluggish fall of the agricultural employment share can be caused by an expansion of exports from the agricultural sector, but these exports were not rising in the 1970s.

tional accounts indicate more than twice that of Sri Lanka in 1980.[10] Thus, there may be a need to look into the national account estimations for the late 1970s.

In any case, both the Philippines and Thailand ended the postwar era with heavy underemployment, although there was probably much more in the Philippines than in Thailand. Comparable data on the underemployment problem are difficult to obtain, as definitions vary greatly. For the Philippines, recent labor force surveys report that those working less than 60 days in three months were about 30 percent of the labor force. Real wages have been falling in the Philippines since the late 1960s, by about 5 percent in the 1970s.

Available data from the labor force surveys on underemployment in Thailand show that the problem was not as severe as in the Philippines. The problem is mainly in the dry, first half of the year when about one-fifth of the labor force is without work and "waiting for the agricultural season to begin." In the second half of the year, with the coming of the monsoon rains, the percentage falls to 3 or 4 percent. The full-time unemployed labor force is only about 1 percent throughout the year, and 2 or 3 percent if those with insufficient work are included. Official data on wages are difficult to locate, but according to one report, real farm wages in the Central Plains did not rise in the 1960s but began to show a slow upward trend in the early 1970s, with the rise perhaps more rapid in the late 1970s (as suggested by the rise in kilograms of rice purchased by the daily wage cited above). How these disparate results in growth rates occurred in the two countries, starting with the agricultural sector, is analyzed below.

Agricultural Development

In Table 7.2 are shown the growth of average yields per hectare for the peasant crops of rice and corn in the postwar decades for the Philippines and Thailand (as well as for Indonesia, Malaysia, and Sri Lanka). The Philippines did not do badly, with combined growth rates of yields as high as Indonesia's and substantially higher than Thailand's, West Malaysia's, and Sri Lanka's. Nevertheless, in the tables in Chapter 3,

---

[10] From Palacpac (1980) and World Bank Reports. Of course, the real wage data are even rougher than the prices in the IRRI report and the above must not be taken as more than orders of magnitude. Wage rates per day in U.S. dollars in Thailand in mid-1977 are shown to be three times those of the Philippines. Surveys of the Food and Nutrition Institute in Manila found only a small increase between 1978 and 1982 in daily calorie intake per person (from 1,804 to 1,808), while protein intake fell substantially, from 53 to 50 grams.

Table 7.2   Average Yields of Rice, Corn, and Sugarcane: Postwar Decades, Southeast Asia (100 kg/hectare)

		Philip-pines	Indo-nesia	Thai-land	West Malaysia	Sri Lanka
1948–52	Rice	11.8	16.1	13.1	19.3	—
	Corn	7.2	7.6	9.1	12.6	—
	Sugarcane	464.0	786.0	175.0	—	—
1952–56	Rice	12.0	17.0	13.5	19.9	15.5
	Corn	5.8	9.2	12.2	13.2	—
	Sugarcane	508.0	936.0	259.0	—	—
1956–60	Rice	11.3	17.3	13.6	—	17.4
	Corn	5.6	9.2	15.6	—	—
	Sugarcane	526.0	747.0	331.0	—	—
1961–65	Rice	12.6	17.6	16.2	25.1	19.1
	Corn	6.6	9.8	19.3	13.9	—
	Sugarcane	481.7	706.0	323.3	469.9	228.4
1966–70	Rice	15.0	19.4	19.3	26.5	23.2
	Corn	7.7	9.6	22.9	31.3	—
	Sugarcane	521.0	763.0	391.0	—	—
1974–76	Rice	17.1	26.1	18.2	29.7	19.7
	Corn	8.4	10.6	23.6	80.0	—
	Sugarcane	494.0	830.0	503.0	414.0	511.1
1978–80	Rice	21.2	30.2	19.7	26.8	23.6
	Corn	9.3	13.2	20.7	12.5	
	Sugarcane	451.0	992.0	384.0	457.0	500.0
Growth percentage rates 1952/56 to 1978/80						
	Rice	2.3	2.9	1.5	1.2	1.7
	Corn	1.9	1.5	2.1	–0.1	—
	Sugarcane	–0.5	0.2	1.6	—	5.0*

Notes: Data for 1948–1952 are left out of the growth rates because of abnormal postwar reconstruction conditions.   * 1961–65 to 1978–80.

Sources: *FAO Production Yearbook*, various years. Coconut growth rate 1952/56 to 1978/80 computed from *NEDA Statistical Yearbook*, 1982 and 1977, p. 255 and p. 213, for Philippines is 1.1 percent.

product per worker in Thai and Malaysian agriculture as a whole grew more than twice as rapidly (5.1 percent on average for the 1960s and 1970s) as in Indonesia and the Philippines (2.1 percent) and five times more rapidly than in Sri Lanka (1 percent). It is product per worker, not yield per hectare, that is related to the growth of GNP per worker and per capita.

In Thailand and Malaysia the peasants were able to expand into new lands during the postwar decades, as documented in Table 7.3 with its data on acreage harvested. Thailand's expansion is substantially

Table 7.3   Rice, Corn, Sugarcane Harvested and Copra Produced: Postwar Decades, Southeast Asia (area in 1,000 hectares, copra production in 1,000 MT)

		Philippines	Thailand	West Malaysia	Indonesia
1948–52	Rice	2,350	5,211	276	5,376
	Corn	969	34	5	2,020
	Sugarcane	159	57	—	45
	Copra production	875	15	141	714
1952–56	Rice	2,693	5,345	278	6,493
	Corn	1,395	56	3	2,199
	Sugarcane	203	95	—	85
	Copra production	1,046	21	156	758
1956–60	Rice	3,151	5,225	—	6,986
	Corn	1,833	157	—	2,390
	Sugarcane	194	137	—	—
	Copra production	1,273	24	140	648
1961–65	Rice	3,147	6,944	382	7,036
	Corn	1,978	422	5	2,870
	Sugarcane	273	138	1	131
	Copra production	1,398	22	132	735
1966–70	Rice	3,164	6,618	457	7,875
	Corn	2,296	664	3	2,984
	Sugarcane	317	144	—	121
	Copra production	1,422	23	145	572
1974–76	Rice	3,560	7,972	577	8,701
	Corn	3,105	1,170	3	2,564
	Sugarcane	495	311	18	177
	Copra production	2,080	41	128	794
1978–80	Rice	3,433	8,695	711	8,911
	Corn	3,277	1,486	10	2,840
	Sugarcane	449	459	20	161
	Copra production	2,014	46	215	855
Growth percentage rate, 1952/56 to 1978/80					
	Rice	1.0	2.0	3.8	1.3
	Corn	5.0	14.0	4.9	1.0
	Sugarcane	3.2	6.5	—	2.6
	Copra production	2.7	3.2	1.3	0.5

Notes: For 1948–1956 West Malaysia, average of 2 years; Indonesia, average of 3 years; Philippines, centrifugal sugar only. Data from *FAO*.
Sources: *FAO Production Yearbook*, various years.

larger for both rice and corn than in the Philippines and Indonesia. In Malaysia, the expansion of acreage is even greater than in Thailand for rice but not for corn. In Malaysia, the increase in irrigation made possible the growing of a second crop of rice, which is much more profitable than corn; and, as we will see in Chapter 8, instead of sugar and coconut, the Malay peasants were able to increase acreages of rubber and oil palm, which were more profitable than sugar and coconut. In addition, the peasants in Thailand were able to expand into coconut, rubber, tapioca, and jute.

In the Philippines, much of the land which might have been opened up was beyond the reach of the peasantry, many of whom were tied to existing farmlands by debts and obligations to landlords. Thus, when in the post-independence period Mindanao was opened up, it was not the small peasants who were able to take advantage of the opportunities but the multinationals, mainly from the United States, and the indigenous landowners from the north who established plantations and large farms. In the 1971 Census of Agriculture, the average farm size in Mindanao was about 25 percent larger than in the Philippines as a whole.

That it was not the physical size of potential agricultural land that mattered most but the institutional forces involved is shown by the statistics on density. If we look not at the conventional density concept (whereby total population is divided by the total physical size of the country), but at what may be termed agricultural density—agricultural population divided by the total agricultural land (inclusive of land under temporary and perennial cultivation)—the data in the tables in Chapter 3 indicate that agricultural density was the same in 1960 and 1970. It is notable that Burma, with density almost as low as Malaysia, did poorly in agricultural growth with lower growth of product than the Philippines, Thailand, and Malaysia in the 1960s and 1970s (see Table 7.4). In Indonesia, despite the vast amounts of land in the outer islands, especially in Sumatra, the failure to develop and resettle Javanese in the outer islands. resulted in sharp density increases.

Though density in the Philippines is about one-tenth higher than in Thailand, it is considerably less than in most countries listed in the tables in Chapter 3 except for Burma and West Malaysia. Moreover, crop lands in the Philippines are more fertile than those in Thailand. About one-half of the acreage in Thailand is in low-yielding and flooded deep-water rice lands in the lower Central Plains where the Chao Phaya River overflows annually, and the rest is in the vast stretches of the northeast with insufficient rainfall and rivers. Rainfall in Thailand is much less than in the Philippines, about 50 inches on the average in the lowlands compared to about 100 inches in the Philippines.

It was the expansion into the low-rainfall northeast in the postwar

Table 7.4   Agricultural Density and Annual Growth of Arable Land and
Land under Permanent Cropping: All Asian Countries

	Annual Growth (in %) of Arable Land and Under Permanent Crops				Agricultural Density*	
	1950s	*1960s*	*1970s*	*Avg.*	*1960*	*1979*
East Asia	1.7	0.2	–0.5	0.5	6.2	5.1
Japan	4.7	–1.0	–1.2	0.8	5.1	2.7
Taiwan	–0.1	0.4	0.1	0.1	6.2	5.8
S. Korea	0.5	1.3	–0.4	0.5	7.3	6.7
Southeast Asia	2.9	1.8	1.3	2.0	2.7	2.7
Philippines	3.5	1.3	0.4	1.7	2.3	2.3
Thailand	5.7	3.7	3.0	4.1	2.1	2.0
West Malaysia	2.2	2.1	0.9	1.7	2.0	1.7
Indonesia	0.1	0.1	0.8	0.3	4.2	4.6
South Asia	0.6	0.4	0.5	0.4	2.5	3.8
India	0.3	0.2	0.3	0.3	2.0	2.6
Nepal	0.1	–0.8	1.1	0.1	2.2	3.2
Sri Lanka	1.4	1.9	0.9	1.4	3.2	3.6
Burma	—	—	–0.4	–0.4	—	1.8
Bangladesh	—	—	—	—	—	7.9

Notes: *Agricultural density refers to agriculture population per hectare of
arable land and land under permanent crops. Arable land refers to land
under temporary crops (double-cropped areas are counted only once),
temporary meadows for mowing or pasture, land under market and kitchen
gardens (including cultivation under grass), and land temporarily fallow or
lying idle. Land under permanent crops refers to land cultivated with crops
that occupy the land for long periods and need not be replanted after each
harvest, such as cocoa, coffee, and rubber; it includes land under shrubs,
fruit trees, nut trees and vines, but excludes land under trees grown for
wood or timber. The agricultural density for Japan in 1950 is 7.5 persons per
hectare.
Source: Various issues of *FAO Production Yearbook*.

decades that produced the slow rise in rice yields and the heavy underemployment in the dry seasons in Thai agriculture, although crop
diversification in the wet season opened up opportunities for work on
other farms and off-farm, and reduced idleness between planting and
harvesting on the rice farms.

Just as important in the differential growth of labor productivity
in agriculture, particularly when exports are considered, is the performance of crops other than grains. Here too, as in rice and corn, the
Philippines performed better in yields per hectare except in the most
important crops: sugarcane and coconut. But the total expansion of
production, export, and productivity per worker were substantially

higher in Thailand as new lands were brought under cultivation. This was also unexpected since the Philippines started the postwar decades with a large, efficient plantation sector and brought in experienced multinational plantations in banana and pineapple. In Thai livestock, poultry, fishery and forestry production, the growth rate of product was also nearly twice that of the Philippines, in units of constant value added, and their exports rose faster.[11] In the two plantation crops where indigenously owned estates were large, sugar and coconut, the performance was disappointing and fell short of Thai achievements, but in others such as banana and pineapple where the multinationals were conspicuous, the results were good (Tables 7.1 and 7.2 and Oshima, 1983). It was particularly disappointing in the major Philippine export crop, sugarcane, of which yields per hectare averaged about 52 tons per hectare in the 1950s, but fell to about 47 tons in the 1970s, compared to Thailand's 30 tons in the 1950s and 45 tons in the 1970s. The Thai small peasants in the 1970s were producing about as much as the Philippine plantations. In the early 1980s Philippine production costs were twice world market prices even though wages paid to plantation workers were among the lowest.

Nor was it public expenditures on agriculture that contributed to the differential agricultural growth of productivity, since both governments spent only about 1 percent of GNP on the agricultural sector in the 1960s and 1970s (Tables 7.5 and 7.6). One reason for the low expenditures in agriculture in Thailand was smaller outlay for extension agents since much of the guidance to the peasants was supplied by middlemen-traders who proved to be more efficient and enterprising than the extension agents in the Philippines. Nor were rice prices received by the producers more attractive for the Thai farmers since prices in U.S. dollars were about 50 percent higher in the late 1970s in the Philippines, far more than could be offset by the overvaluation of the peso relative to the baht. Moreover, the growth was attained with less use of fertilizer in 1972, only one-half that used in the Philippines per arable hectare, two-thirds that used in India and Indonesia, and one-fifth that used in Malaysia (Intharathai et al., 1976). Thus, the growth of Thai agriculture was much more efficient, owing largely to the vigorous efforts of the farmers. In many respects, it resembled the

---

[11] See data for Philippines in *Journal of Philippine Development,* op cit., Table 5, and for Thailand, World Bank, *Thailand, Selected Issues in Rural Development,* Table 3, Background Working Paper No.4 (Nov. 1978). Value-added figures from the national accounts of each country. Despite the very much larger coastline and fishing waters surrounding the Philippines, the Thais caught 2 million tons of fish compared with 1.5 million in the Philippines, 1977–1979.

Table 7.5   Annual Average Expenditure by Function of General Government: Thailand

	1950s Average			1960s Average			1970s Average		
	Amount (Mn. baht)	% of Total	% of GNP	Amount (Mn. baht)	% of Total	% of GNP	Amount (Mn. baht)	% of Total	% of GNP
General administration	887.9	27.0	2.4	3,389.7	35.5	3.7	10,163.5	24.5	2.8
Defense	879.5	26.7	2.4	2,471.7	25.9	2.7	14,272.0	34.4	4.0
Justice and police	456.3	13.9	1.2	929.0	9.7	1.0	3,700.5	8.9	1.0
Education and research	811.1	24.7	2.2	1,898.7	19.9	2.1	9,720.0	23.4	2.7
Health and services	126.9	3.9	0.3	344.0	3.6	0.4	1,815.0	4.4	0.5
Special welfare services	13.9	0.4	0.0	57.1	0.6	0.1	211.0	0.5	0.1
Transport and communication	71.9	2.2	0.2	423.5	4.4	0.5	1,384.0	3.3	0.4
Other services	42.9	1.3	0.1	43.8	0.5	0.1	227.0	0.5	0.1
TOTAL	3,290.0	100.0	8.9	9,557.5	100.0	10.5	41,493.0	100.0	11.6
As % of total expenditure		29.0			24.1			28.3	
As % of GNP		2.5			2.6			3.3	

Notes: (1) Local government expenditure accounted less than 6 percent of total government expenditure. (2) Based on *Thailand—Toward a Development Strategy of Full Participation*, IBRD, the percent share spent on agriculture in the 1970s is 8 percent of total government expenditure and 1 percent of GNP.

Sources: Various issues of *National Income of Thailand*.

Table 7.6 Annual Average Expenditure by Function of Central Government: Philippines

	Average 1950s			Average 1960s			Average 1970s		
	Amount (Mn. pesos)	% of Total	% of GNP	Amount (Mn. pesos)	% of Total	% of GNP	Amount (Mn. pesos)	% of Total	% of GNP
General public services	92	9.2	0.8	380	15.7	1.1	3,180	15.2	2.2
Defense	182	18.1	1.7	271	11.2	1.2	3,224	15.5	2.3
Education	253	25.2	2.3	698	28.7	3.2	2,591	12.4	1.8
Health				138	5.7	0.6	820	3.9	0.6
Social security & welfare	70	7.0	0.6	36	1.5	0.2	411	2.0	0.3
Housing & communities amenities							510	2.4	0.4
Other community & soc. services							120	0.6	0.1
Economic services				755	31.1	3.5	8,361	40.1	5.9
Gen. adm., regulation and research	74	7.4	0.7				1,120	5.4	0.8
Agriculture, forestry, fishing				202	8.3	0.9	1,705	8.2	1.2
Mining, manufacturing and construction	55	5.5	0.5	65	2.7	0.3	513	2.5	0.4
Electricity, gas, steam and water							1,060	5.1	0.7
Roads	206	20.5	1.9	390	16.1	1.8	2,324	11.1	1.6
Inland and coastal waterways							72	0.3	0.0
Other transport and communication				98	4.0	0.4	638	3.1	0.5
Other economic services				150	6.2	0.7	928	4.4	0.6
Other purposes	73	7.3	0.7				1,647	7.9	1.2
TOTAL	1,005	100.0	9.2	2,428	100.0	11.1	20,864	100.0	14.6
As % of total expenditure		32.2			35.9			21.3	
As % of GNP		2.9			4.0			3.2	

Sources: Data for 1970s computed from *IMF Government Finance Statistics Yearbook, 1982*; data for 1960s computed from *NEDA Statistical Yearbook of the Philippines 1976*; data for 1950s computed from *UN Statistical Yearbook*.

performance of the Taiwan peasants, who, without much help from the central government, were able to grow rapidly, contributing greatly to the development of the rest of the economy, especially in export earnings and in generating surpluses (see Chapter 5). In these respects, agriculture's contribution to industrialization was substantial in Thailand and Taiwan.

The different historical circumstances conditioned the pattern of labor productivity growth in agriculture in the two countries—one never occupied by foreign powers, and the other occupied for long centuries by unprogressive, predatory, feudalistic conquerors who did little to furnish even minimal protection to the peasantry from the exactions of its own economic elite. More than in other Asian countries colonized by foreign powers, the Philippine indigenous elite grew into a rich and powerful oligarchy taking over lands from Spaniards on the one hand and from the peasants on the other as they took advantage of the growth of Western markets for tropical crops. By the end of the United States occupation, there were a few hundred families with land holdings of 50 hectares and more, a hundred or so with more than 2,000 hectares, and a score with 4,000 hectares (Wurfel, 1979). In comparison, the large landlords in Thailand, even in the Central Plains where land concentration is greatest, were much smaller, and the largest consisted of not much more than a few hundred hectares (Takahashi, 1976). In Malaysia, Sri Lanka, and Indonesia, too, the estates of indigenous landlords were in the hundred-hectare class rather than the thousands. The Philippine situation in many ways resembled more that of French-occupied Vietnam with its large rice estates, only on a larger scale.[12]

There is nothing particularly wrong with concentration of economic and political power in an indigenous elite. In Japan, the oligarchy spearheaded modernization and development in the prewar Japanese Empire, and while the whole effort ended disastrously in the 1940s, there were enough constructive elements in the prewar efforts to survive the disaster; in the postwar decades these blossomed into the spectacular growth of Japan, Taiwan, and Korea. The Japanese oligarchs' efforts contained a strong element which was directed to *national* development as distinct from their own *vested* interests. The Thai oligarchy, while neglecting agricultural development, facilitated the efforts of the peasantry to expand and concentrated its attention on catching up with the neighboring countries in enlarging physical in-

[12] The economic power of the Philippine oligarchs is shown by the private armies they maintain, more numerous than anywhere else in Asia and perhaps the root of the violence that has plagued the country.

Table 7.7 Incremental Capital Output Ratio and Savings Rates, Various Countries

	ICOR	Average Internal Savings Rate	Share of Total Savings in GNP
	1960–80	*1970–81*	*1970–81*
East Asia	3.40	28.9	32.0
Japan	4.15	33.8	33.3
China	4.91	30.6	31.1
Taiwan	2.81	28.6	30.7
South Korea	2.92	23.0	29.4
Hong Kong	2.49	27.6	26.7
Singapore	3.12	29.7	40.7
Southeast Asia	3.14	23.1	25.3
Philippines	4.04	23.9	28.7
Malaysia	3.08	26.6	26.1
Thailand	2.82	20.8	26.1
Indonesia	2.61	20.9	20.2
South Asia	5.46	15.2	20.3
India	5.71	20.1	21.6
Sri Lanka	5.75	12.0	22.7
Burma	4.93	13.6	16.5
United States of America	4.93	19.5	19.0
Low-Income Countries	4.89	—	—
Middle-Income Countries	4.17	—	—
Industrialized Countries	5.24	—	—

Notes: ICOR calculated as unweighted average of opening and closing investment ratios, divided by growth rate of GDP. The excess of share of GDCF in GDP over that of internal savings rate reflects the extent of GDCF financing by foreign savings either by borrowing or equity.

Sources: ICOR computed from *IBRD World Development Report, 1982*, other data computed from *IBRD World Tables*, Third Edition, vol. 1, 1983.

frastructure for modern national development. This cannot be said for the Philippine oligarchy, brought up for centuries under the shadow of rapacious Spanish rulers.[13]

After decades of neglect, the Philippines in the 1970s was compelled to turn its attention to agricultural and rural development. A grandiose plan for agrarian reform patterned after the East Asian experience was enunciated under martial law conditions, and some successes were

[13] See Simbulan (1965) for a discussion of elites in each province.

achieved in the first half of the 1970s, but these fell short of East Asian achievements, with only 19 percent of the tenants having received certificates of land ownership after a decade of land reform. The ruling elite in the second half of the 1970s turned to the building of its own new economic oligarchy, financed with borrowings and other aid from international sources.[14]

Industrial Development

The tables in Chapter 3 show that the overall industrial sector product grew at 10 percent a year in Thailand and 7.3 percent in the Philippines; Thai growth exceeded Philippine growth in each of the three decades, narrowly in the 1950s but by wide margins in the later decades. Since Thailand's industrial levels at the beginning of the 1950s were far below those of the Philippines, it is important to look at industrial product per worker, which underlies growth of product per capita. The margin between the two countries is even larger, with Thailand growing at twice the Philippine rate, 3.2 percent to 1.5 percent. Thailand's growth of industrial product is highest of the ASEAN agrarian Four; its growth of product per worker is nearly as high as Malaysia's, 3.9 to 4.0, respectively, with Indonesia at 2.8 and the Philippines lowest at 1.9. The Philippine performance is even more disappointing in view of the fact that in the early 1950s it had a head start in industrialization which put it ahead of even South Korea, Taiwan, and Malaysia; by the early 1980s it had fallen so far behind them that any "catch-up" in textiles, garments, shoes, wood products, consumer electronics, and engineering is going to be difficult despite the lower wages. These are all labor-intensive industries whose expansion is badly needed to absorb the large pool of unemployed and new workers coming into the accelerating labor force in the 1970s and 1980s.

If we look into the industrial subsectors for details of the differential growth of labor productivity, every one of the five subsectors registered higher productivity growth in Thailand except for construction (Philippines' 1.9 as against –0.9 for Thailand). The differential was widest in the public utilities (9.4 for Thailand as against 0.4); lowest in mining 2.1 and –0.2; and middling in manufacturing (3.7 and 1.6) and transport and communication (3.6 and 1.6) (Oshima, 1983d: 92).

The wide disparity in public utility productivity growth is plausible to anyone who has lived in the capital cities of the two countries. In

---

[14] The assured market in the U.S. for sugar at guaranteed prices for long periods contributed to inefficiencies, akin to the loss of vitality of British entrepreneurship with assured industrial markets in the colonies.

Manila, since the 1950s and 1960s telephone and electricity services have steadily worsened as maintenance, repair, and replacement were neglected; with the best system among the ASEAN capitals during the 1950s, Manila had perhaps the poorest among the ASEAN agrarian four by the late 1970s. In contrast, Thailand, without a colonial background, had to substantially expand meager and inadequate facilities beginning in the early 1960s. Similar impressions hold true for transportation. The Thai bus and rail systems today are superior to the Philippines' obsolete railways and dilapidated buses. Philippine Airlines started out in the 1950s as the largest airway in East and Southeast Asia (except for JAL), but today Thai International Airways has become one of the largest and most profitable carriers. In all these fields, Filipino management was generally inefficient and often ineffective; its problems compounded by insufficient funding for replacements and maintenance. The postal system by the late 1970s had degenerated into one of the worst in Asia, inviting the proliferation of private messenger services and telegraph companies.

In the manufacturing sector, the low (1.6 percent) rate of growth of output per worker can be traced mainly to the labor-intensive branches of textiles, footwear, garments, and leather products (−3.4 percent), to the more capital-intensive branches of chemicals, petroleum, and non metallic minerals (−1.3 percent), and to basic metals, machinery, and transport equipment (−2.7 percent) (Echavez, 1981). In Thailand, for the period 1963–1976, labor productivity in firms with 10 or more workers grew at a rate of 3.7 percent.[15] These figures are not quite comparable as the Philippine data pertain to firms with five or more workers and are for 1956 to 1974: the differences are due to differences in the coverage of the establishment censuses and surveys in the two countries; the output data are from the national accounts and the employment data are from labor force surveys. But they are in line with the broad results shown in the overall coverage of tables in Chapter 3 and other data cited.

In the Philippines, the manufacturing sector was troubled from the

---

[15]From Paitoon Wiboonchutikala,"The Total Factor Productivity Growth of the Manufacturing Industries in Thailand, 1963–1966," National University of Singapore, Economics Department, 1982/83, mimeo. The estimates of total factor productivity in this study are difficult to interpret as the capital stock estimates were derived from capital data reported in the Industrial Censuses where only half of the sample replied. Such data were applied to the Ministry of Industry's Surveys of Industrial Output which covered a much larger universe. In *Productivity Growth in Philippine Manufacturing*, PIDS, 1984, Richard Hooley comes up with estimates generally consistent with ours, though they pertain to a longer period but a much smaller group of industries, 20 workers and more, only 4 percent of the total in manufacturing in 1980.

early 1950s by an import-substitution strategy which lasted into the early 1980s in one form or another. Much has been written on the nature of Philippine import-substitution policies, starting with the pioneering studies of John Power and Gerardo Sicat. To summarize briefly the findings from these and other studies: the import-substitution policies, despite changes in the 1960s and 1970s, left a badly distorted economy which was biased against exports, producers' goods, labor-intensive industries including agriculture, smaller units of production, regionalization, efficiency, employment creation, and income equality.[16]

The literature on Philippine import-substitution policies is the best in Southeast Asia; many countries have profited from the analysis contained in these studies, but its impact seems to be the least felt in the Philippines. The question arises: why was it that such economic policies were pursued so long, throughout the 1960s and 1970s, when they militated against overall national interests—while industrial successes were being achieved in the 1950s in nearby Japan and Hong Kong, and in the 1960s in Taiwan, Korea, Singapore, Malaysia, and Thailand? In contrast, India, Sri Lanka, and several of the Latin American countries with similar structures of protection were faltering. Communist China was slowing down in the 1960s and 1970s, with a different structure of incentives militating against efficiencies and more in the direction of the Sri Lankan and Burmese systems of welfare and socialism. (See Chapter 8 on Sri Lanka and Malaysia and Chapter 9 on India and China.) Questions like these are difficult to answer, and it is understandable that trade economists with a strong bent toward quantitative studies are loath to go beyond quantitative findings. But in a study of the secular growth of nations it is difficult to evade them, and a beginning must be made.

The answer may be similar to that proposed in the discussion on agricultural development. The ruling elites who emerged from a colonial past were too powerful in political, economic, and social life to be forced to make major concessions to small businesses and workers (or to the peasants and the landless workers in agriculture). As in the case of Latin American countries with a Hispanic colonial past, the oligarchies perceived family destiny to have higher priority than that of the nation which they ruled with little opposition.[17] In such a political setup, the urge to lower tariffs and to boost exports is weak, partic-

---

[16] In particular, see Power, 1966; Power, 1971; Baldwin, 1975.

[17] Spain and Portugal were the slowest growing nations in Western Europe throughout the 19th and 20th centuries, along with Southern Italy, which was occupied for two centuries by Spain.

ularly with the large masses of consumers too weak in political power to protest. In South Korea, the military regime that came into power in the early 1960s worried about the effects of a stagnating, import-substituting industrialization on the nation's defense efforts against the North; similar concerns were foremost among the Kuomintang leaders who fled to Taiwan and imposed their rule on the island population. To the British in Hong Kong and the labor-supported government of Singapore, there was absolutely no alternative but to find markets abroad, since these city-states must export to pay for their large food imports and to substitute for domestic demand from the agricultural sector. (See Chapter 6.) In Malaysia, the Malay political leadership had no desire to pay high prices for protected industrial products made internally by Chinese and other foreigners. The military-dominated Thai regime had similar leanings.

There may be other reasons. The Filipino ruling elite was richer than its counterpart elsewhere: land reforms in Taiwan and South Korea, colonial protection of the peasantry in Malaysia and Indonesia, and land policies in Thailand weakened the landed oligarchies. Not only could the Filipino oligarchs transfer their large surpluses from agriculture to urban investments, but additional funds were supplied by the government and private banks, most of which they controlled.

Nevertheless, by the late 1960s it was obvious that exports could be profitable as supplements to stagnant local markets, thus reducing excess capacities which had emerged in many Philippine industries. If the latter had become efficient enough to make it worth while to go international, Philippine industry could have maintained some measure of protection at home and competed abroad, as Taiwan and South Korea did. Apparently this was not the case, and the reason must be sought in the quality of Filipino entrepreneurship, which many past observers had assumed to be of relatively high quality.

But entrepreneurship to match or surpass the Asian NICs must be exceptionally good since it must compete with their strong Confucian work ethics.[18] We are also led to look beyond protection into the quality of entrepreneurship by the fact that in the service and non-manufacturing industries where protectionist policies did not apply, the growth of labor productivity was even more disappointing than in protected

---

[18] John J. Carroll (1965) points out: "Many ... do appear to work hard; but few of them gave evidence of the compulsive need to work and to amass wealth which appears in Skinner's description of the self-made Chinese business leaders of Bangkok. ... Rather, they seem to enjoy their work and the varied satisfactions which it brings them—including the opportunity to live well and to spend freely, for there is little evidence of Calvinist asceticism among them."

manufacturing, with the lowest growth rates among all the East Asian and ASEAN countries.[19] Many of the favorable comments about Philippine entrepreneurship (by Caroll and Golay) were based on statistics on the rapid growth of industrial output in the 1950s but which paid little attention to the growth of output per worker so important in judging growth performance. It is not difficult to increase industrial output at the outset of industrialization if the state doles out huge amounts of cheap loans and subsidies, but it is another matter to improve productivity.

Reading the pre-World War II literature, one is struck by the references to the propensity of the indigenous oligarchy to absorb the lifestyle of the Spanish, especially their luxurious indulgences. In fact, one reference goes so far as to remark that the culture of the indigenous oligarchy became even "more Spanish than the Spanish." This behavior surprised the colonial administration during the American period, and it appeared to have continued into the postwar period after independence. In Asia, just as the Japanese businessmen are known for their groupism, the Koreans for their dynamism, and the Javanese for their mysticism, the Philippine ruling elite are known for their luxurious lifestyle. Such a lifestyle is not likely to be conducive to strong entrepreneurship, which is particularly necessary in the early stages of industrialization.

Philippine management styles were studied by Mamoru Tsuda (1978) from the perspectives of about 98 Japanese investors, mostly large firms, in joint ventures in the Philippines. These firms not only were in highly protected manufacturing, but the majority were protected minimally, including several corporations in finance, commerce, services, fishery, agriculture, and construction. The Japanese investors were appalled at the differences from the management styles to which they were accustomed in Japan, and to which they attributed the high productivity of Japanese firms. Tsuda describes the common pattern in the Philippines as authoritarian decision-making, extensive nepotism and the dominance of familial interests over those of the corporation, contemptuous attitudes toward workers, short-term profit maxi-

[19] It is often said that United States assistance to Taiwan and South Korea was the source of their good performances, but it must be remembered that much of this aid went directly or indirectly to the maintenance of huge armed forces numbering 300,000 to 400,000. In this regard the Philippines probably received more non-military assistance per capita than any of the countries in the region, especially in the 1950s and 1960s through United States aid and Japanese reparations which amounted to a few billion dollars. Destruction caused by World War II was extensive in all three countries, not only in the Philippines. Moreover, U.S. bases at Subic and Clark spared the Philippines from spending much for defense.

mization practices, and a strong tendency to drain profits out of the enterprises into other activities.

Some of these characteristics might have disappeared under more competitive market conditions with less protective markets, but they were also traits which characterized oligarchic behavior in the Philippines long before the postwar decades, originating in plantation management. There is here an interrelation between deep-rooted historical values and the structure of protection, just as the Japanese system of management and industrial relations are rooted in the prewar past. Infant industries were slow to grow into maturity under protection as experienced employees left for other firms in reaction to discriminatory promotion practices and the "learning" effects were dissipated while scale economies were slow to emerge as profits were drained out and put into other enterprises in different industries or else consumed.[20]

Recently an extensive and authoritative study on Philippine management in selected manufacturing industries was carried out by a World Bank team headed by B. A. de Vries (1980). It confirms the findings of the Bautista-Power volume concerning the unfavorable impact of high protection on domestic costs. There were many cases of low protection and high domestic resource costs (glass, glass products, hand tools, general hardware, industrial chemicals, several wood products, cordage, twine, and net), and conversely high protection and low costs (slaughtering, poultry dressing, metal cans, boxes, and containers). These cases may have something to do with cost "cascading" and bottlenecks, which the World Bank team found troublesome in a number of labor-intensive industries (textiles, garments, wood products, leather products, metal products, and printing and publishing), but the quantitative measures of protection and resource costs also cannot take into account major aspects of quality so important in international markets, especially in Japan and the U.S.A.

It is interesting to note that the discussion on management inefficiencies and family controls is reminiscent of the first authoritative economic survey of the Philippines, that of the Bell Mission, made before

---

[20] Tsuda notes that some of the respondents had studied the historical past and attributed this unique entrepreneurial behavior to the long colonial period, both Spanish and American, and the low efficiency of the Filipino workers to their poor treatment; many of them were worried about the near future and unsure of how long political stability would last and were preparing to pull out. Since the time of Tsuda's study many of the Japanese investors have left, according to *Business Day*, Dec. 2, 1982, p. 2. The Bell Report, cited below, also attributed the low productivity of the Filipino worker to poor employment practices. Under different management abroad, the Filipinos are known to be good workers.

the import-substitution regime was imposed.[21] The main focus of this report, which was made at the time of the Philippine government's request for financial assistance in 1948 after the large reserves of foreign exchange were dissipated with imports of luxury goods and transfer of capital abroad only two years after independence, was on the need to improve economic efficiency. These bits of evidence, together with the poor performance of the non-manufacturing industries, indicate that historical factors, in addition to the adverse structure of incentives, played a major role in the postwar growth patterns of the industrial sector. In Japan, the automotive and other industries, though highly protected in the 1950s and 1960s, emerged as internationally competitive industries in the 1970s. More than compensating for the absence of competition from abroad was the fierce competition within Japan and good management practices and industrial policies. This is relevant to the findings of the World Bank team regarding industries with low protection and high costs.

The Thai industrial policy was more pragmatic. After dabbling with public-operated industries in the 1950s, the government was convinced by the poor results to turn to import substitution through private enterprise in the 1960s and fairly good results were obtained. But seeing that import-substitution successes were short-lived, it began to go in for export promotion in the 1970s with measures which compensated for the import-substitution biases. The baht was kept undervalued, unlike the overvalued peso, throughout most of the period (IBRD, 1980). Above all, there was no large class of landed oligarchs who were anxious to move into big industrial enterprises and become tycoons. The Thais left industrialization to the local commercial classes, most of whom were Thai-Chinese. Nor did they license a large group of American enterprises interested only in exploiting the domestic market with no intention to export, or limit export-oriented foreign enterprises to minority shares, thereby subjecting them to the dictates of inefficient indigenous entrepreneurs.

In sum, the Philippines started with an industrial entrepreneurial class whose work ethic was weaker than Thailand's. Because the struc-

---

[21] *Economic Survey Mission to the Philippines, Report to the President of the United States* Washington, D.C.: 1950. This was an even larger mission than the World Bank, one with a higher level of expertise. The recommendations were notable even from the vantage point of the 1980s, and it is tantalizing to imagine what the Philippines would be like today if they had been implemented then and in later decades. As it is, the problems it raised—productive inefficiencies, fiscal and financial mismanagement, misdirected investment, inflation, balance of payments deficits, unequal income distribution, corruption, low credibility of the government and so on —are still unsolved in the Philippines of the 1980s. For the latter see de Dios, 1984.

ture of incentives was less favorable to improvements, productivity per worker did not rise very much as time went on, despite the increasing capital intensity. The Filipino entrepreneurial spirit should improve with a more favorable incentive structure, but this will take time; it is still not too late.

The Service Sector

Service product grew at a 5.4 percent annual rate in the Philippines during the three decades, compared with 7.5 percent in Thailand, but the disturbing thing is that service product per worker did not improve while in Thailand it was growing at 3 percent. This failure can be traced to commerce and government service, in which productivity declined, while personal services registered only a small rise (about 1 percent). These figures can be compared with Thailand's rise of 3.5 percent for commerce and personal services and 1.9 percent for government service (Oshima, 1983: 92). As noted in Chapter 3, even though the S sector grows largely in response to the growth of the commodity-producing sectors A and I, and in response to household demand, it is the main supplier of external economies to these other sectors in the form of financial, marketing, informational, training, sanitation, and security (law and order) services. A large part of the costs of industrial and agricultural product and household expenditures involves the service sector (plus utilities, transport, communication), and as such the efficiency of these other sectors depends on services in one form or another. As noted in Chapter 6, the efficiency of Hong Kong's and Singapore's industries is due partly to their dynamic service sectors. The magnitude of external economies generated by the S sector may be surmised by the size of value added. Even in countries like the Philippines and Thailand, whose industrial transition is far from complete, about two-fifths of GNP, or roughly the size of the industrial value added, is generated by the S sector.

It is necessary to be cautious about interpreting the S data in terms of constant prices. For many of the small units in commerce and personal services, the data on current output are difficult to collect, but even more difficult is the deflation to convert current to constant prices. The problem is compounded by intractable conceptual problems in defining the output of such sectors as government (Oshima, 1979). Public services are normally not sold, so there are no prices for the output of public administration, defense, education, public health, police services, and others, and output must be measured from the costs of inputs in which the overwhelmingly important cost is wages and salaries. These rise mainly with prices. In the Philippine national accounting practice (and also in the case of Thailand and some other countries), government output over time in constant prices is measured by extrapolating some base year value of current output by the number of government employees, which implicitly assumes that the growth of labor productivity is zero. An alternative (perhaps better) method is to deflate the current output over time by the cost of living index, thereby separating out the increases due to prices, leaving productivity increases in the constant output series. The limitation of this method is that government wage and salary changes do not reflect productivity changes of its employees; in the long run, however, there must be some correspondence if the government is to be able to recruit workers for its varied functions, many of which have counterparts in the private sector. When the cost of living index is used as the deflator, the 2.6 percent growth of public output in the Philippines is substantially smaller than in the official estimates for the 1970s (Thailand's was 4.6 percent).

The explanation for the inadequate performance of the service sector in the Philippines is generally consistent with that presented for the commodity sectors. In the vital financial sector, where savings are collected and then allocated, there was a concentration of economic power in the large firms which enabled them to limit competition in a cartel-like fashion. A World Bank/IMF study noted that ". . . concentration in the financial sector tends to create excessive market power for a few institutions. Market power, in turn, will reduce the economic efficiency of the financial sector as a whole, because credit will tend to be misallocated and extended at a high cost" (World Bank/IMF, 1980). And an ILO report concludes: "In general, it seems clear that the resulting allocation of credit has systematically discriminated against the small-scale, labour-intensive enterprise and against the low-income family, through the requirement of collateral to secure loans for small borrowers but not for 'some wealthy or influential individual or firm acceptable to the bank' [and] the heavy emphasis on short-term loans, low interest rates to small savers, and so on."

Since these studies, the government has floated the interest rates on savings by removing the ceiling, but they have remained substantially unchanged at around 9 percent, far below the inflation rate, as the Bankers Association of the Philippines is able to reimpose the ceilings. In addition, a major scandal has shaken the banking system since one of the favored borrowers absconded with large amounts of unsecured loans.

It is well known in the Philippines that the important commercial banks are controlled by the leading business families of the country with their close ties to many of the largest industrial and agricultural corporations (Tsuda; 1978; IBON Databank, n.d.). With such concentrated economic power lodged in the country's major banks the tendency for the allocation of savings and credit to be biased toward the larger firms in the commercial sectors will leave the numerous small firms with inadequate funding, constraining their efficiency and productivity growth. This together with the larger units' slow growth due to insufficient competition, though funding is ample, retards the overall growth of the commercial sector.

There is another factor, perhaps more important than the above. The rapid population increase, particularly in the 1950s and the 1960s, accelerated the growth of the labor supply in the 1970s to the highest level in Asia (over 3 percent per year) according to the National Development Authority of the Philippines National Census and Statistical Office. In the face of insufficient employment opportunities in the agricultural and industrial sectors, the excess labor force must seek employment in the informal sectors of commerce and personal services —in the small shops and stores, in street vending, in food stalls, in domestic services, and so on. The informal sectors can be more flexible about employment expansion, but productivity is extremely low not only because much less land or capital is used but because the intensity of work throughout the day or the number of work days in a week can be varied easily. Thus earnings, either wages or returns to proprietors, are the lowest in the urban sector. The informal service sector (and not the agricultural sector) has become the residual sector of the economy, absorbing surplus workers not needed by the commodity sectors.

Moreover, in the Philippines real wages in the urban economy have been falling since the mid-1960s with no evidence of any perceptible rise before the mid-1960s for blue-collar and unskilled laborers. Such declines in real wages over the decades imply that by the late 1970s the main wage earner in low-income households was unable to bring home sufficient income to maintain the subsistence levels of the 1960s. This must have forced women, especially housewives, into the labor market in an effort to maintain family subsistence levels. This conjecture is consistent with the data from the labor force surveys showing that the unusual rise in the labor force throughout the 1970s was due not to the increase in the working age population but to the increase in the labor force participation rates, which rose to 58.4 percent in 1978 and 62.2 percent in 1983 (first quarter), an increase mainly due to the growth of the female participation rate. With the commodity sector growing slowly, it was the residual service sector which bore the brunt of labor absorption. The share of employment in the commodity sectors declined from around 75 percent in the 1960s to 72 percent in the 1970s while the S sector share rose from 25 percent to 28 percent.[22]

In the foregoing mechanism, the slow growth of output in the commodity producing sectors generates insufficient jobs; the labor surplus grows as the labor supply accelerates, and the poor performance of output per worker in the commodity sectors keeps real wages down. Slow growth of output and output per worker together push the surplus labor into the informal S sectors using minimal amounts of capital and paying the lowest wages, and as real wages in the overall economy fall, the surplus labor force increases more than the working-age population increases (3.3 percent annually) as lower-income families desperately try to maintain a bare subsistence level. But this, in turn, forces down productivity in the informal S sector. This may have been the main mechanism preventing the private S sector from improving productivity because employment in small units with fewer than 10 workers is large in the S sector. In 1972 there were 520,000 in commerce or 55 percent of all business and 910,000 in personal services or 56 percent of the total. In 1978, the employment share of small units in commerce rose to 67 percent and in personal services to 88 percent according to the official Establishment Census.[23] With such large increases in the low-productivity, small-unit sectors, increases in the larger units must be very large to compensate for the lower productivity.

The Thai commercial sector appears to be much more competitive than that in the Philippines. Despite a number of problems and shortcomings, the banking system is ably supervised by the Bank of Thailand, one of the independent central banks in the region. In contrast to the Philippine situation, the competition of the commercial banks for deposits is so strong that the central bank must hold down the interest rates on deposits for fear that competition may make them too high. The wholesale and retail sectors also appear to be more competitive. In food retailing, instead of only 47 central public markets licensed by the Manila government, there are many more central markets and innumerable smaller ones, which can buy easily at wholesale markets and compete effectively among themselves. Entry to food marketing appears to be wide open in contrast to the centralized system in Manila, and food prices are lower in Bangkok: in mid-1977 (in U.S. dollars)

[22] Data from Oshima, 1977a.
[23] Data from Oshima, 1983c. Totals for firms with fewer than 10 workers were taken from the 1972 Census of Establishments and for all firms from the 1972 Labor Force Survey.

a kilogram of rice at retail price was $0.28 in Manila compared with $0.21 in Bangkok (Palacpac, 1980).

In the Philippine government sector, despite U.S. efforts to establish a strong civil service system in the bureaucracy from the early decades of its occupation, the system has steadily weakened over the course of the postwar decades. This began in the Commonwealth period before the war with an increasing number of appointments made outside the system, and by the mid-1970s, two-thirds of government officials were appointed without competitive exams (Corpuz, 1965; Henderson et al., 1976). The bureaucracy became substantially overstaffed with political appointees, and instead of efficiency improving as occurred in Thailand, Indonesia, and elsewhere, matters appear to have gotten worse in the 1970s as the purchasing power of real earnings diminished and the need for supplementation with graft and "moonlighting" increased.

Well-publicized purges of the government bureaucracy were conducted periodically by the martial law government in the 1970s. But in 1984, when another purge was announced, one columnist in a Manila paper remarked that these purges were of limited value as the top echelon of government officials was barely affected, bearing out the views of public administration experts that purges were not the way to improve the behavior of public officials. In other countries, improvements came through quiet and continuous efforts by the top leadership toward the leading officials directly below, who in turn directed efforts toward their subordinates. The notable personnel improvements in a handful of agencies, such as in planning, were outweighed; all this is consistent with data showing negative growth of output per worker despite the limitation of the constant output data. Even more important than the quantitative dimensions captured in the physical output data, the quality of the services appears to have been poor, as complaints from the public began to mount.

Since the population and per capita income of the Philippines and Thailand are about the same, the absolute size of government employment of the two can be compared by using the data from the labor force surveys status classification. Government employees reported for Thailand in 1979 total 1,133,000, while for the Philippines the latest figure, 1,321,000, is from the second quarter of 1978. Since in the first quarter the figure was 40,000 less, one can safely assume the total to be about 1,400,000.

Most of the public institutions in Thailand seem to have modernized and made progress from the early years of the postwar era when traditional remnants were predominant. A World Bank report called for changes to improve interagency cooperation and coordination, better job descriptions, training programs, greater decentralization down to local government levels, and a restructuring of the compensation system as necessary steps in the recent modernization of the Thai bureaucracy. These rather routine recommendations could apply to other governments.

The most distressing aspect of the Philippines experience, particularly during the years of martial law, has been the deterioration of nearly every public institution pertinent to development. Most such institutions in neighboring countries appear to be slowly improving.

Income Distribution

The income distribution data for two countries are not as good or as abundant as those for East Asia. There are about half a dozen surveys for both countries.

As shown in Table 10.1, the income disparities rose both in the Philippines and Thailand in the 1970s compared with the 1960s (the data for the 1950s are scarce and of questionable value). In the Philippines, there was roughly a 10 percent increase in the Gini from the averages in the 1960s to the late 1970s, mainly related to the rise in the share of the highest decile and a decline in the lowest deciles. Various long-term factors can be cited as reasons for these changes in income disparities.

First, Philippine product per worker (or income per worker) in agriculture, the lowest income sector, fell about 15 percent relative to industry in the 1970s from the 1960s average, thereby increasing the disparities of average income of workers between the two sectors. Also the excess of product per worker of the industrial over the service sectors rose by 52 percent. There was, however, a reduction in disparities between per-worker product in the agricultural and service sectors. (See Table 10.1.)

Within agriculture the increased disparities in the 1970s compared with the 1960s were probably due to increases in the number of landless, near-landless, and small farmers as population rose in the rural areas and little new arable land was available. In industry, the real wages of unskilled and semiskilled workers declined more than wages of the more skilled and salaried workers. Above all, mounting surplus labor in the informal S sector (with the lowest wages) in the 1970s was a major factor in reducing the share of the lower deciles.

Based on the above, one would expect a greater than 10 percent rise in the Gini. Counteracting forces must have acted to keep the Gini from rising even more in the Philippines, including the limited land reform in the early half of the 1970s and accompanying rural development programs. These development programs succeeded in spreading the benefits of new rice seeds, credit for fertilizers, and other modern inputs to groups of the peasantry beyond the 30 percent reported in the 1970 Agricultural Census. Irrigation services also spread with the completion of dams and roads, enabling more multiple cropping than in the 1960s.[24]

In the urban sector, the number of earners per family might have risen more in the lower income groups than in the upper groups, as housewives and children sought more jobs and income to supplement real earnings. The increased outflow of Filipinos to jobs overseas was also a major supplement to family budgets of those in the lower income brackets. There was a tenfold increase in the number of overseas workers from the mid-1970s to early 1980s. Finally, various measures such as rent control on low-rent housing and minimum wages in the larger enterprises might have been contributing to greater income equality.

Thailand started the postwar era with fewer inequalities than did the Philippines. This is to be expected in an almost completely traditional and self-sufficient economy. But inequalities began to rise in the 1960s and into the 1970s as the share of the lowest deciles declined and that of the highest deciles rose. Contributing to these results were the impacts of modernization, agricultural commercialization, industrialization, and urbanization which affected in the 1960s only a small number of families living in the Central Region in and around Bangkok and then spread to other households near the main rivers and roads connected to Bangkok in the 1970s. Agricultural product per worker relative to nonagricultural product per worker fell in the 1960s from the 1950s average of about 5 percent but rose 30 percent in the 1970s, and the excess of industrial product per worker over service product per worker declined 20 percent from the 1960s level.

The pattern of agricultural expansion in the 1970s in less fertile lands away from the Central Plains, especially in the less fertile Northeast where rainfall and off-farm jobs were meager, contributed to greater inequalities within the rural sector. This, together with the rising population of landless and tenant peasants in the Central Plains, increased within-agriculture disparities. Nevertheless, throughout the postwar period, inequality levels were substantially lower in Thailand

---

[24] For the tendency of multiple cropping to have a greater impact on smaller farms where surplus labor per hectare is more abundant, see the Taiwan experience discussed in the *Special Issue on Multiple-Cropping in Asian Development, Philippine Economic Journal*, nos. 1 and 2 (1975) and Chapter 5 of the present volume.

than in the Philippines, indicative of the greater importance of oligarchies, tenancy, and the urban poor in the Philippines.

Population Growth

One favorable aspect for Thai development is a faster decline in birth rates than in the Philippines. Thai rates were higher in the mid-1960s but fell to 30 per thousand, lower than the Philippines' 34 in 1981, with total fertility rate 3.9 in Thailand as against 4.0 for the Philippines. Since crude death rates and life expectancy levels were about the same for the two countries in 1960 and also in 1980, other factors were involved in the fall of birth rates since the late 1960s. One might be the more extensive implementation of family planning programs. Fifty-nine percent of Thai women of childbearing age use contraceptives, compared with 48 percent in 1981, although fertility began to fall before the programs were implemented. Literacy levels were higher in Thailand than in the Philippines, 86 against 75 in 1981—up from 68 (against 72) in 1960—even though the numbers enrolled in primary, secondary, and higher education as a percent of the respective age groups were lower in Thailand.[25] It is puzzling that Thailand had lower literacy in 1960 and lower enrollment rates, but Philippine literacy fell below the Thai level by the 1980s. The efficiency of the Philippine education system in the primary sector may be the problem, a former minister of education having noted that substantial numbers of primary school graduates were not literate.

One fact contributing to higher birth rates in the Philippines is Catholicism, but the influence of the Church on the lower classes is difficult to assess. The female work force participation rate in Thailand is higher but has been falling, while it has been rising in the Philippines. The agricultural population in Thailand is much larger than in the Philippines, and per capita incomes in both countries are about the same.

The main forces involved in the faster decline in fertility may not be related so much to the level of the foregoing indexes as to the distribution of income, public health facilities, life expectancy, contraceptives, mortality, and various social amenities. Disparity levels in the Philippines are substantially higher than in Thailand, and the incomes of the lower deciles are higher in Thailand. The Thai total fertility rate is as low as that in Malaysia, where per capita incomes are much higher but with a higher Gini. Philippine fertility may be

[25] Data in this paragraph are from various issues of the *World Development Report*.

higher because the lower income groups are in poorer health and have higher incidences of mortality and morbidity, have lower life expectancy, and receive fewer family planning services. In their poverty and insecurity they view more children as sources of income and security in old age.

Another major difference between the Philippines and Thailand is the law and order situation in the two countries. In the Philippines rural peace has been disturbed by gangs attached to provincial oligarchs, bandits, communist rebels, and even the military. The urban police are also ineffective. As Simon Kuznets has pointed out, such a situation forces families to turn to their own kin to cope with dangers. The frequency of natural disasters such as typhoons and the prevalence of government corruption increase the insecurity of lower income groups. In few countries of Asia is the family so strong as in the Philippines, a legacy of the arbitrariness of the Spanish colonial rulers, including the Catholic friars, which forced the Filipino to rely on family members for protection (Fast and Richardson, 1979).

Concluding Remarks with a Postscript on the Philippines

As a result of the faster growth of Thailand in the 1960s and 1970s, its per capita income by the end of the postwar era had reached Philippine levels, which had been twice as large at the beginning of the era. The Philippine economy slowed down with the poor performance of its industries, particularly in the capital-intensive sector despite large government support. Agricultural growth was mainly responsible for the Thai success.

The story might have been different if the Philippines had helped its peasant agriculture and labor-intensive industries to develop. Its capital-intensive industries faced little competition abroad or at home and never grew up to sell abroad, while the plantation sector stagnated. This disappointing performance in the postwar decades had its roots in the prewar centuries during which local landlords grew into powerful oligarchs by taking over the farms of free peasants and making them into tenants. In Thailand it was the opposite: serfs became free farmers.

In the 1980s, the situation worsened in the Philippines when it was struck with a severe financial crisis. Per capita real incomes in the first half of the 1980s fell year after year, unprecedented in the recorded experience of postwar Asia (Diliman, 1984). In a sense this was a continuation of the scenario of the previous decades, as witnessed by the continued wasteful use of resources in big projects whose public usefulness may be low but whose financial returns to the organizers of the projects are high.

The financial crisis has now intensified into a stagnation of insufficient aggregate demand in a period of falling real wages, slow growth of employment and productivity, and worsening income distribution. The danger is that the economy may be settling down to a low long-run equilibrium level consonant with low aggregate demand. This may further accelerate the loss of valuable skilled manpower, aggravating the degeneration of institutions.

With nowhere else to turn, the economy is being directed, at last, to the all-out development of agriculture and labor-intensive, industrial exports. But it may not be easy to turn the economy around in time as the regeneration of institutions, the redirection of construction to the rural areas, and the rehabilitation of the rural economy may take some time. Most of the dramatis personae in these institutions are tenured officials whose habits are hard to change. Many other institutions need overhauling. The system of primary and secondary education, one of the best in Asia in the early postwar decades, has become one of the worst, with only four years of secondary schooling. Above all, extensive land reform is long overdue.

The potential is still there after decades of neglect. Time will be required for implementation of rural development schemes since they must deal with numerous small units of production. This is so even when the implementing public agencies such as extension services are in good shape. The shift to diversified agriculture, agro-industries, and off-farm employment is complex since it is not a matter of one crop as in rice culture but dozens of products whose growing, processing, financing, transporting, and marketing in the different regions of the country have been experienced only in a limited way.

The export potentials for diversified products in the decades to come are enormous. Real wages in Japan and the NICs will grow at rates of 4 or 5 percent a year, and diversified agriculture will become too costly to maintain. The subsequent restructuring upward to higher-valued production should open up opportunities for countries like the Philippines, Thailand, and Indonesia provided that they can meet the competition in costs and quality from China.[26] Moreover, the internal

---

[26] After suppressing small rural industries for decades, China has recently been encouraging them. Recent reports of the Associated Press indicate that they have grown very rapidly, employing 16 percent of the 370 million rural workforce and producing 3,200 different kinds of commodities in 6,600 distribution centers. Soon exports from some of these will reach other countries as plans for doubling rural employment by the year 2000 are implemented. China has come to appreciate the significance of off-farm activities in a monsoon economy and is racing to make up for the fact that

demand for these products should expand to meet the requirements of a more diversified dietary pattern shifting away from carbohydrates and toward more proteins, minerals, vitamins, and other nutrients.

There are lessons from the Philippine disaster that should be studied by other countries, particularly by those who are prone to make major decisions within a narrow circle. When industrial policies are made by a small group, government (including military) engineers have the greatest voice, supported by a few businessmen interested in obtaining subsidies and credits to invest in them. Excluded are the larger group of more experienced engineers in better-paying private industries, successful entrepreneurs, and scientists, engineers, economists, other social scientists from the leading universities, and leaders of community organizations, all of whom have fewer vested interests in the projects under discussion. Proper evaluations of the projects are often not made and when done are not made available to the public which learns about them when construction begins or is completed. Full disclosure comes only when a major crisis occurs, and even then information is not adequate, as was the case in the Philippines and Indonesia in the early 1980s.

The Special Case of Indonesia

After so much spending of valuable foreign exchange from oil exports on big projects, Indonesia now faces difficult problems of employment creation for its growing labor force. Since this growth in the 1980s was expected a decade ago, preparations to cope with it should have started long since.[27] Perhaps instead of spending so much on costly capital-intensive projects, much more should have been spent on efforts to diversify agricultural production, agro-processing, and labor-intensive industries. This would have been possible if a much greater share of foreign investment had been permitted into the upstream, resource-based heavy industries such as petrochemicals, paper/pulp, aluminum, and iron/steel, And if foreign investment was not forthcoming, that should have been taken as a good sign that the projects were not viable. Greater foreign participation would have made for better management

---

it had the lowest share (only 9 percent) of off-farm income in Asia in the late 1970s. The use of 60 million hitherto underemployed rural workers will not only raise production but also raise farm family incomes and hence aggregate demand.

[27] A study based on Indonesia's input-output tables by A. Kuyvenhoven and H. Poot (1984) showed that based on the past capital-intensive strategy, employment will increase by 1,800,000 compared with 2,500,000 from a more labor-intensive one. The strategy proposed above should create even more jobs than the one suggested in their study.

and larger tax returns (or smaller subsidies). The mere availability of natural resources for these industries does not ensure their early viability, which also depends on good manpower, especially management, and on long-term viability and R&D capabilities, as other countries have found. (For a discussion on the infant-industry argument for heavy industries, see Chapter 9 on India and China.) It may not be too late to sell off some of these industries.

Indonesia should move more slowly in heavy engineering and study the Indian experience. These industries require a good network of ancillary enterprises able to produce high-quality components and parts, but these are the firms which require time to nurture, more so in a country like Indonesia with a small pool of entrepreneurs. It may be better to start with light engineering, permitting time for small industries to gain experience, and then move upwards, as UNIDO (1981) has suggested.

There appears to be an undue emphasis on linkages in identifying lower-stream industries as buyers of or sellers to upstream resource-based industries. As will be noted in the Chapter 9, linked industries are desirable only when they are efficient. If not, the cost-cascading effect will penalize the lower-stream industries, and tariff protection becomes necessary. Many of these linked industries downstream are technologically as complex as those upstream, requiring much capital and high-level manpower, and it may be better to leave them to foreign investors. Indonesian experience in industrialization is minimal, even less than that of India, and it is better to gain experience from the technologically simpler, lower-stream industries which are cheaper and create more employment while learning from employment experience in foreign firms willing to make the investments, take the risks, and pay taxes to Indonesia. If experienced foreign firms are unwilling to do this, Indonesia should take the risk only with the approval of a large group of leaders from all walks of life.

If more funds can be released, they should go into building diversified cropping in the small farms by starting with irrigation, extension, financing, marketing, and other services, together with the promotion of related agro-processing industry as a source of off-farm employment. The increase in incomes of small farms will be spent on some of the agro-industrial products and the rest on the output of the labor-intensive industries and farm inputs. Above all, a country with such enormous need for trained manpower as Indonesia needs more funds channeled into manpower development to speed up growth in the long run.

CHAPTER 8

Plantation Economies in Transition:
Malaysia Outpaces Sri Lanka

*P*eninsular Malaysia and Sri Lanka began the postwar era with fairly high per capita incomes for monsoon economies. Three decades later Malaysia was far ahead, with per capita income about five times that of Sri Lanka. Both are small countries by monsoon standards whose populations number about 15 million and whose economies have been dominated by perennial crops (trees and shrubs) grown in large British-owned plantations and in small holdings. Both countries are fortunate to be watered by two monsoons, a major one in the summer and autumn months, as in other monsoon countries, and a minor one in the winter months, good for perennials which require water throughout the year.

The early 1980s saw peninsular Malaysia completing its industrial transition. Its agricultural labor force declined absolutely and per capita income exceeded that of South Korea. Malaysia was the first country with a large plantation sector to join the Asian NICs. This chapter deals only with peninsular Malaysia, excluding Sabah and Sarawak which became part of Malaysia only in the mid-1960s and for which data do not exist for earlier periods.

Ethnic problems have plagued both Malaysia and Sri Lanka. Sri Lanka started the 1980s with a Tamil-Sinhalese conflict which threatened to disrupt the economy for some time to come and with extremely high levels of unemployment. Ethnic problems have been contained in Malaysia and the economy has attained full employment. How these widely disparate results came about is the subject of this chapter.

Historically, these two countries were atypical of monsoon Asia in that perennial crops dominated agriculture. Tree crops are substantial in both the Philippines and Indonesia, but they are secondary to rice-growing. In Malaysia in 1960 about four times more land was devoted to tree crops than to rice, while in Sri Lanka about one-fifth more land was planted in tree crops than in rice, meaning that the perennial crop sector dominated and that the rice sector was less important than in other monsoon Asian countries. Growth patterns were determined more by the plantations than by the peasant sector, at least in the earlier stages, and it was the fluctuation in the exports of these crops which were of major importance in the movements of GDP.

The peasant sector was relatively important in the past, partly because a large portion of the acreage devoted to tree crops was owned and tended by small holders; this share rose over the course of the postwar decades. Moreover, despite the second monsoon rains in the winter months, seasonal underemployment was substantial in the peasant sector in the first half of the year. The perennial crops (rubber, coconut, tea, palm oil) employed the workforce more evenly throughout the year than did sugarcane in the Philippines and Java, which needed large numbers to harvest and process and then to plant the new crop. These were, therefore, basically surplus labor economies. The large proceeds from commercial crop exports made it possible to buy imported British manufactures. These penetrated the plantation economies through the extensive railroad network built to transport the export crops, contributing to a rapid decline in the traditional handicrafts that once provided non-agricultural income.

Historical Background

The different paths of postwar development taken by the two plantation economies cannot be explained without examining their contrasting colonial backgrounds. Despite seeming similarities, it was these differences in the colonial past which became crucial in the postwar era. The British, unlike the Dutch in Java, established plantations on land not being used by the peasantry for crops, in the mountainous areas of Sri Lanka and in the inland jungles of what was then Malaya.

But in the case of Sri Lanka, communal land near villages was taken over by the colonial government and sold to plantation owners; approximately one million acres were appropriated before this land policy was halted in 1935. For the peasantry, this meant loss of land for vegetables, fruits, wood and other forest products, and grazing, all vital for subsistence and easily purchased. Most important, the loss of crop lands meant little room remained for future expansion as the population grew. Sri Lanka ended the prewar period with agriculture land per agricultural population only one-half that of Malaysia, and two-thirds of Sri Lankan rice farmers were filling less than one-half hectare while 95 percent had less than one hectare (Karuntilake, 1971; Nyrop et al., 1971); Snodgrass (1966) reported that the number of draft animals per peasant declined by 50 percent from 1881 to 1946.

Malaysia, however, was sparsely settled, and there was plenty of land away from the peasant areas for the British to set up their plantations and no need to encroach on communal lands. Even in 1979, agricultural land per farm population was nearly three times greater in Malaysia than in Sri Lanka (see Chapter 6). The reason for this was that unlike other countries in monsoon Asia including Sri Lanka, much of Malaysia is covered by well-drained granite soils too sandy to hold water for paddies, which require more workers than tree crops. In the coastal areas clay soils suitable for paddies existed, and densities there were as high as in Sri Lanka (Grist, 1950).

In Malaya, the British forbade the appropriation of peasant land and attempted to protect the Malay village communities from the demands of their own elite as well as others, perhaps learning from earlier experiences in Ceylon and Burma. Under the Malay Reservations Enactment of 1913, certain land areas could not be sold to non-Malays (Emerson, 1937). In Sri Lanka the colonial government did little to protect the peasantry until the enactment of the Land Development Ordinance in 1935. The 1946 Census indicated that 40 percent of the paddy holdings were tenant-operated, while in Malaysia tenancy was not much of a problem.

Although most government agricultural research was confined to tree crops, in Malaya the British began to work on rice after World War I and introduced high-yielding varieties in 1925 (about the same time Japan discovered new rice varieties). These were disseminated through extension services, irrigation projects, and cooperatives, by providing agricultural education in schools, and by putting new land under rice cultivation. In Malaya, rice yields rose 20 percent from the first half of the 1920s to the late 1930s while the increase in Ceylon was only 7 percent. By the latter half of the 1930s, yields in Malaya were the highest outside of East Asia and yields in Ceylon among the lowest, only about one-half of those in Malaya (Wickizer and Bennett, 1941).

The difference in the colonial policies toward small land holders in Malaya and in Ceylon must have contributed to the difference in the treatment accorded the plantation sector in the post-independence era. In Sri Lanka, this sector together with those in the upper income groups were heavily taxed, and eventually the plantations were nationalized. This contrasts with the successes achieved in agricultural and rural development in Malaysia. There were other elements in the historical background which should be cited before one can comprehend the uses to which the surpluses extracted from the plantation sector were put. In Sri Lanka they were invested in large amounts of welfare services compared with more productive expenditures in Malaysia.

It can also be conjectured that a contributing force to the welfare system in Sri Lanka may have been Theravada Buddhism with its emphasis on charity and the widespread practice of donating food to priests. Historically Theravada Buddhism has been a strong influence in the lives of the Sinhalese, and the practice of giving may have created favorable attitudes toward giving and receiving and therefore to social welfare. The historian S. Arasaratnam (1964) has noted: "Charity was a great ideal preached by Buddhism, and charity to the Sangha was especially recommended as giving great merit. . . . Though larger viharas [temples] were wealthy enough to look after themselves, in the smaller village temples the priests were dependent on the charity of the villagers. . . . This emphasis on charity also had the effect of influencing laymen to undertake works of social welfare. Wealthy people spent considerable sums putting up public works of one form or another."

Instead of being shamed as in Confucian culture the receiver does a favor to the giver by permitting the latter to earn merit. Historically, the Buddhist Sangha stood in opposition to the colonial rulers who sought to weaken the strong hold of Buddhism on the Sinhalese through the promotion of Christianity and English schools (in competition with the temple schools), to reduce temple lands by appropriating them for plantations, and by withdrawing traditional state support for the priests and the Sangha (Nyrop, 1971). After independence, the popularity of Buddhism began to increase and the priests began to participate in politics, associating themselves with the welfare-oriented left.

Thus, the Weltanschauung propagated by Theravada Buddhism was more favorable to a social welfare state than was Confucianism with its emphasis on family-centered reliance and self-help. The shift from placing rice into the bowls of wandering priests to government disbursal of free rations or rice was not difficult to make. What is wrong with taxing the "haves" to give to the "have-nots" when the former will earn merit and the receiver will be better fed, educated, and housed? It is no coincidence that Burma, the other welfare state in Asia, was also strongly Theravada with a highly politicized Sangha which the British antagonized. Even more than in Ceylon, the Burmese peasantry suffered under British rule and lost much more land. In Burma, in sharp contrast to Malaya and even Sri Lanka, the British brought in members of the Indian Civil Service to assist with colonial administration, ignored the Burmese elite, replaced the traditional village headmen, and refused to recognize the Sangha. With the introduction of Western law, land appropriations began, and by the 1930s, two-thirds of the farm lands in lower Burma were lost to absentee landlords, mainly Indian. L. J. Walinsky (1962) wrote: "Not only were land ownership, the government, the civil service, and trade and commerce almost entirely in foreign hands; there had been, in effect, a leveling down of all Burmans, and a destruction of the existing social relations and values." In Theravada Thailand (where the giving of food to priests is still widespread), the absence of foreign rule permitted Buddhism to flourish and remain a political force, although in the postwar decades the power and popularity of the Thai monarchy enabled it to exercise tight controls over the Sangha.

These are some of the historical forces that may have contributed to the different courses economic development took in Malaysia and Sri Lanka after independence. There were other forces such as the influence of the welfare-oriented Labour Party in Britain which enabled both to win independence with relative ease. More important may have been the substantial ethnic Chinese population in Malaya (about 40 percent of the total population), whose distaste for welfare may have been much stronger than that of the minority Tamils in Ceylon, and the greater willingness of the ethnic Malay majority to trust and rely on Western estate owners and advisers, a willingness that was a historical product of the different treatment accorded the occupied populations.

It is astonishing that a comprehensive welfare program such as Sri Lanka's was created in the early stages of national development. The only other country to follow this welfare strategy was Burma, but to a lesser degree and with a more socialist government. This difference is comprehensible in view of the greater destitution of the Burmese under British rule, and the more extensive foreign ownership of land, trade, commerce, and industry in Burma. Ownership of estates, trade, commerce, and industry was also mainly in foreign hands in Ceylon. But with the large sterling assets accumulated during the booming war years, the Ceylonese were able to buy up British holdings as the latter were heavily taxed and harassed. (In contrast, during the war, rubber production in Malaysia sank to zero under Japanese occupation and living standards fell to disastrous levels.)

The Record of Growth

As may be seen in Tables 1 and 2 in Chapter 3, Sri Lanka started out in the 1950s at a somewhat faster pace than peninsular Malaysia. Sri Lanka's GDP growth was 3.9 percent compared to Malaysia's 3.6 percent, GDP per capita growth was 1.3 percent compared to 1.0 percent,

Table 8.1   Average Annual Growth of Product, Input, and Total Factor Productivity in the Four ASEAN Countries, India, and Sri Lanka, 1950–1980

	Product	Employment	Capital	Total Input	Product per Employment	Product/ Capital	Total Factor Productivity
I. Assuming depreciation equal to 1.5% of capital stock							
Thailand	7.1	3.7	6.6	4.9	3.4	0.5	2.2
Philippines	6.0	3.9	6.1	4.8	2.1	-0.1	1.2
Malaysia	6.0	3.1	6.3	4.5	2.9	-0.3	1.5
Indonesia*	5.7	3.1	10.5	6.7	2.6	-4.8	-1.0
India	3.6	2.7	6.6	4.4	0.9	-3.0	-0.8
Sri Lanka	4.2	1.7	5.9	3.4	2.5	-1.7	0.8
II. Assuming depreciation equal to 2.0 of capital stock							
Thailand	7.1	3.7	8.8	6.2	3.4	-1.7	0.9
Philippines	6.0	3.9	8.7	6.3	2.1	-2.7	-0.3
Malaysia	6.0	3.1	8.6	5.8	3.0	-2.6	0.2
Indonesia*	5.7	3.1	12.2	7.8	2.6	-6.5	-2.1
India	3.6	2.7	7.0	4.7	0.9	-3.4	-1.1
Sri Lanka	4.2	1.7	7.9	4.6	2.5	-3.7	-0.4
III. Assuming depreciation equal to 1.75% of capital stock							
Thailand	7.1	3.7	7.7	5.4	3.4	-0.6	1.7
Philippines	6.0	3.9	7.1	5.3	2.1	-1.1	0.7

(Table 8.1, continued)

Malaysia	6.0	3.1	7.4	5.1	2.9	-1.4	0.9
Indonesia*	5.7	3.1	11.4	7.3	2.6	-5.7	-1.6
India	3.6	2.7	6.7	4.6	0.9	-3.1	-1.0
Sri Lanka	4.2	1.7	6.4	3.8	2.5	-2.2	0.4

Sources: Product data computed from various official publications on national accounts (like *NEDA Philippine National Accounts*, *National Income of Thailand*, etc.). Employment data computed from *ILO Yearbook of Labour Statistics*. Capital data computed using the depreciation figures given in *UN Yearbook of National Accounts Statistics* as described below.

Notes: Because capital stock estimates are not available (except Aurora Sanchez's data for the Philippines which are of too short a period for our use), we compute capital stock data using depreciation estimates and based on alternative assumptions that depreciation is equal to 1.5 percent, 1.75 percent, and 2.0 percent of capital stock at constant prices. The range of 1.5 percent to 2.0 percent is selected on the basis of comparisons of depreciation allowances and capital stock data of Japan, Taiwan, S. Korea, and the Philippines. For Japan in 1965, depreciation as percentage of capital stock was 2.0 percent. S. Korea in 1965 was 1.5 percent, Taiwan in 1965 was 1.9 percent, and Philippines in 1965 was 1.8 percent.

* 1960–80 data.

and GDP per worker growth was 2.7 percent compared to 0.7 percent annually. But, in the 1960s and 1970s, Malaysia outpaced Sri Lanka substantially and after three decades had GDP and GNP per capita growth rates about 50 percent higher than those of Sri Lanka. Malaysian growth rates in GDP and GNP per capita improved as the decades went by, but this was not the case with Sri Lanka (or the Philippines).

Although national product data for the 1950s are not as abundant as for more recent decades, Sri Lanka, like the Philippines, was able to get a strong start when independence and nationhood were achieved easily and quickly before 1950, while Malaysia, like Indonesia, was plagued by rebellion and other problems of nation building. Moreover, the British armed forces, driven out of Malaya and Burma in the early days of the war, made Ceylon a staging ground for their military comeback. The war years were boom years for Ceylon, and the country was able to accumulate large sterling assets in London banks.

Capital stock data are not available for either country. A very rough estimation method based on a bold assumption as to the stability of the relationship between depreciation allowances and capital stock in Japan, Taiwan, South Korea, and the Philippines in 1965 yields data on total factor productivity for three variants (Table 8.1). For Malaysia, taking variants I and III (and discarding II for which depreciation is too high since it is based on Japan's depreciation), something like a TFP growth rate of 1 percent per year is indicated—a figure not as high as Thailand's but higher than any of the other countries in the table, including Sri Lanka where the TFP growth was about one-half Malaysia's. One reason for the better performance of factor productivity in Sri Lanka relative to the negative rates of Indonesia and India is the slow growth of capital stock, the lowest in the table for variants I and III, given the growth rate of product for the three countries shown in the first column of the table.

The slow growth of capital stock in Sri Lanka, as Donald Snodgrass (1966) reported for the 1950s, is related to the rapid growth of consumption, the slow growth of private investment, and the poor allocation of public investment. The growth of consumption expenditures, particularly of foreign goods, produced large balance of payments deficits which had to be paid for with the foreign assets accumulated during the war years. By the end of the decade these assets had dwindled to levels which could not be depleted further, and drastic import controls had to be imposed in 1960.

Since capital stock estimates are not available, we must rely on the analysis of labor productivity. Table 8.1 shows that for the three postwar decades Malaysian product per worker rose 3.0 percent per year compared with 2.5 percent for Sri Lanka, despite the 3.1 percent growth of employment in Malaysia, substantially larger than Sri Lanka's 1.7 percent. It should be noted that the data for the 1950s and 1960s are for peninsular Malaysia but those for the 1970s include Sabah and Sarawak for the 1970s. Labor productivity is lower in these two states, and if their data are excluded, Malaysia's labor productivity would go beyond 3.0 percent.

After a slow start in the 1950s when product per worker rose only 0.7 percent yearly compared with 2.7 percent for Sri Lanka, Malaysian productivity grew 4.4 percent annually in the 1960s compared with 3.5 percent for Sri Lanka, and 3.8 percent in the 1970s compared with 1.6 percent (Table 3.2). This together with the faster rise in employment (Table 3.1) enabled Malaysia to complete the industrial transition, as the labor force in industry exceeded that in agriculture in the early 1980s. Sri Lanka, in contrast, ended the postwar era with an industrial labor force only one-third that in agriculture, while Malaysia had one-half its labor force in industry.

In the completion of the industrial transition, the Malaysian economy was retracing the steps taken by the Japanese economy in the 1950s, the Taiwanese economy in the early 1970s, and the South Korean in the late 1970s. Unemployment rates fell throughout the 1970s as GDP grew at 7.8 percent, the highest for South and Southeast Asia (Table 3.1), and in 1980 unemployment was down to about 2.6 percent of the labor force (obtained by adding 2.3 percent actively unemployed and 0.3 percent inactively unemployed) according to Malaysia's Department of Statistics. Since there are problems in the use of unemployment rates in defining full employment in monsoon Asia, particularly with underemployment and rural housewives' employment, I have defined full employment as the point at which the wages of unskilled workers begin to rise as fast or faster than those of semiskilled and skilled workers. Around this point, the pool of unemployed workers, whether unskilled urban workers or rural peasants, begins to disappear. In developing countries skilled and semi-skilled employees are in short supply and are usually adequately employed. Appropriate wage series are not available for Malaysia, but the existing data show accelerated rises of wages of palm oil harvesters, bus conductors, and bus drivers, especially from 1980.

A good substitute for wage data are the differential rises in components of the consumer price indexes produced by workers of varying skills as shown in Table 8.2. In the upper panel of the table, it is seen that service prices began to rise faster than consumer prices as a whole

Table 8.2   Consumer Price Indexes in Malaysia, 1975–1982

I. *Annual Growth Rates of Consumer Price Index in Percent*

	1975 to 1980	*1980 to 1983*	*1975 to 1983*
Total	4.5	6.4	5.2
Durable Goods	8.9	2.9	6.7
Semi-durable Goods	4.4	4.9	4.6
Non-durable Goods	3.9	6.9	5.0
Services	5.1	7.6	6.0

II. *Annual Growth Rates in Percent of CPI in Services (1980–1983)*

Payment for sewing, knitting	14.6
Laundering, cleaning, dyeing, etc.	12.9
Domestic services	11.8
Services of barber and beauty shop, etc.	11.4
Expenditure in restaurants, cafes, and hotels	13.2
Other services	4.8
All Services	7.6

Sources: Upper panel data from *Monthly Statistical Bulletin*, Kuala Lumpur: June 1984; lower panel data from Department of Statistics.

from 1980, faster than semi-durables, durables, and non-durables. This is because most consumer services were produced by less skilled workers, domestic workers (maids, cooks, gardeners), restaurant and hotel workers, and laundry and cleaning service workers. The rates of increase in the prices of these services since the 1980s have been greater than the rise in services as a whole, and much larger than the rates in health, education, recreational, cultural and other services that employ more highly trained workers.

Full employment was attained around 1980, and the workforce in agriculture in West Malaysia began to decline absolutely for the first time even though the real output in agriculture was rising (from 6.3 billion ringgit in 1980 to 7.1 billion in 1983; ADB, 1983). This work force rose to an all-time high of 1,554,000 in 1978 and steadily fell to 1,374,000 in 1981, as mechanization in agriculture began to accelerate along with rising real wages. Employment data in agriculture as a whole for 1982 and 1983 are not yet available, but these trends must have continued. Employment data for rubber estates show that there were 158,000 workers at the end of 1980 and by the end of 1983 only 132,000, despite rising output. Although such data are not available for rice, the area planted has been declining while yields and production have risen. In the 1960 Census of Agriculture, only about 2 percent of the rice farms were mechanized but by 1979/1980 about one-half were. By 1983 nearly all irrigated rice farms were said to be mechanized (according to agricultural statisticians of the Department of Statistics), reflecting agricultural labor shortages. On the other hand, the industrial labor force in manufacturing has been increasing from 321,000 at the end of 1980 to 340,000 at the end of 1983. There were even greater increases in the large construction industry (estimated to employ about 400,000 in 1984) (Department of Statistics, 1984). Hence, it is likely that West Malaysia completed the industrial transition by 1983 or 1984. By June 1984, the influx of foreign workers, especially from Indonesia, was becoming a problem, and an agreement was signed between Malaysia and Indonesia to regulate workers in construction, agriculture, and domestic services. In contrast, Sri Lanka ended the postwar era with unemployment rates approaching 15 percent. The following sections discuss how these widely differing performances of Asia's two leading plantation economies came about.

Agricultural Development

To understand the differential growth in Malaysia and Sri Lanka, we must look at the 1960s and 1970s since in the 1950s growth was somewhat faster in Sri Lanka. The agricultural sector holds the key to the success or failure in the industrial transition (except in city-states such as Hong Kong and Singapore). Thus, it is not surprising that the more rapid growth of national product (4.1 percent in Malaysia and 2.6 percent in Sri Lanka) can be largely attributed to the 5.5 percent growth in Malaysia's agriculture compared with 2.9 percent in Sri Lanka's for the 1960s and 1970s, and secondarily to the combined industrial and service sector growth which was about 8 percent for Malaysia compared with 5 percent for Sri Lanka (Table 3.3). In the early stages, when the agricultural sector is still the largest, the industrial and service sectors' growth is more dependent upon the growth of agriculture than the other way round, and this is particularly so in plantation crop export economies. A growth rate of 5.5 percent for agriculture is the highest found in monsoon Asia in the 1960s and 1970s, although for the entire period including the 1950s, Thailand's 4.7 is the highest.

The major source of the high rate of agricultural product in Malaysia is the 5.2 percent annual growth of product per worker in the agricultural sector, the highest in South and Southeast Asia. Sri Lanka's is the lowest at 1.0 percent for the 1960s and 1970s. This growth rate for Malaysia is substantially higher than the growth rate of product per worker in any of the other sectors of South and Southeast Asia (Table 3.4). The agricultural sector must be the focus of the analysis of Malaysia's successes.

Malaysia spent large sums in the 1950s to build up its agricultural sectors for later decades. An effective program to cut down old rubber trees and replant with higher-yielding ones was carried out in the 1950s on both rubber and oil palm (the main tree crops) plantations and acreage was expanded by clearing jungles. Lim Chong-Yah presented data showing that replanting in rubber reached one-third of the total planted area, and that in the 1960s 8 percent new rubber land was added, while in oil palms there was a 41 percent increase in planted area.

In the other major crop, rice, Malaysia invested large amounts in irrigation projects from the 1960s to expand double-cropping of paddy. In the 1950s only about 1 or 2 percent of paddy fields was double-cropped, but by the latter half of the 1970s about one-half was double-cropped. The improved irrigation increased yields of both rice crops: they rose to about 3.4 tons per hectare in 1980, the highest for South and Southeast Asia and about the same as in Java where several times more manpower is used (Department of Statistics, 1984).

Besides the disruptions of the Emergency and low export prices, it can be seen that the low growth of Malaysian agricultural output in the 1950s was due to the need to cut down old trees for replanting and expansion of acreage with new trees, which required a gestation period of a decade or more before yielding maximum output and then peaking off after another decade or so. Lim Chong-Yah noted that rubber trees are tapped from the age of 6 or 7 but peak yields take 15 to 17 years more to reach; the trees become unprofitable after 33 years; oil palm begins producing after four years with yields rising between 11 and 30 years. Similarly, the irrigation works started in the late 1950s took a number of years before substantial results were obtained. Hence, the high labor productivity in the 1970s was the outcome of efforts in the 1950s and 1960s in replanting, expansion, and building up a physical and social infrastructure.

Even though in the 1950s rubber and coconut yields per hectare were roughly the same in the two countries, yields in Malaysia by the late 1970s were running about 40 to 50 percent higher than in Sri Lanka. For tea, the major export crop of Sri Lanka, yields and quality were falling, and for Malaysia's most promising crop, oil palm, yields were reaching the highest level in the world. (Yields of these crops cannot be compared as tea is not produced in Malaysia and oil palm output is insignificant in Sri Lanka.)

Not only was productivity per worker in Malaysian agriculture rising rapidly, but more important, there was expanding employment in the 1960s and 1970s, culminating in full employment. The large resettlement schemes transferred new lands to small holders for the cultivation of rubber, oil palm, and other perennial crops producing employment throughout the year. In 1950 acreage in rubber was 800,000 hectares for the estates and 640,000 for small holders, but by 1980 small holder acreage rose to 1,200,000 hectares, double the 490,000 for the estates. Increases for coconut, oil palm, pineapples, and other perennials also occurred.

Malaysia's early program of irrigation and double-cropping of paddy farming was largely completed by the late 1970s. This was important in achieving full employment for rice farmers who had been having difficulty in finding adequate work during the dry season. With yields rising in most crops, the domestic market in the rural areas expanded, contributing to increases in off-farm employment. The Department of Statistics estimates that the farmers' off-farm income portion doubled from 14 percent in 1973 to 28 percent in 1979. One can speculate that a larger share went to those peasants with little land since surplus labor per hectare is greater, as was the case in Japan and Taiwan.

Even though the labor force rose rapidly at a 2.9 percent rate from 1960 to 1980, with real farm family incomes rising at annual rates exceeding 5.5 percent, Malaysia was able to reach full employment, as the much faster rise of income meant that agriculture was absorbing the new entries into the labor force and giving more work to the underemployed throughout the 1960s and into the 1970s, when mechanization began to make some headway in the later years. In Sri Lanka, though the labor force grew at a slower pace of 2.0 percent, the 2.9 percent growth of real incomes was not rapid enough to absorb the large pool of surplus labor and the new workers entering the labor market. Thus, Sri Lanka ended the period with reduced but still large unemployment. Unemployment rates were 18 percent in 1971 and 15 percent in 1980 (ADB, 1983).

In fairness to Sri Lanka, it must be said that various government attempts were made to expand acreage and irrigation, promote replanting, and in general to improve cultivation. It was fully aware of the consequences of negligence in replanting tea, rubber, and coconut farms since the competition from neighboring Malaysia, Indonesia, and India in the various export crops was keenly felt in the balance of payments. But these efforts were far less successful than in Malaysia with the possible exception of rice. This may have been due to inefficiencies in administration (which was saddled with too many programs), but in large part, it was the lack of good working relations with the estate sectors and the suspicion and even hostility of the British, unlike in Malaysia, and, perhaps more important, the insufficient government resources for the development of agriculture, despite the stronger financial position that obtained in Sri Lanka in the late 1940s. The reason for inadequate resources in Sri Lanka was the vast amounts channelled into the financing of a very large social welfare program demanded by the people. In the 1950s, 35 percent of the total central government budget (or 7.5 percent of GNP) went to social welfare (including education, health, social security, housing, and other social services), and this rose to 44 percent (or 10.8 percent of GNP) in the 1970s. In Malaysia, the comparable shares were 18 percent of the budget (or 2.1 percent of GNP) in the 1950s and 34 percent (and 5.6 percent of GNP) in the 1970s. In Sri Lanka, not only were education and health completely free for all (even secondary and higher education), but in the 1970s (Tables 8.3 and 8.4) 23 percent of the budget (6 percent of GNP) went to social security and welfare compared with 3.1 percent (and 0.5 percent of GNP) for Malaysia. A large chunk went to free rice rations for all (about 4 pounds per person per week) and substantial subsidies to food producers. In addition, public transport and housing were subsidized.

In economies such as Sri Lanka's with low levels of per capita income (US$270 in 1980) and with relatively low Gini, the share of surplus that can be invested for private and public development is severely limited, and the diversion of 6 percent of GNP for social welfare and security is likely to leave insufficient amounts for private investment and public expenditures to develop the major sector of the economy, agriculture, however good intentions may be for promoting agricultural development. In consequence, Sri Lanka faced chronic deficits in the government current accounts and in the balance of payments, and high inflation rates and frequent devaluations, unlike Malaysia. Of course, the latter was fortunate in discovering petroleum resources which in the late 1970s comprised about one-fifth of total merchandise exports.

The shares of private consumption, gross domestic capital formation, and government consumption as percentages of GDP in constant prices are shown in Table 8.5. Except for India, Sri Lanka has the lowest share in capital formation among all countries—20 percent compared with 27 percent for Malaysia—and for 1960, 1970, and 1980, the lowest average (except India) of 18 percent as against Malaysia's 21 percent. Sri Lanka had the highest private (or personal) consumption in 1980—90 percent compared with Malaysia's 57 percent. Sri Lanka's combined private and government consumption shares are the highest for all three years, except for India's. And if constant price estimates were available for Sri Lanka, the shares for the three years may have

Table 8.3 Average Annual Expenditure by Function of Central Government: Malaysia

	Average 1950s			Average 1960s			Average 1970s		
	Amount (million ringgits)	% of Total	% of GNP	Amount (million ringgits)	% of Total	% of GNP	Amount (million ringgits)	% of Total	% of GNP
General public services	103	17.0	2.0	*	*	*	1,160	16.6	2.7
Defense	162	26.8	3.2	265	12.8	3.1	1,155	16.6	2.7
Education	70	11.6	1.4	429	20.7	5.0	1,540	22.1	3.6
Health	33	5.5	0.6	159	7.7	1.9	461	6.6	1.1
Social security & welfare	5	0.8	0.1				213	3.1	0.5
Housing & community amenities	*	*	*	45	2.2	0.5	44	0.6	0.1
Other social services	*	*	*				117	1.7	0.3
Economic services	65	10.7	1.3	—	—	—	1,111	15.9	2.6
General administration	*	*	*	—	—	—	227	3.3	0.5
Agriculture, forestry, fishing	12	2.0	0.2	189	9.1	2.2	391	5.6	0.9
Mining, mfg. & construction	2	0.3	0.0	—	—	—	10	0.1	0.0
Electricity, gas, steam & water	1	0.2	0.0	—	—	—	49	0.7	0.1
Roads	1	0.2	0.0	124	6.0	1.5	294	4.2	0.7
Inland & coastal waterways							40	0.6	0.1
Other transport and communications	20	3.3	0.4	43	2.1	0.5	86	1.2	0.2
Other economic services	29	4.8	0.6	134	6.5	1.6	15	0.2	0.0
Other purposes	167	27.6	3.3	685	33.0	8.0	1,169	16.8	2.8
Total	605	100.0	11.8	2,073	100.0	24.3	6,970	100.0	16.4
Social expenditure as % of total	17.9			30.6			34.1		
% of GNP	2.1			7.4			5.6		

Note: * Included in the item for other purposes.
Sources: Data for 1970s computed from *IMF Government Finance Statistics Yearbook 1982*; data for 1960s computed from various issues of *UN Statistical Yearbook*; data for 1950s computed from Lee Soo Ann, *Economic Growth and the Public Sector in Malaya and Singapore 1948–1960*.

Table 8.4   Average Annual Expenditure by Function of Central Government: Sri Lanka

	Average 1950s			Average 1960s			Average 1970s		
	Amount (mil.rup.)	% of Total	% of GNP	Amount (mil.rup.)	% of Total	% of GNP	Amount (mil.rup.)	% of Total	% of GNP
General public services	*	*	*	*	*	*	562	10.1	2.5
Defense	40	3.4	0.7	69	3.2	0.8	154	2.8	0.7
Education				372	17.3	4.4	697	12.6	3.1
Health				175	8.1	2.0	357	6.4	1.6
Social security and welfare	423	35.9	7.5	*	*	*	1,297	23.4	5.7
Housing and community amenities				47	2.2	0.6	43	0.8	0.2
Other community & social services				*	*	*	54	1.0	0.2
Economic services	403	34.2	7.1	262	12.2	3.1	966	17.4	4.2
Agriculture, forestry, fishing	—	—	—	124	5.8	1.5	469	8.5	2.1
Mining, mfg. & construction	—	—	—	182	8.5	2.1	33	0.6	0.1
Other transport & communications	—	—	—	*	*	*	434	7.8	1.9
Other economic services	—	—	—				30	0.5	0.1
Other purposes	311	26.4	5.5	919	42.7	10.8	1,407	25.4	6.2
Total	1,177	100.0	20.8	2,150	100.0	25.2	5,537	100.0	24.3
Social exp. as % of total	35.9			27.6			44.2		
% of GNP	7.5			7.0			10.8		

Note: * Included in "Other purposes".

Sources: Data for 1970s computed from *IMF Government Finance Statistical Yearbook.* Data for 1950s and 1960s from various issues of *UN Statistical Yearbook.*

Table 8.5   Percentage Shares of Private Consumption (PC), Gross Domestic
Capital Formation (GDCF), and Government Current Consumption (GC) in Asian Countries

						% GDCF	
(Constant prices) % Shares in GDP			% Share of GDCF*			financed abroad	Govt. deficit
PC	GDCF	GC		Struct.	Equip.	(net)	(%)
EAST ASIA							
Japan							
(1960) 62	26	12	(1960–70)	33.2	66.8	–0.2	–3.2
(1970) 53	39	7	(1970–80)	40.3	59.7	–2.5	–5.1
(1980) 58	33	10	(1960–80)	36.7	63.3	–1.4	–4.2
S. Korea							
(1960) 86	8	15	(1960–70)	64.4	35.6	14.1	–7.5
(1970) 75	28	11	(1970–80)	59.9	40.1	20.2	1.7
(1980) 66	35	10	(1960–80)	62.2	37.8	17.2	–2.9
Taiwan							
(1960) 60	15	31	(1960–70)	47.6	52.4	4.6	–2.9
(1970) 55	26	19	(1970–80)	44.9	55.1	–5.2	–3.8
(1980) 49	30	15	(1960–80)	46.3	53.7	–0.3	–3.4
Hong Kong							
(1960) 91	19	8	(1960–70)	—	—	—	—
(1970) 81	19	7	(1970–80)	—	—	—	–19.2
(1980) 62	33	6	(1960–80)	—	—	—	—
Singapore							
(1960) 94	10	8	(1960–70)	47.0	53.0	—	–9.1
(1970) 71	37	12	(1970–80)	42.3	57.7	31.5	–5.8
(1980) 57	34	10	(1960–80)	44.7	55.3	—	–7.5
REGIONAL AVERAGE							
(1960) 79	16	15	(1960–70)	48.1	51.9	6.2	–5.7
(1970) 67	30	11	(1970–80)	46.9	53.1	11.0	–6.4
(1980) 58	33	10	(1960–80)	47.5	52.5	8.6	–6.1
SOUTHEAST ASIA							
Malaysia							
(1960) 73	16	14	(1960–70)	—	—	—	—
(1970) 60	20	15	(1970–80)	—	—	16.7	34.2
(1980) 57	27	20	(1960–80)	—	—	—	—
Thailand							
(1960) 77	16	10	(1960–70)	45.1	54.9	5.2	—
(1970) 69	27	11	(1970–80)	47.2	52.8	17.8	18.7
(1980) 63	24	13	(1960–80)	46.2	53.8	11.5	—
Indonesia							
(1960) 68	9	13	(1960–70)	—	—	—	—
(1970) 69	13	9	(1970–80)	—	—	20.1	22.1
(1980) 79	26	13	(1960–80)	—	—	—	—
Philippines							
(1960) 79	17	8	(1960–70)	51.6	48.4	1.4	—
(1970) 73	21	8	(1970–80)	48.6	51.4	11.1	24.0
(1980) 64	25	9	(1960–80)	50.1	49.9	6.3	—
REGIONAL AVERAGE							
(1960) 74	15	11	(1960–70)	48.4	51.6	3.3	—
(1970) 68	20	11	(1970–80)	47.9	52.1	16.4	24.8
(1980) 66	26	14	(1960–80)	48.2	51.8	9.9	—

(Table 8.5, continued)

SOUTH ASIA
India

(1960)	76	15	11	(1960–70)	60.9	39.1	10.0	—
(1970)	73	19	9	(1970–80)	57.0	43.0	−1.3	−26.9
(1980)	71	17	13	(1960–80)	59.0	41.0	4.4	—

Sri Lanka

(1960)	78**	16**	15**	(1960–70)	69.3	30.7	20.1	16.5
(1970)	69	16	12	(1970–80)	58.8	41.2	13.4	18.8
(1980)	90	20	10	(1960–80)	64.1	35.9	16.8	17.7

Notes: * Refer to Gross Domestic Fixed Capital Formation. Government deficit as percentage of government revenue (negative denotes surplus)
** Current prices.
Sources: Percentage shares in Real GDP of consumption and capital formation computed from *IBRD World Tables 1980 & Key Indicators of DMCs of ADB* (April 1984). The rest of this table is in current prices and computed from various country publications on national accounts, namely: *National Income of the Republic of China 1981*; *National Income in Korea 1982*; *Annual Report on National Accounts of Japan 1982*; *NEDA Philippine National Accounts*; *Singapore Yearbook of Statistics*, various issues; *Key Indicators of Developing Member Countries of ADB* (April 1983). Data for India computed from *UN Yearbook of National Accounts Statistics 1979*. For Sri Lanka, data are computed from various issues of *Key Indicators of Developing Member Countries of ADB* and *UN Yearbook of National Accounts Statistics*.

been about the same as India's. If the 1950s were included, consumption shares would most likely be higher for Sri Lanka, since India undertook heavy industrialization in the 1950s.

But more is involved than investment. The urge to save for the future is weakened if there is little worry about old age, health care, education, and so on. The decline in thrift affects the volume of personal savings and the incentive to work hard to increase savings for all classes. For the upper income groups, if there is no need to budget for education, health care, transport, housing, food, life insurance, and other needs, incomes will be spent on luxury goods, most of which must be imported. Thus not only the savings and investment account but foreign balances are adversely affected by growing imports of consumer goods. Accordingly, among the countries included in Chapter 3's tables, Sri Lanka has the lowest share of internal savings as percent of GDP.

Replanting expenses are high if sufficient subsidies are not extended by the governments, and not many can afford to forgo income while the crops mature to peak productivity and yield high incomes. Moreover, in the case of tea, the British were reluctant to invest in replanting for fear of nationalization, which in fact materialized in the mid-1970s. If so much had not been diverted to welfare, much more could have been accomplished towards raising the efficiency of commercial crops, particularly in the non-estate sectors of rubber and coconut, and in increasing food production for local consumption long before the 1970s, thereby reducing early food imports. In Malaysia, 50 percent of the First Plan (1956–1960) went to rural development, and this was raised in the last plan (1976–1981) to 55 percent (APO, 1978).

Industrial Development

Industrial growth in Malaysia was 6.8 percent annually in the three postwar decades compared with 4.0 percent for Sri Lanka. Underlying this difference was the faster growth of labor productivity in Malaysia of 4.0 percent compared with 3.3 percent in Sri Lanka for the last two decades. (See tables in Chapter 3.) Here, too, Sri Lanka was in a more favorable position at the outset, as the war boom years saw the mushrooming of several industries while no such opportunities were possible in Malaysia under Japanese occupation. In the 1960s and 1970s Malaysia caught up with and surpassed Sri Lanka. In the years for which comparable data are available, Malaysian manufacturing production grew twice as fast, 13.5 percent per year compared with Sri Lanka's 6.2 percent, and Malaysia made rapid strides in food production, textiles and apparel, wood and paper products, and especially in metal products and machinery. All of these industries were important in laying the basic foundation for future industrialization. The growth of industrial product per worker increased in Malaysia by 3.5 percent a year in contrast to a negative 0.1 percent for Sri Lanka despite the fact that growth in 1977 was one of the best registered by the industrial sector. It is interesting to note that some of those industries in Sri Lanka which were government operated—wood products, non-metallic minerals, basic metals, and metal products—registered the smallest increases in productivity while using more capital (U.N., 1978).

Sri Lanka's industrial policy appeared to have been plagued by shortcomings. In the 1950s, not much was done to foster industrialization as foreign exchange to buy imported industrial goods was plentiful, but after the exchange crisis in 1960, the government rushed in with a whole array of "licensing, quotas, higher tariffs and a complete ban," taxes, and other incentives to promote rapid industrialization, somewhat similar to the situation in the Philippines. Thus, while Malaysia was spending less than 0.01 percent of GNP on industries, Sri Lanka's government spent 1.5 percent. Under the banner of self-reliance so prevalent around that time in South Asia, foreign joint ventures were discouraged. As summarized by Karuntilake (1971) the results were "enormous waste of equipment, raw materials, and foreign exchange because of experimentation, the lack of know-how, and the inability to utilize the new machinery properly. The rejection rates of products were abnormally high because local personnel were inexperienced in handling machinery and a great deal of time had to be spent on training persons on the job. This was true of a large number of industries although there were a few exceptions. In most industries where there has been active foreign participation, controlling the quality of the products, eliminating waste, proper organization, efficient management and the use of the most appropriate techniques have come naturally." Instead of encouraging small, labor-intensive industries, the large ones were promoted with consequent proliferation of capital-intensive industries and high market concentration in many industries. Between 1960 to 1968 the growth rate of manufacturing production rose at an annual rate of 3.8 percent and the increase in productivity per worker was a mere 1.4 percent.

Moreover, like Burma, India, and other South Asian countries, Sri Lanka began to establish state-owned and operated industries and to nationalize others, ending up in 1979 with 125 nonfinancial public enterprises, compared with 21 for Malaysia, and even more than the 45 in socialist Burma (IMF, 1980). These public enterprises have tended to be inefficient. Predictably, as in India and Burma, they were highly protected, badly managed, overstaffed, and underutilized, with a poorly selected and motivated workforce, and have absorbed a great deal of public funds (Radhakrishnan, 1977).

In contrast, Malaysia started serious industrialization only in the 1960s with a relatively mild structure of protection, a liberal policy toward foreign investment, and an early shift to export promotion. An important advantage for Malaysia was its larger domestic market due partly to rural development policies, and the accumulation of sufficient finances and experience before launching industrialization. Hence, it was possible to establish a large system of free trade zones and industrial estates (over 50 of them) which were able to attract a considerable number of foreign enterprises, especially in the export of electronic components, of which Malaysia is currently the world's largest exporter. This type of industrialization has been criticized by some as transitional and costly since linkages with the domestic economy are few and limited. But the purpose of free trade zones is to invite foreign firms to utilize the excess labor force and to create employment and foreign exchange. Even though linkages are forgone, exports are possible by cutting out inefficient linkages. This is far better than to leave the surplus labor force unemployed and demanding handouts as in Sri Lanka. The employed workers learn the work habits, skills, and know-how needed in such industries as electronics, which will stand the country in good stead in the future. As to the costs of establishing the estates, Malaysia can easily afford them, and this is a more profitable investment than doling out free food rations to the unemployed population year after year, or financing inefficient industries whose output may render exporting by firms buying the inputs impossible, as in Sri Lanka. After the multinationals depart, the country is left with a great deal of industrial infrastructure useful for local entrepeneurs.

Income Distribution and the Demographic Transition

One major achievement of Sri Lanka's welfare state has been in improved distribution of income. In the social indicators Sri Lanka ended the postwar era with an income-distribution Gini falling from 0.45 in 1953 and 1963 to 0.35 in 1973 but rising back to 0.44 in 1978/79, compared to Malaysia where the index has risen to about 0.52 in 1976 from 0.50 in 1970. Life expectancy in Sri Lanka has increased to 69 years, and 85 percent of the total population was literate in 1981 compared to Malaysia's 65 years and 60 percent. (The literacy rate for Sri Lanka is higher than Singapore's 83 percent.) The total fertility rate is 3.5 in Sri Lanka, lower than in any country in South and Southeast Asia (excluding Singapore), and substantially lower than Malaysia's 4.0 (Central Bank of Ceylon, 1983; Snodgrass, 1980).

These achievements by a developing country have been made at heavy cost, but it is pertinent to ask if they could have been obtained at much less cost and without sacrificing so much growth at lower income levels. (I assume the rise in Gini in 1978/1979 back to 1953 and 1963 levels is temporary, although there are no grounds for such an assumption.) First of all, this kind of a fall in inequality cannot be said to be a secular decline since the food handouts must be given and paid for every year. If this is stopped, inequality will rise as in 1978/79. There is an old saying to the effect that if one teaches a man how to fish, he will feed himself thereafter, but if one gives him a fish, he will starve without further charity. Thus, if the funds spent on food handouts were put into improving food production, incomes in the lower income families, most of whom are in the rural areas, could have been just as high without the handouts. Through double-cropping in the MUDA Valley scheme Malaysia was able to double farm family incomes, which amounts to more than the 40–50 percent increase in Ceylonese peasant family incomes with the addition of food handouts.

Actually, Sri Lanka's free ration schemes benefit the middle classes most, not the lowest 10 percent who receive only 20 percent of their income in food rations compared with more than 50 percent in the other groups. Alailima's study (1978) on income distribution concludes: "Partly as a result of the rigidities in the structure of subsidies and partly due to a substantial burden from indirect taxes, the net transfers directed towards the lower income groups have been small compared to the total of income transfers and insufficient to materially effect their socio-economic status or prospects. . . . It directed only 5 percent of total tax revenue as net benefits to the lowest 25 percent of the population. . . in comparison, 60 percent was returned in the form of direct benefits to all income groups which affected their willingness and ability to work, save and invest." In effect, the system of social welfare was a scheme benefitting mainly the middle 60 percent of income receivers.

Reduction or elimination of health, education, and housing benefits to the upper half or two-thirds income group would also have lowered the Gini without an appreciable adverse effect on high life expectancy and the literacy rate. Higher and secondary education need not be free if a system of scholarships to deserving students from lower income groups is established. And if the health schemes were confined only to the families who could not afford health care, mortality and life expectancy rates would not be significantly affected. Instead of comprehensive housing subsidies, which resulted in the wealthier groups building several homes for themselves, a program of public housing for low-income groups would have sufficed.

The sharp decline in Sri Lankan birth rates is not easy to understand. The subsidies for food, education, health, and housing should lower the cost of raising children and thereby tend to raise the supply of children. It must have been the demand side on which the welfare system affected the birth rates. Subsidized housing, health, pensions, homes for the aged, and educational schemes must have reduced the need to plan for future and security, thereby reducing the need for children as support in old age, just as they must have lowered the need to save for future contingencies, at least among the upper and middle classes. In lower income groups, the persistence of high unemployment among the young probably lowered the value of children as future sources of income. Perhaps among peasants with only a few acres of land, the traditional birth rates were exceptionally high because of the prevalence of malaria, and with its eradication mortality fell to levels which made a much lower birth rate sufficient to attain desired family size. The smaller size of families on the estates compared with that of small holders may be due to the greater security of employment and income on the estates, and also the greater usefulness of children in doing chores around a family farm than on the estates. Malaria eradication played a major role not only among the lower classes but among the upper classes as well by lowering mortality and raising life expectancy. Thus, unemployment and malaria may have been just as important as the welfare measures in bringing down the fertility rates.

In Malaysia, with its extensive welfare system, the benefits received as a percentage of income are eight times more in the lowest quintile than in the highest and nearly four times more than in the next highest quintile. These differentials are mainly due to the greater share of educational, medical, and social services received by lower income families (Meerman, 1979). Thus, if a detailed revision of the income distribution data for Sri Lanka's 0.44 Gini in 1978–79 and Malaysia's 0.52 in 1976 is made with the benefits from education, health, and social services added into the income of both, the Gini of the two countries may not turn out to be so different. And in the future, with full employment and rising real wages for unskilled workers in Malaysia, one can expect income inequality to be declining faster than in Sri Lanka with its high unemployment.

The high fertility rate for Malaysia (4.0) relative to Sri Lanka is also puzzling since one would expect from economic development and income levels to find Malaysia's fertility rate to be lower than Sri Lanka's 3.5. Elsewhere I have attempted to explain this solely in terms of the comprehensive social welfare system of Sri Lanka (Oshima, 1983a). But more may be involved. The average size of farm operated by the peasantry is considerably smaller in Sri Lanka than in Malaysia, perhaps two or three times smaller. The mechanization of the irrigated paddies has been fairly recent and its labor-replacing effect has yet to affect substantially the desired family size. Moreover, the rain-fed paddies and the tree-crop farms of the Malaysian small holders are not mechanized in the most labor-intensive operations, and the difficulties of obtaining labor under full employment may keep the demand for unskilled workers high. This demand can only be satisfied by a larger family, which may partly explain the larger size of families among Malay peasants compared with the Ceylonese, who work but have much smaller non-mechanized farms.

Concluding Remarks

The contrasts in the postwar experience of the two leading commercial crop economies of monsoon Asia are sharp. They are difficult to comprehend unless we look back into the prewar decades and delve into the differences in historical circumstances. It does not take any training in economics to realize that low-income countries cannot afford to spend as heavily as Sri Lanka did. Unlike Malaysia, it brought in some of the leading British economists (N. Kaldor, J. R. Hicks, J. Robinson, D. Seers, and others) to advise the government in the 1960s. What is surprising is that Malaysia, unlike any other country in South and Southeast Asia, put so much effort, generally in the right direction, into the development of its agricultural sector. Perhaps the Malaysian government in the 1960s depended very little on economists, most of whom were not favorably inclined toward agricultural development. Instead, the political leadership, whose main constituency was the ethnic Malay peasantry, merely followed its political bias.

That the Malaysian example was a rarity in Asia can be appreciated when it is recalled that these were the heady days of development economics which saw poor countries trying to leapfrog into full development by starting with heavy industrialization, accelerated industrialization with rural surplus labor (dualistic theories), big-push and crash investment programs using disguisedly unemployed labor, and so on, most of which looked upon industrialization as the vehicle of success and on agriculture as the obstacle to it. All of these views were based on the general framework of traditional economic theory, which paid little attention to cultural and institutional forces (see Chapter 2). It was also the heyday of Keynesian economics, which condemned high savings as the culprit responsible for high unemployment and looked to redistribution through high taxes and social welfare to reduce savings.

In turning to the question of why Malaysia and not Sri Lanka took the right path in the postwar decades, significant differences in their respective prewar historical backgrounds must be noted. Malaysia started out with population densities much lower than Sri Lanka's, in part due to the unsuitability of much of Malaysia's sandy soils for highly labor-intensive paddy growing. But in the main two factors were crucial: one was Ceylonese hostility to British rule, which led to the unfavorable treatment of British enterprises after independence; the other was the strongly Theravada Buddhist culture of the dominant Sinhalese in Sri Lanka which led to a welfare state.

The loss of communal land in Sri Lanka was unfortunate. In a subsistence economy, the products of the communal land taken together are just as vital as rice. The importation of a large alien population from India meant that in one way or another foreigners would be competing with the local peasantry for the use of resources, particularly when the migrants were likely to work harder for less remuneration than the nearly landless peasants. The British and the Ceylonese landowners of commercial crops thus had an alternative labor supply, which tended to keep wages on the estates and in general lower than if the additional labor supply had not been available. If the British had made some effort to protect the peasantry from its own ruling elite as they did in Malaysia, the hostility could have been minimized, but this was not done until the mid-1930s, when it was already too late. By the mid-1940s, the number of peasants per hectare of arable land rose from less than 2.0 to 2.4 and the number of work animals per peasant fell by one-half, implying an increase in tenants and landless peasants. The British, while taxing the peasantry, did little to improve their lot. If the British had helped to improve rice cultivation and had used the surplus to feed the estate populations, instead of importing food and thereby tending to depress prices, the situation would have been different. As it was, rice yields rose only marginally and Ceylon ended the prewar period with the lowest yields in monsoon Asia, only one-half of the Asian average. Thus, there was a historical precedent for the policy of guaranteeing high prices for rice in the post-independence era beginning in the 1960s, particularly as a device to motivate peasants to shift from broadcasting to more costly transplanting technology, which had been given up as too costly by the end of the British colonial rule.

British attempts to weaken the hold of the Sangha on the peasantry by introducing Christianity and withdrawing traditional state support from the Sangha drove the priests to depend on the peasantry for food, which they accomplished by stressing the importance of charity and earning merit. This in turn obligated the priests to assist the peasantry in many ways, drawing the two closer together. What could be better than using the proceeds from estate taxes for charity in the form of welfare spending?

The prospects for Sri Lanka in the 1980s are brighter as a new government is trying to dismantle the welfare programs and denationalize industry. But progress is slow as the pressures are great to retain much of the welfare program. Denationalization is difficult since public enterprises are so inefficient that no one wants to buy them. Of course, prospects are far rosier for Malaysia, which has completed the transition to an industrial society while maintaining a well-developed agricultural sector. Needless to say, new problems are likely to crop up for the first plantation economy to move into industrial society. One particularly difficult problem is the mechanization of the most labor-intensive phases of tree crops, rubber-tapping and the harvesting of palm oil,

Malaysia's two major export crops. Suitable machines to replace labor are nowhere to be found since Malaysia's estates are the first in the world to reach the harvest-mechanizing stage for tree crops.

In the case of rice growing, the early adaptation of imported technologies has sufficed, although further improvements are being made in transplanters and reaping/threshing combines as labor shortages become acute in the double-cropped areas (Hatta, 1982). Without suitable harvesting machines for rubber tapping and palm reaping, the release of workers to nonagricultural employment will slow down in coming years. It takes time to develop and produce new technologies cheaply. Something like a decade elapsed in the Hawaiian sugar industry to mechanize sugarcane harvesting. In the meantime, Malaysia is forced to bring in workers from other countries.

Although Malaysia's need for foreign workers is helpful for countries like Indonesia, which have plenty of surplus labor, for Malaysia it means that the decline in income inequalities and fertility rates will slow down. With full employment and wages of less skilled workers rising faster than the others, with the shift of the labor force from lower paying industries, and with more earners per family in the lower income groups, income disparities in the 1980s should begin to fall. However, the import of foreign workers will retard these processes, while the delays in mechanization in harvesting may obstruct the demographic transition of small holders and laborers in tree-crop agriculture since the desire for children among unskilled workers on the estates and small holders will remain high. All this will tend to slow down the overall growth of the economy as measured by per capita product.

Malaysia's domestic market will expand as the population increases, but, unlike the rise of the domestic market in East Asia with the completion of the transition, the expansion of the internal market solely through population and labor force increases will not comprise a rise in the demand for higher income-elastic commodities. A lesson from Malaysia's experience is that countries with a large tropical crop sector should start early research in the mechanization of crop growing for which technologies cannot be imported. Once an economy approaches the completion of the transition, there is a rapid conjunction of forces difficult to handle within a short time span.

A major mistake made by Sri Lanka (and India, the Philippines, and others to varying degrees) was to emphasize industrialization so strongly at a stage when the economy was not ready for it, in terms of physical infrastructure, accumulated capital, and manpower quality, especially industrial entrepreneurship. No amount of protection and government nationalization can succeed in nurturing a large class of viable enterprises for many industries in the early stages of development. Sri Lanka is now burdened with numerous industries which are obsolete and inefficient but difficult to replace because they employ a large number of workers and have absorbed much capital, while powerful vested interests in the bureaucracy and the private sector exert pressure to keep them going with rehabilitation spending.

Malaysia was fortunate not to have launched such a group of industries. Its relatively free market policies in the industrial sector in the 1960s and 1970s have permitted a fairly large shelf of efficient, labor-intensive industries which are now beginning to accelerate their exports, even though these are by no means as strong as those in Taiwan and Korea where these types of industries were developed nearly a decade earlier under more favorable domestic and international conditions.

On the one hand, Malaysia's successful completion of the industrial transition with a well-developed agricultural sector, full employment, and prospects for declining income disparities will make it easier in the coming decades to transfer resources to the industrial sector and to import new labor-saving and skill-using technologies. But new and difficult challenges loom ahead for any nation aspiring to higher levels of industrialization, particularly in a multiracial society with a history of ethnic problems which are not easily solved. For Malaysia's commercial-crop sectors the low-wage exports from Sri Lanka and Indonesia may pose strong challenges as Indonesia is trying to improve the management of its estate sector. Malaysia's prosperity in the 1960s and 1970s was in part due to the retardation of the tree-crop sectors in Sri Lanka and Indonesia, but these countries are learning from Malaysia's successes and could stage a comeback.

The old guard of Malaysia's leadership has been replaced by a younger political group with support from a rapidly rising young business circle. In a bullish mood, they have opted to move into heavy industrialization following what then appeared to be a successful Korean strategy in the 1970s. With the prices of oil and other export products now sagging and future prospects uncertain, there should be second thoughts about the heavy industry strategy. Despite strong opposition from economists and the other business groups, no changes have been made so far. The dangers of narrowly centered decision-making on such complex issues as industrial policy are many. It can destroy many of the gains achieved by the older leadership in nurturing a labor-intensive strategy which saw West Malaysia complete the agro-industrial transition in the early 1980s. It may be time for the leadership to look more closely at the problems South Korea is now facing, the difficulties the Philippines has had ever since it moved too quickly into industrialization in the 1950s, and, above all, the experience of Sri Lanka. Both have been able to stay away from authoritarianism, in large part because the rural development program in Malaysia and welfarism in Sri Lanka have been popular with the majority of the people. But as both countries begin to move away from rural development and welfarism, as they have been doing recently, republican governance may begin to run into difficulties unless wider participation of important minorities is permitted.

CHAPTER 9

Slow Growth with Unlimited Labor Supply: Heavy Industrialization in China and India

One of the signal events of recent centuries was the freeing from colonial influence and the early and vigorous start into modern economic growth of the two only remaining ancient civilizations on earth: those of India and China.[1] These nations, the most populous in the world, are so large that even modern census counts can easily miss groups of people the size of the populations of Singapore and Hong Kong. These giants, after stagnating for the last few centuries, finally emerged with powerful leaders and made it their aim to catch up economically with the West as quickly as possible. This chapter argues that it is unfortunate that they chose to develop heavy industries first, postponing the development of agriculture and the lighter, lower-stream industries.

This chapter deals with the adverse impact of such a strategy on the growth of agriculture and other industries, and therefore on the economy as a whole. In order to understand the problems encountered by India and China, we must discuss the heavy industries and their complications at length. Unlike the city-states and other smaller nations, these Goliaths, with their extensive natural resources and large potential markets, had greater options. But on the basis of questionable theories of economic growth, they chose to leap into the most advanced complex industries.

The impact of heavy industries on overall growth is an important subject in view of the continual debate going on in other Asian countries as to whether this or that heavy industry should be launched now or later. Both India and China deliberately embarked on a wide range of heavy industries, arguing that the very enormity of their countries furnished unlimited markets and natural resources to ensure economies of scale without being constrained by the need for export earnings.

[1] Although this chapter is a fresh composition, the main thrust of the argument is found in Oshima, 1962; 1971a; 1983b.

Their sights were mainly set on the goals of self-sufficiency and self-reliance and (unlike the city-states) less on efficiency or exports.

Despite their similarities, there are problems in comparing the growth of these two giants because of the basic difference in their ideological, political, and economic systems: one is a totalitarian Communist country relying largely on comprehensive planning; the other, a democratic socialist-oriented country relying largely on market forces and perspective planning. There are sufficient similarities in their heavy industrialization strategies to make the comparison worthwhile, although account must be taken of various differences in order to draw policy implications for other countries. One basic similarity, however, is that most of the heavy industries established were undertaken by the national governments and given top priority.

Historical Legacies

The historical legacies of the great ancient civilizations of China and India must be traced to periods earlier than the recent centuries of Western penetration. In understanding postwar economic growth, two major legacies should be considered: the religious/ethical institutions of Hinduism in India and Confucianism in China, and the monsoon rice technology of transplantation, both about two and a half millennia old. The Western intruders in Asia did little to change these two fundamental legacies.

As Eckstein's (1975) estimates show, at the beginning of postwar growth, industrial output in India on a per capita basis was about double that of China in cement, crude steel, pig iron, and electric power, and India had three times the number of cotton spindles. But yields per hectare of rice were about two times higher in China and those of wheat about 50 percent higher. GNP per capita in 1952 U.S. dollars were about the same: $60 in India and $50 in China, but because of the difficulties of exchange rate deflation for such vast countries with large regional price differentials the difference cannot be said to be significant (Oshima, 1951).

The legacies of Hinduism and Confucianism are difficult to evaluate. Max Weber's (1964, 1967) judgment that social values derived from Confucian culture were more conducive to modern economic growth than the social values of Hinduism with its thousands of subcastes is probably valid.

The spirit of mutual cooperation is much stronger in Confucian culture than in Hindu caste culture, and regional and national consensus is thus easier to reach. The endogamous caste system of Hinduism makes for strong loyalties to subcastes and castes often transcending loyalties to the village, province, and nation and turns the individual's outlook inward toward his caste rather than outward toward society at large. Confucianism, with its strong emphasis on harmony, cooperation, and moderation among members of a family, among the families within a village, and among villages within a nation, is more conducive to regional and national unity and integration. The strong identification with subcastes, not only in India but in other South Asian countries such as Nepal and Sri Lanka, can be likened to the identification with Islam among Muslims and with the family among Filipinos.

The detailed division of occupations among numerous subcastes is reminiscent of the problems involved in the detailed job specifications promoted by Western labor unions. The local elites are dominated by the highest castes, with frequent physical violence perpetrated against the less privileged lower castes and outcastes. The power of these local high-caste elites is so strong that the various land reform measures enacted in the postwar decades have not yet been implemented to any substantial degree (Agrawal, 1980).

Historically, China was ruled by the Mongols in the 13th century and by the Manchus in the 17th through the early 20th centuries, but in both instances the conquerors were absorbed by Han culture without too much disruption. In contrast, India was invaded very early in its history by fair-skinned Aryans from Central Asia who, in order "to preserve the purity of the race," imposed a rigid caste system. Indian civilization developed as a synthesis of the Aryan and indigenous culture. There is a strong nonmonsoon element in Hinduism, as it was a synthesis of Vedic ideas brought by the Aryans from outside monsoon Asia with the indigenous religion. Weber (1927) regarded it as "a kind of Indian Catholicism." From the 13th to 18th centuries India was ruled by Muslim conquerors; British colonial rule began in the mid-18th century.

During British rule, India included significant groups of non-Hindu peoples (Muslims, Sikhs, and Buddhists), especially in the north, as well as even larger groups of indigenous non-Aryan Hindus in the south, so that the Hindu-Aryans in government were looked upon by other groups as neoimperialists.

Although national income data are inadequate, Indian economists appear to agree that per capita income in the British period did not rise, and probably declined slightly. This stagnation may have been due to the enormous rice sector in which total production failed to rise as the population increased. Total (cleaned) rice production from 1910/11 to 1924/25 averaged 26.63 million tons and from 1925/26 to 1939/40 26.45 million, with average yields per hectare declining from 10 to 9 quintals (Wickizer and Bennett, 1941). Consistent with these trends were the data computed by Daniel Thorner from the Indian censuses (Agrawal, 1980) showing a rise in the share of the male working force in the agricultural sector from 74 percent in 1881 and 1901 to 76 percent in 1921 and 1931.

Comparable data for China are not available. Eckstein (1975) reported that paddy rice yields per hectare in 1931–1937 averaged 25.3 metric quintals compared with 21.1 in 1950, according to the first official report from China. This was about double that of India's 13.3 in 1934–1938 but much lower than Japan's 36.3 in 1934–1938. Japan's yields in the 1880s were lower than China's, being only 21.6, but by 1929–1933 Japan had caught up according to Buck's (1956) study. Taiwan and Korea, under Japanese colonization, raised their yields by 50 percent from the early 1910s to the latter 1930s.

British policy in India (as in Burma and Sri Lanka, but unlike in Malaysia) produced additional burdens for the peasantry. The British used intermediaries to collect taxes and eventually made them landowners. The original intermediaries gradually moved to urban areas and became absentee owners, the tiers of tax collectors multiplied, and by the end of British rule about 40 percent of the peasantry were paying taxes to maintain the British government and several layers of intermediaries.

The decades before World War II were times of great poverty and distress for the peasants in both countries. In China, the decay of the Manchu dynasty had proceeded to the point where warlords ruled the countryside, while the government and absentee landlords exacted ever-higher shares from farmers. And in China and India the penetration of foreign powers had reduced urban markets for the handicrafts produced by the peasants during the slack rice-growing season.

Under these circumstances, one might have expected China and India in 1949 and 1946, respectively, to put major emphasis on agricultural development, using the new Japanese varieties, culture methods, and extension services, and to expand the light industries and physical infrastructure needed by the agricultural sector, as was done in Taiwan, South Korea, and Malaysia. But after a few years of rehabilitation and reconstruction, both began to emphasize heavy industrialization, placing it above agricultural development.

Record of Postwar Growth

There are serious problems with aggregate data such as those from the national accounts for countries like China and India. National networks of transport and communications are much more restricted to major cities and towns than in smaller countries, and connections with the vast hinterlands away from the coastal areas are weak. Therefore, the extent to which national markets connect factor and product prices between villages and smaller towns with those of the cities is limited. Even in cities and major towns that are part of the national network of transport and communications, the costs of transporting goods and labor over long distances render tenuous the operations of national market forces in integrating the nationwide system of output and input prices. In large developed countries like Canada and the United States, the far-flung, efficient transportation and communication systems facilitate the free movement of all but the bulkiest products (such as coal, cement, iron ore, and lumber), and even for the latter the strong linkages of one regional market to the next establish chain relationships in generating a meaningful nationwide system of national prices.

There is an additional difficulty. In the case of both China and India the expenditure for data collection among populations so large has been meager on a per capita basis, so that the underlying information upon which the national accounts have been constructed is small. In the case of China, no modern census was conducted on the labor force until the 1982 Census of Population. (The Communist countries do not subscribe to the concept of a labor force in terms of people who are willing to work, perhaps because they do not recognize unemployment.) Hence, labor force statistics are not available for much of the period under consideration. During the years of the Great Leap Forward in the late 1950s and during the Cultural Revolution (1966–1976), there was a breakdown in the Chinese statistical system when party cadres vied with each other in reporting inflated figures to show how successful their programs were. Not until a new national leadership came into power were the official statisticians free to produce objective data.

The sources of information for Indian estimates are much scantier than for China, where data are regularly collected from an extensive network of monitoring agencies whose record-keeping is necessary for non-market, "command" economies. The multifarious, minor crops comprising a large portion of agricultural activities and the huge informal sectors outside farming are informed "guesstimates," often arrived at through bargaining and negotiations among various ministries. In both countries, the 1970s national accounts are better estimates than those of previous decades.

Particularly confusing is the fact that Chinese estimates appear to be under revision by the official statistical bureau. The *World Development Report* for 1979 reported Chinese per capita income in U.S. dollars to be $390 in 1977, but the 1978 Report figure was $230, although between 1977 and 1978 China's net material product rose more than 10 percent. The World Bank's *World Tables, Third Edition*, 1983, presents Chinese GNP details only for 1978 to 1982.

Until such times as the new estimates become available, specialists in Chinese affairs are using 1977 estimates, which imply much higher estimates for China's growth from 1952 than for India's. Wilfred Malenbaum (1982) a specialist in the comparison of Chinese and Indian growth, has found several puzzling features in the pre-1977 estimates. If the new figures of the World Bank are used, the GNP per capita in 1981 for China of $300 is 15 percent higher than India's $260. Compared with Southeast Asia, China's per capita income is only about one-half the average of Indonesia, Thailand, and the Philippines and the same as Sri Lanka's. The $300 figure appears somewhat low but is plausible when compared with per capita calorie consumption figures. According to *FAO Production Yearbook* statistics, China consumes about 35 percent more calories per capita than India, which may be due to the larger physiques of Chinese, the colder climate of China, more food waste, and the lower prices of foodstuffs due to large government subsidies. Per capita consumption of calories is about 15 to 20 percent higher in Taiwan, Singapore, Hong Kong, and South Korea and 10 percent higher in Malaysia than in China.

One may conclude that although China's GNP growth rate was not as high as Southeast Asia's 6 percent it was probably higher than India's and South Asia's 3.5 percent, perhaps around 4 to 5 percent. If we deflate official net material product in current prices (which is called national income in China) by the official cost of living index, we obtain a growth rate of product of 5.7 percent from 1962 to 1979, of product per capita of 3.8 percent, and of product per worker of 3.2 percent (*Beijing Review*, 1982). These rates are as high as those of Southeast Asian countries in our basic tables, although they may be too high.

In view of these and other problems in the estimates for mammoth countries like China and India, an attempt was made in Table 9.1 to experiment with alternative estimates of growth. In this, use is made only of the current price estimates of GNP converted into U.S. dollars by the exchange rates for the decennial census years (1950, 1960, 1970,

Table 9.1 Alternative Estimates of Growth Rates of Asian GNP in Terms of Their Purchasing Power of United States Goods: Postwar Decades

Country	Period	$GNP per capita at current prices		Annual growth rate between (1) and (2)	U.S. consumer prices: growth rate	Annual real GR of $GNP per capita (minus U.S. inflation rate)	Annual growth rate of aggregate product
		Initial year	Terminal year				
		(1)	(2)	(%) (3)	(%) (4)	(%) (5)	(%) (6)
Japan	(1950–81)	214	10,080	13.2	4.3	8.9	10.0(7.0)
China	(1952–81)	50	300	6.4	4.3	2.1	3.9(6.0)
India	(1950–81)	60	260	4.8	4.3	0.5	2.6(3.7)
Philippines	(1950–81)	171	790	5.1	4.3	0.8	3.7(5.9)
Thailand	(1950–81)	57	770	8.8	4.3	4.5	7.2(7.0)
Malaysia	(1955–81)	252	1,840	8.0	4.8	3.2	5.9(6.5)
Indonesia	(1960–81)	94	530	8.6	5.5	3.1	5.3(5.7)
Singapore	(1960–81)	438	5,240	12.6	5.5	7.1	9.08.5)
Hong Kong	(1950–81)	283	5,100	9.8	4.3	5.5	8.7(9.5)
Taiwan	(1950–81)	106	2,400	10.6	4.3	6.3	9.0(8.7)
South Korea	(1950–81)	49	1,700	12.1	4.3	7.8	9.9(7.7)

Notes: Col. (1) derived by converting per capita GNP in national currency into that of U.S. dollars using the foreign exchange rate of the year; Col. (2) taken from *IBRD World Tables*; Col. (4) computed from country table for U.S.A. in the *IBRD World Tables*, Col. (5) the difference between Col. (3) and (4); Col. (6) population growth rate per year added to Col. (5). Data in parenthesis computed from official estimate of GNP.

Source: Computed from *IBRD World Tables*, Third Edition, Vol. 1

1980) around which the basic censuses of population, agriculture, economics, etc., are taken and near which the sample surveys are most valid since the sampling frames are newly worked out on the basis of the decennial censuses. More important, this approach dispenses with the indigenous price indexes for deflation. The weak part of the approach is the use of foreign exchange rates to convert current price estimates into U.S. dollars, the problem being that the foreign exchange rates understate dollar incomes of developing countries because nontradables do not enter into the formation of LDC exchange rates. In the course of three decades, the share of nontradables has declined so that the bias diminishes. This is probably of minor importance for countries like China and India.

Specifically, what was done in Table 9.1 was to take the dollar estimates of Asian per capita GNP in or near the census years and deflate them by the U.S. consumer price index. In effect what we get is the growth rate of Asian countries in terms of the capacity of their GNP to purchase U.S. goods in constant prices, not the capacity to purchase goods in their own countries in constant prices or conventional growth measures. Column 6 in Table 9.1 gives the former, with the latter in parentheses, taken from World Bank figures. The growth rates in U.S. dollars are substantially lower than the conventional rates for China and India (and for the Philippines) but roughly the same for most other countries. Protection of the industrial sector is the greatest in China, India, and the Philippines.

It appears that the weight of the agricultural (A) sector relative to the industrial (I) sector was understated from the beginning. Although periodically procurement prices of agricultural products have increased, they were still understated even after a 22 percent increase in 1979, since the free market prices were well above the procurement and ration prices even afterwards (World Bank, 1983). Since 1952, base prices have been shifted twice—in 1957 from 1952 to 1957 base prices and in 1971 to 1970 base prices. In the first change, agriculture's output in 1957 was actually lowered from 60 billion yuan in 1952 prices to 57 billion yuan in 1957 prices, but in 1971 it was raised from 74 billion yuan in 1957 prices to 109 billion in 1971 prices. Thus despite the raising of agricultural procurement prices from time to time no significant change in price weights was made until 1971 that did not soon become obsolete. The overstatement in the official growth rates may be partly due to an understatement of the share of the slow-growing agricultural sector, where the growth rate was only one-fifth that of industry, or 2 percent a year compared with 10 percent, 1960–1980 (World Bank, 1983). When such a slow-growing but large sector is underweighted in the deflator in the base year, the upward bias is substantial.

It is mainly the underweighting that produces the puzzling problems mentioned by Malenbaum (1982). The much greater difference between the percentage shares of output and labor force in Chinese agriculture in 1975 compared to Indian agriculture is due to the undervaluation of output and low labor productivity in Chinese commune agriculture (because of poor methods of remuneration and the "iron rice bowl"). The much greater excess of value added per worker in industry over agriculture during 1975 in China than in India largely reflects the same forces as in the differentials of output and employment shares and not just structural imbalances. Nor is the large size of incremental capital-output ratio in industry in both countries indicative only of inefficiencies; it reflects a deliberate policy of heavy industrialization.

If it were possible to obtain detailed free market prices and use them in weighting agricultural product, its relative share in total product would be much larger than the share of industrial product weighted by free market prices. This would give an overall growth rate much lower than that shown officially but more consistent with the low level of per capita product in U.S. prices in China for 1980 as in the above. Since market prices for China and India are difficult to obtain it would be interesting to weigh the sectors according to the shares of employment in the A and I sectors; if this were done it is quite likely that the growth rates for countries like India and China would be considerably lower than those of other countries with a smaller A sector. At any rate, it can be concluded that the GNP growth rates for both countries were low, but India's were lower than China's.

Heavy Industrialization and Its Impact on Overall Growth

Given the extensive poverty in the rural sector, and the huge imports of food in the 1950s and 1960s, it seems strange that neither China nor India gave agricultural development top priority. Along with the expansion of labor-intensive light industries to provide villages off-farm employment during the agricultural slack season, priority to agriculture would have created jobs for underemployed peasants in an era when markets for handicrafts have been reduced by the availability of machine-made products. Instead, both China and India began to emphasize agriculture only in the 1970s. It is now known that the average Chinese consumption of grain fell from 198 kilograms in 1952 to 164 in 1960, and by 1976 had recovered only up to 183. Similar declines were recorded in vegetable oil consumption and probably for protein intake, despite large imports of cereals and soybeans. As a result of falling rural output, and large subsidies and benefits for urban populations, the excess of urban over rural incomes increased continuously from the mid-1950s to the mid-1970s as farm incomes in real terms remained unchanged. The farming population fared particularly badly during the late 1950s during collectivization and the Great Leap Forward and in the Cultural Revolution of 1966–1976. Nevertheless, the Chinese peasantry, freed by the Communists from the demands and oppression of landlords, did well during the relatively liberal first half of the 1950s and the 1960s when left alone to produce, free from the heavy-handed intervention of the bureaucracy (Lardy, 1983). In India, the peasantry fared even worse as rice yields, after rising in the first half of the liberal 1950s in the First Plan, barely rose during the next three plans when resources were shifted to heavy industrialization.

The lower priorities accorded to agriculture by Mao Tse-tung and Jawaharal Nehru in the early stages of development are puzzling in view of their power bases. Mao rose to power through his strategy of depending on the peasants and the countryside before moving on to the conquest of the cities, and Nehru inherited Gandhi's mantle as the champion of the peasantry. It may be that intellectually the distrust and scorn of the peasantry found in the Soviet Marxist and British socialist intellectual traditions were deeply embedded. Indeed, the view that the peasantry was traditional, backward, intractably unprogressive, and incapable of modernization was widespread and extended among nonsocialist intellectuals as well as Communists (Chenery, 1980; Lewis, 1954; Nurkse, 1952).

In the socialistic thinking of Mao and Nehru, the most persuasive arguments were contained in the Feldman model of growth of the USSR, transmitted to India in a more elegant form by the physicist Professor Mahalanobis, the chief planner for Nehru in the 1950s. This theory, when bolstered by models of surplus labor in underdeveloped agriculture by Nurkse Land ewis and by the arguments about infant industries growing to maturity, the importance of the size of the domestic market for scale economies, and the importance of linkages in conventional economic thinking, presented a formidable configuration of arguments for developing the heavy industries first (and for industrialization in general in all LDCs).

Chinese and Indian Experience in Heavy Industrialization

The problems in industrialization were great in India and China since they attempted to establish nearly the whole range of heavy processing and engineering industries starting in the early 1950s when their economies were underdeveloped and overwhelmingly agricultural. In India, planners set out to establish iron and steel, aluminum, cement, heavy industrial and electrical engineering, shipbuilding, automobile manufacture, heavy chemicals, paper and pulp, and glass industries, and in the 1960s, others such as copper, zinc, and lead, petrochemical complexes, consumer appliances, and atomic energy were added. In China, with Soviet aid, an even more ambitious heavy industrial program was established, beginning a few years earlier than in India. In 1953–1957, 156 major construction projects were launched, mainly for heavy industries. Of these, iron and steel projects were most important, following Mao's 1950 order to "take steel as the key link." But after more than two decades of experience, Indian planners were talking of "technological complexity of the industries" entailing a "slower learning curve" as one of the reasons for the difficulties encountered in many of the heavy industries. Despite the shift to an agricultural strategy, 12 percent of GNP in 1979 was still spent by the government for industrial public enterprises. Even in 1984, obsolete methods such as open-hearth furnaces and ingot castings were being used, and the energy consumed to produce one ton of steel was 60 percent more than in Japan.

Plan reviews in India throughout the 1960s and 1970s repeat over and over the problems of underutilization of capacities in these costly heavy industries, with utilization ranging from two-thirds to three-fourths of rated capacities. The same reasons are given in each plan review for the inability to attain full utilization: shortages of raw materials, power, and transport, strikes and lockouts, poor management, inadequate technology, and quality and regional imbalances.

Similarly, China's heavy industries do not appear to be any more efficient, although they grew at twice the speed of those in India. China's heavy industrial share in total industrial output in the late 1970s was 64 percent, compared with 70 percent for Japan, the United States, and Italy; 56 percent for South Korea; and 74 percent for West Germany. Chinese authorities hold that their industrial equipment is inferior and 20 to 30 years outdated. China's own design capabilities have been slow to improve; levels of technical know-how and management are low. Poor quality, shortages, and unused capacities similar to those in India compound the problems of obsolete technologies. Another problem is overstaffing—a result of the "iron rice bowl" syndrome.

Due in part to unused capacities and severe shortages of foreign ex-

Table 9.2   Annual Growth Rate of Manufactured Exports (1970–1980, except for China 1976–79)   (%)

	China	India	Malaysia	South Korea	Hong Kong	Singapore	Philippines
Total mfg.	26.0	14.4	23.5	37.2	20.8	31.3	21.5
Food and tobacco	18.7	16.6	27.5	40.3	16.8	19.8	16.7
Textiles and clothing		13.2	39.8	33.9	20.0	24.9	47.5
Wood and wood products	28.2	24.2	24.8	18.5	13.1	26.5	23.7
Paper and printing		3.9	11.7	65.0	25.5	23.0	26.1
Chemicals and plastics	29.0	13.8	13.3	45.7	17.5	31.5	23.4
Nonmetallic minerals		18.8	15.3	54.0	25.8	24.5	31.5
Basic metals	17.9	2.6	13.7	57.0	16.7	38.9	31.2
Mach. and equip.	24.8	18.0	46.4	55.0	28.5	39.5	41.5
Other		24.7	39.5	16.8	13.6	23.5	37.5

Sources: Data from IBRD *World Tables, 3rd Edition*, vol. 1, except for China which are from *China, Socialist Economic Development*, vol. 2. Taiwan's growth of exports in the 1970s were 30 percent for chemicals, for machinery and transport equipment, from Taiwan's official *Statistical Yearbook*, 1983.

change, the growth of manufactured exports in India and China fell far behind those of South Korea, Taiwan, and Singapore in the 1970s and were even somewhat lower than those of Malaysia and the Philippines (Table 9.2). China's growth rates, which are available only for the 1960s the late 1970s, would have been much lower in the early 1970s due to the disruptions of the Cultural Revolution. The growth of heavy industrial output for India is even less impressive, especially in basic metals and machinery.

Another way of looking at the industrial export performance is given in Column 5 of Table 9.3 which lists industrial exports in 1980 U.S. dollars on a per capita basis to adjust for the large size of countries like India and China. Despite the stupendous investments in heavy industries, per capita industrial exports of heavy industrial pro-

Table 9.3   Per Capita Manufactured Export in Asian Countries (1980)

Country	Manufac-tured Export (million US$) (1)	Heavy Industry Export (million US$) (2)	Total Popula-tion (million) (3)	Per Capita Manufac-tured Export ($) (4)	Per Capita Heavy Industry Export ($) (5)
East Asia*	206,794	158,565	1,179.9	1,978	1,359
Japan	127,489	117,065	116.8	1,092	1,002
China[1]	14,443	6,989	1,000.0	14	7
Taiwan	19,257	7,373	17.6	1,094	419
South Korea	16,458	8,537	38.1	432	224
Hong Kong	13,421	5,763	5.0	2,684	1,153
Singapore	15,726	12,838	2.4	6,553	5,349
Southeast Asia*	17,012	7,283	256.5	156	72
Malaysia	6,120	3,148	13.7	447	230
Philippines	3,215	636	48.3	67	13
Thailand	3,950	1,443	46.5	85	31
Indonesia	3,727	2,056	148.0	25	14
South Asia*	5,270	1,475	689.8	17	8
India	4,894	1,266	675.1	7	2
Sri Lanka	376	209	14.7	26	14

Notes: [1] 1981. * Regional averages for each column are simple, unweighted averages.
Sources: Computed from *IBRD World Tables, 3rd Edition*, vol. I except for China from *Statistical Yearbook of China 1981* and Taiwan from *Industry of Free China* (February 1984).

ducts in the two countries in 1980 were only about 1 to 2 percent of Taiwan's, 10 percent of Thailand's, and less than one-half of Indonesia's, Sri Lanka's, and the Philippines'. India's performance was even worse than China's, with per capita exports only one-third the Chinese levels.

The consequences of a heavy industrial strategy during the beginning of the industrial transition go beyond poor export performances. Both Nehru and Mao made fateful decisions in the 1950s when they embarked on heavy industrialization strategies that were difficult to reverse even in the late 1970s when economists began to have misgivings about heavy industries. Enormous sums were budgeted to launch heavy industries and even more to keep them afloat. The costs incurred by the heavy industries for maintenance, repair, and replacements left insufficient amounts for agriculture and light industries, since underutilization of costly capacities meant low rates of return and an inability to replace and expand out of internal earnings.

Agricultural Development

As Table 9.4 shows, Indian government expenditures for agriculture and rural development (including irrigation) in the First Plan (1951 to 1956) were 33 percent of the planning budget, for social services (education, health, and family planning) 21 percent, and for industry 5 percent. In the Second Plan, when the heavy industry strategy was adopted, agriculture received only 15 percent and social services 16 percent, while the share for industry was raised to 23 percent, of which heavy industries were allocated 16 percent. The industrial share

Table 9.4   Percentage Distribution of Outlays in Indian Development Plans, 1951–1979

	1st Plan 1951–1956	2nd Plan 1956–1961	3rd Plan 1961–1966	4th Plan 1969–1974	5th Plan 1974–1979	6th Plan 1980–1985(est.)
	(1)	(2)	(3)	(4)	(5)	(6)
Agriculture and Rural Development	10.5	5.9	8.5	16.7	11.0	12.6
Irrigation	22.1	9.1	7.6	3.9	10.7	13.9
Energy	7.6	9.7	14.6	14.6	24.9	30.3
Industry	4.9	23.4	22.7	22.2	18.7	17.2
Heavy	—	16.4	15.9	14.4	11.9	10.9
Light	—	7.0	6.8	7.8	6.8	6.3
Transport and Communication	26.4	28.3	24.5	23.2	17.6	6.4
Social Services	21.0	15.9	16.5	14.7	15.8	16.0
Education	—	—	6.9	5.1	3.3	2.9
Health and Family Planning	—	—	—	4.5	3.0	3.2
Others	7.4	7.8	5.6	4.6	1.1	3.6
Total	100.0	100.0	100.0	100.0	100.0	100.0

Sources: (1) and (2) from pp. 738–39 of *Third Five-Year Plan*, (3) from pp. 72–74 of *Fourth Five-Year Plan* (*A Draft Outline*), (4) from p. 83 of *Draft Fifth Five-Year Plan* (*1974–79*) *Vol. 1*, (5) from pp. 17–18 of *Draft Five-Year Plan 1978–83*, and (6) from pp. 57–58 of *Sixth Five-Year Plan 1980–85*.

Table 9.5 Industrial Growth and Structure of China

	1st Plan 1950–1952	2nd Plan 1953–1957	Adjustment Period 1958–1962	3rd Plan 1963–1965	4th Plan 1966–1970	1971–1975	1976–1980	1950–1980
I. Average Annual Growth Rate of Gross Output (%)								
Agriculture	14.1	4.5	–4.3	11.1	3.9	4.0	4.9	4.2
Industry	34.8	18.0	3.8	17.9	11.7	9.1	9.3	12.8
Heavy	48.8	25.4	6.6	14.9	14.7	10.2	7.9	15.5
Light	29.0	12.9	1.1	21.2	8.4	7.7	11.1	10.9
National Income	19.3	8.9	–3.1	14.5	8.4	5.6	6.3	7.1
II. Distribution of Capital Construction Funds (%)								
Agriculture		7.8	12.3	18.8	11.8	11.3		
Industry		52.4	61.3	53.7	61.4	60.2		
Light		5.9	5.2	3.9	4.0	5.4		
Heavy (including metallurgy)		46.5	56.1	49.8	57.4	54.8		
Metallurgy		(10.5)	(14.8)	(9.3)	(11.8)	(10.6)		
Other Sectors		39.8	26.4	27.5	26.8	28.5		
Total		100.0	100.0	100.0	100.0	100.0		

III. Composition of Gross Output of Agriculture and Industry (%)

	1949	1952	1957	1965	1975	1979
Agriculture	70.0	58.5	43.3	29.7	28.5	25.7
Industry	30.0	41.5	56.7	70.3	71.5	74.3
Light	(22.1)	(26.7)	(30.1)	(35.4)	(30.9)	(32.1)
Heavy	(7.9)	(14.8)	(26.6)	(34.8)	(40.5)	(42.2)

Sources: Panels I & II from Table 9 and Table 4, respectively, of Xu Dixin and others, *China's Search for Economic Growth, the Chinese Economy since 1949*; Panel III computed from Part IV, page 4, of *Almanac of China's Economy 1981*, both volumes published in Beijing, 1982.

continued to be large thereafter, averaging about 20 percent (1961 to 1980) with a constant 7 percent for small industries. The share for agriculture remained the same throughout the 1960s (about 15 percent) and then rose to 21 percent in the 1970s. The share for social services remained unchanged at around 16 percent throughout the 1960s and 1970s.

Larger shares were devoted to heavy industries in China where the First Plan emphasized heavy industries; the share to industry increased during the Great Leap Forward and Cultural Revolution periods (Table 9.5). As in India, the investment share of agriculture fell after the Second Plan while the share of heavy industries rose. In 1952 the share of agriculture was 59 percent and that of heavy industry 14 percent in terms of total output of commodity production (light industry had 27 percent). In 1979 the share of heavy industry reached a peak with 42 percent, while light industry had 32 percent and agriculture only 26 percent.

Besides biases in budget allocations, the prices of industrial products or such agricultural inputs as machinery, fertilizer, and pesticides were kept high and agricultural product prices low. In China, the raising of agricultural product prices before 1979 did not offset the large increases in input prices with the result that farm returns were poor. The peasantry, forced to turn over a large portion of output to the state, were left with very little, and the income gap between rural and urban areas widened. Moreover, Mao's policy of taking more and more from the peasantry without putting much back into agriculture meant that the peasants were forced to work harder and harder in order to contribute to industrialization.

In India the position of the peasants may have appeared better since prices and incomes were largely determined by market forces. But a free market does not ensure adequate allocation and efficient use of resources in a situation where the forces meeting in the marketplace are unequal in bargaining power. This is similar to a labor market where workers who are not organized into unions must bargain individually with a large corporation. In developed countries the market works well because laborers are organized into unions and farmers into strong cooperatives and associations backed by law. In India, where the small, marginal, and landless peasants are usually in debt, the sale of their output and labor to moneylenders, traders, and landlords occurs at unfavorable times: grains are sold immediately after harvest when the supply is greatest, and labor must be sold during dry seasons when the labor surplus is maximum. With so many resources going to heavy industries, only a little over one-fifth of India's arable land has been irrigated, making it difficult for most farmers to take advantage of high yielding crop varieties requiring a stable water supply.

In China, the moneylender, landlord, and trader classes were wiped out in the 1949 Revolution. Except for the elimination of the British-created zamindars, no agrarian reforms to assist the overwhelming bulk of small and marginal peasants, tenants, and landless workers were implemented. The increasing rural population meant further land fragmentation, tenancy, landlessness, and joblessness, weakening the already low status and economic power of a large segment of the rural population. From the 1951 to 1971 Census, rural population rose from 298 to 439 million, and the 1981 census is certain to show further increases of about 25 to 30 million. I. Singh (1979) showed that landless households as percent of rural households rose from 9.3 percent in 1961 to 9.6 percent in 1971, from 6.8 million to 7.6 million. The extensive protection accorded the industrial sector probably produced negative protection for the agriculture sector, the case in the Philippines. Therefore, dependence on market forces did not help the poorer rural families in India because the market worked against them in the determination of prices and income. In addition there were discriminatory government practices in favor of the urban and industrial sectors.

Light Industry

Tables 9.2, 9.3, and 9.4 show that the export of manufactures of labor-intensive, light industries such as food, wood products, and textiles grew slowly in the 1970s in China and India despite their much lower wage levels compared with ASEAN countries and East Asia. Per capita manufacturing export (the subtraction of per capita heavy industry exports from total manufacturing exports) leaves China with only $7 of light industry exports and India with only $5, compared with much larger amounts for other countries (Table 9.3). And yet India has the longest experience of textile manufacturing in Asia, and Chinese textiles were once highly competitive internationally.

This was due not only to heavy-handed bureaucratic planning, capital-allocation discrimination, and materials shortages but also to the cost and poor quality "cascading" from the highly protected, upstream, capital-intensive industries. Downstream industries were compelled to buy obsolete and poorly made machinery from the engineering industries and poor quality products from the heavy processing industries, and were unable to buy more sophisticated equipment which Chinese industries could not produce.

In the Indian system, equipment and material inputs must be purchased from indigenous industry; only after downstream industries show that these are not locally available can they buy from abroad. Since under the principle of self-sufficiency most of the equipment and other inputs are produced in India, downstream industries ". . . were forced to rely on inferior-quality domestically produced inputs and capital equipment" (Bhagwati and Desai, 1972). Thus, more so than in many other countries of Asia, Indian exporters found themselves disadvantaged, and despite their prewar experience and lower wage levels found themselves losing out, not only to Japan and Hong Kong during the 1950s, but to Taiwan, South Korea, and Singapore from the 1960s, and to Thailand, Malaysia, the Philippines, and Indonesia in the 1970s, where exporters can buy the most efficient machinery, materials, components, and parts in the cheapest markets abroad. In the case of firms producing for domestic markets, these and other difficulties caused a large number of private firms to close down. So-called sick industries developed in the 1970s, and the government was forced to take them over in the interest of maintaining employment and production. A similar situation existed in China in the 1970s.

Nearly three decades of heavy industrialization in China and India have produced what may be termed a heavy industry syndrome, i.e., an economic structure revolving around a wide range of inefficient heavy industries with associated clusters of downstream capital-intensive industries and upstream mines and side-stream utilities and transport. In Malaysia and Thailand, where there is a strong shelf of efficient labor-intensive export industries and agriculture, the driving forces of the capital-intensive syndrome are self-sufficiency in production and self-reliance in technology. In the city-states of Singapore and Hong Kong and in Taiwan, Malaysia, and South Korea the motive force is efficiency for exports and internationalization. In the autarky-oriented heavy industry syndrome, the needs of the heavy and associated industries create a large part of the demand for the other's supplies. Thus a dualistic economy has been created which can be conceived of as two separate circus rings which overlap minimally. One ring comprises industries such as iron and steel, petrochemicals, nonferrous metals, heavy machinery, and chemicals, together with the industries to which they sell and from which they buy (railways, electric power, and mines). The other ring includes most of the agricultural sectors and cottage, village, and small-scale industries in areas where technology is traditional.

There may be nothing wrong with such a dualistic economy except that the future growth of the economy will be slow, not only by the standards of the NICs but also by the standards of the traditional sectors of countries like Malaysia and Thailand. The reason is that the modern sector is geared not to efficiency and export but to self-sufficiency and self-reliance, and is unable to export sufficiently to finance the needs of the sector. As one Indian report put it:

> Twenty-five years after the Second Five-Year Plan the Indian economy (industrial) is largely a licensed one. . . . While it has the third-largest reservoir of trained scientific manpower in the world, the R & D does not meet the needs of the country.

The modern sector continues to depend on foreign technologies and capital for the expansion of the automobile, steel, aluminum, petro-chemical, machinery, and other industries, even though the establish-ment of costly machinery, design, and consulting enterprises was in-tended to dispense with foreign expertise. Much of these imports must come directly or indirectly from loans from foreign governments and international agencies, since the traditional sectors' ability to export has been constrained by the need to support the building-up of the modern sector.

This type of dualism tends to be inflexible, and it is difficult to break out of the rings or to create more overlap. Increases in population and the difficulties of progress in the traditional sectors have meant that by the late 1970s the Chinese and Indian governments turned more to the development of the agricultural sector and exports. But planners in both China and India have found that it is not easy to shift to a labor-intensive agriculture-based development strategy. The needs of the heavy industrial sector cannot be ignored or it will collapse, and it is too costly for the state to permit such enormous investments to go to waste. Hence, as the Chinese and Indian planners have found in their attempts to make the shift, the requirements of heavy industries continue to mount.

Once a developing nation embarks on heavy industrialization for several decades it is difficult to turn the economy toward labor-inten-sive, export promotion because the export industries are not efficient enough to make much headway in the international market, and there is a built-in demand for the products of heavy industries which cannot be met by importation. Nor can the system of licensing and protection be altered expeditiously to promote efficiency. The dissolution of the segmented dualistic economies will take some time; the modern sector cannot be opened up to meet competition from imports, and the traditional sector cannot make much headway with exports.

Not only has the heavy industry sector generated a life of its own, it also has created a powerful vested interest in the bureaucracy, profes-sions, and military which cannot be ignored by today's political leaders. The final product of the modern sector goes into the lifestyle of the modern elite, who include not only bureaucrats, both civilian and military, and professionals, but industrialists, merchants, and landlords who make up no more than 10 percent or so of the populace but wield disproportionate power. In short, the economic dualism of the heavy industry syndrome creates its own social and political dualism.

The affluent tend to consume a diet based on bread, meat, poultry, temperate zone vegetables and fruits. To produce these in monsoon Asia requires land/capital-intensive agriculture, which is costly.

Consumer durables such as automobiles, refrigerators, washing machines, television sets, and other electrical appliances are also costly to produce locally, and their import requires a great deal of foreign exchange and puts pressure on the balance of payments. The outcome can be chronic deficits, as the 1950s and 1960s experience in Sri Lanka and the Philippines illustrated so well. The overwhelming majority of the population must keep to a traditional lifestyle and are too poor to buy many of the outputs of heavy industry. This is true not only of consumer products but also of mechanized equipment. Work continues to be done with traditional tools and there is continued dependence on children for additional labor supply.

China's dual economic system is kept intact by simply forbidding rural labor to migrate to the cities. The communist mayors of cities in the state of Bengal find progress difficult to achieve as each new construction of facilities invites more of the rural poor to migrate to the cities.

Income Distribution

Data on household consumer expenditure distribution in the Indian Sixth Five-Year Plan show that the lowest 30 percent of the population, which received 13.1 percent of total expenditures in 1958–1959, got 15 percent in 1977–1978 in the rural areas, and in the urban areas the figures were 13.2 percent and 13.6 percent twenty years later. It is difficult to make too much of such slow progress in expenditures, if indeed they can be said to be progress at all. For these figures to be taken to mean a reduction in the size distribution of *income*, it must be ascertained that borrowing among lower decile families has not risen and that their family size has not increased faster than among the higher deciles. Most important, the higher share in the lower deciles must not be largely due to a decline in regional price differentials as road networks and transport have become more extensive. There is a need to examine these issues, since it is not expected that a capital-intensive strategy mainly benefitting only a small segment of the nation (10 to 20 percent) and neglecting the much larger labor-intensive sections would lead to improved distribution of income. In a dualistic economy and society such as India's, it is likely that there are islands of high incomes here and there surrounded by oceans of poverty.

To convert family expenditure distribution into income distribution, one must take into account positive savings in the upper deciles and negative savings in the lower deciles. (Incomes are equal to expenditures plus savings.) There are no data available on the trend in the distribution of savings. The Rural Household Survey for 1962 (National Council of Applied Economic Research, 1965) reported that families in the highest quintile were responsible for 97 percent of total family savings, with the highest 1 percent of households saving 59 percent of the total. The lower half of income receivers showed negative savings or borrowing to pay for family expenditures which could not be covered by current income. Household savings were estimated in the national accounts to have climbed from 10 percent of net domestic savings in 1950–1951 to a hefty 33 percent in 1978–1979. If we assume that the highest 30 percent was responsible for most of the savings by the household sector throughout the three decades, then it is clear that incomes of the three highest deciles must have gone up considerably more than their expenditures, of which the share in total expenditures went down slightly from 53 percent in 1958–1959 to 52 percent in 1977–1978. This was because a tripling of the share of household savings in total domestic savings in a slow growing, low-income country like India reflects a rapid rise in the household incomes of upper income groups. It is possible that some of the savings were loaned through banks and other institutions to lower-income groups to cover daily expenditures.

These conclusions are plausible because productivity per worker in Indian agriculture, where most of the lower-income families work, did not rise and probably fell. In the basic statistical tables in Chapter 3, product per worker in agriculture showed no rise in the three decades, and in fact showed a 0.1 percent decrease, while product per worker in the economy as a whole grew at about 1 percent. Income among agricultural population thus did not grow as rapidly as that among the rest of the population.

Within the different sectors, real wages have been constant in industry throughout most of the postwar era except in 1975 and 1976. In agriculture wages were constant in the 1960s and fell in the early 1970s. These unfavorable trends in real wages, together with a 1 percent rise in GNP per worker, indicate that income disparities within sectors may have risen, unless employment per year rose. Employment could have expanded because the shift to an agricultural promotion policy had raised production considerably by the late 1970s. The possibility that lower-income families shared somewhat more than did higher-income families in the increased production cannot be dismissed.

Data on growth differentials in family size in India are not available, making conjecture unavoidable. Crude death rates have fallen, especially among children under five years old, indicating that public health measures have affected the lower-income groups more than upper-income groups. If family size has indeed increased faster among lower-income families consumer expenditures have to be shared by a larger number than among the upper-income families. It is plausible to conclude (pending better evidence than expenditure data) that toward the end of the postwar decades there were relatively more people in the families in the lower quintile groups than in the upper ones, and thus per capita family income inequality did not improve.

China's income disparities are substantially lower than India's (a TDI of 0.5 compared 0.6 for India) but higher than in Japan and Taiwan, although due to the greater regional heterogeneities in China, comparisons with Taiwan may not be warranted.[2] If data existed, it would be better to work out disparity measures for each province in China and average them for comparisons with Taiwan, eliminating much of the between-province disparaties. China's obsession with egalitarianism, especially during the Cultural Revolution when equalization of the wages of unskilled, skilled, and white-collar workers was attempted, has resulted in astonishingly small differentials among the three groups. In 1980, TDI within the urban sector was only 0.24 (corresponding to a Gini of 0.16) compared to the within-rural TDI of 0.46 (corresponding to a Gini of 0.31), or roughly one-half. This is the opposite of non-socialist economies in monsoon Asia where the urban sector's within-disparities are usually larger.

Urban households in China receive considerable subsidies; the total amounted to 32 billion yuan in 1982. If this is reduced to a per urban household basis it comes to about 150 yuan per capita, and added to the average 500 yuan urban income it means that per capita income is about 650 yuan, further widening the disparity with the agricultural sector. China's income disparities under a heavy industry strategy are less but not qualitatively very much different from those in India. However, China's within-industry sector disparities are very low, in fact, too low for a rational system of incentives to improve productivity. A more balanced strategy would have cut down the between-sector disparities by generating lower urban and higher rural incomes through more investment in agricultural infrastructure in the rural low-income regions in both countries. In China this would have offset, if not cancelled out, the larger within-sector variations due to a more dispersed wage structure, allowing higher growth. By the late 1970s, India and China had shifted to a more balanced strategy.

Population Growth

Population growth has recently slowed down much more in China than

[2] On TDI, see Chapter 10.

in India. Growth in China was 1.5 percent per year in the 1970s compared with 2.1 percent in India, while it was 2.3 percent in both in the 1960s. The total fertility rate has fallen to 2.9 in China compared with 4.9 in India (IBRD, 1983). These big differences reflect the higher levels of per capita incomes, their better distribution, and lower mortality levels, particularly in the urban areas where Chinese family size is substantially lower than in rural areas. Rural-urban differences are small in India according to census figures.[3] The extensive system of social security and health insurance plus the employment security available in China are all but unknown in India.

In India, children from five years of age are counted in labor force surveys. In 1967, working children under 15 composed about 8 percent of the labor force. The percentage may be much larger because it is said that organized industries commonly falsify reports to comply with the requirements of child labor legislation and because unorganized household industries which commonly employ children make no official reports. Despite large pools of surplus adult labor, industries resort to hiring child workers for unskilled work because their labor is cheap, reminiscent of the first half of the first industrial revolution in the West.

In India, the number enrolled in primary schools, as a percentage of each age group, was 76 percent in 1980 compared with China's 100 percent by 1960. Adult literacy in India in 1980 was only a little over half the Chinese figure. Effective prohibition against child labor in industry and in commune farm work means that the benefits of child labor are severely limited in China, or at least were until commune agriculture was virtually abolished. There was strong opposition to India's attempt at compulsory family planning measures in the 1970s in contrast to the wide compliance in China. Recently, since the commune system was replaced with family "responsibility," the demand for child labor for farm work has gone up. Peasants are opting for larger families since farm machinery is not available.

China's accomplishments in the demographic field are more the outcome of social welfare than of socialism, similar to the case in Sri Lanka. There have been major tradeoffs with growth, particularly in work and investment propensities, but increased mechanization may

---

[3] *The Beijing Review*, October 24, 1983, reports a 4.2 average for urban areas compared with 5.5 for rural areas. For India the 1971 Census shows little difference: 5.5 in the urban areas and 5.6 in rural areas. The average family size data may overstate China's situation relative to India because of the greater prevalence of the extended household system in China, perhaps in part reflecting the economies of scale in Chinese cooking.

persuade parents to keep their children in school longer as they begin to realize the need for secondary schooling for their children's future employment. At present, China's secondary enrollment is relatively low at 34 percent of the relevant age group in 1980, compared with 51 percent in Sri Lanka in 1980.

Concluding Remarks and Implications for South Asia

It is tempting to visualize what might have happened to India and China, which together have two-fifths of the world's population, had Nehru and Mao opted for labor-intensive, agriculture-based development programs in the 1950s and then gradually shifted to more capital-intensive, industry-based strategies.

If they had started with a labor-intensive strategy, perhaps there would not have been any NICs, and ASEAN today would look different. Shanghai and Bombay would be thriving world centers, rivaling Tokyo and Osaka. Why, then, did the two countries adopt such difficult strategies of development at the outset? Questions such as this are difficult to answer, but cannot be evaded in a study purporting to learn from the past.

No one could have foreseen that postwar technological progress would change the nature of heavy industries into such complex and formidable groupings. Nehru proudly informed his economists that India possessed the third-largest pool of scientists in the world, not realizing that most of them were teaching in high schools and had no industrial experience. Nor were economists at the time aware of the critical importance of technological change in growth. Only one economist out of 20 summoned by Nehru to prepare the Second Five-Year Plan objected to the shift to heavy industrialization. The originator of the heavy industry strategy, the Soviet economist Feldman, had little to say about technology. Nor did economists two decades later, who remained unaware that the economies of scale, markets, linkages, manpower, and so on are affected by the nature of technologies assumed in their models.

Of course, it may have been that these large countries, endowed with sufficient natural resources, domestic markets, and manpower skills, could afford to ignore the need to export and aim for self-reliance, self-sufficiency, and isolation, unlike the city-states and Japan, Taiwan, Korea, and Thailand. China and India could take the risks of leaping into the ranks of industrialized nations by starting with the sinews of modern industry, without counting the costs too closely.

India and China have now shifted to a more labor-intensive strategy with emphasis on agriculture. The influence of this change on smaller countries in the region such as Burma, Sri Lanka, and Bangladesh, may be more favorable to growth in South Asia.

Socialist institutions as well as prewar institutions inhibit growth in South Asia. Hinduism and caste in India, Islam in Bangladesh and India, and Theravada Buddhism in Burma and Thailand need to be modified to be more conducive to modern economic growth. Without the burdens of nationalized industries and economic intervention, the governments of South Asia may have more time and resources for participating in the improvement of the indigenous institutions which are so important for economic growth.

Finally, there will be more resources for the development of small industries and agriculture and the human resources needed in them. Without widespread education (currently only available in Sri Lanka) and industrial and agricultural extension, the small industries and agriculture cannot benefit. As self-sufficiency in rice is approached, the shift to diversified agriculture in peasant farming must be made. And with this there will be an expansion in agro-industry processing, creating off-farm employment and helping to raise family incomes and increase domestic markets for labor-intensive industries. But all these require resources unavailable if too much is spent on capital-intensive industries.

PART III

Implications, Prospects, Summary

CHAPTER 10

Income Distribution in the Industrial Transition

*I*n the study of economic growth, the distribution of income should not be neglected; not only does it influence the incentives to work, the level and pattern of consumption and savings, and therefore the structure of production and imports; it also has various connections with population growth. In this chapter, the discussions in the country chapters are brought together, comparing the experience of the various countries to determine to what extent economic growth and structural changes are related to distributive changes in the transition.[1] Other forces cannot be ignored, some of which, like communalism in Malaysia and regional differences in large countries, are of major importance. But my chief concern is to integrate the analysis of growth and accompanying structural changes with income distribution in a monsoon setting. This involves a more detailed discussion of Thai, Malaysian, Philippine, and Indonesian experiences. As in the study of growth, my interest lies more in the distal than the proximate forces.

Measures and Statistics

In dealing with incomes, consumption, and savings, the family is the unit of decision-making on problems of livelihood and living. Ideally, therefore, boarders and live-in servants should be excluded, but most surveys find this difficult as boarders and servants share food and shelter with the family. Incomes are personal incomes as defined in the national household account but excluding incomes of nonprofit enterprises and associations. Although my interest is in long-term changes in distribution, most countries in Asia find it too costly to conduct annual surveys. For the prewar decades, there are no representative surveys because mathematical sampling methods were applied only

[1] This chapter makes use of estimates and discussion in Oshima, 1962; 1977a; 1982.

in the postwar decades. Besides the limited supply of data, there is the more difficult problem of the comparability of one survey with another when various changes are made in the size of the sample, the survey design, and the definitions of various items. Most troublesome is the quality and reliability of income and consumption data. There is now a consensus that incomes in surveys are substantially understated, mostly in the upper deciles, and particularly for proprietary and property incomes, and also among the lowest deciles since family earners in these groups do a number of odd and miscellaneous jobs throughout the year and are unable to recall some of the income earned. For these and other reasons, the totals of personal incomes from surveys are substantially lower than estimated in the household sector in national accounting systems. Inequality is usually understated because understatement in the upper levels tends to be greater than in the lower levels of the distribution. This assumes that the incomes in the middle are better reported as they are largely the wages and salaries of regular workers.

Since the quality of the data varies from one country to the next as well as from one survey to the next, it is clear that the scattered data available are far from ideal for a study of comparative trends. One actually needs income distribution data for each year which can be averaged out for a decade. It is encouraging, nevertheless, that there is no unusual "jumping around" of the data over time or between countries that is difficult to accept, although part of this may be due to the care and control exercised by statistical units before reporting survey results.

In consequence, only broad and large changes in the data can be taken seriously for interpretation. This implies that a simple approach is better suited than a more sophisticated one which uses methods presuming precision in the data and comparability in the concept and data-gathering methods. For this reason and for simplicity and brevity, I used only the percentage shares of income in five groupings of families, or quintiles. Thus, the highest quintile (Q) or 20 percent of families contains the highest income receivers, the next Q contains the next highest income receivers, and so on until the lowest Q, containing the lowest 20 percent of income receivers. This approach is convenient because experience indicates that it is usually the shares in the highest and lowest Qs that change most frequently. Another important justification for using this approach is that because it is simple, with the fewest assumptions and statistical manipulations, the analysis of distribution is straightforward and not cumbersome.

The measure of overall inequality used is that of quintile inequality.

This measure is the difference between the share of income and the share of families in each Q, and the differences of the two shares are summed up without regard to whether they are pluses or minuses. The sum will be zero if each Q receives 20 percent of income, thus indicating perfect equality. Conversely, the highest inequality is obtained when the highest Q receives all the income and all the others zero. The highest inequality is 160; i.e., the difference between 100 percent (share of income) and 20 percent (share of families) is 80 for the highest Q and 20 for each of the other four Qs (20 × 4 = 80 percent). Thus, if the total quintile inequalities of a country is 80, the quintile inequality index is .50 (= 80/160) and if the total is 40, the index is .25. Table 10.1 presents these indexes for various countries for which data are available. This inequality index (QII) is about one-fifth lower than the Gini index for the Lorenz curve. As argued elsewhere, the Gini overstates income inequalities through the process of cumulating shares of the lower groups, thereby giving undue weight to the lowest shares throughout the cumulation up to the last cumulation by including all the lower shares in all the upper shares. The cumulation of lower shares into higher shares produces a smooth, well-behaved curve cutting through one half of the area of a square so that statistically it gives a neat presentation. But what is the economic rationale for the cumulation? In a study of income inequality, we are interested in how much the richer families, the middle income families, and the poorer families contribute to inequality. Thus, cumulative shares including all the lower income groups are inappropriate and confusing.[2] The extent of the upward bias is considerable, amounting to 20 to 25 percent, judging by the difference between the QII and Gini for half a dozen Asian countries. While in the studies on poverty and other special problems it could be argued that this bias may be appropriate, for our purpose, we need a more general and less tampered-with measure for studying growth. The QII is easily rendered additive, as will be discussed below.

Most important, the reason for the use of quintile inequalities instead of the Lorenz curve and the Gini is the convenience in analysis. In the latter, due to the cumulation of frequencies, no segment of the curve can be identified as belonging to a particular group except the lowest, so that it is difficult to single out each segment for separate study.

In the case of the lognormal curve, the assumption of lognormality is often not fulfilled, especially for the agricultural sectors in monsoon

---

[2] The area between the Lorenz curve and the diagonal is, strictly speaking, not an area in the sense that it is bounded by width and length but a solid whose height rises from the lowest point of the curve to the top at the highest point of the curve.

Table 10.1   Income Distribution Trends in Postwar Asia: Quintile Inequality Index

	1950s			1960s			1970s		
	National	Agr.	Non-Agr.	National	Agr.	Non Agr.	National	Agr.	Non-Agr.
Japan	.30	.22 (1)	.20 (1)	.31 (2)	.27 (2)	.28 (2)	.30 (3)	.28 (3)	.27 (3)
Taiwan				.30 (4)	.28 (4)	.30 (4)	.26 (5)	.25 (5)	.25 (5)
South Korea				.37 (6)	.26 (6)	.44 (6)	.33 (7)	.28 (7)	.39 (7)
Hong Kong				.48 (8)			.39 (9)	.31 (*)	.41 (*)
Singapore				.45 (8)	.35 (*)	.47 (*)	.40 (10)	.37 (*)	.42 (*)
Philippines	.46 (11)	.37 (11)	.44 (11)	.46 (12)	.37 (12)	.46 (12)	.46 (13)	.42 (13)	.39 (13)
Thailand				.38 (14)	.34 (14)	.38 (14)	.45 (15)	.42 (15)	.39 (15)
Malaysia	.36 (11)	.34 (11)	.38 (11)	.48 (16)	.42 (16)	.44 (16)	.48 (17)	.42 (17)	.47 (17)
Indonesia							.47 (18)	.49 (18)	.39 (18)
Sri Lanka	.43 (19)			.42 (20)			.35 (21)	.30 (21)	.38 (21)
India							.38 (22)		
China							.28 (23)	.26 (23)	.14 (23)

Notes: See text for description of Quintile Inequality Index. (1) Averages for 1953–1959; non-agriculture refers to employee households; (2) averages for 1962–69, excluding 1966; national refers to total ordinary households; (3) averages for 1970–1974; (4) averages for 1966 & 1968; (5) averages for 1970–1979; (6) averages for 1967–1969; (7) averages for 1970, 1971,

& 1976; (8) 1966; (9) averages for 1971 & 1976; (10) 1975; (11) 1957, refers to data for rural and urban households; (12) averages for 1961 & 1965; (13) 1971, national average refers to 1971 and 1979 average; (14) averages for 1962–1963 and 1968–1969, refer to rural and urban households; (15) 1971–1973; (16) 1967–1968; (17) averages for 1970 & 1976; (18) 1976; (19) 1953; (20) 1963; (21) averages for 1973 and 1978–1979, refer to rural (including plantation) and urban sectors; data are for spending units; (22) 1975–1976; (23) 1979, refers to rural and urban sectors. (*) Indicates that the figure for agriculture pertains to industry and that for non-agriculture to services for the city-state.

Sources: T. Mizoguchi and N. Takayama, *Equity and Poverty Under Rapid Economic Growth: The Japanese Experience; Report on the Survey of Personal Income Distribution in Taiwan Area, ROC,* various issues; H. Choo, *Factors Determining Income Distribution in Korea,* vol. 1, KDI; L.C. Chau computations based on Hong Kong Census data; H. T. Oshima and T. Mizoguchi, eds., *Income Distribution by Sectors and Overtime in East and Southeast Asian Countries,* CAMS, Manila, for data on Singapore (Rao's article) and Thailand (S. Wattanavitukul's article); Lim Lin Lean, *The Pattern of Income Distribution in West Malaysia, 1957–1970; Income Distribution in Indonesia 1976,* Jakarta: Central Bureau of Statistics; H.N.S. Karunatilake, "Long-Term Changes in Income Inequalities in Sri Lanka," mimeograph; **IBRD** *China Socialist Economic Development,* vol. 1; and *IBRD World Development Report 1980* (for India).

Asia. For example, if the distribution of family incomes is to be linked to the analysis of savings, consumption, and fertility in the demographic chapter below, it is convenient for us to use the quintile groupings to relate incomes and savings to the size of families and birth rates for the different sectors of the economy.

In the quintile share approach, we ask why the upper quintiles' shares of income increase faster than the lower quintiles' shares when the index of inequality rises, or, conversely, why the upper shares decrease more than those in the lower shares. In the next chapter, we ask why the upper quintile families which possess skills, property, and enterprises (and hence higher incomes) desire smaller families and the lower quintile families with few or no skills, property, or enterprises (and hence lower incomes) want larger families. The dynamics of fertility behavior for those with skills, property, and enterprises differ among groups depending on the income sources. The impact of growth and structural change on differential incomes and fertility with and without different sources of income can be studied, as will be attempted in the next chapter.

The approach adopted in this chapter is to look at the main sources of higher incomes as being fourfold: property or wealth ownership, the ownership of enterprises (farms or firms), trained skills, and number of earners. The more of these possessed by the family the higher the income and vice versa, both generally speaking and in the long run. The relative importance of the four sources is in determining the family income changes with the passage through industrial and demographic transition as the demand for trained skills increases and the enlarged supply of wealth makes possible more borrowing as a way to obtain capital for enterprises and differs with respect to the income bracket to which a family belongs. The lowest income families have to depend on the number of earners since they possess very little property and few enterprises and skills. This approach is also used in the fertility discussion in the next chapter.

The economy is divided into two major sectors, agricultural and nonagricultural, on the basis of the sector attachment of the head of the family, and the forces impinging on the three sources of income which influence inequalities must be determined within each sector. But the quintile inequalities for the economy as a whole are not confined to the (weighted) average of the two sector disparities. In addition, there are disparities due to the differences in the mean of the family incomes in the two sectors. These are the between-sector quintile inequalities and are equal to the differences in the national QII and the weighted average of the two sectors (Fei, Ranis, and Kuo,

1979). Mathematically, the national QII can never be smaller than the sector averages and the lowest it can be is equal to the average, signifying that the between-sector QII is zero or that the average farm family income is equal to the nonfarm family income, as is nearly the case for Taiwan in the 1970s (Table 10.1).

Although statistically one can neatly decompose the national QII into three QIIs, analytically the forces responsible for changes in disparities usually affect both the between- and within-sector QIIs directly and indirectly. For example, when South Korea put billions of dollars into heavy industries in the late 1970s, this policy directly raised the between-sector QII by raising non-agricultural incomes and indirectly tended to lower agricultural incomes by reducing the share of resources going to farming. It also increased disparities within the non-agricultural sector by putting more resources into higher-income-generating industries and less into the labor-intensive, low-technology industries.

Family Income Distribution in Monsoon Asia

It is unlikely that the distribution in most countries at the very beginning of the transition in monsoon Asia would have been very unequal. The reason is that in these overwhelmingly agrarian societies, with four-fifths of the labor force in agriculture, the scarcity of land and high densities would preclude the possibilities of wide differences in farm size such as in the West. If 10 million hectares are operated by 1 million farms instead of 10 million farms, the probability of wider dispersion in farm size is greater for the former case.

Disparities in income among peasants might have been narrower than in the later colonial period when populations began to increase and land was taken away from rice for perennial crops, and with the emergence of a landless or near landless working class. The main groups making for disparities were the landlords, the nobles, and their slaves in the precolonial period, but these classes were not large considering the low productivity of traditional agriculture. Nor would mercantile enterprises in the cities have been large given the smallness of the markets and of the urban sector. Moreover, in the precolonial period, the markets for the craft products made by the peasants in the agricultural slack period commanded good prices. Premodern monsoon peasant incomes were probably bunched together, and the resulting distribution curve would have been highly peaked with a short tail to the right in a frequency distribution with the number of families in the vertical axis and incomes in the horizontal axis, compared with the less peaked mode with a much longer tail to the right in later periods (Council for Asian Manpower Studies, 1975; Oshima, 1976). Most peasants produced for subsistence with little left for sale.

Under these circumstances, the coming of the colonialists tended to widen the traditional disparities as plantations employing low-paid laborers were established; rice land in some cases or village forest and community land was appropriated; and machine-made industrial products were imported. There was an increase in tenancy in the case of the Philippines and land became concentrated in the hands of the Catholic Church and indigenous landed elite; in Korea and other countries land was mainly held by the colonizers. The urban sector expanded and trading widened the disparities between the rural and urban sectors. The disparities increased within each sector as older class divisions differentiated and new classes, such as foreign traders, laborers, and so on, came into being. The peak of the mode of income distribution would decline and the share of upper-income groups to the right of the mode tended to increase as the share of the lower groups decreased.

Of course, income inequalities would nowhere rise to such magnitudes as in Latin America where the Spanish conquerors took enormous quantities of the best land from the natives, enslaving many of them and driving others to the hills and other poorer lands. In countries such as Thailand, however, the coming of Westerners was not accompanied by occupation of the country, and large enterprises such as plantations were not established. Instead the nobility lost much of their land and the peasants were able to produce rice to export to nearby countries where rice farmers shifted to production of commercial crops for export. The income distribution may have improved although the importation of Western manufactures took away some slack season jobs.

In Java, the Dutch forced peasants to grow sugarcane, which, on top of the labor needed for rice production and the decline in the amount of land for grazing of work animals, meant that agricultural and population densities rose. In contrast, the British in Malaya brought in foreign labor for the plantations hacked out of the forests, and there was little increase in densities. Most of the commercial crops had to be worked throughout the year, and the seasonality of labor demand was less than in the sugar crops of the Philippines and of Java. Accordingly, income disparities increased less in Malaya than in Java, and less in Java and Ceylon than where large chunks of rice land were taken over by foreigners and indigenous landlords in the Philippines, Burma, South Korea, and India. Probably least affected was Taiwan where the Japanese started out with moderate land reforms and provided irrigation and extension agents to promote higher yields and more crops per land unit. Japan's inequalities were high due to tenancy in the rural areas and sharp dualism in the urban sector as modern, large-scale industries appeared alongside very small firms making traditional low-value products with hand tools.

Hence the different countries in monsoon Asia had different levels of income disparity on the eve of World War II, although in the Philippines, Burma, and Korea disparities were most evident. That is to say, if we imagine the starting point of the Gini or the quintile inequality index on the vertical axis of a diagram with time on the horizontal axis, the intercept or the starting level for each country differs. Unfortunately, there are no data on any of the countries of Asia in the latter 1940s, and only for a few countries in the 1950s. In Table 10.1 the Philippines in the 1950s shows the highest inequalities, followed by Sri Lanka and by Malaysia; Japan's were the lowest. In the countries with higher disparities, low rural densities (and hence wider variation in land ownership) and greater variations in ethnicity, compared with land-reformed, racially homogeneous Japan, existed.

Table 10.1 also shows the following: (1) lower levels of inequality indexes existed in Taiwan, Japan, and South Korea compared with the Philippines, Thailand, Malaysia, and Indonesia throughout the postwar decades; and (2) higher inequality indexes occurred in Hong Kong and Singapore, compared with India and China. The index for Malaysia in the 1950s may be too low as it was taken from a small survey of which the main focus was expenditure data for constructing a cost of living index for employees.

The surprisingly high levels of inequality in the city-states were mentioned in Chapter 6, where it was pointed out that the disparities within the service sector are typically larger than in the agricultural sector of larger countries. In Table 10.1, QII in services is much larger than in industry for both city-states and was the highest in Singapore in the 1960s. This was probably due to the existence in the 1960s of a large sector of traditional services earning low incomes alongside a large sector of modernizing and modern services. With the shift to mechanized industrialization and the relative decline of the service sector, particularly the decline of traditional occupations like domestic services, peddling, hawking, and the like, there was a sharp decline in the inequality indexes from the 1960s to the 1970s for the city-states in consequence of full employment and rising real wages.

Nevertheless, the disparities in the city-states are higher than expected considering the much greater regional homogeneities of small countries compared with continent-sized countries like India and China where geographical differences are compounded by ethnic, religious, and language variations among the regions. Monsoon densities and paddy agriculture may cut through these heterogeneities, enforcing uniformities which tend to even out family incomes, but this tendency is negligible in city-states. The relatively lower levels of the index in welfare-oriented nations like China and Sri Lanka were also discussed in Part II.

The higher inequality indexes in the ASEAN agricultural Four compared with East Asian countries (Table 10.1) not only were high to start with but did not appear to fall in the 1970s. The levels of the indexes are high in both the agricultural and non-agricultural sectors.

In agriculture, it was not only the absence of comprehensive land reform programs such as those carried out in Japan, Taiwan, and South Korea (the Philippine reforms were only partial) but also the degree of effectiveness of the rural development programs in ASEAN compared with the greater successes achieved by the Japanese and Taiwanese programs, in raising yields and crops per hectare, in diversification, in infrastructure, and in institutional improvements discussed in Chapters 4 and 5. With the exception of Malaysia, rural development programs were not sustained over a sufficient length of time. Even in Malaysia, the successes achieved were not comprehensive enough to reduce farm income disparities within the sector as a whole. In fact, the scattered successes might have increased disparities within agriculture in Malaysia where multiple-cropping schemes were carried out in only three regions. Comprehensiveness was not achieved, perhaps partly because rural institutions such as cooperatives were not adequately established.

Without a greater rise in multiple cropping and crop diversification, a great deal of underemployment remained and off-farm incomes were low. Higher off-farm incomes would have benefitted the smaller peasants more, as Chapters 4 and 5 indicate. Generally in Japan, Taiwan, and Korea, off-farm incomes of farm families on smaller farms rose faster than those on larger farms.

By the end of the 1970s off-farm incomes as a share of farm income were low in Southeast Asia (Thailand 60 percent, Malaysia 39 percent, the Philippines 20 percent) and still lower for South Asia compared to 390 percent in Japan and 180 percent in Taiwan. For tropical monsoon Asia, where the dry period is longer than in East Asia, the Southeast and South Asian shares could be considerably higher. It can be conjectured on the basis of East Asian experience that higher off-farm incomes will contribute more to the incomes of smaller farm families since the approach of full employment will open up more job opportunities for those in the lower-income levels. After full employment both the rise in wages and the release of workers to off-farm jobs or to urban migration promoted mechanization in South Asia which eventually spread to all farms, although in Southeast Asia mechanization was confined to the larger farms and contributed to inequality.

As population and labor force growth accelerated, starting from the 1960s, the number of landless or near-landless rural families increased in the Philippines and Indonesia. In Thailand and Malaysia new agricultural land was carved out of the forest. In Thailand the new lands in the northeast were marginal, and without adequate water, yields were low; second crops were difficult to grow without irrigation. Accordingly, population growth contributed to income disparities within the agricultural sector, through landless workers and/or through under-employment which was extensive. Malaysia, after two decades of rural development and accelerated expansion of labor-intensive industrialization, approached full employment in the early 1980s, but income inequality was still rising.

Those who were unable to find work in the rural sector migrated to the cities, and those unable to find jobs in the factories and offices drifted into odd jobs in the informal service sectors. Incomes were low among the latter group and together with the jobless they constituted the lowest income groups in cities. They created more disparities in urban incomes, unlike East Asian urban migrants who found employment in mechanized factories for higher wages.

The new factories and modern service offices opened up jobs for the educated segment of the labor force in Southeast Asian cities. These enterprises were profitable, particularly because many of them operated under government protection. The bureaucrats, the educated labor force, and the urban rich made up a new urban upper class, and this increased the share of the upper income quintiles. In contrast with East Asia, the continuous flow of workers not needed in the rural sector held down real wages, so that income disparities in the urban sectors continued to remain high and in some cases rose. The more rapid rise in product and productivity in the non-agricultural sectors compared with agriculture tended to increase the disparities between the two sectors. In East Asia, not only off-farm jobs but subsidies and protection from governments kept farm family incomes high.

The foregoing are some of the major forces underlying the trends in income disparities in the two regions. Historical circumstances discussed in the country chapters are related to these forces. The development of rice culture and human resources, especially education, in the prewar period in East Asia and the plantations in Southeast Asia (except in Thailand), together with the prevalence of Confucian values, are influences behind some of these forces. But there were others unique or special to each country in Southeast Asia. These will be singled out and compared below.

Thailand. Thailand emerged from the past with insufficient modern infrastructure and sought to expand the economy through farm exports. Regions near rivers and railways connected to cities benefited the most. However, because the overwhelming majority of farms were far from transport facilities, farm incomes did not rise and subsistence farming remained the rule. The commercialized farms, mainly in the Central Region near Bangkok, tripled chemical fertilizer use while irrigated areas and the use of tractors both doubled. The volume of exports increased by 50 times between 1962 and 1969. Although data are not available, land concentration in the Central Region probably increased. The large increase in QII for the agricultural sector (from .34 to .42) reflected the widening disparities between the small commercial and the large subsistence sectors.

In the urban sector, the proportion of household heads with higher education in the Bangkok-Thonburi area nearly doubled to 15 percent in the second survey compared with the first of the official household income/expenditure surveys. The numbers of modern industries and paid employees rose as indicated by the decline in the number of proprietors and family helpers from 48 percent to 40 percent. The increasing disparities reflected the spread of commercialized agriculture in the rural areas and of industrialization and modernization in the urban areas. In the 1980s, the disparities should become less important as the spread effect is completed, although other forces may emerge.

West Malaysia. The agricultural QII rose from .34 in 1957 to .42 in the 1960s and remained the same (or higher) in the 1970s in West Malaysia. The rise in the 1960s reflected confusion arising from the emergency in the 1950s and a land resettlement program which reclaimed jungle to create 15-acre farms for commercial crop production (tapioca, sugar, cocoa, maize, rubber, etc.) while rice farming was neglected. Policy shifted in the 1970s to improvement of rice farming which helped to raise the income of many small farms through multiple cropping, extended credit, and so on. The high QII in agriculture even in the 1970s may be largely due to the uneven impact of the improvement program on rice farms in various parts of the country, particularly on rain-fed farms, which composed one-half of rice farms. Thus, unlike the overwhelmingly rice-producing agriculture of East Asia, Malaysia's farm sector is highly heterogeneous and features uneven development of agricultural regions, especially in the lagging eastern portion of the peninsula, accounting for the highest QII in the 1960s (Table 10.1). The impoverishment of traditional fishermen due to the encroachment of trawler fishing has increased.

In the urban sector, the secession of Singapore from the Malaysian Federation had an important effect on the high QII level in the 1960s and the 1970s. Enterprises in Kuala Lumpur, Georgetown, and other cities began to take over commercial and industrial activities formerly conducted in or through Singapore. Many enterprises moved out of Singapore into Malaysian cities, especially Kuala Lumpur, and began to expand, while new ones were also established. Financial, trading, and rubber, oil, and tin processing firms plus import-substitution manufacturers all moved across the causeway from Singapore. With political assistance, the upper classes in Malaysia began to demand their share of the growing enterprises, jobs, and profits, and their income share rose. There was the emergence of a dualistic structure which widened urban income disparities while the higher incomes generated increased the between-sector inequalities from the late 1960s and into the 1970s.

On top of agricultural, industrial, mercantile, and regional diversities, Malaysia's ethnic diversities are more pronounced than in any other ASEAN country. Besides Malays, there are sizable groups of Chinese in the cities and Indians on the plantations, in addition to smaller groups of Westerners and Indonesians. The Westerners and Chinese are in the upper quintiles and most of the others in the lower quintiles, with concomitant differences in education, occupational experience, and religion. The ethnic diversity in Malaysia is responsible for some of the income disparities. The full employment attained in the early 1980s and the completion of industrial transition may erase the disparities in future. But unlike the situation in East Asia, their elimination may be delayed by lack of mechanization in the harvesting of tropical commercial crops, the need to bring in Indonesian laborers, and the government's efforts to establish capital-intensive industries.

Philippines. If income tax reporting improves, the Philippine QII may in reality be as high as or higher than that of Malaysia, where tax administration is better. Except for the moderately successful land reforms in the first half of the 1970s, there is little evidence the Philippine QIIs fell during the postwar decades. Just as diversity underlies the high QII for Malaysia, it is the landed oligarchy in the rural areas who accumulated urban wealth, enterprises, and human capital that underlies Philippine income disparities. Diversities are not unimportant in the Philippines, although the differences between ethnic groups are less pronounced than in India and Malaysia.

In the rural sector, the increase in disparities from the 1950s was partly the outcome of the uneven spread of new rice varieties. In 1971 the new varieties were being used on only one-third of the farms and chemical fertilizers on one-fourth, according to the 1971 Census of Agriculture. Those using the new varieties were probably the richer, larger farms with resources to purchase fertilizers, which in turn require irrigation. Two-thirds of the farms without irrigation operated less than half the year and were producing largely for subsistence. Smaller farms of less than one hectare increased from 11.5 percent of all farms in 1960 to 13.6 percent in 1971, as a result of population pressure. Thus, the disparity indexes rose in regions where the new rice varieties were introduced (mainly in Luzon); where they were not introduced disparities remained unchanged from the 1960s to the early 1970s.

Preliminary data from the official 1979 survey of households show that the disparity index in the Philippines has risen by about 10 percent from 1971 to reach the 1960 levels. This is somewhat surprising because one would expect that even with a limited land reform program (limited to about 10 to 15 percent of the total farm land) and rural development programs, income distribution in agriculture might have improved or at least not worsened. What probably happened was that tenants who became owners benefited and went up on the income scale but many others failed to obtain land and improve their positions. The 1981 Census of Agriculture's preliminary figures show that the average farm size declined from 3.6 hectares to 2.6. If the distribution of farms by size is published in the census, it is likely to show that the larger farms grew more than the smaller ones despite the impact of land reform which was overwhelmed by the population surge in the countryside. Inequality was increased further by the rise in the number of landless peasants, as implied by the increase in wage workers in agriculture from 0.9 to 1.3 million (a 40 percent rise), according to official labor surveys from 1971 and 1978. The landless workers' families have the lowest incomes in the rural sector, even lower than the smaller fishermen, whose output declined as the number of commercial fishing enterprises using trawlers nearly tripled in the 1970s, based on National Census figures.

In the non-agricultural sector, the larger establishments employing 10 or more workers grew much more rapidly than the smaller ones. The census of establishments showed a 24 percent growth in the former and a 25 percent decline in the latter in terms of employment from 1972 to 1978. Nominal wages per worker rose nearly twice as fast in larger firms, thus reducing the relative share of the lower quintiles. Similar trends appeared to prevail in the wholesale and retail sectors; data for transport, construction, mining, and public utilities are not available. If we turn to overall wage statistics, various studies show that real wages decreased more among unskilled than among skilled workers. The decline in real wages, probably due to unemployment, is surprising when compared with the increase in real product per worker in industry of about 4 or 5 percent (see tables in Chapter 3).

Between-sector disparities also rose somewhat as product per worker in industry relative to product per worker in agriculture rose from an average ratio of 2.6 in the 1960s to 2.8 and relative to product per worker in services rose from 0.9 to 1.2 (see tables in Chapter 3). The relative decline in the services might be related to the influx of surplus workers unable to find jobs in the commodity sector. Off-farm employment for farm family members could have offset the above effect but the available data show a 1 percent decline in the share of off-farm incomes to on-farm incomes from 1971 to 1975 and an increase from 12 percent to 20 percent from 1965 to 1971.

These data are difficult to reconcile with the 2 to 3 percent growth of GNP per capita shown in the official national accounts. That these accounts may have overstated growth can be seen from the report of the first nationwide nutrition survey in 1978 by the Food and Nutrition Research Institute. Per capita calorie intake in the second quarter averaged only 1,800 per day and protein intake only 53 grams per day per person, among the lowest reported figures from nutrition surveys in Asia. One wonders where all the 3.4 percent GNP growth during three decades has gone. Even if it is assumed that the GNP per capita growth was only 2 percent, still one must ask what quintile of families benefited from even that low growth. It is also surprising that between 1978 and 1982, when GNP growth per capita was supposed to have equalled about 1.5 percent, the second national nutrition survey showed no increases in the per capita intake of calories and protein.

Indonesia. The 1976 nationwide income and employment survey (known in Indonesia as *Sakernas*) was a large sample survey, consisting of about 95,000 households. I use the Gini as computed in this report. It is to be noted that the total income implicit in the survey comes to only one-half of the estimated personal income from the national income statistics (Central Bureau of Statistics, 1979). The low income shares of 4 percent and 7 percent, respectively, for the two lowest quintiles of households and 57 percent for the highest do not resemble the distributions of Thailand and the Philippines but come close to those of West Malaysia in 1970. Indonesia's growth after a decade of stagnation began to pick up in the mid-1960s and then accelerated to an impressive rate of 6 percent GNP per capita in the 1970s, a performance comparable to that of Malaysia and Thailand. There were many similarities in the pattern of growth, suggesting that common forces making for inequality from the 1960s were present. This growth was associated with the more rapid growth of non-agricultural sectors in which real product tripled between the first half of the 1960s and the last half of the 1970s, in contrast with a 60 percent increase in agriculture. This meant that family incomes in agriculture were growing much more slowly than those in industry and services. For the same period, the increase in product per worker in agriculture was only one-half that in industry and services. In the first half of the 1960s, product per worker in non-agriculture was 2.4 times that of agriculture but during the latter 1970s it rose to 3.0 times.[3]

The rapid growth of the non-agricultural sector in the early stages of the transition meant that large establishments with machine technologies and modern practices were introduced. This raised within-sector disparities, as in the Philippines in the 1950s and 1960s and Thailand and Malaysia in the 1960s and 1970s. The financial sector was generating incomes per family four times that in agriculture; the public utilities, two and a half times; and mining and quarrying (mainly oil), commerce, construction, transport and communication, and the services (mainly government), two times that in the agricultural sector. The growth in incomes was also related to the establishment of modern physical, economic, and political infrastructure needed for the rise of modern industry and commerce.

Coincident with and overlapping the growing industrial sector disparities were regional disparities both between and within sectors. Most of these modern technological and institutional infrastructures were established in the large cities of Java, especially Jakarta. Jakarta's income per family was three times that in the rural areas of Java. Even higher income per family was being generated in the modernizing sectors of Jakarta (mining, industry, public utilities, finance, and public services, none of which were particularly large but were large enough to raise the disparities within Java and in the income share of families belonging to the highest 10 percent who had 40 percent of the nation-wide income). There is no evidence that incomes in the traditional

---

[3] These and other data cited below are from the Central Bureau of Statistics, Government of Indonesia, and also from Oshima, 1978.

and informal sectors of manufacturing, transport, construction, and services rose rapidly. Unskilled workers poured into the urban areas from the rural sectors, and it is unlikely that the earnings of laborers and small family enterprises kept pace with those in the newly established, rapidly modernizing firms. It is likely that within the cities income disparities rose in the 1970s. Certainly under conditions of inflation, it is difficult for laborers and smaller enterprises to do as well as the smaller skilled labor force and larger firms.

A unique aspect of Indonesia's 1976 income distribution is the high 0.53 Gini in the rural areas, particularly in densely populated Java, compared with the 0.45 urban Gini. This is unusual in monsoon Asia where Ginis are no higher and generally lower in the rural sector in all countries for which there are surveys. Urban Ginis should be higher, because urban incomes are higher and therefore can vary more, and because given the high monsoon rural densities, especially in Java, farm size and incomes cannot vary much. Another interesting aspect of Indonesia's income distribution, setting it apart from other countries of monsoon Asia, is that per capita incomes on the main island of Java and on Bali were lower than on the outer islands. The reason may be that most parts of Sumatra, Kalimantan, and others nearer the equator receive even rainfall throughout the year: thus the larger farms produce perennials. Thus, with much less paddy-rice agriculture and more year-round farm work, the sparser populations could earn more in a year than the Javanese and Balinese peasants who experience dry monsoon months but engage in labor-intensive paddy growing on tiny farms in the wet months. Therefore, the outer islands resemble Mindanao and Malaysia.

One reason for the high rural Gini may be the growing number of landless, near-landless, and small peasant families, particularly in Java, as well as the uneven spread of various new technologies associated with IRRI rice varieties. Dr. Sayuti Hasibuan of Bappenas (the National Planning Agency) has called my attention to the following data from Report No. 3 of the 1980 Population Census of Indonesia:

Farm Households by Type of Land Used

	Agricultural Census 1973		Population Census 1980	
Households cultivating	No. in 1,000s	%	No. in 1,000s	%
(1) Owned land only	10,747	74.8	12,849	73.6
(2) Land of others only	456	3.2	2,602	14.9
(3) Owned land and others	3,171	22.0	2,017	11.5
Total	14,374	100.0	17,468	100.0

The sharp increase in (2) may be interpreted to mean that small peasant workers from 1973 on lost the meager plots they possessed as payment for debts to speculating land owners, to others who had knowledge of future plans for construction of dams and other irrigation structures, and to urban dwellers. Many of them became pure share-tenants, pure farm laborers, or a combination of the two. Table 15 of the 1973 census showed that landless households operating farms of less than a quarter hectare made up 45 percent of the total of landless farm households (of 2.6 million), and 77 percent operated less than one-half hectare. Java had 57 percent of landless households.

The 1976 Sakernas total of farm households is substantially lower than that of the 1980 Census (17.5 million) and even lower than the 1973 Agricultural Census (14.4 million). There is nothing odd about the discrepancies, even when assuming that farm households were rising throughout the 1970s, because it is usual for the definitions of farm households to vary from one survey to the next. If one assumes that the definitions in the two censuses were the same, then the 1976 Sakernas definition was more restrictive. Thus, instead of 31 percent of all farmers working farms .10 hectare or smaller, the figure may have been closer to 35 percent in 1976.

Information on the quality of the land worked by different farm household income groups is difficult to obtain. One census table showed that of the total of farm households using less than .10 hectare of *sawah* land, 87 percent had no irrigation. Since new rice varieties and technology require water control for effective fertilizing, it is not likely that the spread of the new rice varieties made much headway on these tiny farms, most of which may be assumed to produce mainly for family subsistence.

Based on the the above discussion, it seems that the number of landless and near-landless farm households increased during the 1970s, and that because of the lack of irrigation on small farms, multicropping was not feasible. Further impoverishment of small-farm households could only be prevented by increasing the amount of off-farm work alongside increases in pay for both farm and off-farm work.

The lowest income groups in rural areas depend on a multiplicity of odd jobs here and there, particularly during the dry season and between planting and harvesting. This is true in all monsoon agricultural countries but particularly so in Java where densities are among the highest in Asia. Underemployment is extensive in Indonesia in both urban and rural areas.

Various more or less reliable surveys seem to indicate that in areas where the modernization of agriculture and the mechanization of industry are being introduced, labor-saving devices are reducing the number of jobs done with traditional tools at harvesting and in traditional threshing. In the industrial sector, mechanized production and more modern equipment are superseding the traditional labor-intensive methods of food processing, spinning, weaving, and garment making, and in wood and other handicraft shops, construction, transport, and so on.

Time series on wages were not available for Indonesia until the late 1970s. Monthly wages of regular workers on the plantations as shown in Central Bureau of Statistics figures rose less than the cost-of-living index until 1970 and since then have more or less kept pace with it. Considering the limitations of both wage and price data, the safest conclusion is that real wages have been more or less constant or fell somewhat if the period from 1966 to 1979 is included. If this real wage movement can be taken to be representative of the returns to unskilled and semiskilled workers in industry as well, then it is not unlikely that profits and proprietary income rose more than prices, thereby contributing to inequality in the non-agricultural sector. In part, profit increases may have been due to import substitution protection. The low share in the second and third quintiles may have been a result of smaller farm size in Java compared with the rest of Southeast Asia.

Finally, the official national accounts show that while private consumption expenditures went up threefold, gross national savings rose fivefold and tax revenues on upper income groups from personal and corporate incomes rose fourfold between 1972 and 1976. The sharp fall in the Engel coefficient, particularly in urban Java, where there was a drop from 76 percent in 1964–1965 to 58 percent in 1976, compared with moderate rural declines of 81 to 78 percent, may be indicative of the ability of the upper income groups to save. With food expenditures as high as 78 percent among the lower half of the distribution, it is unlikely that positive savings will exceed negative savings or dissavings. Hence, increased personal savings must have come from the upper quintile of families, indicating growing disparities.

No simultaneous family income and expenditure surveys have been carried out in Indonesia. As a substitute, the share of expenditures for the official National Socio-Economic Survey for January-April 1976 for the highest quintile of families was estimated to be 49 percent, which when compared with the share of incomes of 55 percent from the Sakernas may indicate that there were positive savings in the upper groups but for the rest of the quintiles expenditure shares exceeded income shares. For the lowest 40 percent, expenditure shares were 16 percent compared with 12 percent for income share, and for the next 40 percent the respective figures were 36 percent and 33 percent. Similar patterns of savings and dissavings are found in Thailand, the Philippines, Malaysia, and other countries.

Concluding Notes

The inverted U curve depicting the trend of income disparities in the course of growth has been frequently attributed to Simon Kuznets but he has protested the attribution. It should be noted that the steepness of the rise and then decline is by no means as sharp as in the inverted U. Most important, the curve is not related so much to time per se but to phases in the agro-industrial transition and the type of development strategy pursued by a country. In Latin America, where capital-intensive strategies are pursued it takes a very long time for disparities to fall; where agrarian and other reforms are pushed through, the fall is quick, as in East Asia, Sri Lanka, and socialist countries (Table 10.2). Other forces and mechanisms that must be considered are noted below in the summary for Asia.

In the early phase of the agro-industrial transition, income disparities in a monsoon economy beginning modern growth are typically low. This is because the innumerable small farms produce almost entirely for subsistence or for sale within a locality. As growth begins, commercialization of agriculture and increases in output for sale outside the locality occur. Output and income increase on these farms but not in the rest of the country. As commercialization spreads to the other sectors with the construction of modern means of transportation, income disparities rise. Within the urban sector, incomes of firms (and their employees) participating in the industrialization and modernization process increase faster than in those that continue to pursue traditional activities.

These processes can be seen clearly in South and Southeast Asia, particularly in Thailand which began the postwar era with the least amount of modern infrastructure and institutions. As population increased, countries with limited land for expansion found the growth of rural population exceeded the increase in farm acreage. Those with the lowest incomes, tenants and landless farmers, began to increase, further aggravating income inequalities not only in rural areas but in urban areas as those unable to work in agriculture migrated to the cities. Due to capital-intensive industrialization, adequate employment could not be found in the cities, and disparities increased between those in the formal and informal sectors. This took place in the Philippines, Indonesia, India, and other South Asian countries, but not in

Table 10.2   Quintile Shares of Household Income

		Q₁	Q₂	Q₃	Q₄	Q₅	Q₁/Q₂	QII
East Asia		*7.2*	*12.2*	*16.4*	*22.5*	*41.6*	*0.58*	*.30*
Japan	(1979)	8.7	13.2	17.5	23.1	36.8	0.66	.25
Taiwan	(1976)	8.9	13.6	17.5	22.7	37.3	0.65	.25
S. Korea	(1976)	5.7	11.2	15.4	22.4	45.3	0.51	.35
Hong Kong	(1980)	5.4	10.8	15.2	21.6	47.0	0.50	.36
Southeast Asia		*5.2*	*8.5*	*12.9*	*21.0*	*52.3*	*0.62*	*.42*
Malaysia	(1973)	3.5	7.7	12.4	20.3	56.1	0.45	.46
Philippines	(1971)	5.2	9.0	12.8	19.0	54.0	0.58	.43
Thailand	(1975/76)	5.6	9.6	13.9	21.1	49.8	0.58	.39
Indonesia	(1976)	6.6	7.8	12.6	23.6	49.4	0.85	.41
South Asia		*6.1*	*9.7*	*14.0*	*20.1*	*50.1*	*0.63*	*.39*
India	(1975/76)	7.0	9.2	13.9	20.5	49.4	0.76	.37
Sri Lanka	(1978/79)	5.7	10.3	14.3	19.8	49.9	0.55	.37
Nepal	(1976/77)	4.6	8.0	11.7	16.5	59.2	0.58	.49
Bangladesh	(1973/74)	6.9	11.3	16.1	23.5	42.2	0.61	.32
Western DC's		*6.2*	*11.1*	*16.0*	*22.9*	*43.8*	*0.56*	*.34*
Italy	(1977)	6.2	11.3	15.9	22.7	43.9	0.55	.33
U.K.	(1979)	7.0	11.5	17.0	24.8	39.7	0.61	.31
France	(1975)	5.3	11.1	16.0	21.8	45.8	0.48	.35
W. Germany	(1978)	7.9	12.5	17.0	23.1	39.5	0.63	.28
U.S.A.	(1978)	4.6	8.9	14.1	22.1	50.3	0.52	.41
Latin America		*3.1*	*7.3*	*12.1*	*20.4*	*57.2*	*0.42*	*.48*
Brazil	(1972)	2.0	5.0	9.4	17.0	66.6	0.40	.58
Mexico	(1977)	2.9	7.0	12.0	20.4	57.7	0.41	.48
Argentina	(1970)	4.4	9.7	14.1	21.5	50.3	0.45	.40
Venezuela	(1970)	3.0	7.3	12.9	22.8	54.0	0.41	.46
Miscellaneous		*5.0*	*9.8*	*15.4*	*21.0*	*48.9*	*0.50*	*.38*
Yugoslavia	(1978)	6.6	12.1	18.7	23.9	38.7	0.55	.28
Turkey	(1973)	3.5	8.0	12.5	19.5	56.5	0.44	.46
Sudan	(1967/68)	4.0	8.9	16.6	20.7	49.8	0.45	.38
Tanzania	(1969)	5.8	10.2	13.9	19.7	50.4	0.57	.38

Source: Based on data from *IBRD World Development Report* 1984.
Note: Q₁ = lowest quintile; QII = quintile inequality index

Malaysia and Thailand where additional agricultural land could be opened up. Income inequalities slowly rose during the early half of the transition in Southeast and South Asia.

The situation was different in Japan, Taiwan, and South Korea, where the earliest phases of the transition started several decades before World War II. Commercialization of agriculture was already extensive at the beginning of the postwar era, enabling a speedy transition. The steep fall in income disparities was the result of comprehensive land reforms and agrarian development in the early years. When population began to increase, despite the lack of further land for expansion, employment was sustained by extensive irrigation to cultivate additional crops, particularly diversified produce which gave rise to agro-industries and off-farm employment. For those who migrated to the cities, jobs were available in the labor-intensive industries which expanded along with larger incomes and spending in the rural areas and along with rising exports abroad. As productivity increased, real wages rose, and mechanization on farms and firms began to accelerate further the growth of productivity. Passage through the transition was swift as full employment approached. Farm incomes kept pace with nonfarm incomes through mechanization and release of workers to urban industries. Despite the shift to more capital-intensive industries, disparities in the urban sector were kept low by the mechanization of labor-intensive industries and services when wages rose with full employment. Japan completed the transition in late 1950s, Taiwan in the late 1960s, and Korea in the latter 1970s, but China, India, and other South Asian countries were still in the early phase while Thailand, the Philippines, Indonesia, and Sri Lanka were midway and Malaysia was in the late phase of the transition at the end of the postwar era.

Unlike the steepness of change suggested by the inverted U curve hypothesis, the quintile inequality indexes in Table 1 changed very little in Japan and the Philippines throughout the three postwar decades, and only minimally in other countries, despite the vast transformations Asia witnessed. One reason for this is that changes in economic development created related influences on income inequality which were both favorable and unfavorable. The major ones take time to work out, with the exception of "once and for all" episodic events such as land reform. Thus it is better to think of the shape of the curve as a flatter curve whose degree of curvature depends on the speed of transition, historical heritage, specific physical and social endowments, and so forth.

Cross-section data as a proxy for time series used by economists to test the hypothesis should be viewed with a great deal of caution because the intercept of the disparity curve varies in different countries. City-states start the transition with higher inequalities than countries with an agricultural sector. Data for countries in and outside monsoon Asia should not be lumped together in one diagram as inequalities in agriculture will differ between monsoon Asia and, say, Latin America. And within one region a country with a long historical legacy of concentration of wealth, as in the Philippines, will start with higher inequalities than countries such as Thailand. Nor should one expect a country with a huge plantation sector in the tropics and one without in a temperate zone to start with the same level of disparities even though per capita incomes may be the same. Other characteristics of a country are more important than per capita income levels in influencing income disparities, so cross-sections should be avoided as much as possible.

With these and other caveats, the income disparities in a country during the transition are likely to increase in the early period of the transition, perhaps taper off at the peak, and then begin to decrease in the latter period, although the exact points of directional change will differ.

Finally, trade-offs between growth and distribution of national income are minimal as long as a country starts out with labor-intensive industrialization and a rural-based strategy as Taiwan did. The main forces maximizing sustained growth are also consonant with a wide spread of resources, wealth, income, and employment. If a country starts out with capital-intensive industrialization at the neglect of agriculture, not only will resources and wealth be concentrated in the hands of a smaller group but rapid growth will not be sustained, as shown by the experience of India, China, and the Philippines. Thus there are no trade-offs. Trade-offs occur when countries intervene with measures to regulate wages and create permanent jobs, or to establish welfarism. As noted elsewhere, extensive welfare policies are also very expensive, siphoning off resources needed for the development of agriculture and small industries. If rapid growth is sustained with full employment under a labor-intensive strategy as in East Asia there will be much less need for such interventions.

CHAPTER 11

The Demographic Transition and the Industrial Transition: A Comparative Perspective

*T*he main interest in this chapter is the impact of growth and structural changes on birth rates in lower-income families during the latter half of the demographic transition.[1] Birth rates among peasants and workers' families must fall substantially if the demographic transition is to be completed. The importance of this problem is underlined by the 1984 IBRD World Development Report's finding that after the beginning of the transition, fertility declines have slowed down in South and Southeast Asian nations.

It was noted in Chapter 2 that it is not satisfactory in a growth model to have population growth and therefore labor supply growth exogenously determined or given. Nor is it adequate to link it directly to per capita income since population grows in the early part of the agro-industrial transition mainly because modern medical technologies reduce mortality. Income growth affects fertility in the later parts of the transition but only as part of a mechanism whose main component is the spread of education among the lower classes. A summary of this mechanism is given below, based on the industrial and demographic transitions as they occurred in Japan during the 1950s and in Taiwan during the 1960s.

It was seen in Chapter 3 that the passage into an industrial society is accompanied by rising yields per hectare, multiple, diversified cropping, off-farm employment, and higher farm family incomes. With increased incomes, aggregate demand for industrial products rises, employment opportunities in the cities open up, and soon full employment is reached. Rising wages induce mechanization on farms and in firms as a substitute for workers, especially unskilled workers, who migrate to the cities. The farm labor force declines not only relatively but absolutely. As pointed out in Chapter 10, the impact of these and other changes is favorable on incomes and savings among peasants and laborers who achieve higher productivity.

[1] This chapter elaborates on Oshima, 1983a.

315

This chapter contends that these changes contribute to fertility declines in lower-income families during the latter half of the industrial transition. The progress of mechanized and other modern technologies in the economy calls for secondary education for children as parents begin to realize that the future labor demand will be for more skilled and educated workers. The parents' higher incomes earned from the use of modern technologies and through more employment with housewives working makes it possible to finance more education even while forgoing incomes teenagers could earn. Savings after children are educated can be used to purchase real and financial assets and insurance for the parents' future more secure. The widespread dissemination of modern technologies in labor-intensive growth is crucial in the decline of fertility in lower-income groups to levels low enough to complete the demographic transition. Since this is related to the spread of mechanization, there is a rough concordance with the completion of industrial transition.

The approach in this chapter is to look at fertility patterns by dividing families according to the occupations of household heads cross-classified by status (proprietors including own account workers, employers, and employees), or better still socio-economic classes. These classes in the agriculture sector are landlords, large, medium, and small farmers, tenants, fishermen, and landless workers; in the non-agricultural sector: employers, proprietors, own-account workers, salaried employees, skilled workers, unskilled laborers, and unemployed workers. In the previous chapter, it was noted that the sources of family incomes are the ownership of property, enterprises, skills, and the number of earners in the family. The upper quintiles of families own more property and enterprises and have more skills than the lower quintiles who have more earners. The poorest families have no property and no enterprises and therefore must depend on larger numbers of earners without skills in order to raise their incomes.

In the course of the transition, the upper quintile families acquire more property, enterprises, and skills and do not need many children to increase their incomes. They can save to provide for present and future contingencies and security in old age. The lower quintiles, even though their incomes rise in the early stages of the transition, must still depend on a large number of children to provide for current and future needs. As the economy proceeds through the transition, the lower quintiles begin to earn more as their productivity improves, especially as teenagers go to work after receiving primary education. Toward the end of the transition, most families in the economy earn enough to send their children to secondary schools. With longer years of schooling, young people postpone marriage in order to work long enough to help with family finances. Families of better educated younger parents in the lower quintiles begin to desire fewer children than their parents did.

Underlying these changes in attitudes towards education are the growing complexities of modern society in an age of scientific technologies on farms (chemical fertilizers and insecticides, genetically bred seeds, internal combustion machines, and electrically operated equipment); in factories, offices, and stores; in the operation of urban mass transport infrastructure, mass communications, and public health and sanitation; and in modern homes, all of which demand more and more scientific and vocational training, literacy, and numeracy.

In brief, 20th-century technologies tend to reduce the demand for uneducated labor and increase the demand for educated workers, as well as increasing the number of jobs that females can do as well as males. Moreover, the structural changes associated with productivity growth have reduced the size of the classes and occupations with higher levels of fertility: the peasantry, landless workers, unskilled laborers in factories, and proprietors of small stores and handicraft shops where mechanization is not applicable. The size of classes and occupations with lower fertility—employers, managers, professionals, and white-collar and skilled employees—increases.

Prewar Background

In prewar monsoon Asia, whenever the secular demand for workers rose, fertility increased to meet the demand, and as more food became available more work was done and mortality fell. This is not quite the Malthusian mechanism which starts out with more food, making possible better health and lower mortality. When transplantation of rice seedlings originated during the early centuries of the first millennium in China, more hands were needed during planting, and birth rates had to rise if the innovation was to be put into operation. After more and more hands were available the food supply increased, furnishing food for the additional workers, and more could be fed as output per worker rose and transplantation improved. Morbidity fell and life expectancy rose. The Asian process started with increased labor, not food supply. But in the case of multiple cropping in the second millennium when short-duration rice seeds were introduced, the demand for labor did not rise as much because the construction of irrigation and work for the second crop could be carried out largely by the same labor force in the slack months of the year. As in the Malthusian case, food supply increased first, resulting in reduced morbidity and mortality and even increased fertility through better nutrition.

In the colonial period, the introduction of plantation crops for export to the West increased the demand for workers although the demand was different for perennial crops such as rubber, oil palm, tea, coconut, etc., and those like sugarcane which required workers mainly at harvest and planting. The introduction of tropical perennials for export in Asia meant that some additional workers were needed throughout the year, and birth rates rose as the peasants needed more hands. Under Japan's Empire, the extension of irrigation made more transplantation, multiple cropping, fertilizer use, and intensive cultivation possible, and birth rates increased. Data on birth rates show increases in Malaya from the 1920s, in Sri Lanka and Singapore from before the 1900s, while in Japan they rose from the 1880s to the 1920s, and in Taiwan and Korea from the early 1910s to 1930s.

Work on the plantations did not require formal education for the lower quintiles since few mechanized or scientific techniques were used. The impact on the demand for work differs among premodern or modern technologies, as noted in the discussion in Chapters 4 and 5 regarding farm technologies. These differences have varying impacts on the demand for children and fertility behavior and must be considered in any analysis.

Postwar Changes in Fertility and Productivity

Simon Kuznets has noted that the sharp declines in birth rates in East Asia telescoped into a decade or two what took nearly a century in the industrialized West. Table 11.1 reveals some striking associations between economic and demographic trends: the rapid growth of productivity and product, and the sharp decline in birth rates in Japan, South Korea, Taiwan, Hong Kong, and Singapore which contrast with the slower growth of productivity and decline in birth rates in the Philippines, Thailand, Malaysia, and Indonesia. The contrasts in declines of crude birth rates between East Asia and Southeast Asia would be even greater if data prior to the 1960s were included. For instance, birth rates began to fall in the 1950s in Singapore and Taiwan and in the 1920s in Japan when they were still rising in other countries; crude birth rates in the three fell by about 50 percent between 1950 and 1980. Data for the 1950s and earlier periods for other countries are not available for comparison.

These sharp birth rate declines could not have occurred without a reduction in agricultural family size, as farm families have the highest

Table 11.1   Changes in Birth Rates and in Growth of GDP Per Capita and Per Worker in Monsoon Asia

	GNP per Capita (US $), 1981	Percen- tage Change in Crude Birth Rate, 1960–81	Total Fertility Rate, 1981	Growth of GDP per Capita, 1950–80 (%)	Growth of GDP per Worker, 1950–79
East Asia (simple avg.)	4,170	−42.7	2.3	6.0	4.6
Japan	10,080	−24.9	1.7	6.9	6.0
Taiwan	2,600	−43.4	2.2	5.7	5.3
South Korea	1,700	−43.7	3.0	5.7	4.2
Hong Kong	5,100	−45.0	2.2	6.0	—
Singapore	5,240	−53.0	1.7	6.2	—
China	300	−46.3	2.9	5.4	2.7
Southeast Asia (simple avg.)	983	−28.7	4.2	3.5	2.8
Philippines	790	−27.4	4.6	3.1	2.0
Thailand	770	−32.1	3.9	4.2	3.4
Malaysia	1,840	−31.0	4.0	3.2	3.0
Indonesia	530	−24.4	4.4	3.3	2.7
South Asia (simple avg.)	208	−13.8	5.3	1.5	0.9
India	260	−18.8	4.8	1.8	0.9
Sri Lanka	300	−24.3	3.5	2.0	—
Bangladesh	140	−12.2	6.4	0.7	—
Burma	190	−13.7	5.2	2.2	—
Nepal	150	0.1	6.4	0.7	—

Sources: World Bank, *World Development Report 1983* and *World Tables 1980* (for growth of per capita GNP in the 1950s) except for Taiwan, data for which are from that country's *Statistical Yearbook*. Data in the last column, taken from *ILO Yearbook of Labour Statistics*, represent the growth of total real GDP divided by total number of employed persons.

fertility in Asia, and in the nonfarm family size in the lower-income groups. As shown in Table 11.2, the decline in family size recorded in farm household surveys in Japan, Taiwan, and South Korea was substantial, not only in the highest quintile by farm size but also in the next two or three quintiles. Declines were smallest in the lowest one or two quintiles where mechanization was limited. On Japanese farms between 1959 and 1979, by which time mechanization of the most labor-intensive operations in rice growing had been achieved on nearly all farms, average family size declined at a rate of 1.1 percent a year

Table 11.2   Changes in Family Size in Japan, Taiwan, and South Korea (farm families by size of farm; nonfarm families by income group)

Farm Families	Japan			Taiwan			South Korea		
	1959	1979	Annual Growth Rate (%)	1966	1981	Annual Growth Rate (%)	1968	1979	Annual Growth Rate (%)
Farm Size									
All Families	5.80	4.45	-1.3	8.48	6.48	-1.8	6.02	5.20	-1.3
Less than 0.5 ha.	5.07	4.06	-1.1	6.90	5.83	-1.1	5.09	4.40	-1.3
0.5–1.0 ha.	5.69	4.35	-1.3	6.91	6.13	-0.8	5.63	4.97	-1.1
1.0–1.5 ha.	6.39	4.66	-1.6	8.01	6.62	-1.3	6.58	5.63	-1.4
1.5–2.0 ha.	7.05	4.95	-1.8	9.53	8.05	-1.1	7.05	5.94	-1.5
More than 2.0 ha.	7.74	5.53	-1.7	11.81	6.73	-3.7	7.68	6.19	-1.9

Nonfarm Families	1951	1959	Annual Growth Rate (%)	1966	1981	Annual Growth Rate (%)	1964	1979	Annual Growth Rate (%)
Income Group									
All Families	4.69	4.41	-0.7	5.30	4.60	-0.9	5.80	4.70	-1.4
Lowest One-third	4.09	3.96	-0.4	4.20	3.70	-0.8	4.80	3.40	-0.7
Middle One-third	4.66	4.43	-0.6	5.20	4.70	-0.7	6.30	4.60	-2.1
Highest One-third	5.24	4.89	-0.9	6.70	5.10	-1.8	7.30	5.10	-2.4

Note: For Japan and South Korea, families headed by employees only, excluding those headed by proprietors.

Sources: Data for Japan from Ministry of Agriculture, *Farm Household Economy Survey* (Nōka keizai chōsa) and *Family Income and Expenditure Survey.* Data for Taiwan from *Report of Farm Record-Keeping Families in Taiwan* and *Family Income and Expenditure Survey.* Data for South Korea from *Report on Farm Household Economy Survey* and *Family Income and Expenditure Survey.*

on the smallest farms (of less than 0.5 hectare) and by 1.7 percent a year on the largest farms (of more than 2.0 hectares). Similar rates of decline were recorded for farms in Taiwan from 1966 to 1981, and in South Korea from 1968 to 1979. In all three countries urban families also declined in size, albeit less than in rural areas; a similar pattern by economic status was seen.

Data on changes in average family size do not give a direct indication of fertility declines since, on the one hand, the number of nuclear families and thus the number of households in the denominator was on the increase in all three countries, compounded by labor force migration from rural to urban areas and falling mortality. A clearer picture would be given by fertility rates for each income group (or by occupation of the head of household) adjusted by age group to take account of life-cycle effects. Such data are not available, but a useful approximation may be found in Paul Liu's fertility rate analysis in Taiwan according to the wife's age and educational attainment (illiterate, literate, primary, junior high, senior high, and higher) for 1966–1980 (Liu, 1983; Mueller and Cohn, 1974). Liu's data showed substantially higher fertility declines among families among the less educated groups than among those with more than primary schooling in the age cohorts 25–29, 30–34, and 35–39 (in the 20–24 age group, the decline was large only in 1975–1980).

The transformation to an industrial society involved: (1) the attainment of full employment with rising real wages; (2) the quick spread of mechanization; (3) the acceleration of family incomes and savings, and (4) substantial structural changes (Figs. 11.1, 11.2, and 11.3). How each of these changes affected fertility in East Asia and Southeast Asia is examined below.

Effects of Full Employment

Full employment refers to the long-term full employment levels attained as a result of more or less permanent improvements in cooperatives, education, agrarian and industrial relations, physical infrastructure such as roads, and technologies (see Chapters 4 and 5).

Figures 11.1, 2, and 3 show trends in unemployment rates since 1950 in Japan, South Korea, and Taiwan. As the surplus pool of unskilled workers was exhausted, wages in unskilled occupations began to rise as fast as and then faster than those in skilled occupations. The urban labor market attracted not only workers from rural areas but also workers from the informal sector and urban housewives. The great rural-to-urban migrations in Japan in the 1950s and 1960s, in Taiwan

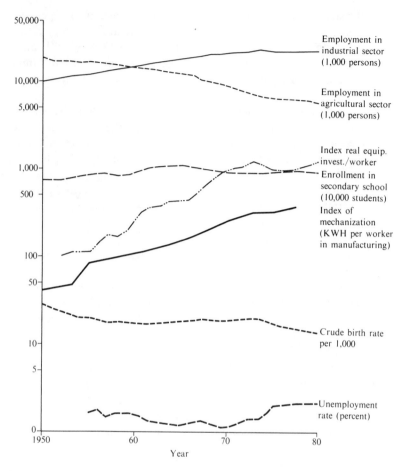

Figure 11.1   Trends in employment, fertility, education, and mechanization in Japan, 1950–1980.

Notes: Industrial sector includes mining and quarrying, manufacturing, construction, public utilities, transport, storage, and communication.
Agricultural sector includes farming, livestock, hunting, forestry, and fishing.
Investment refers to the concept of flow, not stock.

Sources: Mainly from various issues of *Japan Statistical Yearbook*, except for index of real capital formation on equipment per worker, computed from *Annual Report on National Accounts*.

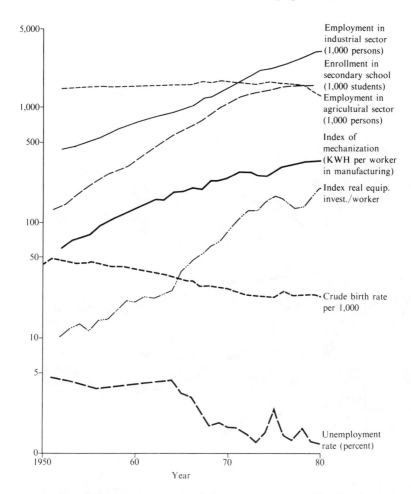

Figure 11.2   Trends in employment, fertility, education, and mechanization in Taiwan, 1950–1980.

Notes: Same as for Figure 11.1.

Source: All data from various issues of *Statistical Yearbook of the Republic of China*.

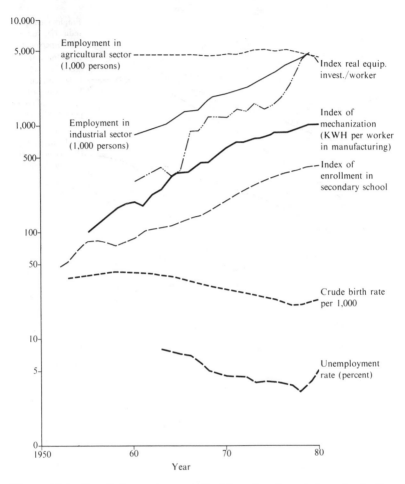

Figure 11.3 Trends in employment, fertility, education, and mechanization in South Korea, 1950–1980.

Notes: Same as for Figure 11.1.

Sources: Mainly from various issues of *Korean Statistical Yearbook*, except employment data for early years from *ILO Yearbook of Labor Statistics*.

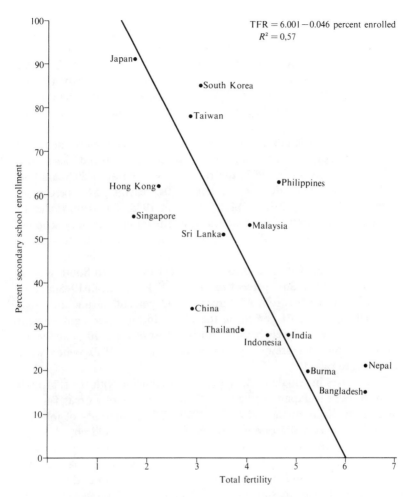

Figure 11.4   Relation of secondary school enrollment as a percentage of the entire age group to the total fertility rate in Asian countries, 1980.

Source: World Bank, *World Development Report 1982*.

and South Korea in the 1960s and 1970s, and the influx of workers from China and Malaysia, respectively, to the city-states of Hong Kong and Singapore are testimony to this process. Domestic servants became difficult to hire in Japan from the late 1950s, in Taiwan from the late 1960s, in South Korea from the mid-1970s, and in Hong Kong and Singapore from the early 1970s. The share of employment in the personal service sector began to fall in these countries, while it was rising in Southeast Asia.

In Japan, female labor force participation rates among women aged 15 years and older rose to a high of 56.2 percent in 1956 and then slowly fell to 53.4 percent in 1962; the rates for women aged 20 years and older continued to rise into the late 1950s, reaching 54.7 percent in 1960 and falling slightly to 54.2 percent in 1975. The drop is due to the increasing number of teenaged girls attending secondary schools. In Taiwan, the female labor force participation rate for those aged 20 years and older rose from 19.3 percent in 1966 to 27.2 percent in 1970, to 41.9 percent in 1975, and to 47.1 percent in 1980. In South Korea, the rate rose from 36.7 percent in 1966 to 37.9 percent in 1975, and in Hong Kong it rose from 37 percent to 43 percent during the 1960s and fell slightly to 41 percent in the 1970s. In Singapore, government policies kept wage levels constant during most of the 1970s, and female participation rates grew only slowly until the late 1970s when wage levels were raised.

These rises in female participation rates coincide with the sharp fall in birth rates in Japan during the 1950s, and in South Korea, Taiwan, and Hong Kong in the 1960s and 1970s. The availability of jobs for women increased the opportunity cost of rearing children, although it is difficult to say how important this factor was in fertility decisions relative to other factors discussed below. The rise in participation rates probably understates the contribution, because these rates do not take account of the increasing productive activity of housewives on the farms, in factories and shops, and in urban own-account enterprises as the economy began to reach full capacity growth and labor shortages ensued. In Taiwan, with the expansion of multiple cropping, housewives in farm households became occupied throughout the year; in Japan, as men commuted to jobs in towns, many housewives took over the operation of family farms. Moreover, many jobs opened up in labor-intensive industries like textiles and attracted housewives from working-class families as light-handed work using small machines expanded.

These trends, together with rising earnings of females, raised the opportunity costs of rearing children. This was particularly so in households without live-in grandparents to give child care since domestic servants became increasingly difficult to hire and teenagers were occupied with schooling.

The situation in the ASEAN agricultural Four was different. There was a great deal of underemployment among the lower quintile families, especially in the rural sector, and female participation rates changed very little. Real wages increased only in the late 1970s in Malaysia when the labor market began to tighten. Thus, the decline in fertility rates was slow and probably confined to the upper quintiles.

Effects of Mechanization

It is not widely recognized that the mechanization of agriculture and industry can have major consequences on the costs and benefits of having children in lower-income families. With full employment, the demand for labor rises; if mechanization does not spread rapidly and replace unskilled workers, the effect of full employment is to raise the demand for children and thereby encourage larger families. This is happening in rural China today after the abolition of the commune system and the institution of the family responsibility system, as it happened during the first half-century of the Western Industrial Revolution. However, as mechanization spreads, the economic benefits of children fall and childrearing costs rise. In monsoon rice farming, the mechanization of highly labor-intensive operations during the peak seasons of planting and harvesting can render child labor redundant, thereby lowering their value to parents. The mechanization of menial, unskilled operations in urban households has a similar effect.

The mechanization of agriculture and industry and other technological advances soon persuade parents to educate their children (now no longer needed as much on farms and in factories) beyond the primary level to provide them with the skills and education needed to obtain better jobs as the demand for uneducated laber falls. As productivity rises and full employment is attained, higher family incomes enable parents to bear the costs of education and forgo the incomes teenagers would have earned if they had started working after primary school.

The degree of mechanization is difficult to measure. One method used in manufacturing industries is to look at the use of kilowatt-hours (kwh) per worker. The growth rate of kwh per worker in industry during 1955–1970, when fertility dropped sharply in Japan, was 7 percent a year; in Taiwan and South Korea from 1960 to 1978, the rates were 5.4 percent and 9.4 percent, respectively. Comparable data are not available for Southeast Asia, but in peninsular Malaysia (which has the highest capital intensity in Southeast Asia) in 1978 manufacturing averaged 7,125 kwh per worker, as compared with about 8,922 kwh per worker in South Korea, around 10,000 in Taiwan, 23,500 in Japan, and 36,200 in the United States. Similar data for Indonesia among firms with 20 or more employees, and in the Philippines and Thailand among firms with 10 or more employees overstate the electric power used in comparison with Japan and Taiwan (for all firms) by perhaps as much as one-third to one-half. As noted in the chapters on Japan, Taiwan, and South Korea, the rapid substitution of machines for handwork on farms and in firms was related to rapid growth. In contrast, in Southeast Asia the vast majority of small farms and workers in industry used hand-operated or animal-powered tools, with the exception of West Malaysia in the late 1970s.

Effects of Higher Incomes and Savings

Not only were incomes and savings in East Asia higher, but they were more equally distributed (see Chapter 10). Thus the lower quintiles were able to earn and save more than those in the ASEAN agricultural Four. Higher incomes meant that even the lowest quintiles could pay for more secondary education and forgo the earnings of teenagers; the higher savings made possible the purchase of machines and became working capital for expansion.

To be relevant to long-term demographic analysis, higher income levels must be viewed in the long term. They must originate from lasting changes such as improved institutions and technology; shifts to crops with higher cash values and to multiple cropping; rural industrialization, mechanization, irrigation, and drainage programs; improved roads and transport systems; and higher education levels. Long-term full employment during which wage rises are sustained over one or two decades assures parents that incomes will continue to be high in the future and contributes to fertility declines.

Belief in a more secure future has had important repercussions on family size decisions in East Asian countries. In China, Japan, and Singapore, private and public insurance schemes are extended to most earners, and housing schemes are available in Singapore and Hong Kong. South Korea has made the least headway in this direction, and this together with a slower pace of mechanization may have had some bearing on the fact that its total fertility rates were the highest in East Asia (somewhat higher than China's); the lowest rates were in Japan and Singapore, which have the most extensive mechanization and the most comprehensive insurance schemes. The extensive land reforms in Japan, Taiwan, and Korea were also important. Japanese life ex-

Table 11.3 Income Per Household and Per Person by Size of Household

Household with	Philippines (1971)		Taiwan (1972)		Thailand (1962/63)		USA (1972)	
	Income per Hh (Pesos)	Income per Person (Pesos)	Income per Hh (NT$)	Income per Person (NT$)	Income per Hh (Baht)	Income per Person (Baht)	Income per Hh ($)	Income per Person ($)
1 Persons	2,279	2,279	27,200	27,200	3,322	3,322	5,140	5,140
2 Persons	2,503	1,252	41,100	20,550	4,850	1,877	10,580	5,290
3 Persons	2,839	946	50,200	16,733			12,720	4,240
4 Persons	3,437	859	55,100	13,775	6,113	1,368	14,380	3,600
5 Persons	3,549	710	59,900	11,980			14,640	2,930
6 Persons	3,661	610	61,700	10,283	7,176	1,138		
7 Persons	3,960	566	65,900	9,414	8,969	981	14,120	2,040
8 & over	4,819	504	78,700	8,545				
Average	3,736	639	60,500	10,800	6,644	1,211	12,630	3,640
Ratio of largest to small size	2.11	0.22	2.89	0.31	2.70	0.30	2.75	0.40
TDM	16.2	20.6	12.8	18.4	19.0	18.2	26.4	26.2

Sources: Philippines, Taiwan, and United States computed from Simon Kuznets, "Demographic Components in Size Distribution of Income," *Income Distribution, Employment and Economic Development in Southeast and East Asia*, vol. II, CAMS-JERC, July 1975; Thailand data computed from S. Kuznets, "Size of Households and Income Disparities," *Research in Population Economics*, vol. 3, 1981.

Notes: TDM is the sum of differences between percentage shares in the two relevant totals (households and income, persons and income), signs disregarded. They were calculated by Kuznets and taken from the tables in his articles cited above.

pectancies have become one of the highest in the world. Taiwan's life expectancies in 1980 came close to the average of those of the industrialized countries. South Korea's progress has not been as good as Taiwan's, but it has achieved life expectancies about midway between those of Taiwan and those of Thailand and the Philippines.

The effect of income and savings on the size of families and fertility levels has been commented on by Simon Kuznets. Kuznets has found that when families are grouped by size in terms of the number of members and ranked from smallest to largest, there is a clear-cut negative association with income per person in the families in three Asian countries (see Table 11.3). As families became larger, the income per person in the family became smaller in the United States, Germany, Israel, Taiwan, the Philippines, and Thailand. This is the opposite of what happens when family size is associated with size of the sum of incomes going to all members of the family, as shown in Table 11.3.

In Table 11.4 the average number of children born to families classified by the husband's occupation is shown. The largest numbers of children are found in the lowest skilled occupations, in agricultural

Table 11.4   Mean Number of Children Born to All Married Women, by Husband's Occupation

	All Married Women				Children per Hh
	Thailand (1977)	Phillippines (1978)	S. Korea (1974)	Malaysia (1974)	Taiwan (1979)
Professional, technical	3.2	3.7	2.9	3.2	1.89
Clerical	2.5	3.4	2.8	3.3	1.95
Sales	3.6	4.1	3.1	4.5	2.36
Agr. Self-Employed	4.3	5.1 ⎫		4.7	2.54
Agr. Not Self-Employed	4.4	5.0 ⎭	4.6	4.5	2.47
Services	3.4	4.1	3.1	3.4	2.14
Manual, skilled	3.2	4.4	3.0 ⎫		2.46
Manual, unskilled	4.2	4.6	3.8 ⎭	4.2	2.39
Total	3.9	4.6	3.6	4.2	2.28

Sources: *National Fertility Survey* of each respective country, except Taiwan data from Report on the *Survey of Personal Income Distribution in Taiwan Area, ROC, 1979*, whose figures represent average number of children per family.

families, and among unskilled workers. The smallest families are in white-collar occupations, professionals, and technical and clerical workers, with sales and services in between. It is well known that average length of education and incomes are positively associated with the skill levels in the occupations. Thus, one can plausibly speculate that families with little, if any, property, wealth, enterprises, or trained skills need to have many children who can be put to work as soon as possible. Since these families cannot afford to invest as much as others in education, the lower earnings of unskilled children must be offset by their numbers.

In Table 11.4, farmers who are self-employed tend to lead all other occupations in the number of children. This may be because they are too poor to hire farm workers or buy machines and need family helpers in the busy season of the year. It is interesting to note that in Japan, too, farming families have the largest family sizes. This is also true among self-employed workers in urban enterprises in both industry and services.

Effects of Structural Changes

As the labor force moves from agriculture to industry, there is a parallel shift from rural to urban society, with all the attendant implications in social, cultural, and political life. Many of these changes have been discussed in the literature, including the higher costs of urban living, more modern and secular ways of living and thinking, fewer work opportunities suitable for children, the need for more education since city life is mechanized and complex, and so on. Likewise, the modern city with its amenities, health and sanitation facilities, protection from natural hazards, wider availability of pension and health insurance schemes, and extended opportunities to save and invest assets for the future reduces the long-term benefits of children as a form of insurance. In addition, the shift away from agriculture reduces the number of peasants and landless workers, who have the largest family size and the lowest incomes. The reduction in the labor force in agriculture was far less in Southeast Asia than in East Asia, while in India there was only a small drop in the size of the agricultural labor force, from 74 percent of the total labor force in 1960 to 71 percent in 1980. Within East Asia, the Korean shift was also far less than in Taiwan and in Japan (see tables in Chapter 2). Structural shifts within each major sector in East Asia were from smaller to larger farms and firms, from proprietory to corporate enterprises, and from less skilled to more skilled occupations, all of which tended to reduce the desired family size.

Secondary Education as a Link
Between Industrialization and Fertility

A negative association between education and fertility is commonly found both in cross-sections and over time, although the causal mechanisms remain elusive. It is argued here that the key variable is secondary school enrollment as far as the lower quintiles of families are concerned. The spread of secondary education is a response to the labor force requirements of a mechanized society, which in turn is a major factor exerting a downward pressure on fertility.

Table 11.5 shows enrollment rates in secondary and higher educational institutes in Asian countries for 1960 and 1979–1980. In both years, school enrollment in East Asia as a percentage of the age group 12–17 years old was roughly double that in Southeast Asia. By 1979,

Table 11.5   Enrollment Rates in Secondary Schools and Higher Education in Asia (simple average)

	Number Enrolled in Secondary School as % of Age Group		Number Enrolled in Higher Education as % of Population Aged 20–24	
	1960	1980	1960	1979
East Asia	37	68	6	13
Japan	74	91	10	30
Taiwan	30	82	3	12
South Korea	27	85	5	14
Hong Kong	20	62	4	10
Singapore	32	55	6	8
China	21	34	—	1
Southeast Asia	16	43	1	14
Philippines	26	63	13	25
Thailand	13	29	2	13
Malaysia	19	53	1	3
Indonesia	6	28	1	—
South Asia	14	27	1	4
India	20	28	3	9
Sri Lanka	27	51	1	3
Bangladesh	8	15	1	3
Burma	10	20	1	4
Nepal	6	21	1	3

Secondary school age is generally considered to be 12–17 years inclusive.
Sources: World Bank, *World Development Report 1983*, Table 25. Data for Taiwan from *Statistical Yearbook of the Republic of China 1982*.

more than one-half of this age group was in school in East Asia. Japan led the way with 90 percent.

Figure 11.4 shows the close association of total fertility and secondary school enrollment in cross-section. The association would have been even closer had it been possible to adjust for differences between countries in the age groups covered by secondary enrollment. In the Philippines, for instance, primary and secondary education comprise only 10 years (six years of primary and four years of secondary education) instead of 12, as is usual in the region; secondary education is for those aged 13 through 16. Since younger children are more likely to be enrolled than are those 17 years old, the Philippine enrollment rate is overstated relative to other countries; a correction would drop it below 50 percent. China's secondary school age group is also 13 through 16, and Nepal's is 11 through 15; in both instances, adjustment would also bring the enrollment percentage down closer to the regression line. Enrollment in Thailand (ages 14 through 18) and Indonesia (13 through 18) would move up closer to the regression line, according to UNESCO 1981 figures.

Several countries are higher in the scatter of Fig. 11.4 than one would expect from their per capita income levels. China has the same fertility rate as Taiwan, although Taiwan has an average per capita income about seven times that in China. Sri Lanka has a lower fertility rate than Malaysia, which has an average per capita income five or six times higher. It is important to take note of these cases in which development levels and fertility are not associated. China and Sri Lanka are two outstanding cases of comprehensive welfare states in the region (the third being Japan). In both countries, not only is income fairly equally distributed but also lower-income groups have a number of benefits that diminish the security value of children to parents in their later years. In China the very high rate of female labor force participation is also a factor in reducing fertility. Thus, these two countries in which agricultural mechanization is far below the levels of Taiwan and Malaysia are interesting deviations from the mechanization hypothesis.

Thailand's educational enrollment rate is close to that of India, but Thai fertility is lower and Thai income is double that in India. Part of the explanation may lie in the extraordinary rate of Thai female labor force participation, which at 60 percent in 1980 was one of the highest in the world.

Of course, sociocultural forces differ from country to country in any cross-sectional comparison. But it is interesting to note that over time the effects of many of these forces, which are slower to change than

Table 11.6 Trends in Total Fertility Rate and Secondary School Enrollment in East Asian Countries

	1910	1920	1930	1940	1950	1960	1965	1970	1975	1980
Japan										
Total fertility rate		4.3	4.0	3.6	3.4	2.0	2.1	2.1	1.9	1.8
Secondary enrollment (per 1,000)	786.2	1,385.7	2,382.9	2,672.6	7,268	9,139	11,031	8,949	9,095	4,952[a]
as % of age group 10–19		12	18	23	42	45	55	53	56	56[a]
as % of males aged 20–44		15	22	29	53	54	57	—	40	42[a]
Taiwan										
Total fertility rate	4.6	4.4	5.0	4.8	4.9	4.4	3.7	3.1	2.0	2.5
Secondary enrollment (per 1,000)	1.5	0.8	18.9	42.0	120.0	355.3	663.8	1154.6	1,497.8	1,598
as % of age group 10–19	1[b]	1	2	2[c]	7	16	22	31	38	41
as % of males aged 20–44	0.2	1	2	5[c]	9	20	33	47	56	47
South Korea										
Total fertility rate	3.2[d]	4.6[e]	4.4[f]	4.6[g]	4.9[h]	5.6	4.9	3.9	3.2	3.0
Secondary enrollment (per 1,000)				81[i]	322	792	1,257	1,909	3,150	—
as % of age group 10–19				2[i]	7	16	20	26	36	—
as % of males aged 20–44				2[i]	10	19	27	37	52	—
Hong Kong										
Total fertility rate					3.0	4.7	3.7	2.6	2.4	2.2
Secondary enrollment (per 1,000)					26.5	88.7	195.8	270.4	368.7	424.5[j]
as % of age group 10–19						17	23	27	—	41[j]
as % of males aged 20–44						14	33	40	—	49[j]
Singapore										
Total fertility rate					5.5[l]	4.6	3.7	2.8	2.2	1.8
Secondary enrollment (per 1,000)						59.3	115.9	150.5	186.1	189.6[k]
as % of age group 10–19						17	—	28	—	35[k]
as % of males aged 20–44						21	—	43	—	40[k]

[a]1979 [b]1915 [c]1935 [d]1912 [e]1922 [f]1932 [g]1942 [h]1953 [i]1944 [j]1977 [k]1978 [l]1951

Notes: For Japan, secondary enrollment data are not comparable before and after World War II. Earlier data include enrollment in 5th and 6th grades, which constitute about one-third of total primary enrollment.

Sources: Japan: *Hundred Year Statistics of the Japanese Economy* for prewar years and *Japan Statistical Yearbook* for postwar years. Taiwan: Samuel P. S. Ho, *Economic Development of Taiwan 1860–1970*, updated by *Statistical Yearbook of ROC 1981*. South Korea *Korea Statistical Yearbook*, various issues; and N. F. McGinn and associates, *Education and Development in Korea*. Hong Kong: *Hong Kong Statistics 1947–67* and *Hong Kong By-census 1976*. Singapore: Institute of Developing Economies, *Performance and Perspectives of the Singapore Economy*, and *Yearbook of Statistics 1977/1978*.

economic factors, can be sidestepped and the demographic transition readily completed if the economy grows rapidly. For example, family size declined rapidly despite continuing strong preferences for sons in Korea and Taiwan.

Long-term trends in total fertility rates and secondary school enrollment in Table 11.6 are presented to bring out the timing of the declines in the five East Asian countries and to supplement the data on absolute numbers of students enrolled in secondary schools in Figs. 11.1 to 11.3. In Table 11.6, since data such as shown in Table 11.5 are not available for the earlier years, I took secondary school enrollment as a proportion of the age group 10–19 and as a proportion of adult males aged 20–44, the latter serving as a rough index of the proportion of families with children in secondary school. Japanese declines in total fertility started before World War II, when about one-fifth of households sent their children to secondary schools, but an acceleration in fertility decline occurred in the 1950s when over one-half of households seem to have had children enrolled in secondary school. Similarly in Taiwan, the decline in the total fertility rate from around 3 to 2 occurred when half of the households had children enrolled in secondary school. For the city-states of Hong Kong and Singapore, the fall from 3 to 2 seemed to have started somewhat earlier, when about two-fifths of the households had children in secondary school.

Historical accounts and contemporary analyses both strongly suggest that in traditional societies in East and Southeast Asia the costs of rearing children up to, say, the age of ten years could be recouped and often exceeded by the benefits derived from children working during adolescence and supporting parents in their old age. Sir Thomas Stamford Raffles, writing about Java in the second decade of the 19th century, stated: "Children which are for a very short period a burden to their parents, become early the means of assistance and the source of wealth . . . a species of valuable property, a real treasure, while during their infancy and the season of the helplessness, they take little from the fruits of his industry but bare subsistence. Their education costs him little or nothing; scarcely any clothing is required, his hut needs very little enlargement, and no beds are used." B. N. F. White (1976) found in a Java village that persons below 20 years of age did about 60 percent of the total work of those aged 20 and above and consumed 74 percent of the food of the older group. Also, children aged 12–14 not attending school worked nine hours per day, while those attending school worked only 4.5 hours.

In preindustrial societies, adolescents contribute through productive work on the farm and in the market, and also by performing tasks around the house (cooking, sweeping, fetching water, weeding, collecting firewood, running errands, marketing, caring for younger siblings), which frees adults for more productive work. The early Asian censuses defined the minimum working age as 10, or failed to specify a minimum. Since World War II most Asian censuses have continued to set the cut-off at 10 years of age, although recently this has been raised to between 11 and 15 years except in Indonesia. Thus, children were generally thought of as potential members of the work force from age 10 on.

In addition to the foregoing benefits derived from adolescents, working parents incurred the direct costs of secondary education, which are substantially higher than for primary education. Parents began to demand that after secondary schooling adolescents postpone marriage to help with family finances, and age at marriage rose. There was also a shift away from arranged marriages, suggesting that very early marriages were previously enforced by parents. No wonder, then, that the traditional literature in Asia often alluded to children as the wealth of the family.

The large cross-national study of the value of children organized by the East-West Center's Population Institute in the 1970s supports the ideas expressed above (Bulatao, 1979). In Fig. 11.4, in countries with high fertility and low post-primary school enrollment, such as Bangladesh, India, Indonesia, Thailand, and Malaysia, respondents consistently cited the economic benefits of children as a factor in family size decisions, whereas respondents in countries like Australia, West Germany, Belgium, Japan, the Netherlands, and the United States cited the cost of raising children, particularly of educating them, as a factor in their decisions. The industrializing countries of Taiwan, Hong Kong, Singapore, and South Korea fell between the high and low fertility countries in their responses.

The importance of the net value of children is a factor in fertility differences not only between countries but between classes within each country. Educational requirements for children have the greatest impact on middle-income peasant families in rural areas, on families headed by skilled workers in industry, and on clerical and sales workers in urban areas; these categories comprise roughly one-half of the families in East Asian countries in Table 11.6. The sharp drops in the average size of middle-income families were noted earlier. These are the families most affected by the mechanization and modernization process taking place throughout the economy. They are quick to realize that the future will bring more mechanization and modernization and that the demand for unskilled, uneducated workers will fall.

Many parents in Asian countries want their children (at least the males) to get as much education as possible. This is true not only in the Confucian countries of East Asia where learning is extolled but also in other parts of Asia where the colonial tradition placed a high premium on education. For these parents, their inability to pay for secondary education and to forgo the earning capacity of adolescents are the major constraints on extended education. But for most parents in the lower-income groups it is the perception that jobs will be difficult to find if the children are not educated beyond primary grades which impels them to work hard and save for more education. It is this per-

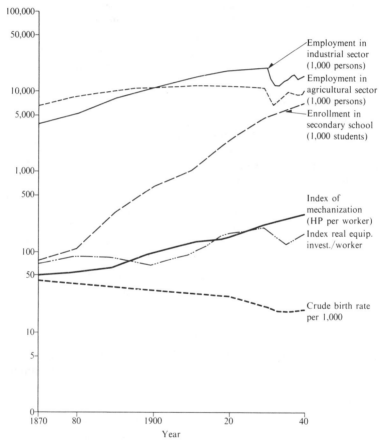

Figure 11.5 Trends in employment, fertility, education, and mechanization in the United States, 1870–1940.
Sources: Various series of *Historical Statistics of the United States*.

ception that leads to close spacing of births and, after the children are old enough to enter school, the need for housewives to go to work.

In Japan the premature introduction of compulsory primary education in 1872 was resisted with peasant uprisings. Carl Mosk (1977) has noted, however, that in the decades before World War II, compulsory primary education laws in Japan created an excess of actual over desired natality, and the legalization of abortion in 1948 (by cheapening the control of fertility) contributed to the speed of the fertility decline.

It is instructive to look at the situation in the United States when it completed its industrial transition around 1900. The decline in birth rate was slow until the 1920s, when there was an accelerated spread of new electric- and gas-driven machines from the emerging second industrial revolution, which replaced unskilled labor and caused with it a spurt in secondary education enrollment (Fig. 11.5). In the same period income disparities began to fall and total factor productivities rose sharply. Figure 11.5 shows an absolute decline in the farm labor force in this period, and there was an accelerated growth of cities with populations of one million or more. Female participation rates for those aged 20 years and older rose with real wages. It is interesting that the accelerated rise in secondary education and mechanization and a decline in fertility occurred in several countries in Western Europe: the United Kingdom, France, Norway, Sweden, and the Benelux countries. According to the United States Census for 1980, for the first time white-collar workers outnumbered blue-collar workers (52 million to 47 million). These trends may continue in coming years with the emerging third industrial revolution. But not all new technologies have the same impact on labor demand or supply. Biological ones such as higher-yielding rice varieties that require more fertilizing, weeding, water control, and threshing by hand may actually increase the demand for labor.

Concluding Notes

The important points of this chapter could be summarized by Table 11.7. Average investment in equipment (mainly machines) and in education per person aged 24 years or less was highest in Japan, then in Taiwan and South Korea, and lowest in the Philippines and Thailand (line 9). In line 10 is shown the average number of children born in the 1970s per 100 population, which was lowest in Japan and highest in the Philippines. My interpretation of this negative association of average investment in line 9 and the number of children born is that Japan and other East Asian countries were using investments in machines and education as substitutes for children. The countries where expendi-

Table 11.7   Average Annual Investment in Equipment and Education in Selected Asian Countries, 1960–1979
(In billions of national currency units)

	Japan	Taiwan	South Korea	Thailand	Philippines
1. Average investment in current prices	22,262.6	116.1	1,747.6	47.2	17.3
2. Equipment	15,543.0	89.4	1,390.0	37.0	12.7
3. Education expd.	6,719.6	26.6	357.5	10.2	4.6
Public	3,859.6	16.2	189.5	7.6	2.7
Private	2,860.0	10.4	168.0	2.6	1.9
4. Persons 24 yrs. old or less (1,000)	44,240.0	9,195.0	20,068.0	22,907.0	27,282.0
5. Average exchange rate (US $)	290.0	38.0	440.0	20.5	7.1
6. Average investment in equipment and education of persons 24 years old or less	503,223.0	12,625.0	87,081.0	2,062.0	634.0
7. Item 6 in US$	1,735.0	332.0	198.0	101.0	89.0
8. Number of children born in 1970s (100 persons)	1.77	2.45	2.56	3.00	3.25

Notes: (1) Item 5 is the exchange rates of local currencies per U.S. dollar, average for 1970 to 1979; (2) item 6 is in units of national currency and is obtained dividing item 1 by item 4; (3) item 7 obtained by converting item 6 into U.S. dollars using exchange rate in item 5.

Sources: All data on investment computed from official national account statistics of each respective country, population aged 24 or less, from official statistical yearbook.

tures on equipment and education were low needed more children as sources of future income and security.

The dynamics of population growth vary in different phases of the transition. This is to be expected because of changes during the transition in the nature of the demand for and supply of labor, and in the institutions and endowments which make up the labor market. At the beginning of the transition, cultural factors and physical endowment may dominate fertility behavior, but later, as modern technologies substitute for labor, sociocultural forces may become less important. Not all technologies substitute for labor, as noted above. The technologies of the first industrial revolution created a demand for unskilled labor, especially for child labor, and birth rates rose in the first half of the 19th century in the West. Moreover, in addition to the labor market, the institutions providing for the future security of the elderly play an important role in population dynamics. These change with the different phases of the transition, beginning with the importance of the extended family and shifting to public institutions of health, social security, and so on.

This chapter dealt mainly with the latter phase of the transition and with economies passing swiftly through it. The factors underlying fertility change can be linked with economic growth and structural changes since population growth underlies labor supply. Without this linkage, labor supply becomes exogenously determined. Also, if fertility dynamics are not linked to economic growth, independent variables such as changing marriage age, years of schooling, wives' employment, family incomes, and others important in the decline of fertility will be largely exogenous in the explanation of fertility changes in various groups. Of course, not all of the forces affecting marriage age, educational enrollment, etc., are due to economic growth. But because of the widespread association found between development and fertility change, the most important factors probably arise in the process of economic growth and structural change.

One issue emerging from this chapter that needs to be looked into is the education that affects fertility in lower-income families. This chapter focuses on secondary school enrollment; demographic literature refers frequently to primary enrollment and also to mothers' educational attainments. Recent World Fertility Surveys show that the impact of primary education on fertility is insignificant. But these surveys treat populations in large aggregations without examining peasants and workers separately. It may be that primary education is more important than I think among peasant families, and that the importance of mothers' education may be confined to upper-income families in Asia and also families in advanced countries where maids are expensive to hire and secondary educational enrollment is universal. Thus, the relation of secondary enrollment to primary enrollment and to mothers' education needs to be studied.

Another issue is the relation of education to technologies. How is the perception formed in lower-income families that more education is needed with technological progress? Is it directly related to working with machines, or indirectly through the mass media, neighbors, and other general influences? Nor should influences from technologies other than labor-replacing ones be neglected. Biological, chemical, agronomical, and other agricultural technologies may increase the demand for labor but not for uneducated labor. Working with these technologies requires just as much if not more education than working with machines. In the cities, to what extent does the use of modern technologies in transportation, communications, construction, government services, and in urban homes call for education beyond the primary level?

Still another issue is to what extent parents invest in children's education because of a concern for their future welfare, to what extent because the costs of raising more children relative to their benefits have gone up, and to what extent because their incomes have increased so that they can afford to. The interplay of these three factors is complex and will vary among different socioeconomic groupings, but has implications for population and education policies.

On the whole, the policy implications of the findings in this chapter are encouraging, since policies to speed up economic growth with more employment, education, higher incomes and savings, and so on are consistent with lower fertility and slower population growth, which in turn react favorably on further economic growth with modern technologies. But the negative association between the rapid growth of income and education and slower population growth during the transition has one disturbing consequence for the future when viewed cross-sectionally in a given country. Better educated parents tend to have fewer children than parents with less education. Political leaders in Singapore, India, and Bangladesh have seized upon this and devised programs to encourage the better educated to have more children. One would think that it would be better to encourage parents with less education to have fewer children through all-out efforts to promote more education and employment opportunities. Perhaps more studies on some of the issues listed above would be useful in devising future population policies.

CHAPTER 12

Lessons from the Past:
Guideposts Toward the Pacific Century

*M*uch has already been said about the implications of the discussions in previous chapters for policies. In this final chapter the various strands are woven together, the major lessons from the past are identified, and their impact on the future of Asia are discussed.[1]

The End of the Postwar Era

The beginning of the 1980s appeared to be a watershed marking the end of the postwar era and the beginning of a new one. The high GNP growth rates of nearly 5 percent registered in the industrialized countries during the 1950s and 1960s were associated with an investment boom induced by an increase in aggregate demand for capital and consumer goods. Underlying the growth of demand were not only secular factors but also compensation for the low investment and consumption levels during the depression of the 1930s, and a shift of resources to military activities in the first half of the 1940s. Moreover, many countries were able to take advantage of the many new technologies that were developed in the 1930s and 1940s. Other factors that led to high growth were the low debt burdens of firms and households, flexible labor supply, very liberal international trading conditions, and favorable institutional environments in which there were low levels of spending on social welfare and taxes, few oligarchies, and weak labor unions. As a result of the investment boom, there were large overcapacities in most of the capital-intensive industries, to which were added the overcapacities in the NICs by the second half of the 1970s (Oshima, 1981). By the mid-1970s, most of the factors which had led to the high 5 percent growth were no longer in operation, and growth slowed down to about 2.5 percent from 1973 to 1983.

In the early postwar years about 100 or so countries became inde-

[1] Some of the papers underlying this chapter are Oshima, 1962; 1971a; 1973; 1978b.

pendent and proceeded to buy materials and equipment from the industrialized countries to expand and modernize their physical infrastucture and other facilities necessary to develop their agriculture and move into industrialization. According to various IBRD and World Development Reports, merchandise imports of the developing countries increased from $126 billion in 1960 to $234 billion in 1970 and to $354 billion in 1979, accounting for an average over the two decades of nearly 40 percent of the merchandise exports of the industrialized countries.

Around the mid-1970s, to counteract the tendency for exports to the industrialized countries to grow slowly, the Asian NICs and ASEAN countries borrowed heavily from the large flow of petrodollar loans to sustain their high growth rates. The resulting construction boom continued into the early 1980s, but when oil prices began to fall, the loans stopped and the construction boom collapsed in the mid-1980s. In 1985 the growth rates for the NICs and ASEAN in the 1970s were cut in half to 3 percent and 4 percent, respectively, ending both the construction and export boom. These countries (except Taiwan) are now saddled with large external debt burdens whose servicing in 1983 as a ratio of the government budget amounted to 30 percent in the Philippines, 26 percent in Korea, 16 percent in Indonesia, 15 percent in Thailand, 12 percent in Malaysia, and 10 percent in Singapore. Even if external funds are available, these high servicing shares will constrain borrowing, so that the construction boom cannot be revived for the rest of this decade. Since the growth rates of exports and construction combined were higher than the growth of GDP in the 1970s in all the industrializing countries, the major props supporting high growth are likely to be too weak to sustain high growth in the near future.

Without these factors favorable for high growth in the West and in Pacific Asia, the 1980s may be the beginning of a new era of moderate growth. Slower growth with rising or high unemployment may increase a tendency toward higher income disparities. If the changeover from the electric-power technologies of the past into new electronic technologies takes some time to be completed in the industrialized countries, unemployment may persist, so that the return to a period of high growth and low inequalities cannot be expected to return soon. In any case, the conditions which made the post-World War II era a notable one in the history of modern economic growth are now gone, and the world is moving into another, less exuberant, less turbulent, slower, but perhaps more stable era.[2]

[2] The foregoing was written before the yen rose sharply in 1986. The growth of the

The Emerging New Era: The Pacific Century

It is frequently said that the center of modern economic growth has begun to move westward to the Pacific rim. Historically, the center moved westward to the North Atlantic from the North Sea around the turn of the last century, and now the center may move again to encompass Japan, the NICs, ASEAN, and Australia on the western rim. This is a vision of the future that should motivate Asians to exert the efforts needed to fulfill the dream of once again becoming the center of the world economy.

Japan has caught up with the West's leading countries, and the prospects are good that the Pacific century will be achieved, if not at the turn of this century, then in the first or second decade of the new one. However, growth can come to a sudden stop, as in the case of the Latin American NICs, Mexico, Brazil, or the Philippines.

The slowdown in the North Sea Basin is more than the slow growth of aggregate demand and of technological advance: it is a deterioration in institutions vital for productive activities. Management became increasingly dominated in the larger industries by executives trained more in finance than in technology, and by stockholders impatient for quick dividends who opted for short-term profit maximization and ignored more important long-range interests. Labor unions demanded higher and higher wage settlements and managers acceded, relying exclusively on wage incentives and neglecting other types of incentives to raise the quality of production. All three colluded to raise wages and prices at the expense of consumers, instead of improving productivity through investments. Competition between firms declined as firms became more oligopolistic and labor unions more rigid.

While there was much collusion between firms within industries and cooperation among workers within the unions, the values of individualism and independence remained strong within the factory, where workers demanded that each job be classified and specified in detail and all work was strictly "to rule." Management kept powers of administrative decision-making centralized in its own hands, and owners reserved the right of exclusive policy making. Each of the groups, and each individual within the groups, guarded individual rights. Cooperation was limited.

All this might not have been very damaging in the 19th century, but in this century, with its sequentially arranged, interconnected systems

---

NICs is likely to be high in the future, but this will be at the expense of Japan's growth, which can more than cancel out the effect on the rest of Asia of the NICs' high growth.

of machines and equipment, the interdependence of the entire process rather than the independence of individual workers or machines is important. Moreover, the interconnectedness of the chain of operations in the factory calls for high quality in all the means and materials of production since a breakdown in one portion means a stoppage of the whole process. Machinery industries have superseded the material-processing industries to dominate the entire manufacturing sector, and the qualitative aspects of production have become paramount. In contrast, 19th-century manufacturing was dominated by the processing of goods such as food, textiles, and wood products.

Adversarial industrial relations, authoritarian management, individualistic working habits, and undue dependence on wage incentives, which all originated in 19th-century technology, do not motivate workers to produce high-quality products. As pointed out in Chapter 4, the Japanese use more humane, personalized industrial relations with more participatory decision-making and vest fewer policy-making powers in the owners. There is more emphasis on group work, and nonwage incentives motivate workers to higher diligence and quality work. The countries of the industrialized West have begun to worry about their industrial relations and management styles. However, attempts to change to more egalitarian styles have met with objections not only from management but also from workers steeped in centuries of class-structured thinking. Institutions change slowly and in these instances more time than the few decades left in this century may be needed.

The Asian NICs, unlike Japan and the Western industrialized countries, have some time before the frontiers of technology are approached. They need not be held back by the dearth of new technologies and can continue to import them to speed up growth. Institutions concerned with importing technologies have improved in past decades, and cooperation and participation are more common than individualism and adversarial relations. The work ethic in the NICs is quite strong as a heritage from Confucianism.

Increasingly science- and technology-oriented education in the West is gradually eroding belief in the basic doctrines of Christianity rooted in the relations between man and God. But Confucianism is based on human relations and has been less affected by the spread of scientific culture. Aspects of its teachings that extol learning, harmony, cooperation, order, and diligence may be strengthened if the demands of emerging new technology are consistent with these ideals. The strong reliance on the family and kinship groups in Confucian thinking encourages less dependence on the state in old age and in ill health. The heavy demand on Western governments for social security and welfare has had ultimately unfavorable consequences on work ethics and saving propensity.

The above are some of the reasons that Pacific Asia may be able to catch up with Western Europe and the U.S.A. in the next few decades. But there are other factors to which attention must be paid, particularly in the ASEAN countries, that are becoming increasingly important in the development of the NICs. In the remainder of this chapter, lessons of the past are reviewed to identify major areas where improvements are needed to facilitate the passage into the Pacific century.

Strategies for Sector Development

This volume has stressed the importance of agricultural development under conditions of monsoon seasonality and low rural incomes, and labor-intensive industrialization under conditions of high population densities and low levels of industrial manpower development. If agriculture remains undeveloped, aggregate demand and savings will be low, and the limits of urban industries will quickly be reached, long before scale economies, externalities, and manpower experience are sufficient to allow manufacture for export. Even Japan, which had a fairly long industrial experience, started with agricultural development and labor-intensive industries in the immediate postwar period and shifted to capital intensiveness only after full employment had been reached.

Difficulties are compounded when countries like India and China plunge into heavy industrialization or countries like the Philippines and Indonesia start with too strong an emphasis on industrialization from the very beginning. Even Korea, which had a good start on agriculture and labor-intensive industries, ran into trouble when a premature, sudden shift to heavy industries was made in the later phases of the agro-industrial transition. All these countries are now backtracking to focus on agricultural development. However, turning the economy around is proving a time-consuming task since the physical infrastructure and institutions have been developed in a different direction. Although it is "better to be late than never," the losses involved in correcting mistakes are difficult to recoup.

It is more efficient, no matter how large a country may be or how rich in natural resources, to start with development of agriculture, by raising yields per hectare, multiplying crops per hectare, shifting to diversified production as grain production nears self-sufficiency, and expanding off-farm employment, thereby eliminating idleness and low productivity in the drier half of the year.

Agricultural development is more efficient than industrialization in the early phase of the transition because the traditional physical infrastructure, institutions, and manpower skills and experience already exist to allow a fast start of growth. Improvements can be made without too much external assistance, and while the economy begins to take off, infrastructure, institutions, and skills and experience for industrialization can be accumulated. If a country begins with industrialization, too much of the resources and skilled manpower must be mobilized for it, creating not only internal imbalances but undue dependence on external resources as well, as the experiences of China, India, and the Philippines have shown. Even so, these countries are not likely to end up with efficient industries able to export. Hence, in monsoon economies the passage through the transition is quicker, easier, and cheaper if agriculture is developed before industrialization is attempted. The lesson of postwar experience is that shortcuts are few and leapfrogging is hazardous. In short, the first and most important guidepost to the Pacific century reads: "For full speed ahead, the economy should be operating at full employment with maximum aggregate demand." If this is not the case, it may be that the agricultural sector has not been sufficiently developed and cannot buy enough products from urban industries and services since peasant incomes are too low. Without higher yields and multiple diversified crops, demand may be only one-half or less that needed. If this guidepost is missed, backtracking will be necessary.

The Government and the Market

Postwar experience clearly points to the greater success of open, free, and private-enterprise economies over the more regulated, nationalized, protected economies. But the issue is not as clear-cut or as simple as the more enthusiastic advocates of the market system make out. The successes of Japan, Taiwan, Hong Kong, Malaysia, and Thailand should not be credited too much to market forces. As noted above, these countries started out with labor-intensive strategies. One of the virtues of such a start is that market intervention, protection, and nationalization are needed less than in countries like China, India, the Philippines, Indonesia, and other South Asian countries which started out with industrialization, since labor intensity is closer to endowments and is a more efficient path. Moreover, in general these were countries where historical legacies had left better developed bureaucracies. Even in sectors which they did regulate, protect, and nationalize, governments did a far better job than in other countries. Most important, market forces and the marketplace were better developed in these countries. Nor should early postwar developments be ignored, for example, the arrival of a large contingent of experienced Shanghai entrepreneurs in Hong Kong, or the secession of Singapore from the Malayan Federation, or the arrival of American mass distributors in Hong Kong and Japan. Even so, the contribution of the market should not be underestimated, especially in the latter portions of the transition when infrastructure for and experience working in the market are accumulated. The issue, then, is the proper role of the government and the market in the transition and how they are to work together.

As economists know, the market is not an impersonal deus ex machina operating with clock-like precision. It is, like the government, a complex institution run by human beings and requires as much time to become an efficient institution. It is no more efficient than the quality of human beings buying and selling in it. No country in Asia had as little experience with modern markets as China after three decades of comprehensive planning. When attempts to shift to a market economy were made recently, chaotic conditions emerged, including illegal imports, bribery, black marketeering, overproduction, shoddy goods, cheating, and so on. It took the Western countries over a century to develop the market forces to present levels of effectiveness and responsibility; one does not have to go far back in U.S. history to read of robber barons and the like. Like government forces, market forces are the product of development and must be carefully nurtured.

Markets work best in activities where bargaining is central. But when sellers are few and powerful and buyers are numerous, the results of bargaining do not make for the efficient operation of the economy. Poor peasants must sell at low prices to powerful merchants, borrow at usurious interest rates from moneylenders, and pay high rents to landed oligarchs in villages. Workers without unions are at the mercy of employers, especially when labor is plentiful. Small industries buying from giant manufacturers pay high prices for raw materials and financial cartels pay low interest to depositors. The state is called upon to regulate prices, wages, rent, interests, and so on, and when indigenous entrepreneurs continue to be inefficient, tariffs and subsidies cannot be lowered. But these interventions, often by bureaucrats with little experience and knowledge of markets, have consequences which are highly detrimental in the long run, even if they are momentarily effective.

The solution to this dilemma may be for the government to intervene just long enough to correct unequal bargaining power. To make the intervention brief enough so that undesirable, long-term effects are minimal, government forces must move quickly and vigorously to equalize the bargaining powers in the market. As occurred in the early postwar years in Japan and in Taiwan, agrarian reform to distribute land more equally, and establishment of credit, cooperatives, extension services, and irrigation works should be given top priority. Labor unions should be legalized, consumer organizations promoted, monopolies and cartels destroyed, and competition encouraged. Funds to establish institutes and centers for assistance in technology, management, marketing, and training for small business must also be provided. In short, the major developmental function of government, institution building, must be carried out with dispatch in order to dispense as quickly as possible with market intervention.

One problem remains: what should be done with the large collection of public enterprises that is a major burden on national budgets and reduces the resources available for improving institutions. The most costly and inefficient of these are the capital-intensive industries. Several countries have taken steps to privatize them, which should be done even if large losses are incurred and employment reduced or if they have to be sold to foreign enterprises. There are at least two reasons why governments are less efficient than the market in operating enterprises. One is the absence of competition among government units; the other is the lack of rivalry among workers within public organizations who are tenured civil servants and cannot be fired or promoted as easily as in private firms. Even if these obstacles are overcome, their efficiency is still less than in private firms which depend on profits and not on the public budget for survival.

The argument that national enterprises must be kept in the interests of self-sufficiency, self-reliance, and national independence may be a holdover from colonial days when foreign enterprises were exploitive and beyond the control of the natives. Why should the government or a handful of local entrepreneurs exploit the consuming public with costly and shoddy products, while paying wages lower than in foreign firms? If local enterprises after a long period of protection cannot become efficient, it is best to let them go. The "survival of the fittest" is capitalism's way of improving efficiency. Countries like the Philippines, India, and other South Asian countries took nationalistic slogans seriously, but after three decades their nationalized industries are still performing poorly and need protection and subsidies. In the meanwhile, consumers have paid dearly for them.

It is instructive to observe that there is no more fiercely independent country than Singapore, which has the largest share of industrial output produced by foreign enterprises, most of them powerful multinational corporations. At one stroke and with little notice, Singapore destroyed the foreign companies assembling cars in the republic by abolishing tariffs on car imports. This is no longer the pre-World War age of imperialism when Western countries could send out marines and gunboats to collect debts and enforce treaties dictated by the West. Today, a nation's sovereign power is weakened not so much by foreign enterprises but by native enterprises and governments too inefficient to move the nation rapidly to the completion of the industrial transition. A stagnant and slow-growing economy becomes too dependent on foreigners for assistance to be ruggedly independent. Note the recent experience of the Philippines, which after spending so much on dubious public enterprises is stuck with huge debts which cannot be serviced and is now virtually under the thumb of the IMF and foreign banks. Excessive spending on public enterprises left too little for other institutions which have deteriorated sharply over the past decade. In addition, the Philippines pampered the multinationals, protecting their products with tariffs, giving them tax breaks, and permitting monopolistic practices.

The second guidepost to the Pacific century should read: "Let the government establish as soon as possible the conditions necessary for the efficient operations of the market and get back to the more essential work of developing the institutions necessary for development."

Manpower and Institutional Development

This volume has stressed the importance of institutions in their interplay with technology in the progress of developing countries. The effectiveness of institutions is not greater than the quality of manpower operating them. In the distant past, economists used to give greater importance to material resources, land, and capital, but when technology in this century began to diversify, the skills needed by manpower also multiplied. Simultaneously, the institutions needed to operate and service this vast array of production complexes became infinitely more complex. Hence, today the NICs with minimal natural resources and capital but with skilled manpower can emerge as dynamic economies.

Monsoon Asia is not held back because of shortages of manpower. In fact it has too much, so that full employment becomes the first requisite on the road to rapid progress. The problem of equipping the "teeming millions" with modern skills lies at the core of modern development, particularly because Western colonial rulers made only meager efforts to develop modern skills in the agrarian countries they controlled in the prewar decades. When independence was achieved, the new governments established schools. The record of achievements has been good, and Asia succeeded in surpassing Africa and catching up with Latin America in literacy and school enrollment. Nevertheless, Japanese experience teaches that schools are not the only source of manpower development, nor are literacy and numeracy the only dimensions of manpower quality. The average years of schooling completed by the labor force ranged from four years in Indonesia to 12 years in Japan by the end of the 1970s, although time spent in the home and workplace where the culture of work and skills are learned is also important. The sources of skills and attitudes toward work go beyond the schools, homes, and workplace and into the community at large.

The need to expand education systems as rapidly as possible overshadowed quality in some instances. The emphasis has been on general and liberal education and on primary schooling because they are cheaper than technical, vocational, or general secondary education. Secondary education must be upgraded as the ASEAN countries use more sophisticated levels of technologies in agriculture and industry. In addition, schools in Asia are heavily influenced by Western education and may need to emphasize the modernization of social values, the development of national unity and consensus, and knowledge of new institutions since most Asian students come from traditional homes. All this implies that students should spend a longer time in school than their Western counterparts. Modernization must be taught within the context of indigenous, traditional culture, requiring well-trained, competent teachers.

Western religions, especially Protestantism, played an important role in the rise of capitalism. The religions of Asia emerged in response to the needs of traditional societies in ancient times. The new type of economy calls for responsible moral leadership in government and the marketplace; the religions of Asia can greatly facilitate the passage through the transition if they can instill the moral behavior and work ethics required by the new institutions. This may entail modifications and extensions of the theological structures in the various religions, just as during the Reformation in Western Europe new sects such as Calvinism and Puritanism rose to modify Catholicism.

The mass media (newspapers, radio, and television) can be a major source of manpower development, especially in supplementing and extending the education of adults after schooling. In a rapidly changing world, past knowledge can become obsolete, and there is a need for constant renewal and replenishment of skills and culture. Developing countries where formal educational facilities are fewer than in the West can ill afford to neglect the mass media as a tool for continuing education.[3] Yet the mass media are purveyors mainly of entertainment in most developing countries.

In the monsoon tradition, children were taught at home to get along with others as smoothly as possible, a virtue indispensable for group work in busy seasons on the farm. Within this frame of harmonious relations, the importance of responsible, prompt, and careful work habits needs to be emphasized, and some modifications may have to be made, such as in the development of initiative, innovativeness, ingenuity, and integrity, while loyalty and dedication to family and group need to be extended to the national level.

Learning and training in the workplace can be the single most important source of manpower development since more time is spent in the workplace than in schools and community organizations. This requires a system of industrial and labor-management relations different from those in the West which have influenced systems in Asia. The Japanese system (Chapter 4) of extensive worker participation, consultation, and cooperation may be too difficult to transfer elsewhere, but modifications can be made, as is being done in the United States. Management must be prepared to invest more in training, both on and off the job, and in retraining. Since the most suitable machines and skills for training are found in the workplace and the training can be carried out as work proceeds, more use should be made of the workplace as a source of manpower development. If properly carried out, not only will skills be enhanced but productivity and efficiency also will improve as workers become more motivated.

The national government can play a strategic role in initiating, guiding, and coordinating the development of manpower. It can initiate study groups to modernize indigenous social values and work culture, their members composed of respected leaders from academia, politics, business, labor unions, professions, and the bureaucracy. The study groups will draft tentative codes of ethics and values which can then be widely discussed in the media and by other groups before being put into final form.

To raise the quality of manpower, Asia cannot rely on schools alone; more attention must be paid to other sources of manpower development. Schooling is too slow: according to various official statistics, the average years of schooling completed for the entire labor force in

[3] For example, Filipino primary school students spend in school annually only two-thirds of the time that U.S. students do, and secondary schooling in the Philippines is 4 years compared with 6–7 years in other countries.

Japan, Taiwan, and Korea during the 1960s and 1970s rose by only 0.1 to 0.2 years.

Participatory versus Authoritarian Decisions

Whatever may have been the benefits relative to the costs of authoritarianism in the past, the costs appear to be greater than the benefits now. Asians turned to authoritarians who promised faster growth with order and discipline, but in retrospect, results were produced only for a short time and several countries today are still counting the costs, while others have yet to feel the full brunt of the damages.

The costs of heavy industries pushed through by Park Chung Hee and his small circle of advisors in the mid-1970s, the costs of dubious projects secretly launched by former president Marcos and his friends and by Suharto and his generals, the shoddy construction of Bangkok's infrastructure by the military regime in the 1960s, the decision to isolate Burma by Ne Win, and the tragedies of Mao's Great Leap Forward and the Cultural Revolution all were too large and obvious to need careful calculation before passing judgment. However, not only authoritarians but also democratically elected leaders can make costly mistakes if participation is denied to many who can speak knowledgeably on issues.

The advantages of broader participation go beyond monetary savings from better policies and decisions. Even though participatory decision-making takes more time than authoritarian methods, it is more than offset by quicker and better implementation if the participants include some who may be hurt by the decision. Concessions to those who oppose a plan will win them over to cooperate in the implementation and help to maintain the social consensus so important for sustained growth. Cleavages occur when authoritarian decisions are rammed down the throats of opponents left out without a chance to voice their views. With consultation, implementation often need not be enforced through the enactment of laws with severe penalties. The Hong Kong government is not elected but appointed from London, but it has a more democratic image than the elected Singapore government because of its extensive use of consultation and persuasion instead of laws, penalties, and threats.

In the heterogeneous countries of Southeast and South Asia, wider participation is crucial in maintaining social stability. In issues where ethnicity is relevant, the leaders of all ethnic groups should take part in policy discussions, including religious leaders who are often inseparable from ethnic leaders. This eventually helps to forge a more positive attitude to national development instead of each group promoting its own interests. The greater the diversities, the greater is the need for broad participation. Authoritarian methods have been responsible for some of the more serious ethnic rebellions: the Muslims in Mindanao, regional tribal groups in Burma, and religious and ethnic groups in India under Indira Gandhi.

Participation also contributed to manpower development. Extensive consultations with the industrial sector in industrial policy-making in Hong Kong and Japan enable the bureaucracy to learn about technology, management, and industrial relations in ways more practical than textbook knowledge, while at the same time industrialists become acquainted with the problems of government. Both government and market forces are improved, particularly when policy implementation avoids heavy-handed legal enactment.

In quality improvement circles, managers, engineers, and workers identify problems together and work out solutions, and each group gets to know the problems of the others. The quality of manpower is improved in ways far better than from instructions from the top or lessons in training programs. Knowledge and skills are transmitted downward, and experience and practice from the factory floor are transferred upward. Participation improves worker motivation, initiative, cooperation, and loyalty to the firm.

Decisions made in a narrow circle invite corruption, in that they make diversion of funds easier. Fast, autocratic decisions, even though they happen to be correct, bring about the weakening of institutions. They sap the vitality and vigor of staff members, blunt innovativeness and initiative, and damage decision-making capabilities. This happened in the Philippines in nearly all institutions during the martial law era (Chapter 7).

In short, whatever may have been the reasons for authoritarianism in the past, today the labor force is no longer predominantly an illiterate, tradition-bound group. Workers need to participate more in the governance of the nation and in policy and decision-making in the factories, marketplace, and elsewhere. If the Pacific Asian countries are to join the democracies of the United States, Canada, Australia, New Zealand, and Japan in the coming century of the Pacific, they must follow the guidepost pointing to greater participation.

Long-Range Planning and Internationalization

As market forces grow more efficient, the operation of the economy can be increasingly left to the marketplace, and governments can attend to the more important problems of institution building, a longer-term task than the workings of the market. Accordingly, long-range planning must take precedence over short- or medium-term planning.

Most of the difficult problems countries face are easier to solve with more time. This is true not only of social problems of human resource development, ethnicity, regional imbalances, income inequalities, and poverty but also of some national economic problems. One area that needs special attention is the task of expanding trade among countries in the region in the coming years, since trade with the rest of the world is expected to grow only slowly.

As this volume has emphasized, the faster progress of East Asia over Southeast Asia has produced a group of countries which have completed the agro-industrial transition and another group which has not. The problem is to take advantage of this uneven development to improve trading between the two groups. One promising area is the export of agricultural products from one group in exchange for industrial products from the other. To generate employment, countries in Southeast Asia must create more jobs in diversified agriculture and agro-industries that will raise farm family incomes and thus levels of aggregate demand to support faster growth of industries for the domestic market. This will enable the monsoon economies to improve income distribution and achieve full employment. Food consumption needs in Japan and the NICs are shifting away from rice and carbohydrates, but wages are rising to levels where agriculture is rapidly losing its comparative advantage. These countries should begin to phase out the more labor-intensive sectors of their agriculture, and buy from the countries of Southeast Asia, which in turn can buy more of the machines and equipment needed for industrialization. And yet barriers to agricultural trade are going up in East Asia and protectionism is expected to increase in the future, as was the case in Western Europe.

Problems rooted in the structure of the economy will take time to solve as they involve strong sociopolitical pressures. But the issue is most important for all of Pacific Asia in its journey to the Pacific century. One way out is for regional cooperation to establish long-range plans for phasing out various sectors of East Asian agriculture and to increase purchases of industrial goods by Southeast Asia. The plans should include the transfer of the more labor-intensive industries from East to Southeast Asia, which will contribute to a slowdown in the establishment of too many capital-intensive industries in Southeast Asian countries. Such long-range cooperative plans will send out signals to investors and entrepreneurs as to the potential industries of the future for each country and alert the young to train for skills needed in such industries.

In conclusion, it must be stressed once more that many of the major problems of today are rooted in the history of the distant past. This volume has tried through comparative studies to bring out the nature of these problems, hoping that by comparison with neighboring countries a better understanding can be achieved and valuable lessons learned. But nations, like individuals, differ in their inclinations and propensities to learn from others, and this, too, may be a matter of historical background. The world has changed since the Ming emperors boasted that China had nothing to learn from other nations, and since the Tokugawa shoguns isolated Japan for over two and a half centuries.

Today's world is one of incessant technological change which must be met with rapid institutional adjustments and improvements. The most advanced countries in the West are not necessarily the best for developing countries in monsoon Asia to learn from, but the experiences of all countries of whatever ideology should be examined before the most appropriate policies for development are selected and implemented.

Postscript

In mid-1986, something unexpected happened. The yen rose sharply, from around 240 to the dollar to about 160, or by about 40 percent in a matter of just a few months. This is certain to raise a number of problems for Japan in the short run, not least of which relate to the last vestiges of the monsoon economy in Japan—the low productivity in the small unit sectors of agriculture, industry, and commerce. It may turn out to be a blessing in disguise in the long run if imports of diversified products from the ASEAN Four and elsewhere, and of small industries from the NICs and ASEAN, can enter Japan more easily. This will help eventually to wipe out the small units with their high costs, since a higher-value yen may be appropriate for large-scale industries but too high for smaller units. If so, Japan may become the first non-monsoon economy in Asia.

For other Asian countries, the higher yen is a godsend as it makes them more competitive in world markets and also makes them attractive to Japanese companies looking for overseas factory and investment sites.

BIBLIOGRAPHY

Abramovitz, Moses. 1973. "Reinterpreting U.S. Economic Growth." *American Economic Review*, May.

Agrawal, A. N. 1978. *Indian Economy: Nature, Problems and Progress*. 4th rev. ed. London: Croom Helm Ltd.

Alailima, P. J. 1978. *Fiscal Incidence in Sri Lanka*. Geneva: International Labor Organization.

Arasaratnam, S. 1964. *Ceylon*. Englewood Cliffs, N.J.: Prentice-Hall.

Asian Development Bank. 1983. *Key Indicators of Developing Member Countries of ADB*.

Asian Productivity Organization. 1978. *Rural Development Strategies in Selected Member Countries*. Tokyo: Asian Productivity Organization.

Baldwin, Robert E. 1975. *Foreign Trade Regimes and Economic Development: The Philippines*. New York: National Bureau of Economic Research.

Bayley, D. H. 1976. *Forces of Order*. Berkeley: University of California Press.

Beijing Review. 1982. *China Today, Economic Readjustment and Reforms*.

Bhagwati, J. N. and P. Desai. 1972. *India: Planning for Industrialization*. Oxford: Oxford University Press.

Buck, John L. 1956. *Land Utilization in China, Statistics*. (A volume in the series *China During the Interregnum, 1911–1949, The Economy and Society*, ed. Ramon H. Myers.) Chicago: University of Chicago Press. (Reprinted 1981 by Garland Publications, N.Y.)

Bulatao, R. 1979. "On the Nature of the Transition in the Value of Children" and "Further Evidence of the Transition in the Value of Children." Paper Nos. 60-A and 60-B of the East-West Population Institute, Honolulu.

Carre, J. J., P. Dubois, and E. Malinvaud. 1975. *French Economic Growth*. Stanford: Stanford University Press.

Carroll, John. J. 1965. *The Filipino Manufacturing Entrepreneur*. Ithaca, N.Y.: Cornell University Press.

Central Bank of Ceylon. 1983. Report on Consumer Finances and Socio-Economic Survey, Sri Lanka, 1978/9, Part I. Colombo: Central Bank of Ceylon.

Central Bureau of Statistics, Government of Indonesia. 1979. *Distribushi Pendapatan de Indonesia 1976* (Income distribution in Indonesia). Jakarta: Central Bureau of Statistics.

Chang, T. T. 1977. Chapter in *The Early History of Agriculture*, ed. Joseph Hutchinson et al. Oxford: Oxford University Press.

Chang, T. T., B. S. Vegara, and S. Yoshida, eds. 1976. *Proceedings of the*

Symposium on Climate and Rice. Los Baños: International Rice Research Institute.

Chenery, N. 1960. "Patterns of Industrial Growth." *American Economic Review,* September.

Choki, A. M. 1979. "State Intervention in the Industrialization of Developing Countries: Selected Issues." World Bank Staff Working Paper No. 341. Washington, D.C.: World Bank.

Cipolla, Carlo M. (ed.). 1969. *The Emergence of Industrial Societies.* New York: Norton.

Corpuz, O. D. 1965. "Notes on Philippine Economic History." In G. P. Sicat et al., eds., *Economics and Development.* Quezon City.

Cummings, W. K. 1980. *Education and Equality in Japan.* Princeton: Princeton University Press.

Deane, Phyllis. 1980. *The First Industrial Revolution.* 2nd ed. Cambridge: Cambridge University Press.

Deane, Phyllis, and W. A. Cole. 1969. *British Economic Growth, 1688 to 1959: Trends and Structures.* 2nd ed. Cambridge: Cambridge University Press.

Denison, Edward F. 1967. *Why Growth Rates Differ: Postwar Experience in Nine Western Countries.* Washington, D.C.: Brookings Institution.

Department of Statistics, Government of Malaysia. 1984. Monthly Statistical Bulletin, February 1984. Kuala Lumpur.

Devine, Warren. 1983. "From Shafts to Wires: Historical Perspective on Electrification." *Journal of Economic History,* June.

de Vries, Barend A. 1980. *Philippines: Industrial Development Strategy and Policies.* Washington, D.C.: World Bank.

de Dios, E. (ed.). 1984. *Analysis of the Philippine Economic Crisis: A Workshop Report.* Quezon City: School of Economics, University of the Philippines.

Djang, T. K. 1980. *Industry and Labor in Taiwan.* Taipei.

Domar, Evsey D. 1957. *Essays in the Theory of Economic Growth,* Chapter IX. New York: Greenwood Press (1981 reprint).

Echavez, F. S. 1981. Output Growth and Structural Changes in Postwar Philippine Manufacturing. Master's Thesis, University of the Philippines School of Economics.

Eckstein, Alexander. 1975. *China's Economic Development: The Interplay of Scarcity and Ideology.* Ann Arbor: University of Michigan Press.

Elvin, Mark. 1973. *The Pattern of the Chinese Past.* Palo Alto: Stanford University Press.

Embree, John F. 1939. *Suye Mura.* Chicago: University of Chicago Press.

Emerson, R. 1937. *Malaysia: A Study in Direct and Indirect Rule.* New York.

Fairbank, John K., and Edwin O. Reischauer. 1960. *East Asia: The Great Tradition.* Boston: Houghton Mifflin.

Fast, J., and J. Richardson. 1979. *The Roots of Dependency: Political and Economic Evolution in 19th Century Philippines.* Manila.

Fei, J., G. Ranis, and S. Kuo. 1979. *Growth with Equity, The Taiwan Case.* Oxford: Oxford University Press.

Food and Agricultural Organization. 1981. FAO Production Yearbook.

Geiger, Theodore, and Geiger, Frances M. 1979. *Tales of Two City-States: The Development Progress of Hong Kong and Singapore.* Washington, D.C.: National Planning Association.

Ginsburg, N. (with J. E. Brush, S. McCune, A. K. Philbrick. J. R. Randall, and H.J. Weins). 1958. *The Pattern of Asia.* Englewood Cliffs, N.J.: Prentice-Hall.

Glazer, Nathan. 1976. "Social and Cultural Factors in Japanese Economic Growth." In *Japan, Asia's New Giant* (ed. by Hugh Patrick and Henry Rosovsky). Washington, D.C.: Brookings Institution.

Grist, D. H. 1950. *An Outline of Malaysian Agriculture.* London.

Hatta, S. 1982. "MUDA Irrigation Scheme." *Agricultural Information Development Bulletin,* Economic and Social Commission for Asia and the Pacific, September.

Hanks, L. M. 1972. *Rice and Man.* Ithaca. Cornell University Press.

Hayami, Yujiro. 1975. *A Century of Agricultural Growth in Japan: Its Relevance to Asian Development.* Tokyo: University of Tokyo Press.

Hirschman, A. 1958. *A Strategy of Economic Development.* New Haven: Yale University Press.

Ho, Samuel P. S. 1978. *Economic Development of Taiwan, 1860–1970.* New Haven: Yale University Press.

Hooley, R. 1968. "Long-Term Growth of the Philippine Economy, 1902–1961." *Philippine Economic Journal,* Vol. VII.

IBON Databank. *The Philippine Financial System: A Primer.* N.d.

Ingram, J. C. 1971. *Economic Change in Thailand, 1850–1970.* Stanford: Stanford University Press.

International Monetary Fund. 1980. *Government Financial Statistics.*

Intharathai, K., et al. 1976. *Performance and Perspectives of the Thai Economy.* Tokyo: Institute for Developing Economies.

Jones, L., and Il. Sakong. 1980. *Government, Business and Entrepreneurship in Economic Development: The Korean Case.* Cambridge: Harvard University Press.

Kanamori, Hisao. 1968. "Economic Growth and Exports." In *Economic Growth: The Japanese Experience Since the Meiji Era* (ed. by Lawrence R. Klein and Kazushi Ohkawa). Homewood, Ill.: Richard D. Irwin, Inc.

Karuntilake, H. N. S. 1971. *Economic Development in Ceylon.* New York.

Kuyvenhoven, A., and H. Poot. 1984. *Industrial Development in Indonesia.* Rotterdam: Erasmus University.

Kuznets, Simon. 1965. *Economic Growth and Structure.* New York: Norton.

———. 1966. *Modern Economic Growth: Rate, Structure, and Spread.* New Haven: Yale University Press.

———. 1971. *Economic Growth of Nations: Total Output and Production Structure.* Cambridge: Harvard University Press.

———, ed. 1975. *Income Distribution, Employment, and Economic Development in Southeast and East Asia.* Manila and Tokyo: Council for Asian Manpower Studies and Japan Economic Research Center.

———. 1980a. *Growth, Population and Income Distribution: Selected Essays.* New York: Norton.

———. 1980b. "Notes on Theories of Economic Growth." *Philippine Review of Business and Economics,* September/December.

Lardy, N.R. 1983. *Agriculture in China's Modern Development.* Cambridge: Cambridge University Press.

Lewis, Arthur. 1954. *Economic Development with Unlimited Supplies of Labor.* Manchester: Manchester School of Economic and Social Studies.

Liebau, E. 1980. *Labor-Management Relations in the Republic of Korea.* Seoul: Korean Development Institute.

Lim, E. R., and Shilling, John. 1980. *Thailand: Toward a Development Strategy of Full Participation.* Washington, D.C.: World Bank.

Liu, P. 1974. "Role of Education in Fertility Transition of Taiwan." Academica Sinica Discussion Paper 8302.

Lockwood, W. W. (ed.) 1965. *The State and Economic Enterprise in Japan: Essays in the Political Economy of Growth.* Princeton: Princeton University Press.

Malenbaum, W. 1982. "Modern Economic Growth in India and China: The Comparison Revisited." *Economic Development and Cultural Change*, October.

Mason, E. S., et al. 1980. *Economic and Social Modernization of the Republic of Korea.* Cambridge: Harvard University Press.

Matthews, R. C., et al. 1982. *British Economic Growth: 1856–1973.* Stanford: Stanford University Press.

Meerman, J. 1979. *Public Expenditures in Malaysia: Who Benefits and Why.* Oxford: Oxford University Press.

Minami, Ryoshin. 1976, "The Introduction of Electric Power and Its Impact on the Manuifacturing Industries, with Special Reference to Smaller-Scale Plants." In *Japanese Industrialization and Its Social Consequences* (ed. by Hugh Patrick). Berkeley: University of California Press.

Minami, Ryoshin. 1973. *The Turning Point in Economic Development: Japan's Experience.* Tokyo: Kinokuniya.

Mizoguchi, T., and M. Umemura. 1981. *Quantitative Studies in the Economic History of the Japanese Empire.* Tokyo.

Mosk, C. 1977. "Demographic Transition in Japan." *Journal of Economic History*, September.

Mueller, E. and R. Cohn. 1974. *Relation of Income and Fertility Decisions in Taiwan.* Ann Arbor: University of Michigan Press.

Myrdal, Gunnar. 1972. *Asian Drama: An Inquiry into the Poverty of Nations.* New York: Pantheon.

National Council of Applied Economic Research. 1965. *All India Rural Household Survey.* New Delhi: National Council of Applied Economic Research.

Needham, Joseph. 1969. *The Grand Titration: Science and Society in East and West.* London: Cambridge University Press.

Nurkse, Ragnar. 1953. *Problems of Capital Formation in Underdeveloped Countries.* New York: Oxford University Press.

Nyrop, R. F., et al. 1971. *Area Handbook for Ceylon* Washington, D.C.: American University.

Ohkawa, Kazushi, B. Johnston, and H. Kaneda (eds.). 1970. *Agriculture and Economic Growth: Japan's Experience.* Princeton: Princeton University Press.

Ohkawa, Kazushi, and Henry Rosovsky. 1973. *Japanese Economic Growth.* Stanford: Stanford University Press.

Ohkawa, Kazushi, and Miyohei Shinohara. 1979. *Patterns of Japanese Economic Development: A Quantitative Appraisal.* New Haven: Yale University Press.

Oshima, Harry T. 1951. "National Income and Product and the Price

System." *Review of Economic and Statistics*, Vol. 33.

—— 1958. "Underemployment in Backward Economies." *Journal of Political Economy*, June.

—— 1961. "The Linkages Effect and Agricultural Development. *Indian Journal of Economics*, October.

—— 1962. "A Strategy for Asian Development." *Economic Development and Cultural Change* (University of Chicago), April.

—— 1967. "Food Consumption and Economic Development in Asian Countries. *Economic Development and Cultural Change*, July 1967.

—— 1971a. "Labor-Force 'Explosion' and the Labor-Intensive Sector in Asian Growth." *Economic Development and Cultural Change*, Vol. 19, No. 2.

—— 1971b. "Seasonality and Unemployment in Monsoon Asia," *Philippine Economic Journal*, Vol. X, No. 1 (First Semester), pp. 63–97.

—— 1973. "A Labor-Intensive Strategy for Southeast Asia: A Multiple-Cropping Model for 1970." *Kajian Ekonomi Malaysia*, Vol. 10, No. 1.

—— 1977a. "Notes on Differential Growth and Structural Changes in Postwar Asia." *Philippine Economic Journal*, Vol. 26, No. 3.

—— 1977b. "Postwar Asian Growth: The Interplay of Income Distribution and Rural Development." *Economy and Finance of Indonesia*, Vol. 25, No. 4.

—— 1978a. "The Necessity for Labour Intensive Growth in Indonesia." In: An Employment and Incomes Distribution Strategy Proposal, Vol. 1. Jakarta:

—— 1978b. "The Role of Manpower in Postwar Asian Differential Growth." *Philippine Review of Economics and Business*, Vol. 15, No. 4.

—— 1979. "Postwar Growth of the Service Sector in Asian Countries." *Philippine Review of Economics and Business*, Vol. 28, No. 4.

—— 1981. "Policy Implications in the Low Growth Decades of the 1980s. *Philippine Review of Economics and Business*, September/December.

—— 1982. "Reinterpreting Japan's Postwar Growth." *Economic Development and Cultural Change*, October, pp. 1–43.

—— 1983a. "The Industrial and Demographic Transitions in East Asia." *Population and Development Review*, Vol. 9, No. 4, December.

—— 1983b. "Issues of Heavy Industrialization in Asia." *Philippine Review of Economics and Business*, Vol. XX, No. 1 (March).

—— 1983c. "Sector Sources of Philippine Postwar Economic Growth," *Journal of Philippine Development* (National Economic and Development Authority, Manila), First Semester.

—— 1983d. *The Transition to an Industrial Economy in Monsoon Asia*, Asian Development Bank Staff Paper No. 20, October.

—— 1983e. "Why Monsoon Asia Fell Behind the West Since the 16th Century: Conjectures." *Philippine Review of Economics and Business*, Vol. XX, No. 2.

—— 1984a. "Growth of Factor Productivity in the U.S.: The Significance of New Technologies in the Early Decades of the 20th Century." *Journal of Economic History*, March.

—— 1984b. *The Significance of Off-Farm Employment and Incomes in Post-War East Asian Growth*. Asian Development Bank Staff Paper No. 21, January.

—— 1984c. "Toward a Model of Monsoon Asian Economic Growth." *Singapore (formerly Malayan) Economic Review*, October.

—— 1985. "Levels and Trends of Farm Families' Non-agricultural Incomes at Different Stages of Monsoon Development." *Philippine Review of Economics and Business.*

—— 1986. "The Transition from an Agricultural to an Industrial Economy in East Asia." *Economic Development and Cultural Change*, January.

Palacpac, A. C. 1980. *World Rice Statistics*. Los Banos: International Rice Research Institute.

Potter, J. 1979. *Thai Peasant Social Structure*. Chicago: University of Chicago Press.

Power, John. 1966. "Import Substitution and Industrialization Strategy." *Philippine Economic Journal*, Second Semester.

Power, John. 1971. "Philippines Industrialization and Trade Politicies." In *Philippine and Taiwan Industrialization and Trade Policies* (John Power, Gerardo Sicat, and Mottuan Hsiang). OECD/Oxford University Press.

Radhakrishnan, P. N. 1977. *The Public Sector in Sri Lanka—Its Significance and Potential*. Colombo: Ministry of Planning and Economic Affairs.

Raffles, Sir T. S. 1965. *History of Java*, Vol. 1. Singapore: Oxford University Press.

Ranis, Gustav, and John C. Fei. 1964. *Development of the Labor Surplus Economy*. Champaign: University of Illinois Press.

Rao, R. V. (ed.). 1960. *Asian Studies in Income and Wealth*. New York: Asia Publishing House.

Repetto, R., et al. 1981. *Economic Development, Population Policy and Demographic Transition in the Republic of Korea*. Cambridge: Harvard University Press.

Shen, T. H. (ed.). 1974. *Agriculture's Place in the Strategy of Development*. Taipei.

Shinohara, Miyohei. 1970. *Structural Changes in Japan's Economic Development*. Tokyo: Kinokuniya.

——. 1982. *Industrial Growth, Trade, and Dynamic Patterns in the Japanese Economy*. Tokyo: University of Tokyo Press.

Simbulan. 1965. *A Study of Socio-Economic Elite in the Philippine Government, 1946–63*. Canberra: Australian National University.

Singh, I. 1979. Small Farmers and the Landless in South Asia. *World Bank Staff Paper No. 320*, February.

Snodgrass, D. 1966. *Ceylon: An Export Economy in Transition*. New Haven: Yale University Press.

Snodgrass, D. 1980. Inequality and Economic Development in Malaysia. Oxford: Oxford University Press.

Steinberg, D. J., et al. 1971. *In Search of Southeast Asia: A Modern History*. Oxford: Oxford University Press.

Suh, Sang Chul. 1978. *Growth and Structural Changes in the Korean Economy, 1910–1940*. Cambridge: Harvard University Press.

Sumiya, Mikio. 1973. "The Emergence of Modern Japan." In *Workers and Employers in Japan* (ed. by Kazuo Okochi, Bernard Karsh, and Solomon B. Levine). Tokyo: University of Tokyo Press.

Sumiya, Mikio, and Koji Taira (eds.) 1979. *An Outline of Japanese Economic History, 1603–1940.* Tokyo: University of Tokyo Press.

Takashi, A. 1976. In *Rural Employment and Land Reform Policy* (Ahmad, ed.). Bangkok: ILO.

Tohata, Seiichi. 1958. *An Introduction to Agriculture in Japan.* Tokyo: Agriculture, Forestry and Fisheries Productivity Conference.

Tsao, Y. 1982. *Growth and Productivity in the Singapore Economy: A Supply Side Analysis.* Ph.D. diss., Harvard University.

Tsuda, M. 1978. "Understanding Industrial Relations in the Philippines: The Perspective of Resident Japanese Investors." *Philippine Journal of Industrial Relations*, First Semester.

Umemura, M. 1969. "Labor Supply in the Meiji Era." In *Agriculture and Economic Growth: Japan's Experience*, by K. Ohkawa, B. Johnston, and H. Kaneda. Tokyo: University of Tokyo Press.

Umemura, M., and T. Mizoguchi. 1981. *Quantitative Studies on Economic History of the Japanese Empire, 1890–1940.* Tokyo: Institute of Economic Research, Hitotsubashi University.

UNIDO. 1979. *World Industry Since 1960: Progress and Prospects.* New York: United Nations.

UNIDO. 1981. *First Global Study of the Capital Goods Industry: Strategies for Development.* Brussels: United Nations.

Vogel, Ezra F. 1979. *Japan As Number One: Lessons for America.* Cambridge: Harvard University Press.

———— 1975. *Modern Japanese Organization and Decision-Making.* Berkeley: University of California Press.

Wada, Richard. 1975. "Impact of Economic Growth on the Size Distribution of Income: The Postwar Experience." In: *Income Distribution, Employment, and Economic Development in Southeast and East Asia* (ed. by Simon Kuznets, 1975).

Walinsky, L. J. 1962. *Economic Development in Burma, 1951–1960.* New York: Kraus Reprints.

Weber, Max. 1964. *The Sociology of Religion.* Boston: Beacon Press.

———— 1967. *Religion of India.* New York: Free Press.

———— 1968. *Religion of China.* New York: Free Press.

White, B. N. F. 1976. *Production and Reproduction in a Javanese Village.* Bogor, Indonesia: Agricultural Development Council.

Wickizer, V. D., and Bennett, M.K. 1941. *The Rice Economy of Monsoon Asia.* Stanford: Food Research Institute.

Wong, John (ed.). 1979. *Group Farming in Asia.* Singapore: Singapore University Press.

World Bank, IMF. 1980. *The Philippines, Aspects of the Financial Sector.* Washington, D.C.: World Bank.

World Bank. 1983. *World Development Report 1983.* Oxford: Oxford University Press.

Wurfel, D. 1979. "Elites of Wealth and Elites of Power, the Changing Dynamic: A Philippine Caste Study." *Southeast Asian Affairs, 1979.* Singapore: University of Singapore, Institute of Asian Studies.

Index

agricultural development, 60, 66, 70, 347–48; China, 266, 271–72, 277–79; India, 266, 271–72, 276–77, 278–79; Japan, 111–16; Korea, 149–52, 157–61, 173–74; Malaysia, 207–9, 245–53, 258; Philippines, 206–16, 304; Sri Lanka, 245–53; Taiwan, 144, 149–52, 158–61, 169–70; Thailand, 206–16, 302

agriculture, capitalistic, 25, 35–36, 37–38, 39, 45

agro-industrial transition, 56–64, 68–69, 134–35, 137–38, 170, 184, 199, 243, 245, 310–13, 315, 321, 348; *see also* demographic transition

authoritarianism, 106, 107, 354–55

birth rates: Hong Kong, 193–95; Japan, 133; Singapore, 193–95; *see also* fertility patterns

Buddhism, 93; Theravada, 238, 258, 287

Burma, 79; historical background, 199, 201; economic development, 95, 209; social welfare system, 238–39

calorie intake, *See* food consumption

capital-intensive syndrome, 280

caste, 93, 265

Ceylon. *See* Sri Lanka

children in the labor force, 96, 336–37; India, 285

China: agricultural development, 266, 271–72, 277–79; agricultural labor force, 38, 39; economic growth, 79, 97–98, 267–71; exports, 274–75; food consumption, 268, 271–72; historical background, 33–35, 41–43, 177, 265; income distribution, 282–84; industrialization, 272–82; industrialization policy, 263–64; social welfare programs, 285

colonization: British, 94, 180–81, 236–39, 258–59, 265–66; Japanese, 94, 138–45; Spanish, 201, 214

competitiveness, 226–27

Confucianism, 30, 32, 67, 93, 138, 179, 180, 238, 264–65, 346

consensus, 127–28, 174, 177, 195–96, 262, 354–55

crop diversification, 60, 61, 112, 150–52, 174, 210

debt, external, 169, 174, 344

democratization, of Japan, 109, 110, 111, 125, 134, 136

demographic transition, 54, 56, 68–69, 168, 193, 316; *see also* agro-industrial transition

density, agricultural, 209, 236, 237

development models, 52, 272

development planning, 354–57

development theories, 47–57, 70

East Asia: economic growth, 92, 97; region defined, 73, 79

economic growth: defined, 87; measurement of, 87–91, 269–71; in Western development, 94

education, 68, 69, 133, 135, 193–94, 285–86, 287, 315–16, 317, 332–33, 341–42

efficiency: economic, 195, 197; industrial, 178

electrification, 120–24, 157

employment: agricultural, seasonality of, 17, 25, 26–27, 59–60, 85, 113, 147; full, 61–62, 64–65, 66, 117–18, 243, 301, 321–27, 348; lifetime, 117; off-farm, 25, 32–33, 38, 59, 61, 64, 66, 112–14, 124–25, 148, 153, 247, 300–1

entrepreneurship, 186–87, 219

ethnic diversity, 93, 235, 303, 304